Listening to America

HARPER'S
MAGAZINE
PRESS

LISTENING TO AMERICA

A Traveler Rediscovers His Country

☆

by Bill Moyers

A HARPER'S MAGAZINE PRESS BOOK

Published in Association with Harper & Row
New York

For Cope, Suzanne, and John
and their mother, who also listens

STANDARD BOOK NUMBER: 06-126400-8

LIBRARY OF CONGRESS CATALOG CARD NUMBER: 79-144185

Contents

CONTENTS

☆

For ten years I listened to America from a distance. As Deputy Director of the Peace Corps, special assistant to the President, and publisher of Newsday, I lived and worked on a narrow strip of the Eastern Coast. In Washington I helped to draft legislation which we hoped would make this a better country. In New York I belonged to a profession whose express purpose is to communicate with people. But I learned that it is possible to write bills and publish newspapers without knowing what the country is about or who the people are. Much changed in America in those ten years. There were thirty-five million more of us, we seemed more raucous than ever, and no one could any longer be sure who spoke for whom. I wanted to hear people speak for themselves. In the summer of 1970, carrying a tape recorder and a notebook, I boarded a bus in New York to begin a journey of thirteen thousand miles through America.

★ ★ ★

On its way north the bus cuts across the heart of Manhattan's life, through clogged streets (seven minutes to move one block on West Forty-first), past the rotting buildings and vacant lots filled with refuse, along Tenth Avenue, where children play baseball in the streets, past boarded-up stores and pushers on the make, and suddenly, in one of those startling contrasts of New York, past Lincoln Center rising like some Parthenon from a junk yard. A few blocks from its splendor I saw a child, nine or ten years old, who had cut his foot and was washing the wound in the filthy gray water cascading down the gutter.

The city is tolerable if you can leave it occasionally. These people cannot. For them the air is always trapped, the inversion is permanent.

And, as the Greyhound inches through the traffic, the rhetoric of the sixties—the slogans about quality of life, a livable society, qualitative liberalism—seems to be choking in its fumes. A language far less grandiloquent is emerging. At St. Nicholas and 162nd a store conspicuously boasts: POLICE LOCKS, DOOR LOCKS, WINDOW GATES INSTALLED. The sign is painted red, white, and blue.

Once the bus clears the blighted spread of the city and moves beyond Bridgeport and New Haven the scenery and the mood of the passengers change almost simultaneously. Strangers introduce themselves to one another and the bus hums with conversation. The elderly man next to me is going north to visit his son, who took his family to New Hampshire on a vacation once and refused to bring them back—"he has a child with a breathing problem that just don't seem to bother her as bad up there." He offers me a cigar, which is against regulations, but it is thin and inoffensive and we light up, pleading self-defense against the cigarette smoke creeping over the seats around us.

For an hour we talk about nothing important, the way travelers on a bus do when they have first met. Ultimately they will discuss Spiro Agnew, inflation, the war and other grave issues of the day, but they prefer to begin the trip with small talk about children, minis and midis, and the sorry state of American newspapers, a grievance I will hear more often on this trip than complaints about taxes. My companion retired last year after forty years as a newspaper vendor in New York, and the only regret he now expresses is that he did not keep a copy of the last edition of every newspaper that died in New York during his career. "I might have had one for every year I worked," he says. This is only a slight exaggeration and we both chuckle.

The day before my departure, I received from a friend, Clare Wofford, the wife of the president of Bryn Mawr, a letter urging me not "to go out earnestly in search of America's problems but rather in search of its humor, its ironies, its human-ness. Since we are obviously on the frontier of every new and old problem suffered by mankind, we need to be reminded that we are no worse than the rest of the human race. How can the United States find some humility—and from it the chance to offer decent leadership—unless we can laugh a little and stop our endless self-flagellations?"

I folded her note into my wallet to remind me of a gentle mandate I very much wanted to honor. But ancient scriptures teach that man is born to trouble, and experience teaches that he endures those troubles

*by talking about them. Whenever I traveled, and no matter how inno-
cent or casual my purpose, the people I met wanted to talk about the
tribulations of America: war, campus unrest, crime, inflation, pollution,
racism, and drugs. Hardly a day passed that would be free of some
demonstration of our woes.*

Hartford, Connecticut

WITH THE OPENING OF THE POLITICAL SEASON I HAVE COME TO HARTFORD for my first state convention. During the sixties I took part in two national conventions and attended a third as an observer. In those conventions reformers clamored for changes that would increase the number of people who participate in party activities. As the decade ended it was clear that such goals could be achieved only if significant reforms were introduced at state levels. Except in presidential years, the national parties are little more than loose congeries of ambitious men. The work of organizing goes on in the states. For the last twenty years it has gone on quite well for the regular Democrats in Connecticut. Under the leadership of the state chairman, John Bailey, they have not lost a major race. But the organization has wearied, age has set in, and the political convulsions of 1968 brought new and independent forces to the Connecticut political scene. These were largely younger people more interested in issues than organization. Although they failed in their challenge to the regular Democrats at the state convention two years ago, they were trying again in 1970. "If you're going off to see what is happening in the country," a lawyer wrote me from New Haven, "come on up here. You may see the end of an era."

I also wanted to see the Reverend Joseph Duffey. As a candidate for the Democratic nomination to the United States Senate, he is the leader of the reformers seeking change in the Democratic party in Connecticut. I had met him only once, at lunch in New York in 1969, where I realized that the stereotypes created by his press coverage were misleading. He is an ordained minister, with the face of an altar boy, but

3

his manner is free of smug religiosity. He led a walkout of the Connecticut convention in 1968 when the regulars refused to give the McCarthy forces more than nine delegates to Chicago, but he had come to believe that only if reformers organize "to beat the pros at their own game" will anything good come from their efforts. Yes, he had said at lunch, he was thinking of running for the Senate; "If I do, it will be to force a primary. People who don't and can't attend a state convention are not given a share in the selection of their candidates. I would like to take the issues to those people." He would go out into the villages and towns, he said, to seek his delegates not only among students and hard-core idealists but among housewives, shopkeepers, and blue-collar workers.

The odds were against him. Although in 1955 the Connecticut legislature passed a law providing for a primary if a candidate collected 20 percent of the votes of the delegates to the state convention, the organization always managed to thwart its opponents; there had never been a primary. Duffey has opposed the war in a state in which Senator Thomas Dodd has made a career of fighting Communists. And he is a Protestant in a party whose chairman would rather run naked through the insurance district at noon than enter the November elections without an Irish Catholic on the ticket. Once he entered the race, Duffey knew, it would be an uphill fight.

But late in 1969 he decided to run. Now, months later, I wanted to be here for the convention, to see if Connecticut politics is changing and if Duffey has been able to bring new people into a party benevolently protected against upstarts and upsets.

I arrive on Thursday evening—the day before the convention is to open—and go to the Duffey headquarters in the Hotel Sonesta. Duffey is downtown answering questions on a television show and his people are putting the final touches on the suite that will be their command center.

I managed to corner Anne Wexler, co-manager of the Duffey campaign. She is a charming and magnetic woman, and the *New York Times*'s national political correspondent R. W. Apple considers her the country's foremost practitioner of participancy electoral politics. In other words, she believes all registered Democrats who wish to have their voices heard in the selection of delegates to the national convention and nominees for political office should have a chance to take part in the selection process. Translated again, she is for open primaries.

She carried her fight from her Westport home, where she and her friends would gather to lament the closed corporate structure of their party, to the Democratic National Convention in 1968. She helped to write the minority report of the rules committee, which, surprisingly, the convention of the whole adopted; the old unit rule, by which many states had for decades kept control of the party in the hands of the rich and the regulars, died a hard death that day. Mrs. Wexler later became chairman of the advisory committee to the McGovern Commission on Party Structure and Delegate Selection that would try to carry forward the reforms voted in Chicago.

For the last six months she has been directing volunteers combing Connecticut precincts for those 192 delegates who will assure Duffey a place on the primary ballot. Forty-eight hours before the roll call, she says they will make it.

"Two years ago Joe was anathema because he took on the regulars at the state convention and everyone said he was a radical. The bitter hostility is gone today," she says. "It isn't that Joe has changed. Politics up here is changing. Two years ago most of the delegates who came to this convention were elected officials. We've opened it up to newcomers. This may well be the last convention to select nominees for party office. From now on I'm sure there will be primaries."

The Republicans have already nominated their candidate for governor, an Irishman, Thomas J. Meskill. The Democratic nominee, agreed upon by the organization before the convention opens, will be Emilio ("Mim") Daddario, a congressman, the first nominee of Italian ancestry to be selected in Connecticut for either senator or governor. Irish Democrats grumbled uneasily but agreed to Daddario and the party leaders want to mollify them with an Irish Catholic nominee for the Senate. Their choice is Alphonsus ("Big Al") Donahue, a businessman. Bailey needs an overwheming victory on the first ballot to show the Irish they still matter.

How does Bailey honestly feel about Duffey?

"He doesn't really have anything against Joe any longer. The thing is, John has a long record of victories ever since he took over this party back in 1946 and he doesn't want to break it now by ignoring the rule that has worked so well so long."

What rule is that?

"Balance your ticket if it means bouncing your mother."

Do I detect a measure of affection in her voice when she talks about Bailey?

"Yes. I wish all 'bosses' were of his caliber," she says. "He's not been a dictator as much as a power broker, making alliances out of the inevitable. He's a superb technician. I get along with John. That's why the New Left jumps all over me. They don't trust me because I talk to the regulars."

It is ten o'clock and the staff begins to relax. The conversation drifts to the roll call on Saturday and the importance of Mim Daddario's abstaining when the Hartford delegation of which he is a member is polled early in the balloting. If he passes, he will be signaling his acquiescence in, if not approval of, an open fight for the Senate nomination. It will mean that he intends to exact no retribution from delegates who vote for Duffey instead of Donahue.

"He might vote for Donahue just to stampede the convention," Fred Jackson suggests.

"No," someone else says. "He won't do that."

"Why not?" Anne Wexler asks. "Conventions exist to be stampeded."

At this point Joe Duffey arrives.

It is hard to think of him as a politician. He smiles almost incidentally, as if he is anxious to get beyond the pleasantries and small talk to larger matters. Later, when delegates come to meet him privately, he will dispense with the normal exaggerated affectations of a political convention and ask pointblank: "Can I count on you?" He is not an obsequious man.

Joe Duffey is thirty-seven. His mother died when he was ten. His father was a coal miner in West Virginia (and a part-time prize fighter whose opponents once included Jack Dempsey) until, at the age of twenty-three, he lost a leg in an accident and turned to barbering and politics. Joe Duffey began his political experience when he was twelve by wrapping sample ballots around "nip bottles"—two-shot bottles of whiskey—and passing them out as an encouragement to vote. He worked as an apprentice carpenter on the railroads, went to college and quit, got a job in the steel mills, married, went back to college, became a minister of the United Church of Christ, joined the faculty and administration of Hartford Theological Seminary, earned his doctorate, became active in urban affairs, and moved from advocating to practicing the politics of disciplined rage.

"My great unhappiness with the McCarthy and peace movements," he says, "was their failure to overcome the idea of protest for the sake of protest, by people who can afford the luxury of protest. I wanted to go beyond the Beautiful People Peace and Protest syndrome to a campaign concerned with the distribution of wealth in this country, one that would ask questions about the human role in this world."

What do you think is the goal now of liberalism in politics?

"My New Left critics would be very unhappy to hear me say it, but I would say a return to stability. But I mean biological stability, not worship of the status quo—biological stability, in which society is seen as a growing and changing organism. I think our test is to prove that we can govern ourselves efficiently enough to prevent anarchy and wisely enough to realize the system is unjust, really unjust, to a lot of people.

"I hope I've been able to see things in perspective since 1968. If you provoke a head-on confrontation with entrenched power, the establishment becomes intimidated, uptight, defensive, and protective. It doesn't feel your pain, only its own. So I knew we had to organize, to stay with the job after the shouting died down. When the '68 election was over we organized the Caucus of Connecticut Democrats and twelve hundred people attended the founding convention. The press was surprised that we could turn out so many or that we could sustain their interest. One serious flaw in regular politics is that the politicians only call upon people during campaigns and conventions. We kept on struggling through '69 with the problem that has always bothered reformers: how do you employ tough, pragmatic political activity in the service of reformist goals? It's not enough just to express your rage. American reformers have been better prophets than politicians, and some of us knew it was time to become effective politicians. Connecticut politics have always been a closed shop run by the power brokers, disciplined by patronage, and centered in the governor's office and the law office of the party chairman."

Has that been all bad?

"All bad? No. There's a place for the organization in politics. I even think Richard Daley has been a good mayor of Chicago. Look at the public services there and compare them to New York.

"Connecticut is a favored state, with wealth and privilege, and John Bailey and the men he has supported have not been reactionaries. But the progress in this state has been mostly progress for the upper and middle classes rather than the equalization or distribution of wealth to people on the lower rungs of the economic ladder. Liberals have always been eunuchs in the court in Connecticut, using the princes and the kings as they could to do what they could, and they've done

7

some good things with the blessing of the organization, but there has been no sustained assault on the inequalities of society."

Aren't people frightened by terms like "distribution of wealth"?

"I first used it in a debate with Bill Buckley and he survived, although he has more to distribute than most of us. I have used it judiciously in the campaign. It is possible to use it today. What I'm talking about is taxes: where does the budget go? what happens to the money we send to Washington? Education is as important as agriculture subsidies, and both are means of distributing wealth. People are beginning to understand. They are less likely today to react to the term as a cliché. They want to know what it means. I don't know if we will get to enough of them in time, but every political campaign that tries to move the boundaries of public discussion further out contributes to public understanding and in the long run makes a difference.

"Don't take this to mean I think we can't win. We can. This party has many more new people in it than it did in 1968—what I call a conscience constituency—young lawyers, doctors, younger union members, older people who had never been asked. We're going to get our 20 percent because we went out to the little towns and asked people to take part who had never been to a caucus in their lives. On the basis of their participation we went to the town regulars and bargained for recognition from strength. The way-out radicals have attacked me for playing the game, for bargaining with the organization, but I don't know how else we're ever going to change things."

Duffey puts a cold French fry in his mouth and finishes a Coke. It is almost midnight and he has not eaten all day. He asks someone to get clam chowder. "In the past John Bailey wanted to avoid primaries. He feared they would divide the party before the general election in November. Anyone who seriously threatened a primary almost could have had the nomination. Mim Daddario threatened a primary and John went with him. Abe Ribicoff first talked to me about running back in December, 1968, after the election, and he said, 'Threaten a primary, Joe, and they'll give it to you.' That's why Dodd got it in '58. The polls showed Bowles to be more popular, but Bowles had said that if he didn't win at the convention, he wouldn't run. But Tom Dodd said, 'Hell, no, if I don't get the nomination I'll run in the primary,' and Bailey went for Dodd."

If that is the case, I ask, why don't they give it to you? You've threatened a primary.

"Because since 1968 John has regarded me as a menace to his organization, and he still does. I went to him just before I announced and said, 'John, I'm going to run. I don't want to run against Bailey but against Dodd.' Bailey said he understood. He didn't think then that I could win in the general election although he did think I would beat Dodd. [Ill and bitter over his censure by the Senate for allegedly misusing campaign funds, Senator Dodd has announced that he will not seek renomination by the Democrats. He is thinking of running as an independent in November.] John thought then that this would be a conservative year. He wants a candidate who isn't so clearly defined, one who appears as conservative as possible without offending the progressives. But there are more independent voters in Connecticut than there are registered Republicans or Democrats and I think I can pull it off in November, although Dodd would hurt if he comes in."

What about blacks?

"They're in a tragic dilemma just now in Connecticut. The black politicians, who are being pressured by the militants, are where they are because of the organization's favors. They could have enormous power in this party if they played to their constituents, but the power they have is dispensed power; it's sure, it's safe, and it involves few risks. They should be shoving the party, not living off it."

★ ★ ★

It is Friday night and the first formal session of the convention is over. The delegates have returned to the hotel for what to most of them is their one big fling of the year. With or without their wives they travel from one candidate's hospitality suite to another, and by midnight almost everyone I see over forty is in his cups, except the staffs of the candidates.

Upstairs in one room of the Duffey suite Anne Wexler, and campaign aides Wendy Robineaugh and Hubert Santos, sitting yogalike and barefooted on a king-size bed, are making their final delegate check:

Hartford: "11 for Duffey, 23 for Donahue, none for Marcus. This is John Bailey's district and the first time in years it hasn't been unanimous for the organization's man."

Windsor: "—— has to vote for Joe or his wife say's she will divorce him."

Newington: "We've got to get an Italian onto this guy." "Listen, only the Pope could pull him away from Donahue." "What's the number for the Vatican?"

9

Canaan: "Mrs. —— is very much against Joe. She thinks he's a defrocked priest."

The count goes on until almost 3 A.M. Their tally shows Duffey with 202, ten more than he needs to get into the primary. But they are nervous and no one wants to sleep.

In the next room Duffey is meeting one by one with delegates. His wife, Pat, is with him. A black delegate introduces himself to me and says he is committed to Donahue on the first ballot but actually prefers Duffey. I remember what Duffey said earlier about the black politicians in Hartford and ask, "If you prefer one man, why do you vote for another?" He is not at all defensive when he replies, "That, friend, is the name of the game."

★ ★ ★

On Saturday morning the Duffey headquarters shifts to the thirty-foot, two-room air-conditioned trailer outside Bushnell Auditorium. They have rented it for the weekend at a cost of $250. No other candidate has one. Duffey's logistics and floor organization are comparable to anything I have seen at national conventions: a battery of telephones, including a direct line to the hotel; walkie-talkies for constant contact between the six floor coordinators and the campaign managers in the trailer; television sets and the most up-to-date intelligence operation of any candidate. The file includes such precise facts as:

BLUM: Two daughters, oldest is Jean (Pronounced Jan), who is a student at Emmanuel College in Boston (age 20). Principal of Louis Mills High School in Burlington, member Dem. town committee, formerly on library board. Former justice of peace. Was with Knights of Columbus—not active. Against student violence. Thinks primary a good thing. Prefers gin with anything or scotch. Plays good poker. Big Humphrey man. Is looking for the strongest candidate on issues and character. DONAHUE or DUFFEY.

The cards are vignettes of America:

Mandanki: "Son in Peace Corps, son in state police."
Zumbroski: "Tends toward conservative side."
Hart: "Ex RFK fan."
Johnson: "Anti-war."
Barnes: "Anti-McCarthy."
Del Maestro: "Little League manager."
Behuncik: "Doesn't get involved."
Copertino: "Young, bright, ambitious."

Zielski: "Support your local police."
Cornell: "Strict organization man but always scrupulously fair."
Guglielmi: "Controls the women on town committee."
O'Brien (Lawrence): "Came to town with kind of Kennedy image."

Inside Bushnell Auditorium the organization is having a hard time. John Bailey's choice for secretary of state, a Jewish woman from Watertown, has lost out in a dramatic upset to a political newcomer, a popular television personality named Gloria Schaffer. There are rumors of dissatisfaction toward "Big Al" Donahue, whose Irish conviviality has not overcome his lack of political experience. The grapevine says that Ed Marcus, who is supposed to have more delegates than Duffey because of his power base in the state senate, is slipping, giving rise to still more rumors that the convention might draft the retiring governor, John Dempsey. Duffey wants Marcus in the primary, to split the race into a three-way contest and hopefully dilute the organization's unity. Some of Duffey's lieutenants suggest that a few of their people vote for Marcus on the roll call just to keep him in the primary. "We can't do that," Duffey says. "They came here to go on record, to vote for us."

Mim Daddario, who has been unanimously nominated for governor, has decided that he will pass when the Hartford delegation is polled. He does not want to alienate Duffey's supporters publicly for fear they will retaliate by staying at home on election day. Duffey receives the news in his trailer and says to Anne Wexler: "That's a compliment to your organizing. They don't respect anything but strength."

Senator Abe Ribicoff drops by to see Duffey, whom he has already endorsed. "Abe had his bar mitzvah in Chicago," Anne Wexler had told me the previous evening. "That speech [the one criticizing Chicago police] was the most spontaneous thing he's ever done. I'm sure he wanted to appeal to independent voters in Connecticut, but I don't think that speech was planned. He came back a different man, started speaking to high schools and college groups instead of only to women's clubs and religious groups and Rotary. You know something, Abe Ribicoff is becoming a real person."

He tells Duffey: "Mim and Bailey were really hoping for another candidate for Senator. They don't like Marcus, and Donahue hasn't caught on. They are afraid you're too independent and John still hasn't forgiven you for '68. They'll settle on Donahue because he's got the least against him. He's also got the money. Things are changing, though. If John's power was what it used to be, there wouldn't be three candidates for

11

the Senate. The old order is changing," he says, "but they'll not go out without thumping and thrashing around like a fight to the death in some prehistoric forest."

The Senator is a prophet.

Outside the auditorium a dozen black-jacketed youths on motorcycles roar by with signs that say: "AP-UPI-Tass—What's the difference?"

★ ★ ★

There is often one moment in every convention when sentiment overwhelms the reality of an accurate nose count and a candidate's people actually believe something extraordinary is going to happen and their man will take it all. That moment arrives in Hartford when Duffey is nominated. The previous night, in a late strategy session, he toyed with the idea of canceling any demonstration in his behalf, to save time and to show that politics is serious business, not a circus. He finally vetoed the suggestion because, he said, "they [his delegates] deserve a chance to sound off." When Sirabella finishes his speech, therefore, a mighty roar explodes in the auditorium, ignited on the floor and fanned by the Duffey partisans in the galleries. There is no abating; it intensifies until in the trailer Duffey, who seems both pleased and embarrassed, whispers to an aide and the word goes out to the walkie-talkies: "Call it off. Call it off." Ten minutes pass before the chanting begins to subside and Hubert Santos, hunched over the legal-size charts of delegates, not wanting the scene on the television screen in the trailer to end, says softly, to no one in particular: "My God, we could take this thing. We could take it."

The roll call begins. Each delegate's name is called from the rostrum, the answer coming back from somewhere beyond the television cameras, where for one long-anticipated second the anonymity of rank-and-file politics yields the floor for that Act of Recognition which is the special reward of the faithful:

"Donna-HOO!"

"Duffey!"

"Donahue!"

"Marcus!"

"Joe Duff-e-e-e-e!"

"I vote for Big Al Donahue!"

The count proceeds exactly the way Wexler and company had expected until the 19th senatorial district, where there are five surprises in a row, all in Duffey's favor. The town of Waterford is called, a delegate by whose name a question mark appears on Santos' work sheet shouts "Joe Duffey!" and Santos beats the table with his left hand and yells: "We got him! We got him!" But then an alternate, supposedly friendly, goes for Donahue, and someone in the trailer replies in a melancholy voice: "They bagged us on that one." At the end of the 20th senatorial district the count is 64 for Duffey (6 more than expected at this point), 126 for Donahue, and 41 for Marcus. "Duffey has been out working for months," Alan Green says with just a touch of anger, "and Donahue hasn't. But Donahue will get the convention nomination. That's the problem with conventions—most people still vote the way other people tell them."

Duffey is eating a sandwich. Mrs. Duffey stands beside him, watching the screen, three fingers of her right hand covering her mouth. She is the daughter of a coal miner and I wonder how many women like her have stood outside the mouth of a mine and waited for some news from below. It is a thought apropos of nothing at the moment except the way she is standing, and I quickly push it aside. Pat Duffey asks Anne Wexler: "Are you sure we'll get 20 percent?" "Yes, I'm sure, I think."

It is 9 P.M. and the count is 108 for Duffey, 182 for Donahue, and 75 for Marcus. The roll call becomes a shouting match, the Irish belching forth the name of Donahue as if he were a Notre Dame fullback one yard from the goal with thirty seconds to play, and Duffey's people retorting with sharp ringing responses to the call from the platform for each delegate's choice. There are thirty-eight people in the trailer, about three times as many as there should be, but Duffey is moving closer now to the magic number of 192 and no one leaves. It is even possible that he will finish second, ahead of Marcus, an upset of a sort. Now it is 9:45 and Santos, sweating like a Texas cowhand, is projecting three votes ahead. "Oh, Jesus," he says, "it's coming. Oh, Jesus, and Pierz is going to do it. Pierz is going to do it."

Who is Pierz?

"He was my Little League coach," Santos replies. "He was my sweet lovin' Little League coach, and he's going to put Joe over."

And at 9:46 P.M. Steven P. Pierz, a Fuller Brush man from Enfield, Connecticut, Hubie Santos' Little League coach, rises to his feet, and with altogether too much calm for the occasion, replies to the rostrum: "Joe Duffey."

And the galleries and the trailer are bedlam.

Duffey's hand reaches for his wife's. Anne Wexler leans against her chair and says: "This is what they came for. Two years ago Joe said he would stay in the party and work to change it from within. This is what they came for."

"Hot dang," someone says, "I'm still on the payroll."

* * *

Duffey is the first to get the required number of delegates. He will lead Marcus when the roll call ends, 231 to 221. But Donahue is 17 votes short of a convention majority of 481 and consternation prevails in the backstage headquarters of John Bailey's organization. If there is a second roll call Donahue's strength could fade quickly and Duffey, or some dark horse, could go all the way. The word is passed: "Get Kennelly and he'll put the final twist on." James J. Kennelly is a state legislator and the son-in-law of John Bailey. Delegates are located who passed on the first roll call. Other delegates are switched and now Donahue has 480.

He is still one short.

I have gone to the stage and am looking out toward the convention floor. The delegates are perplexed and restless. A local television producer is standing behind me and I can hear through his two-way transmitter the excited voice of a cameraman out there in the wilderness of delegates: "Where's the action? For God's sake, where is the action?"

The action is there, to the right of the stage, in a long and crowded aisle down which one very husky man is leading by the arm a bespectacled, prim, fragile woman of some years, her eyes transfixed far above the chaos on the floor, as if she has just seen some dark specter plunge through the high windows of Bushnell Auditorium and descend on a straight course toward her. By now they are coming up the steps to the wing of the platform and a second man puts his right arm around her shoulder and begins to pat her arm. The first man grips the elbow of her other arm. I edge close enough to read his badge—Martin Fisher, the sheriff of Bridgeport, short, balding, his tie loosened at the neck, baubles of sweat dropping from his mustache to his lower lip and running on down his neck. Both men are looking her directly in the face and smiling as if they were lawyers probating a will. She is staring off toward the rear of the stage, still obsessed with that private dread. The anti-organization delegates, aching for a second roll call that could break the whole thing apart, sense what is about to happen.

14

"No . . . No . . . NO!" they shout.

Behind me, at the rear of the stage, John Bailey tells a television interviewer: "I'm always happy to have just one vote more than I need."

The chairman of the convention tries to quiet the crowd: "Ladies and gentlemen, these are the rules you adopted. They permit a delegate to switch."

And a guttural volcano erupts again across the hall: "No . . . No . . . NO!"

"How does the delegate from Naugatuck vote?" the chair asks.

She opens her mouth but nothing comes out.

"How-does-the-delegate-from-Naugatuck-vote?"

Again she opens her mouth and again nothing.

This time the sheriff of Bridgeport speaks: "The lady from Naugatuck asks me to tell you that she wishes to change her vote for Joe Duffey to vote for Alphonsus Donahue."

"What's that?" the chair inquires, banging the podium and shouting in another vain effort to still the crowd.

"I SAID SHE'S VOTING FOR DONAHUE."

And now two puissant roars, one terrible with anger, the other exultant in victory, rise from the floor and meet in raging dissonance above the lights and smoke.

A man on the stage beside me buries his head in his hands and says, "My God, didn't they learn anything at Chicago?"

"They're crazy," a reporter says. "Don't they know television is carrying this all over the state."

Duffey, who has also come to the stage, shakes his head and says: "This will hurt in November."

It is over. Donahue has 481. Seven other delegates switch and his final tally is 488. Duffey is second and Marcus third. The Democrats of Connecticut will have their primary.

The sheriff of Bridgeport turns and very graciously escorts the lady from Naugatuck down the stairs to the aisle. Alone she walks past jeering, booing delegates toward her seat.

★ ★ ★

The next morning I decided to call the delegate from Naugatuck, Stella Wityak. Her telephone was constantly busy and it was 4 P.M. before I could reach her. I asked her why she switched.

"Well, I'll tell you truthfully. I was really for Mr. Donahue all the

time, but there's a nice young man here—he's kind of a friend of mine
—who asked me to vote for Mr. Duffey. I met Mr. Duffey two or three
times and read about him and I said I would give him my vote if he
needed it to get into the primary. I voted for Mr. Duffey because they
said he needed me. Then I voted for Mr. Donahue because he needed
me. I was proud to do what I did."

Have you received any threats?

"No. I'm used to these things. I've been in town politics for twenty
years."

Have you been to a convention before?

"No, this was my first. I had the time of my life. Oh, I was a little
scared when that man came and got me and we went up that aisle.
They were certainly a noisy bunch. I'd say this was probably the last
convention like it. We certainly made history, didn't we?"

I subsequently reported this conversation to Duffey, and I told him
that Stella Wityak's account sounded convincing to me. Being a gentleman he replied: "Well, let's just say that at least it's plausible." *

★ ★ ★

Once in 1943 my mother took me early on a Sunday morning to the
T & P depot to wave to her brother, who was passing through town
on a troop train heading for the West Coast. The terminal was always
crowded in those days but we managed to locate a strategic spot, and as
the train slowed to negotiate the curve which would swing it toward
Dallas we saw my uncle. All of us shouted and waved and my mother
cried. It was a long train. Hundreds of soldiers leaned out the windows
hollering at everyone and throwing kisses at all the pretty girls. Because
it was early we could see their stubbly young-man beards. I was surprised, for I had assumed that all our soldiers were as old as Brian
Donlevy and William Bendix, who died defending Wake Island. I
would see a lot of fighting men during the war—Donlevy and Bendix,
John Wayne, Robert Taylor, etc.—and they always struck me as very
mature, not at all the kind who would lean from a passing train and
drop in the midst of strangers a note which read: "Please call my mother

* [Six weeks later Joseph Duffey defeated Alphonsus Donahue, Edward
Marcus, and the state organization to become the Democratic nominee for
the United States Senate. In November, attacked by Vice President Spiro
Agnew as a "Marxist," Duffey was defeated by a moderate Republican congressman, Lowell T. Weicker, Jr. Weicker received 42 percent of the vote,
Duffey 34 percent, and Thomas Dodd, whose entry in the race Duffey
feared would split the Democratic vote, received 24 percent.]

at 7854 in Ponca City, Oklahoma, and tell her you saw Charlie and he's okay and he'll write when he gets where he's going," or who in recent days would go to Disneyland to spend their final weekend before shipping out to Vietnam. As we got back in our '35 Chevy I mentioned to Mother my surprise at the youth of the troops. She was still crying a little and said: "Yes, I'd say half those boys weren't more than twice your age." I was nine.

I remembered the incident as I listened to Ed Miles in Hartford. While reading through newspaper clippings of the senatorial campaign I had come upon a brief dispatch from the Associated Press:

> An Army captain from Westport, Edward Miles, stole the show at a rally for Democratic Senate hopeful Joseph Duffey tonight. Miles, who lost both legs to a mortar shell in Vietnam, appeared in uniform and told the crowd of 4,000 at the New Haven arena: "It was all worthless." Miles said the audience should not be concerned with the body counts of enemy dead. "They're all human beings," he said.

Someone pointed him out to me at a reception that evening and after a few minutes we found ourselves retreating down the hall to a vacant bedroom where we could talk quietly. Although his hands had been injured, he patiently and only slightly self-consciously uses a cane to manipulate his artificial legs. He is twenty-five and handsome, with dark hair and deep eyes in a boyish face whose smile kept taking me back to the troop train in Marshall, Texas. He was reared in Manhasset, Long Island, of Republican and Catholic stock, and until his appearance in New Haven he had never taken part in a demonstration of any kind or made a public speech.

"I was really nervous when I made that speech," he said. "I could hardly remember what I said. It was extemporaneous. I went to this rally with my wife and they asked me if I would say something. I've been going to school down at Fairfield University—I want to go to law school—and I sat around satisfying myself with sending a few telegrams to the President and writing a few letters to Senators expressing my disapproval about this or about that. Then, when the shootings happened at Kent State, I knew I just had to do more than write letters. I went to that rally because I wanted to be with people who felt the way I did and when they asked me to get up and say something, I said, 'Sure.' I didn't know there were four thousand people there. I was so nervous I had to ask my wife what I had said when I finished, and she said, 'You spoke out against the war.'

"The next thing I know I got called in to see the commanding officer. Well, I was reprimanded for being late getting back from my convalescent leave—my wife and I had gone to see her parents in Wisconsin—but I was told that the Secretary of Defense had called down to the general and was upset about something this Captain Miles had said in a speech. I probably got one of the fastest medical retirements in the history of the army. Their paperwork usually would take anywhere from six months to two years. Mine took about four days." He laughed gently and discreetly.

Do you know many other veterans who feel the same way you do?

"I know veterans who feel the way I do about the war and I know veterans who feel differently about it, too. The ones I met in the hospital feel the Vietnamese people have been given a bad deal. They feel they were fighting for something that didn't seem possible to achieve."

How did you come to your own feelings about the war?

"I quit college in Connecticut four years ago and went out to Colorado and Wyoming, the University of Wyoming, and did some ski bumming—I loved to ski—and that's when the draft board caught up with me, early in '66. I was inducted into the army in Denver. I think I was against the war then, but I didn't have a full realization of it at the time any more than most people did. I didn't know anybody personally who had been over there and I had not known anyone who had been wounded or killed there. It's hard to have feelings or impressions about something like that until you have experienced it yourself.

"I went to Officers Candidate School and then to Germany with my division. As soon as we returned, all the officers in my battalion received orders for Vietnam. I had just extended my time in order to make captain, so I got my orders, too. I went to special-warfare school at Fort Bragg and learned guerrilla warfare and the Vietnamese language. It seemed to be good training for the type of war we were fighting, but once you get there, you realize this isn't something you can be trained for. I went over late in '68 and wasn't in the country more than a few days when I got into my first fire fight near the Cambodian border on Highway One, near that Parrot's Beak area our troops went into this spring. It's a funny feeling to realize suddenly that someone is shooting at you. I got pretty scared, and I didn't know exactly what to do, and I saw people running and a few guys get hit with shrapnel from hand grenades, and get knocked down, and I saw pieces of flesh flying around, so I got up and started to run toward where the firing was coming from.

I figured that was the thing to do, try to get some covering fire down, and I ran into a tree limb." He laughed at the recollection and said: "And that was how I went to war—I ran into a tree limb. The Vietnamese got a big kick out of it. I guess I did too, although I felt silly at the time.

"I got to be familiar with that part of the area. They sent me to advise the Vietnamese regional forces and the popular-force troops, who are similar to our National Guard. It didn't take me very long to realize they were not well trained and they were not well motivated. They would rather not have been fighting. They were scared of the North Vietnamese. They weren't too scared of the VC [Viet Cong] because the VC were just like them, except they were on the other side. I lived with these people from December until May, and I got to know them. Most of the GIs I knew were not exposed to the Vietnamese like those of us who were advisers. This is a problem over there because GIs get to thinking of Vietnamese as gooks or slopes, not persons. They were all the same to our fellows. I would probably have felt the same way if I had been in the position of the GIs, if I had been working with an American unit and only occasionally running into the Vietnamese. But I lived with them and their families, I helped to take care of their kids, and I liked them. I really felt sorry for them." His voice broke. There was a long pause. Finally he said: "They really have a bad deal."

How's that?

"They really don't have an understanding of what they are fighting for. They comprehend their family and their village and that's about as far as their experience takes them. Democracy is just impossible for them to grasp out there in the countryside."

What about the argument that we are fighting to give them time to establish the conditions of democracy?

"I think that is our motive. I know people here sincerely believe it, but that's not the way the Vietnamese peasants see it. They just want to live in their village, get enough to eat, take care of their families, and live in peace. The more I saw what was happening, the more discouraged and frustrated and unhappy I became. I can't tell you how unhappy I was. I just—" he paused again—"I just watched too many people getting killed, too many people getting hurt. You can . . . you can just take so much of it. I kept saying, there's no purpose to all this killing. There's nothing to be gained by any more killing."

Did you write home with your reactions?

"I did. I wrote a few letters."

How did your parents respond?

"They weren't too politically inclined about the war one way or another. They were just worried about me. Like when they stopped the bombing, my father was upset because he thought this would put our men—me— in a worse position, that the Communists would be able to infiltrate more weapons and troops. That was possibly true, but by then I thought . . . I just thought we shouldn't be there in the first place. So I really couldn't be against stopping the bombing."

When were you hit?

"Right at the end of April, 1969. I got it from a mortar round."

"Unexpectedly?" I asked, and realized what a stupid question it was.

"Oh, it was unexpected," he said, laughing once more. "I wasn't expecting it at all. When you're having two, three fire fights a week you put it out of your mind. When it happened, I remember lying there telling myself to stay conscious, stay conscious. I never did lose consciousness. I probably would have died if I had gone under, because I was hit pretty bad and I had to stay conscious if I wanted to get out of there on the chopper. At the hospital I received about fifteen units of blood transfusion. I got to the hospital in about forty-five minutes. If it had been five more minutes, I wouldn't have lived.

"I'll tell you this," he said. "The people who worked on me in the medical units in Vietnam—and back here, too—are the greatest. That's where I met my wife, in Vietnam. She was an army nurse, and she treated a lot of the wounded, and she kept wondering what could possibly give meaning to all that suffering. We got married after I was hit."

What about Mylai? I asked. Is it conceivable to you that something like that could have happened?

"Oh, yes. I think it is a very unfortunate thing, but I think it can't be blamed on anyone in particular. The fault lies with all of us for allowing a war to go on in which killing is the only end. Killing is why you are there. Those are kids out there, American kids, soldiers, yes, but they are kids, and they're under fire thirty days, forty days, and they've been watching their friends getting killed, and they've been shot at and getting hit and they're under intense pressure, really terrible pressure, and they don't recognize Vietnamese, they see objects, and when they get a chance to fight back, they don't see women and children— they see gooks and slopes. They're desperate to shoot at something, anything, just to shoot back at whatever has been shooting at them and killing their buddies. And they shoot, blindly, madly—they shoot at anything that moves. You can say, 'Well, they are still responsible for their actions,' and they are, I guess, but we're responsible for sending them over there, for giving them a gun and telling them to go kill, go kill, go kill, and they don't even know who it is they're killing. Yes, it was awful, it was crazy—but I'm not surprised at what happened at Mylai."

Ed Miles had been talking in a low voice, at times so low I could scarcely hear him. There was no trace of bitterness as he spoke, and I mentioned this.

"No, I certainly don't have any bitterness toward the Vietnamese or the army. I had some great officers. Sometimes I get bitter about the things going on in this country. What happened at Kent State made me cry. It brought me up out of my chair when I watched it on television. Suddenly I was back in Vietnam. And the more I watched the scenes on television, the madder I got. Those Guardsmen should never have been given live ammunition. When I received riot-control training for the army at Fort Riley, the only ammunition issued to the unit was issued to the CO—to me. In case of snipers we had a contingency plan built around the best marksman in the company. There was no sense in those Guardsmen having live ammunition. I couldn't believe what I saw on television. It was like a turkey shoot. It was like Vietnam all over again."

Ed Miles reached for his cane and pushed himself out of his chair. He stood silently in the door for a minute before he said: "Sometimes I get to thinking how much killing there's been the last few years. I was eighteen when President Kennedy was killed and I don't remember much killing up until that time in my life. It seems that ever since there's . . . there's been so much killing. So much we don't seem to feel it any more. It didn't take long to forget those kids at Kent State. I can't even remember their names now. Nobody pays any attention to the body counts from Vietnam any more. Killing's bad enough by itself. When you get where you're hardened to it . . ."

He shook his head and moved slowly down the corridor toward his wife.

Richmond, Indiana

THERE ARE VETERANS WHO DISAGREE WITH ED MILES ABOUT THE WAR IN
Vietnam. One can find them in any city in the country. I especially
wanted to talk to veterans in Richmond, Indiana, where the principles
of the American Legion are as deeply rooted as, say, the oil depletion
allowance in Texas.

To get there I flew from Hartford to Columbus, Ohio, and drove in a
rented car west on Highway 40 through farmlands and past glens deep
in summer green. This is the old Wilderness Trail, along which the wagon
trains moved west; in the surrounding bottomlands of the Great Miami
Valley of western Ohio men hacked farms from wild growth and guarded
their families against human marauders and their cattle against wolves.
The countryside now was so pleasant, the small towns were so un-
obtrusive, and the traffic was so infrequent that I suddenly realized
I had been driving on the wrong side of the road.

In the village of Brighton I spotted two boys with .22 rifles riding
their bicycles toward the country. Their hair was close-cropped and their
faces were tanned from the spring wind and the hot June sun. They
waved as I passed. I responded only perfunctorily, for the closer I drew
to Richmond, the more I fastened upon the details of my first visit
eight years before.

I had come in 1962 to refute charges that the Peace Corps had been
infiltrated by Communist provocateurs, charges which the American
Legion in Richmond was circulating with considerable attention from
the Midwestern press. Having sought an audience before which I could

face our accusers, I went to Richmond for the confrontation in a Legion hall. There were at least two hundred men present that evening and they were not in the mood to tolerate the supplications of a twenty-eight-year-old bureaucrat from Washington. "He don't even look old enough to recognize a Communist, much less fight 'em," one man said. Several veterans hooted and hissed and laughed as I spoke, and one huge man with a broad forehead descending down a concave face into a long narrow chin kept picking his nose and flicking the fruits of his labor at my feet. He thought me impudent when I stopped in the middle of a sentence and offered him my handkerchief, and the next thing I knew he seemed about to exchange blows with someone across the room, God bless his soul, who defended my right to speak and tried to quiet the audience. I was scared. Deciding that not even J. Edgar Hoover could convince them of the Peace Corps's purity, I left. Driving away, I could still hear shouts and curses as my beleaguered defender, whose name I did not know, joined my own private list of heroes and martyrs.

I always wanted to return. For some reason the conversation with Captain Miles whetted my curiosity about the attitudes of the veterans in Richmond: had the older men changed? Did their own young men back from Vietnam feel any different? I would find out.

Richmond is an attractive community of forty-four thousand people. As I returned this time I noted just how tidy a place it is. The Wilderness Trail ran through here and people are proud of the heritage. In a park on the edge of town is a monument, "Madonna of the Trail," with a pioneer mother holding one child in her arms, a boy of seven or eight clutching her skirts, and her other hand on a long-stemmed rifle. The grass in the park receives careful attention. A sign advises: "Please drive with care. Our squirrels can't tell one nut from another." The exceedingly polite policeman who gave me directions was wearing an American flag on his right shoulder; I would see more flags in front of the service stations, banks, and houses of Richmond than anywhere else on my journey. The place also seemed gentler than it did when I was here eight years ago, although I might have been deceiving myself; a reporter for the local newspaper would tell me yes, he thinks something happened to the psychology of the community when a thousand pounds of black powder exploded in the basement of a Main Street gun shop a few years ago and killed forty-one people. "It is still conservative," he says, "but the people don't seem as mean any more." The high school is integrated and racial tensions flare up from time to time; but the most difficult problems of adjustment, I was told, are being experienced by poor Appalachian whites who have come here looking for work.

The Harry Ray American Legion Post 65 occupies a new one-story building on Sixth Street, several blocks from the scene of the earlier imbroglio. I considered this change to be a good augury.

Downstairs in a dimly lighted bar and game room I inquired of four men playing cards as to the whereabouts of Robert Kimbrough, the post commander. Without looking up one of the men motioned with his thumb to a small office behind the stairs. There Bob Kimbrough worked at his desk, making final arrangements for the big Fourth of July celebration to which the post would contribute the fireworks, if someone named Homer, to whom he was talking on the telephone, could raise another $600 in the next few days.

Kimbrough cradled the telephone and greeted me earnestly but unsmilingly. He is forty-nine, of medium build, with short black hair, a round and open face, and a slight childhood scar on his right cheek ("My war injuries are where I had better not expose them," he said). A small American flag decorates the clip that attaches his pen to the pocket of his white short-sleeve shirt. He served in France in World War II and is a realtor in Richmond. His four children are twenty-one, sixteen, fourteen, and eleven. I asked him if there is a generation gap at home and he answered, "Generation gap? No, my kids think violence is asinine. As far as young people speakin' their piece, fine, but they don't go for this riotin' and stuff. They think it is Communist-inspired, like I do."

I explained to Bob Kimbrough the purpose of my visit and confessed the almost masochistic desire to return which I have nurtured for eight years. He grinned and ran his hand through his hair. "You got nothin' to worry about," he said. "Some of our oldtimers have died, some have moved away, and others have grown up—you'll find the men real friendly. And, if you want the views of veterans, you've come to the right place. We got about eight hundred men in this post alone. There's another eight hundred in Howard Thomas Post 315, there's about two hundred fifty in the colored post, although we got colored members, too, and there's about a hundred ladies in the Molly Pitcher post. The VFW probably has around three hundred and there are about two hundred fifty Amvets. We got about fifty vets out of Vietnam so far, but they're not active. You take tonight—we've got a meeting and the young boys have a baseball game. They'll go to the baseball game and won't get by here until later. You know, they're young and unsettled when they first get back from Vietnam. When they get older and get kids, they'll come around."

I said that Richmond seemed to have a large number of active veterans.

"Well, I think it's because of Earlham College over there"—over there is west, across the Whitewater River, which divides the town. "There's a lot of folks think some Communists got in there a few years back and were going to cause trouble and they joined the Legion to help oppose them. Now, Earlham College is a fine school and a credit to this town, and 95 percent of the students and faculty are good people. But there was a lot of people who believed some Communist influences were at work. It just takes a few to stir up trouble. Here, let me read you something."

He picked from the table two copies of a one-page flyer, handed one to me, and read aloud from the other:

In May of 1919, at Dusseldorf, Germany, the Allied Forces obtained a copy of some of the "Communist Rules for Revolution." Nearly 50 years later, the Reds are still following these rules. As you read the list, stop after each item—think about the present day situation where you live—and all around our nation. We quote from the Red Rules—

A. Corrupt the young; get them away from religion. Get them interested in sex. Make them superficial; destroy their ruggedness.

B. Get control of all means of publicity, thereby

1. Get people's minds off their government by focusing their attention on athletics, sexy books and plays and other trivialities.

2. Divide the people into hostile groups by constantly harping on controversial matters of no importance.

3. Destroy the people's faith in their natural leaders by holding the latter up to contempt, ridicule and obloquy.

4. Always preach true democracy, but seize power as fast and as ruthlessly as possible.

5. By encouraging governmental extravagance, destroy its credit, produce fear of inflation with rising prices and general discontent.

6. Forment [sic] unnecessary strikes in vital industries, encourage civil disorders and foster a lenient and soft attitude on the part of government toward such disorders.

7. By spacious [sic] argument, cause the breakdown of the old mortal [sic] virtues, honesty, sobriety, continence, faith in the pledged word and ruggedness.

C. Cause the registration of all firearms on some pretext, with a view to confiscation of them and leaving the population helpless.

I was to see these "Communist Rules for Revolution" in town after town, in newspaper after newspaper, and even when they had been exposed as a hoax by no less a Tory than James J. Kilpatrick, the columnist, they continued to circulate widely.

"We've reprinted them and have been passin' them out all around town," Bob Kimbrough said. "The young people should be educated as to what to look for, especially the trickery that Communism represents. And I think we have to take a stand against Communism everywhere we can. We have this undesirable thing in Vietnam. Should never have been there in the first place. The French tried it and didn't make it. But if only the force of arms can stop Communism, we have to use force of arms. You can't back down or they'll take more and more.

"This is why we have to promote Americanism. We try to get to the young with things like baseball, even though it costs us about $3,000 a year, oratorical awards, essays, Boys State, Boy Scout troops, things like that. Last year we got American flags put on the sleeves of all the athletes in the school. We had to put a little pressure on the school officials to get it done but we did it."

Did the kids object?

"Heck, no. They're proud. We also donated flags to the fire department and the mounted patrols. We haven't got to Earlham College yet but we want to get flags on their athletes, too. You see, we got these demonstrations and riots because the Communists are trying to use the kids, but if we wake up we can handle them. I'll tell you—the old Yank sits around on his butt until he gets pushed into the corner and then he comes out swingin'. Just like Pearl Harbor. Sure, we had trouble lately at the colleges and the colored folks have been actin' up. Eleanor Roosevelt started that when she went to England and posed with the colored boys. But I can't blame them because I think every American ought to have equality. It's just that you can't expect a miracle overnight. You can't push a man into changin' his ways just like that"—he snapped his fingers.

What do you think happened in the last decade that most contributed to change in the country?

"Money," he said instantly. "Money. We've all done so much better that we could give the kids what they want and we've spoiled them. They don't have to work and a dollar isn't something you have to sweat for. You just—why, you just ask for it. Things were bad when I was a kid. My dad worked for the railroad company and was gettin' laid off twice a year. He would pick up odd jobs where he could, but I know at Christmastime he would get Carpenter Ripley's children to take sticks and put numbers on them and sell the sticks at ten cents apiece and raffle off his shotgun, enough to raise money to buy us—my sister and my brother and I—Christmas. One year he did the same thing and raffled off my mother's ring, that he had given her when they got married, to buy Christmas for us children. My children haven't known times like those. I have tried not to give them everything. I have tried to make them know the value of a dollar. I'm real proud because my children have all worked—we would give them an allowance or we would make them work for money, for things they've wanted. They want more money, we give them another chore. I'd have to admit, though, my children are probably spoiled, like everyone else. No matter how hard you try, when one of those kids pucker up and want something, you're going to give it to them, especially the girls; they could sure get by Dad."

We were joined by Jack McGill, fifty-one, a past commander of the post. "What bothers me about the kids," he said, "is they got no respect. Why, my father used to demand that I call older men 'Mr.' and older ladies 'Mrs.' But the kids today, you're lucky if they say 'Hey' to you."

What about patriotism? I asked. You felt you were expressing your patriotism when you went into the service and to war. What does patriotism mean to you today.

Jack McGill answered first. "To me patriotism means that no matter which way you voted, you go and support the man who is elected as the majority of the people wanted."

"I agree with that," Kimbrough said. "We've got elections, and a way of government that has come about after lots of trial and error, and I think if you're going to be patriotic, you have to support that system. Too many kids have stopped supportin' the government and too many have gotten away from the church. The American Legion was founded on the slogan 'For God and country.' This country was founded upon religion, and too many parents have let their children get away from religion. 'Course I think it's a known fact that the Communist elements are trying to infiltrate the churches, just like they have the racial incidents and the media. . . ."

Where do you get your news? I interrupted.

"I get mine mostly from the newspaper," McGill answered. "I do very little reading otherwise. Now, you may not believe this, but the only time I have the TV on is when there's a ball game on or the news and weather. I turn it on just for them. Now, that's really a fact. I don't care for the media because it's plain missed the boat on the campus thing. Last fall my boy was going to college and there was a Dad's Weekend where you go down and spend the weekend and stay in the dorms. And on one night the different fraternities and the different wings of the dorms put on little skits, and they judged which was the best. The night I was down there, they had nine skits and you know seven of them were patriotic. Now, something like that never hits the newspaper. But if there had been six demonstrators marching down there with signs, it would have been in the newspapers. I think that if a demonstration goes on in this country, if there's something to demonstrate against, then we should be demonstrating against attorneys."

Attorneys?

"Yessir. They make the laws, and somewhere or the other they can twist them around any way they want to, they can just about get anybody off, no matter what kind of crime they've committed. I'd like to see us put all the attorneys right out in the middle of a big field and just march around and around them all day protesting and demonstrating and raising the devil with them for all the trouble they've caused."

Now there, I thought, is an idea that could get more people together than televised football games on Sunday, and I had begun to conjure up images in my mind of lawyers in New York whom I would enjoy seeing out there on Jack McGill's "big field" when the door to the basement office of the Harry Ray Post opened and four young men entered.

★ ★ ★

The Monday-night baseball game was over and the younger members, most of whom are "Viet vets," in their twenties, were coming by for a beer. They are working now for the Post Office, but three have applied for jobs with the U.S. Immigration Service and want to serve in the border patrol. They seemed younger than their age—boyish, in fact, as Ed Miles had. They cracked jokes, bummed cigarettes from each other, and bought one round of beer after another for all of us sitting in the cramped little office; I thought of the troop train again. Wars seem to be fought only by boys. When I mused aloud, one of the new arrivals, the youngest, figured that "anybody who goes over there will come back either dead or a man, makes no difference how old he was when he went."

I asked them if their feelings about the war had changed since their return.

"If it was to protect my country, I'd go right back," one said. "I felt like I was doing something for my country. I told my father I'd go back if they declared war, if they actually meant business and would go in there and do their thing. But I wouldn't go now if you gave me a million dollars. All they're doing in there now is just playing. They're just draggin' it on and on and a lot of people keep losing their lives for nothing. I think we should fly up to Hanoi and blow hell out of the place if you want to know the truth. You're goin' to kill women and children but that's the only way to get the Communists. Sure, if they'd do that, I'd go back in. I guess I'm some kind of patriotic fool but I'd do it."

"I'm a strict Communist hater," another said. "I've never agreed with anything they do or anything I've heard they do. I definitely feel we were fightin' for freedom in Vietnam. That's why I joined the American Legion. I haven't noticed too many young guys really wantin' to get into this any more. It seems like to them it's a bunch of old fogies and stuff like that." The others laughed. He looked somewhat embarrassed and said, "I don't mean you, Mr. Kimbrough. But no kiddin', that's the way a lot of the young guys think. We could bring them in if the Legion could do more as far as fightin' these college demonstrations the Communists are fomentin'. Anybody who wants to say something against the way the country's bein' operated right now, there's no place to go to actually voice an opinion except the Legion."

Did any of you have any doubts while you were in Vietnam?

The youngest man spoke. "I had lots of doubts. I was in the infantry and I fought among the South Vietnamese people. I found out they didn't no more care whether they had Communism or not. As far as they're concerned, they can go either way. If the American troops are with them, they're for the American troops. When the American troops are gone, they're going to help the Viet Cong as much as they can. All they care about is living."

Do you think we're justified in being there?

"As far as fighting Communism, yes," he answered. "As far as helping the South Vietnamese, no."

"I think we'd do more good in fighting the Communists at home," the first one said. "Dissent is all right, but rioting and burning and looting and shit like that, that's got to stop. I think the American people have taken it for so long, and the time's come, if it hasn't already started, for the silent majority, so called, to take action. And when they do, things are going to get tough."

Do you consider yourself a member of the silent majority?

"I don't think we're too silent tonight." Again there was laughter. One veteran said: "It's time to speak up. I'm worried that the young people will cause such an uprising that the whole United States will be mass confusion, open for any country to take over."

"I don't agree with that. If it really came down to a fight or lose your country, I think there would be a lot of people that would turn into Americans. I mean even the people who are called dissenters and rioters would wake up."

What do you think about the fellows who have gone to Canada to avoid the draft?

"I think they ought to shoot every damn one of them that tries to come back."

What about Mylai?

"I don't believe it happened," one young man said.

"I don't either," Jack McGill said. "I was in the Philippines in World War II and I've seen the time you could hardly see the difference in the enemy and the people on your side. And, when there was any doubt, I was ready to see that I got out alive."

"It might have happened," the youngest veteran said. "I mean, you can't tell a North Vietnamese from a South Vietnamese. There's no way. And you can sit there and drink with them all day and they'll kill you at night while you sleep and . . ."

"And that first shot that's fired," someone interrupted. "Everybody's scared, regardless of what they say, they're scared when they go in and that first shot comes at them. And everybody starts shootin' because the only way to keep from gettin' killed themselves is to wipe out everybody they can."

"What bothered me is that our attacks were from under bushes and trees," said a veteran of the air force. "You never seen any of them. You just fired. Shoot down towards the ground and hope you caught somebody. I never seen one dude in a fire fight in a whole year."

A year?

"Yep, and I was in lots of fights. We made contact on every mission we went on during the first six months I was over there. I fired a lot of rounds—I just kept firing away—but I never seen one dude."

There was a long silence. We drifted into banter. Bob Kimbrough offered to buy another round of beer but we all declined; the little office was smoky, it was past midnight and time to leave. One of the young men asked me what I thought about Richmond. I said, "Well, I had a different experience tonight from my first visit," and told them the story of my appearance in 1962. They laughed and one said: "Lots of changes since then. Did you hear about the biggest thing that's happened to Richmond recently?"

No.

"*Playboy* magazine selected one of our girls as Playmate of the Month. Sold out every copy in town. Somebody said we oughta put up a statue to her out there in the park right beside that pioneer mother. Said they was examples of America before and after."

★ ★ ★

The next day I drove across the Whitewater River to Earlham College, a Quaker school whose espousal of social reform goes back to the 1830s. The paradox intrigued me: a college with a large pacifist constituency thriving in a Midwestern community with almost two thousand Legionnaires. Not long ago, a Legionnaire had said, several students from Earlham obtained a permit to demonstrate in opposition to the Vietnam war. Angry citizens besieged City Hall, one man advising the mayor "to recall that permit because those people aren't coming across that bridge." According to my informant, the mayor obliged, restoring the uneasy truce that governs the relationship between Earlham and Richmond.

But Bob Kimbrough had also said that "95 percent of the students and faculty are good people," specifically placing in this category the name of Dr. Elton Trueblood, a professor of philosophy at Earlham. It was a familiar name to me. Many years ago, in a comparative-religion course at the University of Texas, I had been strongly influenced by *The Predicament of Modern Man*, which Dr. Trueblood had written in 1944 while teaching at Stanford University. Against the backdrop of World War II he argued that ". . . our wisdom about ends does not match our ingenuity about means, and this situation, if it continues, may be sufficient to destroy us. . . . Our predicament is a commentary . . . on the human inability to employ both scientific knowledge and technical achievement to bring about the good life and the good society." * Dr. Trueblood subsequently wrote twenty-seven other books which have made him perhaps the most popular Quaker writer in the country. We had talked once, in Washington, when he had visited the White House, but I had not seen or heard from him in five years. There was now a Quaker President in Washington, with whom I understood Dr. Trueblood had been good friends, and I was curious to know if the Quaker philosopher believed the Quaker President's religion affected his conduct in public office.

He greeted me in his study, a large walnut-paneled room, of brick Georgian design, set adjacent to a small wooded sanctuary on the edge of the English park that is Earlham's campus. The room is flawlessly decorated, the centerpiece an old clock that has been running for eighty years without repair. On the wall hang autographed portraits of Dwight D. Eisenhower, Richard Nixon, and Herbert Hoover, the other Quaker who made it to the White House. Dr. Trueblood is seventy now. His hair has whitened considerably since I last saw him, but his bespectacled eyes still move quickly, his voice retains the vibrancy of a much younger man, and his hands gesture intensely as he speaks.

As he showed me the three photographs on the wall I asked him about President Nixon's Quaker antecedents.

"For one thing his grandparents lived on the Muscatatuck River about a hundred miles south of here. If you saw the movie *Friendly Persuasion*, the heroine in there is based on Nixon's grandmother. In that movie the Southern army—Morgan's Raiders—crossed the Ohio and came up through the Quaker settlements, and my grandmother fed the soldiers in her kitchen, and Richard Nixon's grandmother did, too. The first Quaker settlers who came to this country were stubborn people, very stubborn and independent, like the President. Nixon, you see, represents what would be called the evangelical core of Quakers. There is a fringe that has become merely activist without any real faith, any theology, but nearly all of the California Quakers, where Nixon's parents lived, remain in the evangelical core. I know many of those people personally, including some of the President's relatives. They are absolutely the salt of the earth, the backbone of the Whittier community. Nixon's mother had a deep influence on him, of course. She wanted him to be a conscientious objector. There

* *The Predicament of Modern Man,* Harper & Brothers, 1944.

was Pearl Harbor and all the struggle within him and he decided to go into the navy because it was the lesser of the evils. She cried. She was hurt very much, but she sent her blessing. She was a delightful and very deep Christian mother who taught him the wisdom of serenity. She was herself a very serene person. I think he learned very early the need to be quiet. To listen. You know how he is reported to spend a great deal of time alone."

What about the worship services in the White House? Isn't that a rather public kind—

"I'll tell you. Some of the Friends meeting around Washington are Quakers who are on the fringe. Nixon would not recognize them as valid adherents because they have become mere social activists. They are more political than religious, and the President wouldn't feel comfortable in their meetings."

Some of the most effective social-protest movements have grown out of a special religious conviction. John Wesley—

"Exactly so. If you have mere pietism, it grows stale. But if you have mere social action without the roots of tradition, it becomes bitter. I personally think the President is a man of deep personal beliefs, which is why he doesn't like the Quaker meetings in Washington that are just political."

Is there any special relationship between Quakerism and anti-Communism? I'm thinking now of the President's early political life.

"Certainly the Communist system with its insistence on violence and denial of freedom is repugnant to us. There's a kind of leftist mentality that gets into this. I'll admit that some Quakers have been a little soft on Communism. Even Alger Hiss had Quaker connections. It was the funniest thing; those three men all had Quaker connections: Hiss, Nixon, and Chambers. Nixon found out Hiss was lying. And oh, was this hard on the leftists. They've hated Nixon ever since. He ferreted out their fair-haired boy, you see. They never will forgive him. So these people who set the style for the Washington *Post* and the *New York Times*, who are all a little left of center, they just automatically hate him. Then they find the reasons later. I was glad about Agnew because he had the courage to tell the truth and to point out bias where it existed, and because he spoke for the people who have no spokesman. You see, those other people, the ones who are stirring up all of the trouble, have monopolized the media. After all, if you take NBC and CBS you have most of the country and they have it all their way. I'm glad, I suppose, that television was invented—I'm not sure—but I know that it is intrinsically sensational. It fragments the truth. You never see the nuances; you only see one thing. But the truth is always more than one thing. My wife is pretty but she is also smart. But if you take a picture of her you know she is pretty but you don't know that she is also smart. So Agnew was right about the media. I was disappointed when he was selected for Vice President. I think now it was a brilliant choice."

Dr. Trueblood rose and picked up from his desk an article he had written on campus demonstrations. I read it and said: "This is a very strong statement."

"Yes," he said, "I know it."

What was your reaction to Kent State?

"I was sad that four people were killed, but of course the student population all over the country vastly overreacted."

Do you think they overreacted more than Middle Americans have overreacted to campus troubles?

"That isn't the issue. The students were not honest enough to admit that the students were the aggressors."

The aggressors?

"Yes, sir. The aggressors. They were practically trying to kill the National Guard. Throwing pieces of cement with spikes in them. That's lethal. The kids have the devil theory, you see. So they made the National Guard into the devil."

The devil theory cuts both ways, I suggested. Isn't it possible that many people have made all students into devils?

"What you have to keep in mind is all this denunciation, this attack, this scorching opposition. It's the victory of the judgmental spirit, it's totally irrational, and it's created a very strong response from ordinary people. The kids are saying that to be moral today you only have to be against racism, against poverty, against pollution, and against war—and you are moral, whether or not you are faithful to your wife or pay your debts. They are guilty of the most bifurcated moralism I have ever heard of in my life. In fact, there is too much moralism and not enough morality. That's one reason the kids don't laugh any more—they take themselves too seriously. Why, even *The New Yorker* isn't funny any more."

But how are we going to heal this cleavage between the generations?

"Part of it is to let them grow a little."

That puts all the burden on them.

"But the answer is not to be permissive. The one thing that annoys me is to hear someone say, 'But we've got to hear what they are trying to say.' I've heard that until I'm nauseated. I know what they are trying to say, and some of those things are nice things, but I am unalterably opposed to the cult of irrationalism which expresses itself by shouting. Everybody is so busy shouting at everyone else that he's forgotten how to laugh. Don't you think that is obvious?"

It is obvious that you and the President share more in common than the Quaker faith.

Elton Trueblood laughed and said, "Let's go to dinner. Mrs. Trueblood wants you to join us." We walked to their apartment, a few yards from the study. Before dinner he said, "I presume you still adhere to the tenets of the New Testament?"

That has been the subject of much discussion, I replied, but my mother still prays that I do.

"Well, this evening we shall see to it that her prayers are answered." He opened his Bible to I Timothy 5:23 and read aloud: "Drink no longer water, but use a little wine for thy stomach's sake and thine often infirmities."

And in the manner of old we proceeded to interpret the scriptures literally. I felt better immediately.

Yellow Springs, Ohio

TWO HOURS FROM DR. TRUEBLOOD'S STUDY IS ANTIOCH COLLEGE, WHERE his views of American students would probably be received with all the alacrity of the SDS listening to a speech by Strom Thurmond.

Antioch College has long been a magnet for nonconformity. Here, among the incongruous pastoral scenes of rural Ohio, on a campus of fewer than two thousand students, with an endowment of less than $6 million, the ideas of progressive education found succor in audacious minds. While other schools administered true-false final exams and sought vicarious glory on Saturday afternoons, there flourished at Antioch College the concept of a student directing his own studies; of full participation by students and faculty in the choice of rules and regulations; of undergraduates working at paid jobs for as many months in another part of the country or world as they spend in classrooms on campus; of the honor system. Here deviation became the norm, the rebellious minority constituted itself into a majority, and everyone did his own thing long before the Beatles picked up a guitar. And from here went out missionaries into every endeavor of human affairs, carrying the message of the whole man, Man the Incarnate Renaissance. "Antioch," one of its former students wrote, "acquired a tone that combined Greenwich Village and a Quaker work camp. Antioch took on the personality of a career revolutionary—or say, a hybrid of guinea pig and underdog. It drew teachers and students who saw in it a challenge to conventional ideas of study, work and living. There were earnest utopians and flamboyant dissenters. Despite underen-

36

dowment, scorn from orthodox educators, attacks from local and national rightists, Antioch distinguished itself." *

Its students know it. They carry their elitism casually and confidently.

I arrived from Richmond as the incoming freshman class flocked in for the new summer term. For two hours I sat on the steps of the Student Union and watched. In front of the building the newcomers were greeted by a hand-painted remnant of the spring wars:

> Antioch loves novelty,
> One cause after another. . . .
> Well, finish the first one first.
> Pledge money to the Blank Panther Defense Fund.

A bare-chested young man wearing an Aussie hat strolled by in tight-fitting black Nureyev pants tied with an orange sash. Another wore only a loin cloth. Girls ambled along in bikini halters and blue jeans. A mother walked across the street with a son whom she had come to deposit on the shores of a world she would never understand and could never inhabit; she kept two steps behind him, a white-haired woman in her sixties, her blue polka-dotted dress neatly pressed and a little too starched. Her son was big and carried his more than two hundred pounds on two of the largest bare feet I have seen since the summer training camp of the New York Jets at Hofstra University. His hair curved down his shoulders and his yellow shirt went flop-flop-flop against white-streaked blue jeans. They stopped at an old maroon Ford with Illinois license plates; he leaned over and kissed her forehead and without a word disappeared among the trees on campus. She watched him go, got into the Ford, and drove away.

Near the entrance to the Union two boys of about ten with short hair and tennis shoes offered lemonade for ten cents a cup. Three feet from them two long-haired, shirtless young men opened their van at the curb of the street and displayed colorful shirts, beads, scarves, tambourines and other trinkets, the sale of which, they hoped, would finance a trip to Alaska. The two pairs of peddlers carried on a busy discourse with each other all afternoon and once even exchanged commerce.

Across the street small clusters of students sat or lay on the grass. Some laughed, talked, or sang. Others were sleeping. I was about to draw some profound generalization from the observation that I had

---

* Arno Karlen in the June, 1967, issue of *Holiday*.

seen no couples strolling hand in hand when a boy and a girl turned the corner and spared me the error.

In red paint on the side of a dormitory up the street I could read the words: "Power to the people—remember Kent State."

A small notice on the Union door urged volunteers to help organize Dayton hospital workers at a meeting that night. Another announced the birth of twins to some obviously popular campus couple. A third simply stated: "Dr. Wow and the Psychedelic BMW," which turned out to be a tease for a multidimensional orientation film to be shown the next day to freshmen. One handwritten poster advised: "Schizophrenia may be a necessary consequence of literacy."

A Notice to All Freshmen taped on the Union door read:

> Re: campus security. Certain dorms have what is called a "security problem." What this means in effect is that if you don't at all times keep your room door locked, you are liable to have your property stolen. It can happen to you, because at Antioch it happens to *everybody*. Lock your doors even when you are just going to the toilet— and keep it locked when you're taking a nap. *Women especially* should be sure to lock their doors at night—there have been several rapes in the dorms so far this year (this isn't said to scare you, it's just a fact. . . .) If you do get ripped-off in any way, report it to Maples immediately; usually nothing very effective is done but it is good policy anyway. Behave as though you were living in Manhattan on East 5th Street between Avenues B & C, if that means anything to you. . . . It's not paranoia, people, it's common sense from lots and lots and lots and lots of experience.

Marjorie Freed is one of those delightful women who usually inhabit the registrar's office, the dean's office, or the public-relations bureau, have ceased to confirm their birthdays, are married only to the institution, and can tell a visitor more about what is happening on campus than any dozen trustees. Marj Freed runs the Antioch news bureau. She has been there for eighteen years, sustained through it all by a keen sense of humor. She is the editor of *Freed's Journal*, an irregular compilation of news of interest to the college community, written, she says, according to Richard Hofstadter's "typical procedure of the higher paranoid scholarship . . . which is to start with . . . defensible assumptions and with a careful accumulation of facts, or what appear to be facts, and to marshal these facts toward an overwhelming 'proof' of the particular conspiracy that is to be established."

We met for lunch in the Union. I asked her about the flamboyant and varied dress of the students, confessing that I had suffered a bit of culture shock during the morning watch on the front steps. "It even takes a little getting used to by old hands like me," she said. "But I think they are trying to create an identity for themselves, their peers, and the adults. They're trying to say, 'I am different. I want different things. I want a different way of life.' Dr. Dixon [James Dixon, the president of Antioch] once said you could translate a certain restless student behavior into a statement, 'I am here.' I think there is something to that. Our students are mostly middle-class kids, they're well-to-do, they come right out of a culture where they were stereotyped and identified by a pretty sterile life style. When they get here they dress that way"—she nodded her head toward the campus—"to let everyone know, including their parents, that they are very distinct individuals."

She admitted to mixed feelings about the young. "I think the kids have had great success. They forced President Johnson to change the war policy. They forced him to stop the bombing. I think they forced him out. They got Nixon to get the troops out of Cambodia by June 30. They have been effective but, sadly, they don't know it. They expect gratification now and they are unhappy when they don't get it. I can understand why. Their college career is such a short period of their life that they want to see results before they leave. They're frustrated when the results don't occur.

"Of course," she said, "some kids are bastards. They're just mean and ornery. They speak of reason and behave irrationally, and unfortunately they are the ones who set the image for the majority. Those kids out there"—and she gestured toward the campus again—"are mostly good kids, highly motivated, a little affected now by their self-consciousness—the media pays them enormous attention—but they're decent, and they really do want to do something to improve things, and they're gentle. I guess the thing I dislike the most about them is that they don't want you to stereotype them but they sure as hell will stereotype you.

"Antioch is small," she said. "We're small enough to stay in touch. During the student strike this spring I think we would have blown if we had had one more student."

What was that all about?

"Kent State was the catalyst. The weekend before, just after Nixon's

Cambodia speech, I walked across the campus and kept asking myself: Why are they so apathetic? Then those four kids were killed and our people went into action. They made four demands—that we sever our last defense contract, that we pay all employees during the campus strike, that our top governing body come out against the war officially, as an institution, and that the college contribute $50,000 to the Black Panther Defense Fund. The governing council agreed to the first three but turned down the Panther request because it would have involved us with Internal Revenue. That's when we had some violence—more like malicious mischief—some broken windows and some signs painted on the building. The students occupied the administration building and wouldn't come out or let anyone in until the little old ladies who work in the bursar's office came to work. Students said they could come in because their job is to issue the checks to the workers on campus, but in effect the ladies said, 'Hell, no,' and walked off. They didn't want kids dictating their work habits and they didn't want to be working while everyone else was off. This put the kids on a spot because they had themselves insisted that all employees of the college would be paid during the strike. They saw the absurdity of frustrating the very demand they had won, so they vacated the building.

"You have to give Dr. Dixon his due," she said as we walked to the president's office. "He trusts the kids. He has six of his own and he believes kids are persons. His leadership, which looks to some people like no leadership, is to set a climate. He really observes the processes of democracy. He's a gentle man who is never nettled by rudeness. He doesn't try to be a father figure or a self-proclaimed knight on a charger. He's not patronizing or condescending, and he's the least punitive man I know. He was made for Antioch."

★ ★ ★

James Payson Dixon, president of Antioch since 1959, an alumnus come home after an M.S. from Columbia, a medical degree from Harvard, and eleven years as health commissioner of Denver and Philadelphia. Appointed by three U.S. Presidents to distinguished commissions. Co-chairman, with Dick Gregory, of the "New Party," and a sponsor of the National Council to Repeal the Draft.

He is, as Maj Freed said, "essentially bald," his forehead a road map of wrinkles as he talks and thinks, the forty-nine-cent corncob pipe deceptively elegant.

He is also essentially political. "He has made a consistent policy of accommodating himself to student whims," the Springfield *Sun* once wrote of him. "He has had remarkable success in doing so. His success is remarkable because, precisely, there are all kinds of Antiochians." He is accustomed to the unusual. Once two students came to see him. "They were quite stoned," he reported. "They came to ask me, they said, what I would do if students did come and tell me they were stoned."

How, I asked, do you convince people—newcomers, outsiders—to go beyond the students' dress, their hair, rhetoric, and pot—to deal with them as people?

"You try to find circumstances in which young people can relate constructively to others. It depends on trust. One principal difficulty in the country seems to be that we don't trust our young. We don't trust them to make decisions, we don't trust them to modify the nature of their education, we don't trust them to change their sense of what a career is. The young are terribly idealistic, actually utopian, in their notions of what society could be and what they could do within society. They are very suspicious of authority when authority is conveyed by role instead of by person. They aren't suspicious of authority when authority comes out of a face-to-face contact. It is really a matter of trust."

The visitor to Antioch, I said, initially sees little evidence of authority—

"Oh," he interrupted, "there's enormous authority, so that even when we get passionately involved in the questions of Vietnam or the questions of the use of force on campuses there is authority in this community that means people will deal with these violent questions without having to become violent. It is the authority that comes from our collaborating together as a community."

In what ways?

"Take the Kent State crisis. We had a big community meeting, 65 or 70 percent of the community turned out. We adopted the same pattern that was true across the country, the strike, which simply means, 'Let's change our agenda for a while. Let's accept the fact that these things going on at Kent State are important, and let's set aside our normal agenda and deal with them.' Then gradually we worked out a community agenda for our strike. We set aside business as usual and said nobody gets penalized for participating in this new agenda, what-

41

ever it's going to be. Students don't get penalized in terms of credits. Workers don't get penalized if they decide to do something besides come to work during this period. If a member of the staff—a payroll clerk, a waiter in the dining hall, a janitor—finds something more important at this moment in time to do, he does it. Everybody was on an equal footing—students, faculty, staff. There was tremendous authority in the sense of restraint."

Is there a point at which a university ceases to be a university and becomes an instrument of political action?

"The fact is that the university *is* a political institution, in our plan, and has always been. The argument has to do with how to refine a political position that we take on a given issue. The university has always been a source of political energy and political criticism and it's usually been a source of political action. And these have generally hung together with some sort of theory of pluralism. If you make a series of arrangements to do classified research for the Defense Department, you have become a political institution. What you must avoid are simple-minded, monolithic statements, as if a total institution could take a precise position on a political matter. Such statements are phony because they tend to suggest there are simple solutions to complex problems. What we did here was to protect the right to an individual position. Now this produces a good deal of ambiguity and conflict. For instance, it was clear that many of our people meeting together as a community were able to agree that it would be a good idea to use institutional funds for the support of the Black Panthers. But that turned out not to be a universal position within the institution. The faculty believed that, rather than support the use of institutional funds, we should set up a voluntary social-action program, a kind of self tax. This didn't satisfy the staunchest advocates of the Black Panther position but that's what I'm saying—sometimes the result is ambiguous. The sense of individual commitment arose out of the process of asking questions within the university community."

What do you think happened between 1960, which was a relatively apolitical year on college campuses except in a conventional sense, and 1970, in which the atmosphere is volatile and political?

"Unquestionably it was Vietnam. The Vietnam phenomenon and the relationship of deferment and being in college. That involved every male in the process, and when you involve the men you in some sense involve the women, too. The usual elements of patriotism that often

42

function under these circumstances have not functioned. You had in the university communities a greater concentration of people who were personally affected by the war. The universities therefore became a major focus of dissent to the war. You also had in the 1960s a shift to a new morality. The war was caught up in this, but it isn't the only factor."

I mentioned Dr. Trueblood's reaction to the new morality—his comment that to be moral today one has only to be against the war, poverty, pollution, and racism—without changing his personal standards of behavior.

"I wasn't thinking about political morality. I was thinking about personal morality. Drugs very clearly introduced into the community another kind of environmental possibility in addition to alcohol, and it increased the level of permissiveness for self-expression, whether in art, behavior, or dress. That aspect of morality that has to do with how one conducts himself in terms of manner and dress and style got enormously loosened up, and there was a period in the 1960s of intense individualism. I think that loosening-up has allowed people to accept others for what they are in a much more generous and, curiously, in a much more religious fashion. The kids will say, 'I'm not going to try to put into your head what I think you ought to be. I'm going to try to start with who you are.' Now that's a great moral change—the rediscovery of individualism along with which is a tremendous respect for individual difference. This is a very moral track —you can respect a person with whom you cannot agree. The young have developed a new style, a style that has integrity. And it is a style which through the course of time will have to extend the same kind of dynamics of human action to others than themselves."

I mentioned the warning to freshmen posted on the door to the Student Union. Do you relate that kind of thing to this new morality?

"No. I suppose that an open community does tend not to protect itself with locks and that sort of thing, and in that sense they're very gullible. But as we've moved quite self-consciously and in rather daring ways at Antioch toward increasing the cultural pluralism of the college, we've discovered there are, of course, class differences in morality. White middle-class America is pretty cool to the use of either personal violence or mass violence as a means of solving human problems. Usually they look for a method of accommodating or mediating differences short of personal violence. This is not the acceptable mode of moral behavior for, say, a black kid from an inner-city ghetto. At some point he confirms his morality by beating the hell out of somebody. That for him is a positive confirmation. That makes him feel a man. What in a sense is moral in terms of being consistent with the ethic of the culture for one group is not moral for another. And you've got a real problem under these circumstances in trying to define what's crime."

If a national television network gave you five minutes to address the whole nation about this generation of students, what would you say?

"First, I would try to demonstrate that the changes in young people are coming as a consequence of a long historical background—they're not accidental, they're not random, they're real. Second, the young are astonishingly idealistic and utopian, and this is both part of the charm and part of the difficulty. Third, they are learning different modes of both interpersonal communication and use of communications. They are handling more data and in more different ways than we ever knew how to handle. Their generation is going to have to master the meaning of mass communication in our time. Instantaneous data. They're going to have to set into perspective what it really means to have a report from the battle front twenty minutes after it happens or instantaneously. Fourth, I would try to make the point that we have, like all cultures, tended to shelter our young, by accident not by intent, from raw social interactions. We thought it was terribly important that we cultivate their intelligence and perceptions, and the very procedures by which we've done that have been procedures of isolation. So I would argue that some reform is necessary within the educational sector—away from isolation—to expose kids, including secondary-school kids, to different experiences and other kinds of people. And finally I would argue that in the short run people get hurt, things get stolen, and people get raped, as violence occurs, but there's probably drastically less violence than if we were to polarize the nation along conventional revolutionary lines. We can risk this generation's managing us through a revolutionary time which is essentially cultural, or we can polarize and expect a revolution that will be traditional, bloody, and much more destructive of democratic values."

★ ★ ★

I fell in with two black students who were walking toward the Student Union. When I asked them how many blacks are enrolled at Antioch, one of them, a frail, thin young man from the East, replied:

"That's not the problem. The problem isn't that there aren't enough blacks; it's that there aren't enough poor people here—period. And I mean poor white folks too. Most of the kids here," he said, "come from very well-to-do homes. There's not enough endowment for many scholarships from the college and they wouldn't be here if their old man wasn't footin' the bill for them." He laughed and said: "That's why they get such a big kick out of dressin' and messin' around like they do. They're sayin', 'Screw you, Daddy,' all the time they're livin' on his pork. One thing about those middle-class white cats—they sure as hell don't want to do what their parents are doin', but they sure want their parents to keep on doin' it long enough for them to finish college.

"Well, they're middle class, see, I'd say 85 percent, 90 percent, and so naturally the courses and the work and all the programs are really middle class. Most of us [some 175 blacks] are from poor homes. We wouldn't be here if it weren't for foundation grants and special things like that, and we just couldn't swing those middle-class courses. We set up a black studies program but the folks at HEW in Washington said, Uh-uh, you can't run a segregated program on federal money— 'course this was segregated by blacks for blacks—and we got together and said to the college, O.K., you get some more poor white students in here, and some kids like that, because there'll be more like us and you'll have to make some changes." He laughed again and said: "Now there is a switch—*us* agitatin' for more white cats. But we want 'em *poor*, because even if they're white, when they're poor we got a lot in common."

I asked Marjorie Freed about this and she said, yes, Antioch plans to increase its "pluralism" by enrolling more than 200 "high risk" students in the next three years. Of the first 145 who will enter this year, 65 are blacks and 20 are Indians, Orientals, Spanish-speaking Puerto Ricans, and Mexican-Americans. The rest are from working-class white families—sons and daughters of plumbers, truck drivers, steelworkers, toolmakers, clerks, and butchers. "Our studies have shown that many of our white students who do come from working-class families arrive with attitudes and life goals remarkably similar to those of the more usual white student. Only black students introduce true diversity into the classroom and campus life. We are going out now to recruit a significant number of minority-group students and whites with backgrounds, perceptions, and life aims that differ markedly from those of most students here. Much will be changed," she predicted. "Students will have forced the college to accommodate to what the students themselves saw as their needs."

★ ★ ★

I spent most of the afternoon drinking coffee in the Union with students. They were friendly, frank, and inquisitive. Some of them complained that Antioch's past was more radical than its present, that its imitators have surpassed it in innovation. Others disagreed. "I've got friends at Harvard, Michigan, and UCLA," one boy said. "Compared to the mobility I've got, they might as well be in San Quentin."

A visitor on campus, a young man who had been graduated from Antioch three years earlier, seated himself at the table. I asked him what Antioch had meant to him. He stroked his beard and replied: "It forced me to examine my every reason for being. It left me with no ambition unchallenged—perhaps left me with no ambition—not necessarily a bad thing; Antioch graduates rarely enter the big ego leagues. But mostly it showed me that an institution can exist in a state of constant chaos, that the good of the individual can be paramount even in a functioning bureaucracy. Dixon once said that the survival of Antioch as an institution was not among his highest priorities. He also said that one of the school's great discoveries was that human beings can tolerate a much higher level of conflict than they think they can, and that this conflict can be healthy. It's that kind of place—tumultuous, yet exciting and healthy as an institution. It's one of the few places I know which give me hope that humans can exist better in tandem than alone."

After the students I had been talking to left I sat in the snack shop drinking more coffee and watching the continuing procession. It is not easy to generalize about these young people. Marj Freed was correct, they are gentle. And Dr. Trueblood was also correct, they take themselves terribly seriously. They trifle and joke very little. They seem acutely aware of themselves, acutely conscious that the world is watching them through some giant one-way mirror; they pretend to ignore it, but if they think the world is no longer watching, they become very uneasy. They talk earnestly of momentous issues—of war and peace, of love and justice, of "turning the nation around" and "rebuilding the cities"—but not many of them seemed to be personally engaged in any concrete acts of social change. I wondered how far-reaching their influence ultimately will be. Will they change society by infiltrating it with a "new morality" more enduring than fads of dress and rhetoric? Columbia Records claims the Blue Funk Railroad, a musical group, belongs "to the new culture setting forth on a final voyage through a dying world." And the president of Antioch believes they are already beyond us "into a new sociology." But it is a mistake to romanticize the young. They are quite human, and the qualities that attract a James Dixon repel an Elton Trueblood. The jury remains split and the verdict on this generation is still out.

On the Road in Ohio

VIA THE GRAPEVINE I HAD HEARD OF REVOLUTIONARIES OF ANOTHER KIND
in Gary, Indiana, so I headed north. The road carried me through
Urbana ("Home of Brand Whitlock, Author, Statesman, First Ambassador to Belgium") past a large International truck plant sitting alone
in the country surrounded by hundreds of automobiles and testifying
to the genius of some industrial planner who knew how to bring jobs
to a rural area where people could work in a pleasant environment;
he should be put in charge of the Department of Commerce.

I passed through Westville, a flashing yellow light encircled by no
more than three dozen houses and a two-story red school with boarded
windows; past cornfields and creeks that at one time must have stirred
many a young boy's imagination; and into Lena ("Birthplace of A. B.
Graham, Educator, Founder of 4-H"). The signs welcoming the traveler
to these small towns no longer advertise the size of the population.
It is hard not to lament their decline, although life in these rural
towns was never as idyllic as our poets remember it. People who live
in hamlets can be as mean and petty as any urban dweller. "There is
more harm in the village than is dreamt of," Cervantes wrote; but it
is also true that in a small town, as Lyndon Johnson often said when
he went home to central Texas, "They know when you're sick and they
care when you die."

Such was the debate in my mind as I noticed a sign which announced
"Piqua, Home of Donald Gentile, World War II Air Force Ace, 1920–
1951." I grew suddenly preoccupied with Donald Gentile. Perhaps
these recent conversations with veterans in Richmond and Hartford

provoked my curiosity. Perhaps it was the appearance of Piqua itself: the town lay cozily beneath a veil of fading sunlight, and children shouted across their lawns to one another as I imagined Gentile himself had done when he was ten; it seemed a far place from war and violent death. I was content for the moment to leave my curiosity unsated, for I was anxious to reach Gary, but after passing through the town I spied a cemetery and turned in to see, perchance, if Donald Gentile lay there.

Immediately among the dead the past of Piqua came alive. In the middle of the first spoked intersection stands an old-fashioned water pump. It was rusty and I pumped the handle up and down a dozen times with no result but a vain sucking far below the ground. At one corner, in a miniature Grecian tomb, resides General William P. Orr, home from the wars. One lonesome row of stones marks the line of Johan Schmitz (died 2 Sept 1861) . . . Elizabeth (1913) . . . Anna (1925) . . . Mary (1947—she had been born the same year her father died; I wondered if he ever saw her). Near them is the grave of John H. Lines, Killed in Battle at Dallas, Ga., May 2, 1861, age 22 years, 9 months, 24 days; a newly planted American flag flies quietly above him. The parade of names rolls on: Zimmerlan . . . Haller . . . Strumm . . . Jakob . . . Holtzerman . . . Flatz . . . Schroeder . . . Schemmel . . . all dead before the twentieth century. Down one lane I studied a great bulk of sandstone with thirteen headstones evenly spaced around it. On the centerpiece: Amos Gray (died 1875, age 88) . . . Wife Sophia (1881, age 89) . . . Daughter Phoebe (1819, age 3) . . . Son William (1819—two months after Phoebe; age 10 months; diphtheria? pneumonia? what sudden thing visited Amos Gray that season?) Son John (1839, age 16) . . . Daughter Martha (1841, age 9) . . . Son Daniel (1864, age 50) . . . Son Elias (1896, age 74). Of six children, four died young, and only one survived his parents.

My eye stopped at a headstone with the names "Frisch, Frederick 1832–1909; Margaret 1835–1934." In one more year she would have been a hundred years old. She died the year I was born.

I found the monument to veterans, conspicuous in the center of a round green island, bearing the names of Bull Run, Stone River, Wilderness, Fort Donelson, Cold Harbor, Antietam, Atlanta, Nashville. A bronze cross turning green from the elements honors the veterans of other battles: the Philippine Islands, Puerto Rico, Cuba. An old ball cannon mounted on a concrete base guards concentric circles of the dead from four recent wars, with names like Hall, Hughes, Crampton, Lump, Potter, McGill. But I could not find Donald Gentile.

Leaving the cemetery I headed back to town. The local newspaper was closed, but the proprietor of a cigar store said sure, he knew the Gentile family [it is pronounced Gin-TILL-y]. Donald's father still owns a bar two blocks down Main Street, he said. I went there. The waitress, whom I wager is suspicious of every stranger in town, did not want to tell me when Mr. Gentile would be back. On a liquor license above the cash register I noticed his name—Patsy Gentile—and from the telephone operator I obtained his number. The voice that answered spoke with a solid Italian accent. There was a long pause when I explained that I would like to talk to him about his son. Finally he said, "Okeh. We talk thirty minutes. Come on over and we talk."

Patsy Gentile waited for me on the side porch of the small frame house on South Wayne Street. He is seventy-eight, a short, thick man with large, rough hands, John Henry hands born to the hammer, and although he moves and talks slowly, there is about him a feeling of great strength. He motioned me to a chair on the porch. From the living room came the voice of Harry Reasoner discussing the two hundredth anniversary of the nation's birth.

Mr. Gentile said he arrived in America from Italy on April 30, 1909, and found a job breaking rocks in a stone quarry near Dayton for $1.60 a day. "Then I went to Cleveland, to work on water line; they were putting this line down eight feet deep, and one day the bank come down and killed one guy and I got buried up to here"—he drew an imaginary line from one armpit to the other; "and they had to pull me out through the dirt. I say to the boss, 'Boss, I'm a-gonna quit. I ain't a-gonna die down there.' This time they got me here"—he drew the line again—"next time they get me here"—and he raised his hands above his head.

Young Gentile traveled to Pulaski, West Virginia, to work on a dam project—"twelve hours a day, $1.90 a day, seven days a week, and I don't know Sunday, Easter, Christmas, nothing." He became a coal miner but quit after barely escaping with his life when the roof of a mine collapsed. Arriving in Columbus, Ohio, he walked west along the railroad tracks in search of work. "I walked about four miles. They's a-laying a gas pipe across the railroad and some of them guys they talk Italian language. I ask one fellow, 'What is this? Italian people in there?' 'Most of them,' he say. The boss is Italian, too, his name was

Frank, and I said, 'Frank, I like t' work on job like this.' He said he had enough men. He left but I just stay there a-looking because it's interesting to me. Soon there came a fellow with all white hair and horse and buggy and he walka by where I am and said, 'Hello, boy, are you working?' I said I looka for job but boss say he got no place for me. This white-hair man, he's superintendent, and he says, 'Hey, Frank, put this boy to work.' And Frank jump over fence and come and say, 'If you want to work, go to that tool box over there, get you pick and shovel and go to work at end of ditch,' and I went out and I got that goddamn pick and work lika devil. I work in ditch few months and next few months got my own pipe gang and next year they make me the foreman over the ditch gang and then I got me a subforeman on the right-of-way, next year they made a foreman out of me, and later they made a superintendent out of me and I stayed there thirty-one years and never lost a day. Thirty-one years. Second day July, 1912, I went to work. Thirty-one years I stayed."

He spoke in a very low voice. He seemed to be talking to himself more than to me. From the living room I could hear the sounds of a commercial extolling the "little green sparkles" of some brand of toothpaste.

Tell me about your son, I asked. Was he born here?

About five or six blocks from here. He wanted to fly since he was a kid. I was a little bit against it, you know, because—well, this flying, it was a little bit dangerous. But I couldn't work his mind away from it and I thought, you gotta give these boys an opportunity. They want do something, they's a-gonna do it. Better help them, I tell Mamma, because then they keep on a-talking to you. So when he got in high school he said, 'Daddy, I gonna fly. I want a plane, a biplane. Will you buy it for me? Someday I gonna pay you back.' "

Patsy Gentile laughed. A quiet laugh that was drowned in the roar of a passing truck.

"Finally he spotted a plane advertised over there in Baltimore. I forget the name of the plane but I can see it to this day. I said, 'Don, you can no fly that plane, that's a war plane they used in France.' And he said, 'Aw, Daddy, I can look at it, and I can a-study it, and I can train myself in it.' Every night he give me that kind of music. He was seventeen, see, and I got tired of listening, and I said, 'Well, you writa this guy and you tell him to bring that plane up here, and if the plane will do what he says it will do, I may buy it.'

51

"Well, this guy was to come on a Saturday night and Don, he go running over to the little bit o' landing field we got at Pickaway. Nothin' happens. He comes back and he says to me, 'He never show up, where did he go?' And I said, 'I don't know but I still got my fourteen hundred dollars.' Finally he go back over there about night break and there this fellow is circling 'round and 'round and he land the plane there. Don got this boy down from the machine and brought him down to my bar—the bar I had bought—and he was nice young man; he said he had little trouble a-findin' Pickaway. He said he had to go back to Baltimore and Don said we might as well pay him 'cause it's a nice plane. And I say, 'Look a-here, Don, I don't buy cat in burlap sack.' So we go down to airport and they push the plane out and they start the motor and take off and they circle 'round. I'm on ground, see, but I can see my Don, he's a-having a wonderful time. Then they land and I say, 'Now, I say, can you really fly that plane?' The man said, 'I think he can.' And I say, 'Okay, if you a-trust him, get in, start the motors, go by yourself and we'll see.' So the boy got in that thing and took off and cruised way out there and come back and circled around and came down. He hit the ground a little hard, and this fellow say, 'Well, that happens even on a good flyer.' I said, 'Yes, it wasn't hitting the ground hard that troubled me, it was what happened up there, because up there you're not down here.' Well, we got back to bar and I give him fourteen hundred dollars in fifty-dollar and twenty-dollar bills. And I took him down to the hotel and bought him supper and a train ticket. This boy of mine, he just fly that plane all over the country. Up and down, up and down."

What year was that?

"Late '39. Fall. He used that plane to get ready for Canadian air force. He didn't tell me he was a-gonna be in the air force. But when he could really handle this plane pretty good, he come in one day and he say, 'Daddy, I'm gonna join this Canadian air force.' He wanted me to sign the papers for him and I didn't want to sign the papers for him because he wasn't graduated out of school yet. I said, 'Now, Don,' I said, 'here's a-what I'm a-gonna do. Now do not get mad or do not get disgusted because I'm a-gonna do this to you. What little education I got—I know I come from the old country—maka no difference. You might be good boy to fly, but if you ever go into air force and you be lucky to come out, a little later you gonna need something else besides flying. You gonna need more education than you got now. You come through for me in high school and I sign. But if you do not pass in school, I no sign the papers.' And you know, that kid—he must have studied day and night and the last time in school he got everything an A. All As. Looked like somebody put them on line there who didn't know any other letters in the alphabet—everything A-A-A-A. I said, 'What in hell—how you get so smart all at once like that?' "

Patsy Gentile laughed, but his eyes were moist. Harry Reasoner was reporting on the new draft lottery.

"Well, finally he got a letter back from Canada and he came in to me and said, 'I gotta go up there next week.' I said, 'All right, this what I'm a-gonna do to you.' I said, 'You and I will get into the machine—I had an Oldsmobile—and we go up there together.' And we got in that Oldsmobile and we start over here early in morning and I thought we would not get half a-way between here and there before we get in jail because he speeded that machine between trucks and around cars like something was after him. And we got there and we walk in and there was some officers over there and they said, 'Oh, you are Gentile from Pickaway,' and he said, 'Yes, sir,' and he was smiling and I tried to smile with him but inside I was hurting too much. And they took him in another room for a doctor's examination. One of the guys who was kind of old like me came out and put his hand on my shoulder and said, 'Mr. Gentile, you got a soundproof boy there,' and I said, 'Why, thank you. I appreciate hearing that.' He says, 'Now you be able to go to Cleveland for flying tests tomorrow.' And Don said, 'We gonna go today.' And I said, 'Wait a minute, officer, let me do one thing.' I said, "Thissa only one boy I got and I done everything to raise him up to this age. I don't wanta give it up right off the bat without a-knowing what's it all about. Can you give me an idea so that I can hear what he's a-going into. What's this air force? Is it for period of time or always?' And he said, 'Mr. Gentile, if he be qualified here and in States, he gonna be sent overseas and after he get in British government we don't have anything to say. If this war lasts twenty years, he's liable be there twenty years. I say. 'Don, do you hear now what the story is? Still you wanta sign up?' And he say, 'Daddy, thassa why I'm a-coming here for.' 'Well,' I say, 'I sign your papers.' So he was on one end of the desk and I was on this end of desk, the two officers were on this end of desk, and he kissed me right over the table. He leaned over and he kissed me right over the table."

There was another pause before he continued. "After we got through the boy said, 'All right, we got to go to Cleveland.' I tell you, all state patrol asleep that day, because we was a-going fast. I said"— for the first time he raised his voice and a neighbor across the street appeared startled—"I said, 'What in the hell is the matter with the police that they don't catch you and stop you?' And he said, 'Aw, Daddy, I ain't hurt nothing. I know which way I'm a-going.'

"Well, he gotta to Cleveland when the sun was just about ready to fall down, and he go to this building, an old man was there, the captain of the field, and Don told him why he had come and he said, 'Well, I don't think you cana do that today. It's kinda late, come back tomorrow.' So Don said, 'Do me a favor, because I can't come back tomorrow, because my Daddy brought me over here and he can't be back tomorrow and I want to pass this tonight.' And this guy and another one talked about it and finally they said, 'Come on down,' and they walka down the field, me with them, and they come to a great big plane with pistons sticking out everywhere, and Don he looks it over, the wings, the tail, all over the inside, and he come to me and he say, 'I never flew anything like this,' and I say, 'Well, listen, if you think you can make it, get in, but if you think you can't, then you gonna drown yourself in Lake Erie and I'ma gonna die here where you do. Now you are not in the air force yet,' I said, 'and you can give it up.' And he said, 'No, I'm a-gonna do it.' So the old man got in the front and my Don in the back and they fly all over and pretty soon they come back and the fellow said, 'Now, Don, you take off by yourself.' So Don he started down the field, took off, went round, did a zigzag and a somersault and come back. First time, he hit hard and bounced. And the old man said, 'Try it again a second time, take another trip up there.' It was pretty dark but Don went around and came back and put that plane—I'ma telling you, if you'd put a silver dollar right there, when he came back he could put them wheels right on that silver dollar. Well, this guy says, for what I can see now, you gonna be a pilot.

"Don went out to Glendale, California. Supposed to be there for six weeks but he qualified in three and one day he came home with his uniform and Pickaway was a-playing Troy in ball and he went to the game and I'm a-telling you, they stood up and they cheered for Don Gentile. I was proud of my boy.

"Then he went to Canada and from there to England, where he stayed in Royal air force almost a year. Just two days before the year was up he got transferred into American air force. He gotta two, three airplanes when he was flying in the Royal air force. He gotta seven or eight more in just a short time after he came to American air force. Then they gave him a Mustang and he finally got forty-two in the air and nine on the ground. He had 182 missions and they wanted to let him out but he didn't want out and finally they forced him to coma home on leave. He stayed a while and had to go to Washington and while he was there General Marshall decided not to send him back overseas. So Don came home for another visit. Mamma was still on the couch because she got about half dead when we thought he hada go back over. That's the way she is, she can't help it. And she was down in the bed and I said, 'Your boy is home,' and she wouldn't believe it. But I took him in and I said, 'Mamma, here'sa your boy. Thassa best medicine.' When he came home it was my birthday. I didn't see him four, five years, and he came home on my birthday. I don't know if you heard about it, but twenty thousand people were on the streets . . . cars all over . . . police and state highway and city police all over . . . people from the government . . . big parade. That was some parade. I wasa proud of my boy but I wasa proud of Pickaway, too. This is our home, see.

"Well, they decide send Don to Washington when the war was over. He was flying every day, a-testing planes, and he was supposed to move on to Detroit. Had his furniture all packed and wasa gonna move on Monday to Detroit, where he was a-gonna take charge of the field there. This plane he wasa testing, he flew it on Friday. Something went wrong with it and he didn't fly it all the time he was supposed to. So he put it in a hangar and went back Saturday and it still wasn't right. He only had half an hour to go on this plane and it would have been all tested out. So on a Sunday the 28th of January, 1951, he went to church that morning and after he got back from church he told his wife he was a-gonna go to the field to fly that last thirty minutes so he would be done with it before they left on Monday. He went down to the field and he got in this plane and took off. In no time at all he come back and land. Something was wrong and the mechanic said it was only a small thing and it could be taken care of in 'bout fifteen minutes. So my boy said, 'If it don't take any longer than that, I'll wait.' He waited and when they got ready he took the plane out again. . . . Just about a mile or mile and a half out . . . the plane went down." His voice trailed off.

Patsy Gentile had been talking for more than an hour. I stood up to leave but he insisted that I be seated again. I asked him if he was worried about the country.

"No, no. You see, I heard about situation in this country—what a good country it was—when I was in old country. Someday, I said, I'm a-gonna go to United States. So I just pressed down on my mother and father and they didn't want to let me come because I wasa too young. But I kept on until my father got mad and told Mother, 'Buy him a ticket and let him go—if he wants to go he won't do no good 'round here.' And they bought me a ticket and I came over. You can no compare the United States to any other country in the world. Come," he said, "and I will show you some pictures."

I followed him into the house. He showed me a photograph of his family taken in Italy before he left for America. "Those were my sisters," he said of the young girls in the long dresses and pointed hoods. On a wall nearby hung the picture of his wedding. In the dining room, on a chest covered by a tapestry decorated with the image of John F. Kennedy, he pointed to the picture of Donald Gentile: a sprightly boyish face with dark curly hair and assertive eyes. There, too, were the photographs of Don Gentile's three sons, since grown to young manhood. One will soon complete flying school.

We walked back to the porch. It was now almost dark and Patsy Gentile studied the street beside his house. "When I teach this boy of mine, I say one thing to him—I associated with both my children, Don and my girl—on night like this we would walk up and down that street and we talk—and I say, 'Boy, you gonna be a man in this world. If you do, obey the rule of country. You get somebody try to coach you to do wrong, you say, "Aw, I ain't a-gonna do that, I gotta go." Don't get mad. Find a way to say, I like to be with you but I gotta go, then just walk away.' And I say to him, 'Listen to whata people say, even people you think looka simple—sometimes what they say may seema simple but later on you can use it. Associate with people that knows more than you do. You can learna more than you know now. Because if you just go 'round with ones who know what you know, you no can learn anything. Do that, and don't let anything else control you but yourself. Walk away from trouble.'"

He leaned against the railing and stared down the sidewalk along which on other summer nights he had walked with his son. He said, almost in a whisper, "But he was a man, though."

★ ★ ★

The recollections of Patsy Gentile returned vividly to mind the next morning as I departed Piqua. The route again carried me past the cemetery with its host of occupants who came to America from abroad, men with names like Zimmerlan, Holtzerman, McGill—and Gentile. Until now I did not fully understand why on the previous evening my interest had been suddenly and completely arrested by this place. But as I drove one last time down the quiet lanes beside the gravestones, I realized that in listening to America one must listen to the past.

Now the highway ran through fields of new corn and soybeans into one small town after another, towns with tall spires of old churches; banners proclaiming centennials and sesquicentennials to be observed with parades, fireworks, and speeches; pretty girls flirting with overalled young men sitting in pickup trucks at root-beer stands; freshly mowed cemeteries with small American flags waving on the graves. The people in these towns live heartily, investing the commonplace with importance. And they live with an awareness of the dead, who are buried down the block, by the church, and with a sense of history caught and advertised on markers that declare "General Anthony Wayne's Fort—1795" and "Old Indian Village."

The peace that comes upon a traveler in these parts is deceptive. Down the road at Antioch College, across Ohio in Cleveland, north in Chicago, and in hundreds of other arenas over the continent, powerful forces are tearing at the America delivered to us by the past—the America of centennials and cemeteries, pointing spires and little flags. Those forces seem quite remote now. Even when outriders of the future appear briefly in their midst—a marquee in Warsaw, Indiana, announcing the Beatles' *Let It Be* and a long line of teenagers waiting to get in—the people here are only dimly aware of distant furies and only vaguely worried. There are dragon slayers in the land—Nixon and Mitchell and Agnew, Knights of the Known Order—and in the old movies and in the old books the slayers of dragons always prevailed. But I feel for these people unknowingly lying in the path of a juggernaut. They are being asked to get up one morning as if yesterday never happened.

East Gary, Indiana

UNTIL I ARRIVED IN EAST GARY I'D NEVER MET A TRUCK DRIVER WHO READ *Reveille for Radicals* by Saul Alinsky or *Who Am I? Essays on the Alienated* by Gabriel Fielding, Paul Goodman, Marya Mannes, *et al.* But Paul Dietsch, Tom Gwilt, and Frank Klitzke, who once maneuvered pugnosed diesels hauling big flatbeds of steel down the nation's highways, are now studying the literature of rebellion. There is no doubt about their intentions: they seek the overthrow of an established order. The man who rules that order is James Hoffa.

Their instrument of revolt is the Fraternal Association of Steel Haulers (FASH). According to one trucking magazine, FASH "is the single most important development that could cripple the power of the Teamsters Union." The press has accorded it little attention. It was only casually that I had heard of FASH from a friend in Chicago, who had heard from another friend that "something interesting is going on" between students and workers in East Gary. All I could learn was that FASH had begun in 1967 during a spontaneous protest against the Teamsters by the steel haulers—the drivers who own their own trucks and carry steel over the road to distant cities. The steel haulers are a small minority of some twenty thousand men among the hundreds of thousands of Teamsters who operate locally in trucks owned by the companies. The steel haulers accuse the Teamsters officials of treating them like second-class citizens, of exploiting them, and even of wanting to drive them off the highways permanently. When their grievances went unheeded the steel haulers decided to make a total break, to seek from the National Labor Relations Board authority to be the bargaining agent for the owner operators, and to negotiate directly as a separate union with the companies. Unwilling to lose members or to see a rival union rise in competition, the Teamsters struck back. But in two years FASH has grown to more than ten thousand members, with chapters in Ohio, Wisconsin, New Jersey, New York, Pennsylvania, West Virginia, Illinois, and Indiana.

The Indiana chapter is headquartered in East Gary, a doleful collection of tawdry buildings, truck stops and potholed streets south of Chicago. I had trouble finding the office. "Never heard of it," one man said from the cab of his truck with the bumper sticker: "Don't Blame Me! I Voted Wallace."

"Try down at the Crossroads Restaurant," a woman said. But it wasn't there. By this time I had almost decided that my friend in Chicago was only perpetrating a hoax. I could hear him laughing as he told colleagues of sending me in search of something called F*A*S*H. But at that moment I was rescued by a passing patrol car and pointed in the direction of a gray two-story building down the street where a small yellow sign in an upstairs window indicated my destination. I went up the splintery wooden stairs past a charm and modeling school and into three nearly bare rooms where Dietsch, Gwilt, and Klitzke command the western front of the FASH conspiracy.

It was hot. There was no air conditioning, and summer in northwest Indiana has been known to produce wistful longings for hell. Several young people were busily working at various tasks. "They're students," Paul Dietsch said. "They're attending school at Indiana, Georgetown, Valparaiso, places like that. Most of them are probably moderate when it comes to politics. They're certainly not radicals. I guess you would call them concerned kids. One of Saul Alinsky's men told them what FASH is trying to do and they volunteered to help, circulating petitions, putting out national mailings, cutting stencils, things like that. They were like a breath of fresh air. We had tried to get help from officials of other unions, from town officials, from politicians, from the establishment. But these kids walked in here—eighteen-, nineteen-, twenty-year-olds—and they never asked, What do we get out of this? All they wanted to know was, What do we do? They're sticking it out, too."

Paul Dietsch is the top FASH man in Wisconsin. As a member of the national committee he often works out of Gary. A forty-year-old chain-smoking bachelor whose hair is etched with gray, Dietsch hauled steel for seventeen years before he sold his rig to become a full-time organizer for FASH at a weekly salary of $50.

59

"I got tired of being a bastard son of the Teamsters," he said. "They were supposed to be bargaining for us but they've been working against us." He explained that the Teamsters have closed-shop agreements with the majority of companies for whom the steel haulers carry freight. "We had to join the Teamsters to work for those companies.

"We own our own trucks and are paid a percentage of the gross while most Teamster drivers are paid by the hour. During contract time the Teamsters force the company to sign the master freight agreement which covers the hourly drivers. The steel haulers are just a footnote to that agreement. During negotiations the Teamsters put the company to the wall. They say to the company, 'Don't feel so bad because we'll throw the steel haulers in for nothing.' They don't ask for a thing for us. They aren't bashful about it. When you go to the union hall to protest they shrug and say, 'Why don't you sell your truck?—we can't do anything for you.' Yet they're always demanding our guys pay their dues. We've even had cases where they'll insist a guy from out of town who comes into Chicago has to sign up—$50 to $90 initiation fee and a month's dues—before he can get unloaded. When he goes to Denver they'll catch him the same way. He'll tell them he belongs in Chicago and they'll say, 'That don't count out here.' "

Tom Gwilt interrupted. He is the president of Indiana FASH, a lean, slight man with a small mustache, who has been driving since he was fifteen. He is now thirty-nine. Last September he returned to his frame home in East Gary to find it wrecked by a bomb. On his desk, next to *Reveille for Radicals,* are copies of a tabloid, *The Steering Wheel* (this copy compliments of FASH), with a full-colored American flag on the masthead and bits of patriotic advice: "Write letters—everybody—to top politicians. We're tired of losing wars already" and "Pause a minute to be thankful. We still have young men willing to fight for US."

"Let me give you some idea of how the Teamsters grind us down," Gwilt said. "They negotiate directly with the company for the wages of hourly employees, right? But steel haulers get a percentage of the gross the shipper pays to move his freight. Those freight rates are set by the ICC. From 1956 to 1967 the rates on steel hardly went up at all. Our guy was getting killed. He's got a $25,000 to $30,000 investment in equipment he's paying out every year. His costs are going crazy. I used to buy tires for $60 that cost me $100 to $110 last year. But for almost ten years the carriers don't feel they need to increase their rates, so they don't ask for anything. The inflation monkey was climbing all over us and our income was static. Do the Teamsters help us? Do they bargain with the companies to get us more money? Hell, no, they don't. Our take-home pay today is almost what it was several years ago—$150 to $200 a week. Until we took things in our own hands, the Teamsters didn't do a damned thing.

"This was '67. The contract was up in April. By June we had no word of what they were going to do for us. They got an interim contract that didn't provide anything for the steel haulers. Well, we decided to show them how unhappy we were. Not a strike, just a protest against the Teamsters for letting us down. We weren't mad at anyone else.

"About two dozen guys went to the lawn in front of the Gary local. This wasn't enough so we went over to the mills to see if we could round up some more. We sent a man to each gate to tell the haulers as they came in to park their rigs and come over in front of the union hall. By late evening other drivers, not steel haulers, started coming in and saw the guys standing there and thought it was a picket line. Some of the signs said 'Teamster Protest' and the drivers probably thought it was a teamster picket line. Pretty soon we had, in effect, a picket line in front of all the mills. By the following morning the mills were feeling the pinch, because they were running short on their daily supplies. They run twenty-four hours a day and can get hurt in a hurry. The Teamsters started trying to pacify us—'Go back to work,' they said, 'and then we'll talk'—but that's what they've been saying for years and you never hear from them again. We decided to hang on. First thing you know, we saw that people were beginning to realize what a force we could be. For the first time we realized it, too.

"We personally stayed on the mill gates for eight days. It was a wildcat strike by then and eventually lasted sixty-three days. We didn't know we were getting into anything as prolonged as that—we had thought three, four days at the most. By the end of the first week the guys had beards—all they'd brought was two, three T-shirts at the most. They were sleeping in their trucks and the back seats of cars and living out of restaurants around the mills. But they knew then, see, that the steel haulers had stood up on their hind legs. They weren't never gonna squat again."

Frank Klitzke wanted to speak. A big taciturn man of forty-eight, with a square face, coal-black hair, and the long, solid arms of a pugilist, he is the Indiana vice president. His father was a farmer with nine children "and a truck on the side, so's he could stay away from the WPA and all the other stuff that some of the loafers wanted to get. He was what

61

you'd call a stubborn German." Since joining the FASH movement Klitzke has been the object of two assaults, once by the occupants of several cars who surrounded him at a truck stop only half a mile from where we were talking, and again by a man who leaned from the window of a passing car and fired a revolver at him.

"What Tom said about people beginning to recognize us is important," Klitzke said. "Once that thing got going in '67, chaotic and spontaneous as it was, it spread. It spread because all the grievances and frustrations we felt over the years now had a way to get out."

What were some of them?

"One that got to me was the way they assigned loads of steel. We got this big investment in equipment, and we gotta stay hustling to meet the monthly payments, and sometimes we'd have to wait for a load six, eight, ten hours with no pay—one guy waited thirty-two hours once. Or we'd walk up to the dispatcher and he'd say, 'O.K., this is yours,' and he would give you a load of garbage that you would have to go into your pocket to pay for because it didn't meet your expenses. You're a professional and you tell him you can't survive on that, it will put you out of business, and he'd say, 'You want it or not?' If you said no, he'd tell you to turn in your permit, you're finished. I got one load that I started hauling on Monday and delivered on Saturday night up north, then I had to head back here, and I grossed $522. Just met my expenses.

"We'd ask the Teamsters for help but they didn't give a damn. 'Take the good with the bad,' they would say; 'you can't refuse a load,' they would say. 'If you don't like it,' they would say, 'you can quit.' They wanted to get us out of the business, see, because we're a few pears among their peaches. In fact, they took us on because they wanted to get control of us and then eliminate us, make us sell our rigs and go to work driving the company trucks so we would be hourly, too. You'd go to the union hall and ask them to do something about a problem and they'd say, 'Sorry, you own your own truck.' They ignored the fact that they said you had to join if you wanted to drive. 'Why don't you sell your truck,' they'd say, 'and go to work for the company?' They forced us in and then tried to get us down in the basement to get rid of us."

"We're up against the sweetheart of all sweethearts," Paul Dietsch said. "Take the situation where an over-the-road fellow, our man, comes to town. He's a union member, working for a union company, his dues are paid up, and the union in that town forces him to put a city man on his truck. In some cases he never sees this city man and they deduct his pay from your check. The union contract says that the company pays him. But the company turns around and takes the pay for that man out of your truck check. We'll go to the company that's doing this and say, 'Where's that money?' And they'll say, 'We gave it to the Teamsters.' And we go to the Teamsters and they'll say, 'They never gave us any money.' There's one company here"—he called it by name—"that's taking $15 to $20 a week out of every man's check, and we can't break it."

"Even the grievance system is stacked against us," Gwilt said. "The guy who works in a city for hourly wages starts in the morning around eight and he's off around four or five. He can get to a steward when he has a grievance about working conditions. Our people are out on the road, gone a week at a time, and if he is in town, the only transportation he's got is a truck and trailer which is kind of hard to get around in. Besides, it's tough for him to hang around a union hall four or five hours while they try a grievance—he needs to be out on the road, hustling, or he's not going to make ends meet. We've filed grievances, and they get lost, or they're never processed. Once we did get them to set up a grievance committee and we'd meet to point out—we'd say, 'the companies are taking city-man charges out of everybody in long transportation—$15 or $20 a week—and it's against the contract.' We'd meet with them a month later and ask what happened, and they'd say, 'We're still checking on it.' We'd meet with them two months later and they'd still be checking on it."

Have you sought help from the NLRB?

"We have," Dietsch said, "but I've decided the purpose of the NLRB is to give protection to labor organizations, not to individuals except when an individual has been wronged by a company, by management. When the individual is charging the union with failure to represent him, they all of a sudden turn cold. Like the time we went to the Chicago office of the NLRB to register a protest about the local's failure to process grievances properly. The man there said, 'We can hardly believe this about the —— family (the president of the local is the son of the man who was president before him). Why —— used to bring that boy in here and he sat on our lap. He's a straight shooter. There must be something wrong with you people. You must be malcontents or radicals or something.' They're not very eager to go against the local union, see."

Have you sought help elsewhere?

"Oh, sure, we've been to the Department of Labor, to Justice, to Congress. They all said the same thing, in effect: the system is set up, so go to the union and complain. We said, 'But the union won't do anything about it,' and they said, 'Well, why don't you vote them out?' Have you ever heard anything like that? First, we're in the minority, which is why they take advantage of us to begin with, and second, they rig elections down here until hell wouldn't have it."

Why does a man become a hauler? I asked. With conditions like those you have described, why does he go on the road?

"Doesn't the whole country idolize the driver?" Dietsch asked. "Doesn't everyone like to get his foot on the accelerator out on the highway? The dream of every red-blooded American boy, right? You know you can master that big rig. It's an adventure—over the road. It even has a nice sound to it. Our guys are like sailors. They sail away in that rig and they come back a week or two weeks later with a percentage of what the ship takes in, whale oil or spice or, in this case, money from the shipper.

"Let's say you're a young fellow working in a gas station or in a factory and your brother-in-law is in the trucking business, or a friend of yours, or the guy next door. Inevitably it happens, some big-mouthed trucker comes over from next door or he's standing there in the gas station bragging about all he's seen last week and the money he's made, or he comes into the station and asks you to cash his check and you look at it and you're used to making $150 a week with overtime but here that check is for something like $700 or $800. And you'll say, My God, where did you—how long did you have to work to get that? And the guy says a week. He doesn't mention that $750 of it is overhead, so your eyes pop right out and you figure, Boy, I'm going to get me one of those rigs. Someone is always happy to take you to one of these dealers—"

"They're known as friendly financers," Gwilt said.

"—and as long as you've got any kind of credit rating, you need next to nothing. It's like they're renting the equipment. If you've got the down stroke—$500 or $1,000, which you can usually borrow from your in-laws or get by selling your car—you can get into a $30,000 rig with air conditioning and lots of chrome—chrome air cleaner, chrome stacks, the works—without even being asked where you're going to put it to work. You don't mind the hock because as soon as you get this thing rolling you're going to be making $800 a week. One day you're in it and you've got boundless enthusiasm, and you work night and day, just like you got a hole in the ground and it's pure gold, right around the clock, seven days a week, never come home—"

"Till you wear something out."

"Yeah. The first six months you're in this business you're running, you're like a hog, getting into that money. And you don't realize that $800 isn't really yours until about five years later, when you come up for air."

"Naw," Klitzke said, "you know it at the end of the first month when the $700 payment comes due."

"Well," Dietsch continued, "it takes about three or four years for the truck to really get rundown. Even then you will make an excuse. You'll say, 'I had bad luck this year—my engine blew up.' Next year you'll say, 'I had to buy new tires.' The next year, 'my transmission went out.' The next year, 'I had an accident.' There's always an excuse. And that carrot's hanging out in front of that truck."

"But it's manly," Gwilt said. "That's really what gets them. You're a man in that rig."

What about pensions? Retirement?

"Oh, man," Dietsch said. "You have just hit a sore spot, because this is the next big fraud. Most of the long haulers are under the Central States pension plan administered by the Teamsters out of Chicago, the one that has been involved in one scandal after another. That was started in '54, I believe, and the way they manipulated the qualifications automatically ruled out about nine out of ten steel haulers. We've had men who reach fifty-seven—that's the age when you can claim your pension now—and go down and be told, maybe after waiting six months, they're not eligible. Very few men can hack this business, by the way, until they're fifty-seven. And if a man leaves before he is fifty-seven he has no vested interest. We began to get complaints from fellows who would say, 'I'm still working, I'm waiting to get my pension, and they're telling me I don't have enough credits.' What do I do?"

"The funds keep no records," Gwilt said. "They don't earmark money in your name. The whole burden is on you. Plus the under-the-table deals some of the union officials make with the carriers. They go to them and say, Look, by contract you're supposed to pay $19.50 into the health, welfare, and pension fund for these men, but for $1 a head or $5 a week you can forget it. The union figures it can deal with the poor bastard when he discovers he's not covered—who's got the records, anyway? We've found this in a couple of companies right here in this area. One company was making pension payments for only the first ten men. There is a real sweetheart arrangement. All the time they're lending money to racketeers. *Our* money."

"In twenty five years," he said, "the system has turned the steel hauler into an animal. He's been dehumanized. He's screwed by everybody. The company screws him, the union screws him, the steel mills screw him. The police live off him. He's easy pickings for everybody. Everybody's got his hands in his pocket. They've turned him into a cannibal. Like I'm a dispatcher, I'll say to you, O.K., I've got a load here, who wants it? And you climb over each other like animals trying to get to the carcass. You're up to your neck in debt. You learn to charge a bill anywhere some guy is dumb enough to give you credit. You hear the company guys say: 'My God, what a bunch of gypsies—sleeping summer and winter in their trucks, eating pills as they go down the road, big dumb bastards, crude, tearing at each other's throats, got no respect for each other." You get self-conscious. You're an outcast, an outlaw. If you live within the law you can't make a living. Our guy wants to pay his bills, but he doesn't have any money, he's got this monster of a rig, and he pays between $500 and $1,000 a month on it and he's got the Teamsters on his back. Back home he's got a family that he doesn't see all week that needs money. The only thing in his mind is to keep that truck rolling."

There was suddenly a loud crack! from another room and every man in the office, including me, stiffened in his chair. The veins in Frank Klitzke's temples strained against his skin. Tom Gwilt hesitated, then disappeared into the adjoining room. He returned and said sheepishly, "Boy, are we getting nervous. It was only the breeze blowing a door shut." Everyone laughed but it took a minute before the tension relaxed. Paul Dietsch lit a cigarette although he had drawn exactly two puffs from one burning in the ashtray.

I can't imagine, I said, that the average Teamster supports the kind of conduct you have been talking about.

"They're scared to death," Dietsch said. "We don't think the rough-house gang in the Teamsters are as tough now as they were several years ago, but you know the Teamsters' reputation in this area. And ever since FASH was started, and some other dissident groups, we've begun to see more of the goons around. Eleven cars of them showed up here during the shutdowns this past spring."

He handed me a copy of a magazine called *Team Mate*. "This was started last October by some members of the Teamsters who wanted to work for reform within the union. It had some strong criticism of the pension funds, the leadership of the union, corruption. After the first

issue was published someone bombed the printing plant and it never recovered. Truck stops advertising in it were called by anonymous voices
and threatened. One big truck stop south of Detroit was advertising in
it and someone came in and poured acid all over the place and shot out
some of their large expensive signs on the highways. This is what makes
the little guy afraid. If I go to a man and say, 'You know that $10 a week
you and your wife have been putting in the local bank the last fifteen
years for your retirement? Well, the bank president is giving it all away.'
He'll tear down there and raise hell. But if I tell him that the Teamsters
are giving his pension money away, do you know what he says?"

What?

"I don't care. I don't care. I can't do anything about it."

"Remember Charlie from Michigan, who was in with us three years
ago?" Klitzke asked Dietsch. "Charlie and his half brother Ralph? When
I asked him why he wasn't with us any longer, he said, 'Frank, I know it's
right, I was with you, I understand it all, I know what should be done.
But I'm afraid, Frank. I got a wife and a bunch of kids home there. I
can't afford to get back in with you guys.'"

Klitzke, like Dietsch, is a bachelor. "In this business that's the best
way to be," he said.

What about the two wildcat strikes? I asked. (In addition to the long
shutdown in 1967 the steel haulers were in a seven-week walkout this
spring.) Both were illegal and there was some violence.

"There was no redress," Dietsch answered. "We had no redress in our
union, we'd gone to all the government officials, and nothing happened.
You have to understand the way the whole union bureaucracy works.
The people who were first involved in the creation of the union grow old
in their positions. They're not responsive to guys who believe things must
keep on changing. Try to get in there with any people's resolutions, or a
solidarity resolution between unions. It's a different thing if you're not
part of that family. If you're the auto workers you've got a chance. If
you're FASH trying to walk in and ask for change, it's murder. It's the
guy from the bottom who always finds working in that procedure a very
difficult thing. The system's closed. It's clogged. It's a long way from
down to up, and the guy on the bottom can scream and shout and holler
but nobody can't hear him. Sometime or the other he's going to start
kicking. If they don't hear him maybe they will feel him.

"We don't promote violence. We've got a great guy who's national chairman over in Pittsburgh, Bill Hill,* who looks as tough as the next guy but is always preaching that we don't want to let our passions make us suckers for the goon. There hasn't been any organized violence in those wildcats. We asked our guys to shut down, to show the Teamsters we mean business. And the majority of them shut down, and here comes a scab down the road with a load of steel, and going by everybody's nose, and the guys who are putting themselves on the line to clean this thing up say, 'Look at that son of a gun.' Well, he goes by once, and maybe the second time he goes by you're out there with a few bricks. It's not organized, it's spontaneous. But we know you can't beat the guy who is throwing bricks by throwing bricks back at him. We started FASH so we wouldn't have to play it that way.

"That's been the Teamsters way around here for a long time. They're hooked to the corrupt political system in Gary and interlocked with the other unions and the steel mills and the trucking companies and city and state officials and the people who make up the establishment. That's why things are so bad. Walk around this town—no sidewalks, streets all broken up, poor services. This whole area is poverty row, and yet they've got some of the heaviest industry in the country for a tax base, and you know that somebody's doing a job on somebody. The situation here, for the little guy, keeps getting worse, while the lobby for the steel companies gets special permits down in the legislature for us to overload so's we can take steel out of here to avoid taxes. The little guy's got his whole life and energy in the system—he thinks the system is America—and all the time the system is taking him for a ride and he don't know it.

"The Teamsters are powerful. They could help to change the system. Instead they're a party to it. We want to remedy that. We'd like to see the Teamsters reform. We'd like to see competing unions. Right now if you're a Teamster and they're not performing the job for you, what are you going to do? If we succeed, we'll give guys an alternative. We'll be in competition to try to do a better job of representing the union member. We'd like to encourage other owner-operators to do the same thing—movers and produce haulers and dump-truck operators. Everybody knows the Teamsters Union is corrupt, the politicians, the members of the union, the press. But they're all saying you got to live with it, you can't do anything. That's crap."

*Who is also an ex-trucker, a mustached man with Victorian muttonchops and tattoos, a quiet man who was reading the essays of alienation and *Andersonville* when I met him later.

So spoke the man from FASH.

I will not be surprised if he and his friends succeed. They are patient and earnest men. In the face of intimidation and ridicule they have refused to quit their purpose. A native shrewdness guides their strategy; in addition to Alinsky, they were sharing a copy of Dale Carnegie's *How to Win Friends and Influence People*. Revolutions have been born of stranger alliances.

★ ★ ★

I headed for Milwaukee because the morning newspaper reported that blacks there would celebrate the Fourth of July with a special tribute to Crispus Attucks. As I journeyed north, intending to bypass Chicago, I listened on the radio to a Milwaukee disc jockey conducting a "Computer Cash Call." His technology failed him, however, for the woman who answered the telephone spoke only German. The poor fellow did his best with the few phrases he remembered from those late late U-boat movies, but his efforts were hopeless. With more haste than grace he finally extricated himself, mumbling something about the melting pot and people who program computers.

Old myths die stubbornly, and the myth of the melting pot—the boiling caldron pouring forth its uniform ingots of assimilated Americans—is no exception. The concept that "All men are created equal" has often been interpreted to mean that to be different is to be un-American. I was quite along in years in East Texas before I realized that Catholics were not citizens of a sovereign foreign state, the Vatican. There were always rumors in Marshall that the handful of Lebanese and Syrians who found their way to "our town" kept their eyes shut during public salutes to the flag lest they be unfaithful to the colors "of their own countries." And I remember once hearing the elders at my church—and this was in the early fifties—discuss whether "real Americans" would be separated in heaven from "foreign Americans." They never resolved the issue, but the idea persisted: to be a "good American" one should be as much like everyone else as possible.

But of late there has been a resurgent emphasis on the ethnic differences that give the American character discernible variety and vitality. As I listened to the embarrassed disc jockey, I thought again of the testimony of Patsy Gentile, whose son had given his life in the service; of his father's adopted country; what would the nation have been without these men?

By coincidence I was then only a few minutes from Melrose Park, a

Chicago suburb. From Italian-American friends in New York I knew this to be the home of Father Paul J. Asciolla, C.S., a young priest who works closely with ethnic Americans. I wanted to meet him. Instead of continuing to Milwaukee I turned off the toll road and followed the signs into Melrose Park. The first policeman I hailed, himself an Italian-American, said, "Oh, yes, I know Father Paul. Follow me and I'll show you how to get there."

On the walls of the office of Father Paul J. Asciolla are stickers promoting "Italian Power" and "Schillebeecky for Pope." There are also pictures of celebrities—Jimmy Durante, Angela Lansbury, Ron Santos, Gwen Verdon—who have helped to raise money for Villa Scalabrini, the home for the Italian aged which Father Paul serves as assistant administrator. The average age of its 152 residents is 85½; he is 36, an informal, enthusiastic man who, I am sure, will one day resemble in appearance the late Pope John XXIII. He grew up in Bristol, Rhode Island, the home of many Americans of Italian and Portuguese descent. "We swam on the same beach with the Kennedys," Father Paul said. "They were at one end and we were way down at the other."

Young Asciolla came to Chicago to attend seminary but his father, a restaurant cook, was almost totally blinded as the victim of a robbery. His son went home to work in a shoe factory to help support the family. He worked his way through Providence College, taught in the Bristol public schools, received his master's degree from Fordham, and served as principal at Sacred Heart Seminary in Chicago. Since 1965 he has been deeply involved in the life of Melrose Park, an old community of some twenty-three thousand residents, mostly Italian-Americans, on the west side of Chicago. He works closely with Father Amando Pierini, the administrator of Villa Scalabrini, an extraordinary man of sixty-three, who since 1933 has risen at four o'clock every morning to work, in Father Paul's words, "at helping our people to become good Americans with a deep and rich tradition in their own Italian past."

The three of us dined together, after which Father Paul and I talked into the morning hours. I sought his reaction to demonstrations then being staged by Italian-Americans in front of the FBI office in New York.

"This was inevitable. For a long time people have been yelling and screaming that just because they're Italian doesn't mean they're connected to the Mafia. Innocent people have been harassed on occasions, I know that. Most of the people in organized crime in this country, especially in the Italian-American community, grew up side by side with very respectable citizens. A lot of Italians made it in the system, others didn't and formed their own system, a subculture of crime, by performing services and delivering services that nobody else would give.

"I remember as a kid delivering fish and chips to a place behind the barbershop where a huge bookie ring operated. They used to lift me up and say, 'O.K., kid, point to a number on the chart,' and then they'd play that as the daily double. I didn't know what was going on until later. It was organized crime, all right, but the odd thing is they felt they were performing a service for the little guy who couldn't get to the track. Over the years these guys rubbed shoulders with the legitimate people in the neighborhood, and I think most people who aren't Italian secretly suspect that anyone with an Italian name is somehow connected with the underworld. Guilt by association. Like—I guess most of the Ku Klux Klan were white Protestants but that doesn't mean most white Protestants belonged to the Klan. I think the decent people out in front of the FBI headquarters—and not all of them were decent—were saying, 'Look, judge me for what *I* am, not for what some other guy is.'

"I think there is something else, too. All these years Italian-Americans have known who they are. They've had pride and self-awareness for a long time. But they've also known that in the scheme of things they were supposed to suppress their differences—you know, 'Americans aren't like that.' When the blacks started reacting to their own suppressed identities—the 'Black is Beautiful' thing—ethnic Americans decided they could bring their own values right out in the open, too. People have been defining America for us in the wrong way, trying to drive a wedge between our loyalties—'You can't be Italian and be a good American.' Who says? We've got to know who we are. You can't make friends with a paranoid. You can't make friends unless *you* know who *you* are.

"Take the Italian-American family. They feel very strongly that they're Americans; they don't want to go back to Italy. But their Italian roots have given them very special characteristics as a family. The father does one thing, the mother does another, the children are expected to do certain other things. One of the most important factors in that family is the sense of who the whole family is. It extends past his brother and sister into the wider community. Ask an Italian about his family and he will tell you about his cousins, and not just his blood cousins. The family reaches beyond the blood line to the neighborhood, to their turf, to the larger community. And not only is this true of Italian-Americans. Let's say you go into a center-city situation and find an enclave of third-generation

Polish-Americans. You have to understand why they came to that particular place. Usually the church was there, the industry in which they could work was there, relatives were there. In Poland they weren't property owners, but America gave them the opportunity to own land. They immediately began to identify with their neighborhood. It was their land. I don't care how small it was, they would sit in front of it with a gun if they thought it necessary. Look at Tony Imperiale in Newark. He's a symbol of the guy who says, 'This is my turf and nobody is going to take it away from me.'

"I think the politicians understand this, but the social-service agencies do not. Here is a neighborhood. We call it deteriorating, but the people who live there think it's a very nice place to live. There's a little local grocery store—it's part of the family—the church is part of the family, the ward politician, the milkman, everybody there is part of the larger family. A man's house, all of his equity, is locked into that system. Then urban renewal comes and says, 'You've got to move.' They tell him to do an awful lot of things without understanding why he is there in the first place. They don't factor his sense of family ties, his sense of blood, his idea of turf, into making social change. Without even explaining what they're trying to do, they will take the intransigence of this group of people as racism, obstructionist, reactionary. Perhaps the people should move, but there has to be some mediation between the man and his cultural ties. Even in the most optimum circumstances change is difficult.

"This is why ethnic Americans and blacks need to understand how hard it has been for each of them to make it in America and to realize that they really want the same thing. They want good jobs, they want good housing, they want a good education, and they want the freedom to do their own thing in their own way. They have to see that the progress of one group doesn't have to be at the expense of the other.

"This can happen. It happened in a part of Detroit where a friend of mine is the priest, Father Daniel Bogus. He's Polish-American and for a time this district was heavily Polish. Now it's largely black. This priest realized as the blacks started moving in that they had exactly the same needs as the Poles: jobs, good schools, and political power. In Detroit the councilmen are elected at large, which means that somebody who lives twenty-five miles from you may be your councilman. Somebody said that the Poles and the blacks ought to get together on the same meeting ground. Congressman John Conyers, the black congressman from that district, said he thought that would be a challenge because the Poles didn't know any more about blacks than blacks knew about Poles. So they had a meeting, and they discovered very quickly that they didn't know much about each other's history. It took more than six months to arrange for 300 people—150 blacks, 150 Poles—to get together, and they were tense about it. But it went well and now Poles and blacks are not so willing to believe all the bad publicity about each other. They're fighting together on all kinds of things. Like some alderman wanted to build a school in an area that would have meant knocking a lot of people out. These Poles and blacks got together and said, 'No, we don't want this high school if it's going to displace people. We want to keep our neighborhood.' That's integration. I don't know if they love each other or go to each other's churches, but that's integration.

"I can give you an illustration closer to home. There's a polyglot community in northwest Chicago—Mexican, Puerto Rican, Polish, Italian, Ukrainian, Lithuanian—where the garbage wasn't being collected. The alderman was just going to the party people to collect their garbage. All these people suffered who weren't subscribers to the political philosophy of the alderman. The streets weren't even being cleaned regularly. Now the people didn't talk about brotherhood and they didn't talk about integration. They happened to be living in the same neighborhood next to each other, black and white, although they had practically nothing to do with each other. All of a sudden somebody decided they had a common problem—garbage. It seems very mundane but it was their problem. So they all got together, they worked together, they collected all of the garbage themselves in hired trucks, they went to the alderman's wife, who owns a bar in the neighborhood, and dumped it *all* in front of the bar. Within half an hour it was all cleared up.

"This alderman had been very happy because those people were fighting each other. Politicians survive by playing blacks against Irish, Poles against Puerto Ricans, because then they're kept from understanding their real needs, their common needs. So these people finally got together and said, O.K., we're not going to be played against each other. You keep your political philosophy, we'll keep ours, but let's work at our common problem, whether it's garbage or juvenile delinquency. And they're doing it, but they don't sit around holding each other's hands and singing 'We Shall Overcome.'

"The media very seldom gets this kind of thing. With ethnic Americans the media has tended to pick up people who are reacting—reacting to their own awareness of their identity for the first time. It hasn't been very long since people were 'wops' or 'polacks'—you know, stereotypes. The media keeps trying to shove them into some new category—hardhat or racists or beefy clods—everybody has to fit into a mold. They come in and ask, 'Are you for Wallace? Are you for Wallace?' It's the old Biblical thing—the media tries to pit the Sons of Light against the Sons of Darkness. That's where the action is, and action is what the cameras record.

"When you see the hardhat, who's become the ethnic symbol today, he's beating up students. You're seeing the reaction, not what led up to it. I admire Walter Cronkite a lot, but when he says 'That's the way it is' at the end of his broadcasts, I have to smile, because very often that's not the way it is. That's only the way it seems to be. You're getting part of the effect, maybe nothing of the cause. How many television stations paid serious attention to the Indian until the Indians took over Alcatraz? Television looks at people in a pejorative way. It looks at them as if they were categories. On the *Carol Burnett Show* on CBS someone told a joke about the Polish airlines and played the Polish national anthem for comedy and the Chicago station was flooded with protests. We've got a lot of Poles here. Why were the people who put that show together so insensitive? Because there are no Poles in New York. The people who blue-pencil television shows lead very isolated lives.

"I think Agnew mistakenly tripped against a truth. Which is not only that the media has been a little bit to the left but that in general it tends to oversimplify. I doubt that they do it consciously. The very nature of television is to look for struggle that can be capsuled in one minute.

"The problem with Agnew now is that in going from city to city raising funds and saying the well-turned phrases, he's doing exactly what he criticized the media for doing. He's giving simplistic answers to very complex social problems. He's polarizing. George Wallace was right when he said he should have all his speeches copyrighted because Agnew is repeating them. Wallace appealed to people because he spoke of gut issues, a kind of barroom talk, knocking down the liberal establishment and the liberal press, but in the end they wouldn't go all the way with him because he was—he was Wallace. Agnew is saying the same thing and they like it because it gives high-level approval to their fears and prejudices—he is the Vice President, after all. Agnew makes it respectable to hate. He makes all the blacks into bad guys and all the whites into good guys, which is as bad as saying all students are bums and all white workers are right. He also makes the silent majority all white. It isn't. It's not even silent. It's the anxious majority.

"The working class that belongs to that majority has all the anxieties churned up by city living. They thought they had it made in America— 'Work hard,' they were told, 'pull yourself up by your bootstraps, be industrious, and you'll make it.' So they toiled and struggled, only to discover that they haven't made it at all. Suddenly there's an inflationary economy and they have to have two jobs, which really tears at the old family structure and disrupts the familiar habits. They're making between $5,000 and $10,000 a year but their buying power is the buying power of 1948. They're 1948 Americans. The 1969 statistics in Chicago said an average family of four needs $11,400 to live moderately. But the people I'm talking about don't have any way to escape from that system. No tax benefits. Where are they going to invest, and what?

"Most of the people out here were Southern Italians and land meant very much to them. They wanted to plant and see things grow; they loved flowers. Now they're told they're living on the edge of a deteriorating neighborhood, it's going to take twenty years to pay for their house, and all the time the real-estate people are whispering, 'The blacks are coming, you've got to move. The blacks are coming, you've got to move,' and they're faced with the threat, real or imagined, of the blockbuster. They're terribly anxious. They're arming themselves with guns because they're anxious. They're being defined by everybody as a social problem. 'Me? A social problem?' And they're anxious about it. They're beginning to believe all the publicity.

"If you talk to the average guy in Melrose Park, he doesn't feel responsible for racism. He may have accepted the American dream so much by osmosis that he really is intransigent to social change; he's got it made and he doesn't want to give it up. He doesn't have anything against blacks—he has something against anybody who poses a real or imagined threat to his alleged security. And he certainly doesn't feel part of the power structure that perpetuated the slavery system that committed psychological genocide on the blacks. During all the time the black man was trying to get free the Italian was doing his damnedest in America just to survive. He didn't understand the language; he was breaking his back digging ditches and pushing wheelbarrows; he didn't even know there were blacks down there suffering worse hell than he was. All of a sudden, two or three generations later, he's in competition with the blacks who are immigrating from the South looking, he thinks, for his job. He's called a racist because he doesn't want to give up his job.

"He finds himself pressured by the upper class, the monied class, the privileged class to be the fall guy for correcting institutional racism, something he doesn't feel he created. There are no Italians in the major executive suites of the big corporations in this country. There are no Poles. Only two or three showcase blacks. The people who run the big corporations and the people who talk about brotherhood from their high-rise apartments expect this guy living in the nitty-gritty deteriorating neighborhood to take the rap for them. They needed a repressed group—a 'noble savage'—to justify their own guilt over being so well off and over being a part of the power structure that made the rules of the game, so they decided to save the blacks. Now I believe the blacks need help, although I don't think they like to be patronized, but in going to help the blacks, the liberals, the government, the establishment didn't factor in this whole middle belt of people. And you can't look at the problem of the blacks without looking at the reaction of the whites. What the liberal establishment should be telling the white working class and the blacks is: You have much more in common with each other than you think. In the history books of the country you've both been left out. You're getting short-changed right now the way things are going. Get together. Work to change things.

"But that's not what is happening. Agnew is playing to their prejudices, making them relish their bitterness, and the liberals are going around them directly to the blacks. Both groups are being driven apart. I don't want to romanticize the workingman—he can be a real slob—but I am convinced that you can't program for a revolution unless you program for the reaction to the revolution. That's the only way to keep a social order in stress from flying apart.

"There are visibly deprived people and there are relatively deprived people. We don't like to talk about class in America because everybody's supposed to be equal. We've hidden a lot of neglect, a lot of sins, under *that* myth. If everybody's equal in theory, you don't have to worry if they're not equal in fact. Well, the terrible thing is that the most unequal of all Americans are being exploited and played off against each other.

"The kids of the working class have a lot more in common with the black kids than they do with the children of the middle and upper classes. The working-class kid is starting at the same point his father did—he's got to survive in the system, beat the system, just like the black kid does. You know the pattern: 'Get your house, raise your family, be a good citizen even though it's not the best system, O.K., but get a certain amount of psychological and economic security and you will have it made in America.' The affluent kids, on the other hand, don't have these needs. Somebody is paying their bills through college; they don't have to work. They have no roots, no goal; they think history is going to end tomorrow. They have spent a lot of time watching television and they believe in the instant answer. They drift. They get bored, they move on. They can worry about the large social problems. They're worried about Vietnam. They're worried about the 'noble savages' in the ghettoes. But they're terribly unhappy; they are really a mixed-up bunch of kids. What's happened to the Peace Corps? To VISTA? These were the programs of middle-class kids. Where has the great generosity of the young people gone in the last five years? At least the working-class kid has a specific goal—security. He's got to do the fieldwork so the liberal affluent kid can worry about the world.

"I think the politicians and the clergy are the people today who really have to do something about this class gap. It's hard for people in neighborhoods like this to identify with big government. They identify with the local ward politician who does them favors. What a burden— what an opportunity—this is for the politician. Things can happen if he begins to identify the real anxieties of people and tries to bring them together to work on everyday matters like street repairs and health services and schools. I believe very much in the neighborhood. I think that neighborhood organizations that cut across racial, ethnic, and class lines can be the salvation of this country. If only the politicians will see this and stop playing one group against another, stop giving the impression that if one group advances, another has to fall back. That only divides the working people and the blacks.

"I believe in introspection, but people who criticize themselves too much are usually in mental institutions—they're people who can't get out of themselves, who isolate themselves from the rest of society. I'm for criticism, but criticism and radical rhetoric, if you'll pardon the grammar, ain't social action. The heck with talking, let's do something."

Few people are doing more than Father Paul Asciolla, I thought at four o'clock in the morning as I crawled into the hospital bed he had provided me in a ward of the Villa. At dinner his superior, Father Pierini, had spoken of the importance of "enlarging the provincial mentalities of people and giving them respect and a sense of community without losing pride in their heritage." Through courses in culture, Italian civilization, and Italian-American history, through radio programs, a newspaper, seminaries, and programs featuring the food and costume and customs of Italy, the Fathers Pierini and Asciolla are enriching the special heritage of their people and enhancing their ties to America simultaneously. As I lay in bed waiting for dawn, when I would catch an early bus to Kansas City, I recalled a passage from Kazantzakis' *Journey to the Morea:* "It has been rightly said that every man has under his responsibility one definite circle of things, men and ideas, and if he cannot save this circle then he himself cannot be saved." They are doing quite well by that idea at Villa Scalabrini.

She got on the bus in a little town in Illinois, having cut short her summer vacation for reasons she did not amplify, to return to her home in San Diego. She was about sixteen, with long red hair and a platoon of freckles bivouacked on the crest of each cheek, and she was clearly on the make. From the moment she deliberately chose a vacant seat directly across the aisle from two young men, about nineteen and twenty, it was apparent she was not prepared to endure the long ride to the West Coast without adventure.

By the time we reached Indianapolis the younger fellow with his black hair cut in duck tails had won out, much to the chagrin of his companion. He was seated beside her as we headed for St. Louis and by midnight they had disappeared into the last row of three seats, the only ones not separated by arm rests, and except for an occasional giggle we did not hear or see them again until we pulled into Kansas City at 6 A.M. They emerged rather rumpled and forlorn, for he had connections to make to Dallas, and the last I saw of them they were exchanging addresses and embraces on Platform 7.

Lawrence, Kansas

LAWRENCE, KANSAS, IS A MICROCOSM. LAWRENCE, KANSAS, IS THE EPITOME
of a troubled, spirited, inspired, frightened, complacent, industrious, selfish, magnanimous, confused, spiteful, bewitching country. Lawrence,
Kansas, is a little world.

I did not know this when I decided to come here. The man who invited
me, Dolph C. Simons, Jr., said that Lawrence is a pleasant place to live
and to visit—"A university town in the heart of Middle America should
give you a chance to catch your breath," he had suggested—and I half
expected to enjoy a brief respite from my work before heading west. The
prospect was in fact enticing as the bus left Kansas City early in the
morning. With the early sun behind my back and the twin prairies of
sky and grassland racing westward ahead of me, there was no warning
of what was to come.

THURSDAY MORNING

Dolph Simons, Jr., greeted me in his office. He was born to Lawrence.
His grandfather edited the *Daily Journal-World* for sixty-one years and
his father is editor now. Dolph, Jr., is publisher. If you're publishing a
newspaper in a small town you cannot hide behind either your prestige
or anonymity. Everybody in town knows you and they know you're a
sonuvabitch in the first place, which clears the air. "You live around the
corner from the people you rap over the knuckles," Simons said. "You
want to boost the town but you want to tell what you see, too."

You can't run from your hypocrisy, I said.

Over coffee Simons told me of an effort being made in Lawrence to combat the growing drug traffic. A drug-abuse center, known as Headquarters, was started last year by a few University of Kansas students to help junior-high-school and high-school youngsters in trouble. A volunteer staff maintains a constant "switchboard" service which can refer a drug user in crisis to immediate help from doctors, counselors, teachers, or parents. Its reputation, spreading through the high-school underground and the university grapevine, often attracts pleas for help from a dozen young people in a single day.

I asked Simons to take me to Headquarters; I would spend the day there and leave the next day for Denver—or so I thought. We drove to a three-story frame house directly across the street from the university campus and were welcomed by Brian Bauerle, a soft-spoken bearded graduate student from Harland, Iowa. The idea for Headquarters grew in Bauerle's then-drug-soaked mind as he hitchhiked across country in the summer of 1969. I asked him to tell me the story.

"I started out at KU in '66 as a real gung-ho Joe College," he said. "I pledged a fraternity, ran for the presidency of the freshman class, would only date the right girl—she had to be from a certain sorority, you know. And one day I realized how superficial it all was. Suddenly I was frustrated, dissatisfied; I wanted an escape. So I took a job downtown as a salesman in a hardware store and bang! I was a financial success. A college student making $8,000 a year is rolling in money. But it didn't take long for me to realize I had traded one set of frustrations for another. Some kind of deep feeling in me grew more and more unhappy. I was on a commission basis; when someone walked into that store I would use all my energies and wiles to sell him the television set that had the highest markup, because I would make the most money on it. One day I was trying to sell a woman a set she didn't want, and I said to myself, 'Wait a minute, Bauerle; let her make up her own mind; you're manipulating her.' All the time I was telling people that we were charging them 9 percent on their credit, but I figured out one day that it was really 18 or 22 percent. Black people would come in and buy something on a five-year installment plan and pay for it three times and someone else who could pay cash in ninety days had no carrying charges at all. I'm no puritan cookie or anything but that kind of thing started to wear on me. Maybe I was weak or something, but about this time I was introduced to drugs. I was in debt by now because I had bought things like a new car and a big stereo and I had a nice apartment and I was running in a circle I couldn't get out of. I kept arguing with myself: Is this the life you want? Is this what you're good for? Finally I lived on nothing for six months so I could save my money and pay off my debts and quit. I turned to drugs, really turned to them. I used them extensively for a couple of years—for nine months I was a real acid head, dropping acid every day.

"I was hitchhiking across the United States at this time and got to a place called Forest Hills in Chicago. Through someone who picked me up for a ride I learned about an encounter group they were having at a local hospital. Some suburbanites and some real radicals, this person said; do you want to go along? I said sure, I didn't have anything else to do. I got very much involved with a psychiatrist there and I went to work for him—in a place like this one we're running here in Lawrence. Some people got interested in me and I was able to pull myself out, to get back together again. When I came back to KU in the fall, I asked myself, Is your education going to be relevant or isn't it? I started taking some human-relations courses and going to work at another 'switchboard' operation in Kansas City—counseling, handling the telephones, trying to get to kids in trouble, especially the bad trippers.

"I knew that Lawrence needed something like this. For reasons I don't really understand, Lawrence has become a crossroads of the drug traffic. Maybe because of the location, near a major interstate, in the middle of the country, maybe because of its easygoing atmosphere, maybe because so much marijuana grows wild in the countryside around here. But it's a big problem. We've been in business ten months and I'd say we have had at least three hundred high-school kids from the area and a hundred or more from other places. We deal with runaways here, and more kids are splitting and leaving home. For the first time it's conceivable that a thirteen- or fourteen-year-old kid can run away and exist without any means of income. There's a network all over the country which they can disappear into. When they come to us we try to get them to face up to their problems. We tell them they may run away from their parents but they can't run away from what's bugging them inside. It's vogue these days to have parents who are down on you, parents who are constantly hassling you, and we get all the stories—of beatings and arguments, fathers who are never home. We're only hearing the kids' side of the story, which means we can't make final judgments; all we can do is to make them ask if they really want to be dependent on other people all the time. Do they want to bounce around the country for the rest of their lives? We say, 'You have no money, no means of getting a job, you may be fine for a year—what then? You want to be a bum the rest of your life?' We can't advise, we can only suggest. We try to set up some lines of communication with their folks back home, trying to point out some alternatives to both sides. We can't make decisions for either side; we just try to draw out the possibilities."

There was a girl present, Pat, from a Kansas City suburb. "I'll give you an example," she said. "I was really having a bad trip. I was in Lawrence visiting and someone called Headquarters and they came. They saved me, they really saved me. Brian just walked in and put his arm around me and said, 'Everything's O.K. Our problem is to get you out of any trouble with the police.' He got me to thinking about that. I didn't want trouble with the police. And I couldn't concentrate on the bad trip because I had to concentrate on getting out of trouble with the police. Brian brought me here, to Headquarters, and I found everyone going about their lives as a family. They took me in. I knew that I was wanted, I was needed, that I could stay as long as I wanted. This was my home, they said. My head was in such a bad place, but I knew they were trying to reach me. I wanted to run out in front of a car, but they wouldn't let me. I couldn't convince myself that everything was okay, and their reassurance helped. It was the only thing anyone had thrown my way and I grabbed it like I was sinking for the last time. They didn't do anything but reassure me and love me, and they saved me."

There were thirteen young people living at Headquarters at the moment, Bauerle said. "We try to make each one of them feel welcome but everyone here has to share in the work. We find a lot of parents who try to protect their children too much. They aren't willing to let the kids make some mistakes and to find some forgiveness. They don't know that's a ten-year-old *person* down there. Kids tell us, I just can't talk to my father—he explodes. The parents don't realize the kids are feeling them out—you know, 'Here, try this on for size!'—until they know what he will and will not let them do. Parents are so concerned that their children not make mistakes. You know, they want the first dinner the little girl cooks to be such a good dinner, and when she puts in too much of this or too much of that, the mother blows up and shouts, 'Can't you do anything right?' Here we just throw them into the kitchen. When a girl comes we say, 'O.K., if you want to cook a meal, cook a meal.' There are no recipes, we don't have half the things you need for a meal, but they always come up with something. We burn chickens and we have some pretty lousy meals, but you should see the girl who gets through it. It's hard on the stomach but it's sure good on her ego."

Headquarters is open twenty-four hours a day, staffed by people like Bauerle; John Pettit, twenty-two, a senior at the university, majoring in journalism and education; and Bing Hart, twenty-eight, who is working toward his doctorate in psycho-pharmacology. Like Bauerle, they have found their way through the drug scene. They receive no salary. The $8,000 yearly budget for Headquarters must come from community donations. "Most of the time," Bauerle said, "we're flat broke."

"But we discovered very early that people can't plan their emotional crisis between the hours of nine to five while the doctor is in," John Pettit said. "If you are going to be a friend to these kids, you don't say, 'We handle drug cases on Monday, Wednesday, and Friday, and we're closed on Sundays.' You make yourself available all the time. So Headquarters has become a life style. It's all voluntary. Even though we can't pay salaries, people come in and say, 'Hey, I dig this. How can I help?' And we get people from the community—pharmacists, doctors, lawyers— who donate a lot of their time."

"The more adults who participate," Bing Hart said, "the more people will really understand the youth scene and the more they will clear up misconceptions about drugs. By the mid-sixties a lot of kids were really experienced in drugs. They knew their elders were dispensing preposterous information about marijuana and very unjust penalties for its use. I think much of the estrangement of the generations set in right there. Kids knew their parents were spouting nonsense, and public officials, too, and they lost confidence in the credibility of the older generation. That's one reason they got in trouble with the hard stuff. They thought they'd been deceived about that, too."

What do you tell kids about pot? I asked. Hart replied: "We try to tell them first of all that it's against the law—although as of this July it will be a misdemeanor rather than a felony. We simply point that out. The kid already knows it and you can't convince a person not to use pot by telling him it's illegal. The stuff is too easy to come by for that. And we don't preach. We try to make known the implications, the possibilities of harm, of any drug. We relate our own experiences and hope the kid can make an intelligent decision for himself. We concede there are doubts about marijuana, that the doctors are divided on it, that a lot of the propaganda about pot is misleading. But we try to point out that confusion about pot shouldn't be used as an excuse about the hard drugs—

heroin, speed, stuff like that. We urge them not to give that stuff a chance. We try to be honest about marijuana in hopes that the kids will believe us about the hard stuff, too."

"We'd like to see some honest contact grow out of all this between the kids and their parents, and between kids and the rest of society, too," Bauerle said. "We're running a program that encourages people in town to invite some longhair kid to dinner. If they get to know each other and talk together maybe the guy in town will admit that one longhair hippie type is a nice guy, and maybe the longhair will see that, for an establishment type, the other guy is O.K., too. I know that people in the community look at me, John, Bing, and the others and write us off as long-haired hippie freaks. But if they take a look at the kind of thing we're trying to do for their kids, maybe they'll have to say, 'Well, at least they're hard-working freaks.'"

I left Headquarters in the company of Dick Raney, a member of the organization's board of directors. I asked how a forty-two-year-old pharmacist and drugstore proprietor got involved.

"It was all part of the way I was myself changing over the last few years," he replied. "I was on the city commission for four years and mayor during a racially troubled period. By coincidence I was meeting with some black activists on the night Martin Luther King was shot. God, I will never forget how they looked, how they reacted when the news came. For the first time I realized what it is to be within the frame of reference of a disaffected person. I knew then that blacks have to threaten our way of life; if they're going to get back what the past took away, they've got to look us right in the eye and say, 'Screw you.' I came away from there a different man—not more liberal, not more patronizing. If anything, I took my heart off my sleeve. I knew the black man was going to make it without me. I knew things were about to start changing in Lawrence.

"I worked in my own way for what I could do. We got a fair housing ordinance, a swimming pool, some things like that. And word got around that—well, that I would talk to just about anyone. One night I got a call from a kid who thinks of himself as kind of radical. He's not a student activist, or a stone thrower, or a burner; he's a kid just tottering on the edge. And he asked me to meet him some place where we wouldn't be seen. It's funny; the people in town thought I was a little odd and here's this fellow thinking I'm so establishment that he absolutely can't be seen with me. So I arrange a meeting in a motel room and we wind up talking four hours. He talked about everything he thinks is wrong with

Lawrence and I just listened. When he's finished I suggested that I get some other people in town to listen to him. He said I couldn't produce people who would listen to people like him. And I said, 'Bullshit, I think I can.'

"Although I was off the commission by that time—it was just early this year, in fact—people were willing. The mayor, the city manager, some businessmen. We met for six or eight weeks with the 'street community,' some of the kids who live out by the university. They kept asking for another meeting, another meeting, and one guy said he was having more fun than sitting up in his room getting stoned and talking politics. They wanted human-relations committees and we wanted to tell them about sewers, but they were willing to risk something, to take the time and effort to come. They consider themselves disaffected people, they feel the community has treated them indifferently or with hostility. They said the police in Lawrence are pigs—you know the rhetoric—and they said they wanted a police department where the guy maybe walks his beat through their part of town instead of driving through and flashing his floodlight on them. And we said one good way to get that kind of department is not to string piano wire at neck-high levels in the alleys.

"Talking doesn't solve anything, but people were talking who had been standing at a distance smirking at each other. I couldn't buy a lot of things they said, but I could go with a bunch of bright kids wanting to be good citizens. I was told that some of the fellows over at Headquarters heard that some of us old fogies would listen. They asked me to help. It wasn't a time to hibernate, so I said sure."

Score one for Lawrence, I said to myself as Dick Raney drove away. Thinking that I might now stay longer, I wrote in my notebook: "People here trying to span the generation gap. In Washington the term was 'bridge building.' So far in Lawrence there are rope bridges, but at least they reach from one side to the other.'

I did not know that soon they would be lashed by gales as sudden and as mean as a Kansas twister.

THURSDAY AFTERNOON

I drove through town with Jerry Schwartz, a talented young reporter from the *Daily Journal-World*.

There are roughly 47,000 people in Lawrence, of whom a third are part of the University of Kansas. Without the university Lawrence would be in economic trouble. There are townspeople who think they are in worse trouble with it. In more tranquil times young people came from farms and small towns from all over Kansas to prepare themselves for careers and citizenship. They still come, but with the rise of the University of Kansas to prominence as a major institution, Lawrence has lost its immunity from the world. In the spring of 1969 demonstrators led by the Students for a Democratic Society forced cancellation of the annual ROTC review. Recently there were marches against the war in Vietnam, strong stands by the university senate against certain military research, a visit to the campus by Abbie Hoffman, a reported nude-in, demands and protests by black students, rock festivals, and growing vandalism culminating in a fire which inflicted more than $1 million damage to the Student Union building. Administrators imposed a curfew on the campus, there were more fires (one started by a building and grounds employee who was later declared mentally incompetent to stand trial, creating speculation that he and not a student might have burned the Union building), followed by bomb threats and arrests. After Cambodia and Kent State there was more sporadic vandalism. In a move that particularly galled the politicians of Kansas, the university community— faculty, students, and administration—met in a mass convocation to approve a plan allowing students either to finish the semester in classes or to complete the semester early and take part in some political activity of their choice. Radicals wanted the university to take an official position on the war and to strike. Chancellor Laurence Chalmers insisted that the university stay neutral and open. His compromise succeeded; tension on the campus evaporated after the convocation. But many politicians, editorial writers, and alumni denounced the chancellor for cowardly yielding to student demands. Radicals denounced him for copping out. He became a marked man.

There are other forces stripping Lawrence of its immunity.

One is the "street community," a loose and disheveled cluster of rebels, freaks, drug heads, runaways, drifters, serious radicals, flower children, and just plain thrill seekers—young people in search of a kick, roaming like nomads from one oasis of titillation to another, moving on when boredom comes. Estimates of their numbers range from two hundred to four hundred. Some live in small apartments above stores on Massachusetts Street, the main drag in town. Most live in an enclave on the edge of Mt. Oread, the hill on which the university is located. Some are students, many are not—an important point to remember.

The second source of tension is rising black activism. There are approximately forty-five hundred Negroes in Lawrence. For a long time they were quiet. In the last two years they, too, have changed. Confrontations erupted at the high school last spring when the school board rejected most of the demands sought by black students (there are between eighty and ninety in the school). There were fights between whites and blacks. Armed guards patrolled the corridors and grounds.

"The blacks wanted several things," a prominent citizen told me. "A black cheerleader, for one. The football team here is to Lawrence what the New York Jets are to Shea Stadium. It's been written up in *Life* magazine and all that. Cheerleaders fit right into the scheme, and the blacks were asking for something that they recognized was very important to the whites. They also wanted black counselors, more black teachers, black-history courses.

"The situation is compounded because the blacks in the high school relate to the black students at the university. There's an interesting story there. The blacks at KU put a lot of demands on the table. One of them was for $50,000 for special fellowships and scholarships. The administration said that there just wasn't the money. The blacks seemed to accept that—maybe we're asking for too much, they said. The next thing you know there was a story in the paper announcing the university intended to spend a quarter of a million dollars spreading Astroturf on the football field. The blacks wondered about that.

"The blacks at the university got a lot of their demands. The blacks in the high school didn't. The high-school kids started turning to the university kids for help. The KU kids have organized a Black Students Union— the leader is a brilliant kid named John Spearman, a graduate of the high school here. Do you know that two years ago when he graduated from high school he received an award, top student or something like that, and the black kids wouldn't even stand up and applaud him. The white kids did; they thought he was a helluva nice Tom, you know. He grows up a little, gets involved in the Black Students Union at the university and two years later a warrant is issued for his arrest for a disturbance at the high school [he was later acquitted]. His rhetoric is pretty well advanced from what it was as a kind of Tom kid graduating from Lawrence High School."

Massachusetts Street divides the town east and west. It is a wide street twenty-three blocks long. The East Lawrence section is sometimes called "East Bottoms" because it runs down to the polluted Kansas River, which is the north-south dividing line. The blacks are concentrated in East Bottoms, although the area is integrated, and in North Lawrence, which is also the home for many low-income whites. There is no bus service in the north side of town; the bus company could not operate profitably. Many of the streets there are unpaved because property owners, black and white, refuse to pay their share of the costs. Some of the houses are merely shacks, but they are not the slums of Bedford-Stuyvesant. Most of the homes in East Lawrence appeared neat and well kept. There has been random gunfire in the area, but the culprits disappear quickly.

The attendant at the service station near the bridge across the river leaned his head through the window and said: "Things are changing. Everything's changing. What I don't understand is they call me a racist. Hell, I don't even know what a racist is. I do a lot of business with niggers."

★ ★ ★

I was introduced to Frank Ziln, who is studying architecture and sociology. In April he was elected presiding officer of the university council and the university senate, the first student to hold the prestigious posts. Both groups are dominated by faculty members. During the past two years students have been pressing effectively for greater participation in university governance. Students now sit on the policy committees of every school. The chancellor and the board of regents recently approved a revised "Student Code of Rights, Responsibilities and Conduct," a detailed eight-page document drawn up by the student senate.

"The last few years have demonstrated that students can close a university," Ziln said. "But they have had very little power to change the procedures and operations of a school. We've been working with the faculty and administration to rewrite the whole university government system. The day is gone when anyone but students can say, 'This is what the students want.'

"Change is necessary because students need to be prepared to make decisions, to work in groups toward getting a consensus, understanding the dynamics of collaboration. If an education is only attending lectures in a classroom, you're not going to get people to understand these things. Our country is information rich and understanding poor. We don't understand how to deal with other human beings. I don't know a better way to get at that problem than by taking part in the political process of the university. That's what governance means anyway—arriving at ways to deal with each other."

The very mention of university politics brought a smile to his face. "I'm seen by a certain number of students as a traitor—because I have contacts higher up and because I think process is important. Those people honestly believe this is the most violent country in the world and they think the only way to make people take notice is by violence. They're not talking about violence to human beings; they're talking about violence to property. They missed the Depression, they didn't have to fight to get back things they lost, and so they don't put as much value on material things as older people. When they hit at this property thing, they know they're hitting something that is of real value to their elders. But what matters to them is human life."

I interrupted to ask: What about rock throwing, missiles, bottles?

"I'm not a spokesman for the people who do that kind of thing because I don't approve of it, but I think they would argue self-defense in most cases. If they wanted to have guns, they could have guns; guns are easy to come by in this country. We've had a lot of campus demonstrations and if students wanted to do that kind of violence to people, they could have.

"I take part in the political process at the university because I want to avoid violence of any kind. Like it or not, universities are the places where most of our country's leaders come from. They remain loyal to their universities; if, in response to the troubles we're having, they insist on excessive authority—repression—we'll have an abuse of authority all over the country. I don't want to see things get out of hand. We have to deal politically with each other, not violently.

"KU handled the Cambodia and Kent State crisis very well. I don't think a university should take a stand on the war. I think the people within that university should be free to take any view they want personally. For the entire university to come out and say, 'We are against the war'—that's infringing on your freedom. If the university takes one position and you disagree, what happens to you? This spring we kept the university open and students did what in their own conscience they felt was right. Some abused the freedom, but most didn't. And there was a lot of education in what happened: discussion groups, research, personal initiative.

"Four years ago we were primarily concerned with what color socks to wear on campus. Kids here never really faced the contradictions of life, especially kids from middle-class homes, from all those farms and nice little places in Kansas. They've watched a lot of television; but your mind doesn't have to function when you watch television. When you see reports from Vietnam it's like watching a Western. But when your buddy is killed, or you get a draft notice for a war you know most people in the country don't think is worth the killing, or when a black comes up and says, 'Let's go to the ghetto' and you go with him, you see things your parents never told you about. It shakes you. The kids at KU haven't been exposed to the whole complex of what America is. That's why the shootings at Kent State had such an effect. When those four students were killed the war wasn't on television any more. The world was no longer out there somewhere and you were here, safe and comfortable. Most of the freshmen may be apathetic when they arrive. I don't think as many of them will any longer be as apathetic when they leave."

THURSDAY EVENING

After making several appointments for the following day and dining with the Simonses—father and son—I surrendered to the weariness of the previous night's ride, returned to the motel, and went soundly to sleep.

At midnight sixteen-year-old Michelle Raney, daughter of the former mayor, took a pen with red ink and wrote a note which she left beside her father's bed. It read:

Tiger Dowdell is dead. ½ his head was shot off. Not saying whose fault it was or why. Doesn't make much difference really, this town will go anyway.

Michelle Raney is a fragile child with deep feelings about the way people treat each other. On this night she was quite emotional and her information was not exactly precise—one-half of Tiger Dowdell's face had not been shot off. Essentially, however, she was accurate: Tiger Dowdell was dead enough and the town would go.

FRIDAY MORNING

The death of Rick D. ("Tiger") Dowdell occurred in approximately this manner:

Sometime after 10 P.M. Thursday police began to receive reports of sniper fire in East Lawrence, three blocks from the center of town, in the vicinity of Afro House, an organization supported in part by Kansas

University student-activity fees for the purpose of promoting black culture and solidarity. One bullet pierced the left leg of Mrs. Mildred J. Johnson, a white woman, as she was standing in her back yard. Two black men left the scene of the shooting and disappeared into Afro House. A few minutes later Dowdell and a nineteen-year-old KU student, Franki Lyn Cole, came from the front of Afro House, got into a Volkswagen, and drove toward town. Police pursued the car to an alley less than two blocks away. Police said Dowdell ran down the alley; Miss Cole said he "walked hurriedly or trotted." Police said they observed a long-barrel revolver in Dowdell's left hand; Miss Cole said she did not see a gun. Patrolman William Garrett, who is twenty-seven, pursued Dowdell down the alley and commanded him to stop. The Kansas Bureau of Investigation reported that Officer Garrett, after firing a warning shot,

> . . . commanded the subject to drop his gun. Without reply the subject turned and fired the revolver at Officer Garrett, with his left hand. Immediately Officer Garrett returned one shot at the subject. Officer Garrett and the subject were 60 to 70 feet apart when the two shots were exchanged. The subject then ran west to the alley and south down the alley. Officer Garrett fired three shots at the subject running south. The subject was struck by one of the shots fired by Officer Garrett and fell 259 feet south of Ninth Street and five feet west of the east edge of the alley. A .357 magnum revolver was laying beside the subject. The subject was wearing a shoulder holster on his right side, under his jacket.

The "subject" died there in the alley. Cause of death, the coroner said, was a "cerebral laceration" caused by a bullet. The coroner's inquest exonerated the patrolman. There was no grand-jury investigation.

Word spread quickly through East Lawrence. Someone tossed a bottle with a petroleum mixture into a laundry near Afro House. Minor fires were reported elsewhere. Two patrol cars were hit by slugs. A glass and mirror company near Afro House received several bullets from high-powered rifles fired by snipers hiding behind a school across the street. While witnesses to the Dowdell shooting were being questioned inside the courthouse, Dolph Simons, Jr., and three other men standing outside were fired upon by a sniper stationed in a nearby park.

"It was like a war," Simons said when I found him in his office at 7 A.M. "I have an idea it was just the first skirmish," he added.

There is still dispute about exactly how it all started and what happened. There have been investigations and more investigations and the story still is not complete. Even when the facts are accepted by all sides, people in Lawrence look blank and shake their heads when you ask: "Why?" As in a hundred communities in every part of the country in a season of violence, no one—Presidential commissions, state agencies, police, the participants themselves—could say with authority, "This is why it happened."

★ ★ ★

On August 8, 1967, three years earlier, the Lawrence Human Relations Commission convened in a special meeting to listen to the comments of individual citizens. Several young people were present. The minutes of the meeting include this item: "Rick Dowdell was the next speaker. He complained of the problem of police arrests and relationships between minority youths and the police."

★ ★ ★

I drove through the area. Smoke still hovered around the laundry. Workmen were already cleaning out the debris and preparing to replace the glass window through which the incendiary had crashed. Half a dozen young blacks stood in front of Afro House watching with sullen expressions each passing car. I stopped to get out but they gestured defiantly for me to keep moving and I did.

There were two large bullet holes in the plate-glass window and two in the front door of the Wilson Glass Company across the street from St. Luke's AME Church and the York School. Using guerrilla tactics snipers had pelted the neighborhood. The slugs that hit the Wilson Glass Company tore into the far wall of a second room. One had penetrated a $54.17 framed mirror at precisely the point where my chin appeared in the reflection. Bernard Freeman, the manager, had crouched in here and returned the fire.

He was not in the store this morning. I asked the clerk if working here made her nervous. She replied: "Not as nervous as this place makes the customers." Another woman, a customer, said: "We've only been here a year and Lawrence has changed in that time alone."

How?

"There was this trouble in the spring at the high school and the university. Now this. My friends are all scared. People are talking about getting shot right as they sit in their living room." She was to pick up her husband at another store two blocks away, but to get there she had to pass the Green Gables, a tavern frequented almost exclusively by blacks. She said she would take the long way around because she didn't want to pass the tavern even in daylight. "I'm just a coward," she said, laughing nervously.

The clerk, a large pleasant woman, said: "It's all a shame, I know that. It's a bad thing to happen to the good coloreds. Some of our best customers are good coloreds. They're just as good as you or me. This kind of thing"—she pointed to the bullet holes—"hurts them. The people who did all the shootin' are a minority of riffraff. I wouldn't even be surprised if some of them were white trash. Someone told me already there were four or five cars in there"—she pointed up the street—"from out of town. There's people comin' in to stir this up."

I drove to Raney's drugstore on Massachusetts Street for a cup of coffee. The booths were full.

"This is a small town," one man said. "Everybody knows each other. We ought to be able to deal with these problems."

"Hell," another said. "I know how to deal with them," and he made a gesture with his thumb raised and his first finger pointed toward the first man. "It ain't too late to start killin' niggers," he said. Several of the men grimaced. "Put away your gun," one said. "We got one dead already."

Dick Raney looked like a man caught on a rope bridge in a hailstorm.

"I knew Rick Dowdell," he said. "He was a big fellow—six foot five. All of them were big. There were six brothers. The mother died of cancer when they were just little stairsteps. Their father had been out West; I hear he's on his way back for the funeral. The boys were raised by their grandmother. Rick worked for me for a while when he was a high-school student. He had to handle a car and some money for me and at the time he was one of the best kids I ever had working for me. Sometime after he graduated from high school something happened to him. There were skirmishes with the law. He and his brothers were suspects in several unsolved crimes. Who knows whether they were involved. The word got around, 'It must have been a Dowdell.'"

What happens now? I asked.

He shook his head. "I'd say there's going to be trouble. We've got—we've got some rednecks here. Not as many as there used to be, but enough. How large a group this is, I don't know. I don't really want to know. But they do exist. And we've got some wild black kids. I fear the wild ones and a bunch of those rednecks are going to meet on some street somewhere tonight. And neither one of them has a solution available to . . . A confrontation isn't going to help a thing."

A policeman stopped by for coffee. He had been up all night. He was heading home to rest. He called the name of a black policeman and said: "He won't even be able to leave his house tonight because those kids down there hate him so bad his home won't be safe. They think he's a Tom. He told the chief: 'Look, I'll come to duty if you'll put an officer in front of my house.'" Laughter traveled up and down the counter.

The elder Dolph Simons was in the editor's chair when I returned to the *Journal-World*. He has been in this business a long time and knows his mind. "I want to make sure that the paper tells what is going on," he admonished his staff as they prepared for the afternoon paper that would report last night's events, "but I also want you to keep in mind that this is no time to stir up things. The newspaper's got no business inflaming the situation."

His executive editor wanted to put a picture of Dowdell and the policeman on the front page but Simons said he wasn't sure that was a good idea. "The boy is dead," he said. "His picture belongs on the front page. The officer's on the second."

The executive editor: "The headline will read, 'Negro Youth Dies in Gun Battle.'"

The editor: "It wasn't a gun battle."

Executive editor: "The officer fired a warning shot—the Negro fired back—then the officer fired back."

The editor: "I guess it was a gun battle. O.K."

There came to the office a tall highboned man in his late forties named Harvey Schmedemann, a local liquor dealer. He was there to protest to the newspaper, his only ombudsman that day, a mimeographed newsletter thrust by a hippie into the hand of his eleven-year-old son as the boy walked across the University of Kansas campus. Schmedemann was angry. "Look at this," he said, holding up the newsletter. "Full of obscenities and put in the hands of an eleven-year-old kid. A KID! What is going on up there? Can't someone do something about that place? Look at this"— and I read:

Well the amerikan league lost again. Dic was there. Art Linkletter was there. Hell, even Micky Mantle was there and the amerikan league still lost. I guess the —— just weren't ready. Meanwhile back in River City, we smoke our dope, blow things up and run

about crazy. Next year we'll save the amerikan league from defeat.
Next year we'll be in the all star game. Next year there won't be no
—— game at all. No more. No matter how many plastic infields
they make. Is a big —— fight coming and ain't nobody ready for it
much-maybe. Can you survive. Are you ready for the big roundup
—think about it. Dig it. Get ready. The pigs, granted, ain't ready
either, yet. But they do mean to kill us all. Get ready brothers and
sisters or you too may end up like the amerikan league. Jail ain't cool.
Don't wake up there some morning. So sisters and brothers get your
guns, your friends, your fake id's, your hideouts, your alternatives
and your heads together cuz its just a shot away.

"My kid is eleven," Harvey Schmedemann said. "He can't even go to
a summer program for kids up there without getting something like this
slapped in his face. I ask you, How can we stop it? Can't somebody *do*
something?"

He got consolation if not an answer and then he laughed. "I admit
I don't like this long hair. To me I guess it's a symbol that"—he laughed
again—"that they're against me. I don't know. These kinds of kids are
pretty much a shock to a small town. We have a lot of people in Lawrence
who are liberal-minded and will go along with a lot of things, but generally speaking I think the larger portion of the community does not like
it."

FRIDAY AFTERNOON

The local radio station announced: "A tense situation prevails in
Lawrence this afternoon."

Rumors everywhere:

"Someone said carloads of blacks are comin' over from Kansas City."

"They're gonna burn down the university."

"Someone said a Lawrence nigger was in Kansas City this afternoon
and bought $200 worth of ammunition and paid for it with a university
check."

"All the young black leaders have disappeared. They're organizing war
for tonight."

Whether they were organizing for war I do not know; but the young
black leaders were not to be found. They were not talking to whites.
Men who thought they had ties to the black youths suddenly drew blanks
when they called or inquired.

I located the Dowdell home, but as I stepped out of my car a tall black with a thin mustache said: "Move on, buddy, nobody's home."

But I can see people in there, I protested.

"Sorry, buddy, there ain't nobody home for *you*."

★ ★ ★

Chancellor Chalmers and I kept our midafternoon appointment. It was difficult to believe that this man was at the moment facing the prospect of an upheaval on his campus tonight or that he cared about the pressures building from one end of Kansas to the other to oust him from the position he has only occupied for one year. His office was quiet and he appeared calm.

"It's the old question of the vulnerable center," he said. "If you walk down the middle, you get hit by cars going in both directions. We have a small number of people—some students, some not—who capitalize on tensions. They are as busy recruiting during tense periods as the Marines are during a war. Kent and Cambodia were made to order for radicals. Something like Dowdell's death was made for them: 'The pigs got Tiger. You can't trust The Man. Come on with us.' I can hear them now.

"All of this is straining higher education as it hasn't been strained in a long time. Higher education has always been 'something other' to most Americans, to the large majority of people who were never able to obtain a college education. Remember how they branded Stevenson an egghead? When it comes to getting an education for their children, that is their first priority. But in an abstract way they remain skeptical that higher education is really necessary.

"I'm sure that if we didn't have to deal with external issues, we could solve these problems. The radicals are prone to violence but numerically they are very small. After all, not that many campuses out of more than two thousand closed last year. There are politicians who keep fanning the flames. You've probably heard that our Union building was burned this spring. I'm certain some unstable person or persons were responsible. But Agnew made a speech, from somewhere a long way off, I think Florida, and he asserted that the students burned it down—just like that, the students burned it down. He knew something we didn't know. I wish he would turn it over to the Kansas Bureau of Investigation. But there you have it—he fires a salvo from a safe distance, it makes the headlines, but how does a university answer? How does a university resist the radicals on the one hand and the politicians on the other? The tragedy is they're fighting each other and the university is their battlefield. When it's all over they leave and what do you have left? A charred, crippled, shellshocked institution.

"The media tells just enough to be misleading. There was a newspaper headline that said 'KU killings.' Rick Dowdell's death was not a 'KU killing.' Abbie Hoffman came to KU this spring. After a two-hour tirade which really failed to turn our kids on, he said: 'Kansas U. is a drag. I'm going to Dallas.' And he left. I was delighted. Having him here was the best thing we could do to persuade the students that a guy like Hoffman has nothing to offer. Hoffman is part of a circus—he's the sideshow. If the media were able to present the entire sideshow, Hoffman would be finished. Two hours of Abbie Hoffman and you see right through him. But what happens? The media presents Hoffman blowing his nose in the American flag and the people who see that are thrown into a frenzy and blame the university for having him here in the first place. He's farce, he's camp, but one minute of the media and he's a celebrity who is taken seriously.

"The blacks? Well, the relationship between Lawrence and the university is a symbiotic relationship. If one catches a cold they both take a pill. Each suffers the repercussions of whatever happens in the other. The black demands at the university last year were not that different from black demands at the high school. The black community in town identifies with the black kids up here. And that works the other way. They both want the other to do well, and they think they're in the same boat. That's why we'll probably get some action tonight. When one hurts, they both hurt."

I asked if events of this past spring had affected donations to the university. "Up until those events our gifts were equal to the previous year. We are the seventh-largest recipient of donations among public universities in the country—people here really support us. After everything that happened the number of donors dropped slightly but the total amount of money went up. Some people gave a lot more because they felt the university was caught in adversity. They're loyal to the school. I think our contributions will be up next year unless we invade Thailand."

★ ★ ★

In the late afternoon I drove through East Lawrence. The radio continued to proclaim a tense situation. But wars thrive on incongruities. Five white children played in the yard adjacent to Afro House. On the

101

corner of the same block twelve or thirteen children, white and black, and two chaperones were standing in the yard of the Salvation Army headquarters eating chocolate-covered ice-cream sticks. The window of the laundry had been repaired. The evidence of conflict remained only on the faces of the young blacks standing in front of Afro House.

At Raney's drugstore three white men sat at a table and joked with Willie. Willie is a refugee from the Mississippi Delta, a short, wispy black man who is so relieved to be away from there that he is not about to let local troubles turn back his clock. His father once whipped a white policeman who had attacked him, and Willie wants no more of violence.

"Kansas," he said, "is a mighty good place to be."

★ ★ ★

I talked at length with John Spearman, whose son, John, Jr., a graduate of Lawrence High School and a student now at KU, is a leader of the black youths. "I don't know what my son is doing at this moment," John Spearman said. "I haven't seen him since we left to go down there last night when we heard about Tiger. He's called a couple of times but mostly to tell me where he would be. I can't speak for my son. I only know he's doing what he thinks is right, whatever it is."

The elder Spearman—he is forty-two—is eloquent and soft-spoken. He works in the production department of the local Hallmark plant. A year ago he became the only black on the Lawrence school board. His mustache is as sparse as his frame and he wears his hair in a close natural Afro style. He said:

"I think the young blacks are more willing to consider the alternative of violence today than a year ago or two years ago. They were very young during the Martin Luther King years, during Selma, during all that legislation. They were just babies in the Thurgood Marshall era. They kept hearing us say that one day we were going to be free, but after all that we woke up and found that we weren't any more free, actually. The freedom was on the books. And suddenly there was violence. For a while it seemed to achieve more than all those years of patience and striving. That made a lot of people ask, What's wrong in this country that violence can achieve the things more peaceful means haven't accomplished so well? Older men would counsel against it, but the young men would say, 'But what about Martin Luther King? He was a peaceful man and he died violently by a white man's bullet!' Yes, I have to say, they have violence on their minds. I am not sure it is in their hearts.

102

"When I grew up in Lawrence the blacks were pretty invisible people. There are men on the school board who don't realize I went to school with them. They just weren't aware of me. You seldom saw blacks mentioned in the newspaper, certainly not on the society page. Everything in this town was segregated except the schools. While I was in high school you could only participate in noncontact sports if you were black. Track— not basketball or football. The year after I graduated, a black was nominated by the students to run for class president—the first time— but the principal stepped in and eliminated him. Housing was segregated, the drugstores were segregated, the restaurants were segregated, jobs were segregated.

"I was very resentful. I used to read W. E. B. Du Bois. I got angry about those things. I made up my mind that my children wouldn't spend their high-school years as I spent mine. I started very early making sure they knew they were as good as anybody living, anybody walking on this earth. If they suffered oppressions or injustices, I told them, it had nothing to do with their own worth. It has to do with the white man's ignorance and pride. I told them to strive for what you want, what you know is right. But don't deal from feelings of inferiority, frustration, bitterness. That isn't what I wanted for them.

"There is frustration and bitterness here today. I'm probably very prejudiced, to be honest about it, because I know those Dowdell kids. I knew their mother very well. I know they practically reared themselves, and I thought it was an accomplishment for boys so young to rear themselves with just the help of their grandmother. All of them managed to graduate from high school. They did it on their own. They had jousted with the law, but a good part of it was because they got around. And if somebody was doing something, a Dowdell was always suspected. I can't understand why it was necessary to shoot him. I would have hoped —I'd probably never make a policeman—but if I had no real reason to shoot him, he could have walked away before I would have killed him. I would have let him walk away. I'd have been a poor cop.

"They called me this afternoon and said the Chamber of Commerce and some of the business leaders wanted me to go down in there [to East Lawrence] and talk to the kids. Can you imagine what the reaction would be? In the past four years the black community has been beating from crisis to crisis, and when the crisis is over the white community shoves it under the rug and goes back to the status quo. We'll float on to the next crisis and suddenly the whole town's up in arms. And then the Chamber of Commerce wants to have a meeting. That won't bring Tiger Dowdell back to life."

He paused again. He was thinking of young Dowdell. "I wouldn't say Tiger was a saint or anything like that. He may have done some of the things he did because he didn't understand what black power meant. Maybe all those frustrations just poured out of him. Maybe he just didn't like white people. A lot of blacks don't. And suddenly he has a chance to express it. Maybe he did just hit a black kid or two, get in fights with them. I don't know. He probably did. He wasn't riffraff, though. Just a bitter, frustrated young black kid."

He had mentioned black power. "Well, it doesn't mean the same to me as it did at one time. It used to mean a piece of the pie, a chance to work up to your capabilities, a chance to achieve the potential that you have, a chance to lead a good, satisfying life, a chance not to live in the ghetto if you don't want to live in the ghetto. Now, since we're not getting those things by the usual methods of working with the power structure, perhaps all blacks are going to have to realize these things in togetherness. Maybe we can find dignity that way. And if we can't achieve these things, at least we can struggle together as men and women, and dig that feeling of inferiority out of our guts.

"We have some changes that must be made. I mean *must*. There are only four black teachers at the high school and there are no blacks on the administrative staff. Black people aren't blind. If you want to fill these positions with blacks, you can. You know why it is important to have more black teachers and more blacks on the staff? Because they know what it means to *be* black. A white teacher will unconsciously accept the fact that a kid is black and you don't really expect too much of him. If he doesn't give real attention or he doesn't push, if he doesn't have the competitive urge, it's too easy to just sit back and leave him be. The goal of the white teacher becomes order. So you get bright kids who go into high school who can't spell, who don't use English well at all. They don't feel part of the school system because no one, not even the most golden-hearted white teacher, can understand what it is to be black —to feel scared and out of place, to feel alone, like you don't belong, to have had maybe a doughnut and a Coke for breakfast if you had breakfast, to wonder why everybody else's mamma comes to class parties and yours doesn't—because she feels out of joint there. This is the problem. Unless you are black, what America is doing seems impressive. But while it looks fair to you if you are white, it looks to the black like they're really not giving an inch where it counts.

104

"That's why I say it's up to the whites. I think you're going to have to reach into yourself and shake yourselves up, and I don't think any steps will be made until you hurt yourselves a little, and some of these ideals that you profess so easily are going to have to be brought down to earth and shaken out, and maybe we'll all live up to them. Like what would you do if you were black?

"It's up to you. It's not up to the blacks. They've made their choice. Just keep clear. That's the way it is."

FRIDAY EVENING

There was still light in the sky when it began and I thought of how on the bus in Connecticut the light at this time of day had been mellow and lenient. Here it seemed to gather up a whole town's incredulous dreads and suspend them indecently over the landscape.

The voice of the police dispatcher said tersely: "Some people are moving down Pennsylvania shooting out street lights." They extinguished all but a few of the lamps. Within half an hour a twelve-block area of East Lawrence, two minutes from midtown, belonged to guerrillas. An aerial flare soared silently into the sky and exploded like a Roman candle on the Fourth of July. I drove down New Hampshire one block from the battle area and kept telling myself that these broad, clean streets were not, could not, be a combat zone. A fusillade of gunfire rang out. Three blocks away shots shattered the windshield and right front fender of a passing motorist.

The police received a report that forty-five to fifty blacks, all carrying long guns or sidearms, were marching east on Tenth Street. Someone garbled the message and it came through as "four or five." Only four policemen were dispatched to intercept them. As they approached on foot an assailant stepped out of the darkness across the street and fired a shotgun. One of the policemen, Lieutenant Eugene Williams, was hit. Police who moved in to assist him were pinned down. In the dark the ambulance had trouble locating him. After he was evacuated police pulled out of the area and kept an uneasy guard on the perimeters until the firing subsided and the guerrillas melted away.

From the Kansas Bureau of Intelligence report:

> Witnesses said they could not believe they were witnessing such a scene in Lawrence. They described the group as being led by advance men and followed by rear guard men, fading in and out of

105

the shadows, then concealing themselves behind the bushes and trees when any traffic was observed. The group used low whistles and hand signals for maneuvering. . . . Evidence gathered from the scene of this shooting indicated that shotguns and high powered rifles had been used. . . . Most of the citizens interviewed in this area have lived there for several years. . . . They indicated they could not recall ever seeing most of these Negro males previously, and they felt they must be people from towns other than Lawrence joining some of the local residents. . . .

While these events occurred in East Bottoms there was trouble of another kind near the university campus on the southwest side of town —in an area often referred to as "hippie haven." On this spot almost to the day in 1854 the original pioneers from Massachusetts ate their first meal as they searched for a site to build an antislavery colony in the fight for Kansas. The cry in Boston had been: "Let us settle Kansas with people who will make it free by their own voice and vote." They did, beginning here in Lawrence on this hill, which they named Mt. Oread (Oread: a nymph of the hills). Old Amos Lawrence, benefactor of the emigrants from Massachusetts, said the sight of the tent city spreading below him from this location reminded him of Plymouth Rock.

It was something else tonight. The nymphs of the hills, the street people, were setting trash fires, tossing fire bombs, placing boards with nails into the street to harass firemen and police, lobbing bricks at fire trucks and rocks at firemen. A stone—or was it a fire bomb?—landed in Chancellor Chalmers' house. A burning barricade went across Tennessee Street. Arsonists ignited the "White House," a vacant house near the campus where the freaks hang out. Toward midnight Chancellor Chalmers, Dick Raney, and I drove to the scene. A hundred or more young people, most of them from the street community, had congregated to watch firemen fight the blaze. Police guarded the trucks and the firefighters.

Two longhairs walked up to a stocky patrolman standing in the street with the chin strap of his helmet unbuckled, a twelve-gauge shotgun resting on his hip and a belt of shells hanging over his shoulder.

"How about slippin' me one of those shells?" one of the freaks asked.

"Can't do that, sir."

"Just for a souvenir?"

"I'm sorry, sir, but I can't do it."

"What is it, some pig regulation?"

"That's one reason. But the other reason is that I'm low on ammunition."

"You been shootin' people?"

"No, sir."

"Then why are you low?"

"Because they don't want me to have too much down at headquarters."

"Why? Why won't they let the pig have his slop?"

"Because I'm trigger happy."

He did not smile as he said it.

Another cluster had gathered around a second policeman.

"Do you think you could use that?" one freak inquired of the officer, pointing to his shotgun.

The policeman smiled. A tight smile. He turned his head slowly from side to side to keep the crowd in view.

"Why don't you lay that thing down and take off that uniform?" his interrogator asked. His hair stood out as if it were plugged into an electric socket. He was high. "You don't look like a killer to me," he said.

The cop said nothing.

"Killers are supposed to be lean and tough, like the pig that shot Dowdell last night. You're too fat to be a killer."

No response.

"What kind of mentality is it that will stand in the middle of a street on a hot night like this carrying a 12-gauge shotgun and wearing a helmet and shiny boots like the Gestapo? Huh? What kind of mentality?"

His face and the cop's were no more than twelve inches apart. The policeman continued to swivel his gaze around the street.

"Are you aware that that thing can hurt someone? Are you aware that last night one of your guns not only hurt but killed someone?"

A young black man stepped up. "Yeah," he said to the policeman. "How would you feel if a policeman was killed? You'd feel that a brother was dead. Well, that's how I feel 'bout that boy who was killed last night. He was one of my brothers and he was killed by one of your brothers. Now what do you think I should do about it?"

The cop did not answer. At this moment he was joined by another policeman. He appeared relieved.

Two other street types tried to provoke another officer.

"If a cop is a pig, what is the son of a cop?" the first one asked.

"A piggy?"

"No, a son of a bitch."

They laughed. The cop was silent, absolutely silent. But from the look in his eyes you knew he had heard.

I was introduced to George Kimball. He is reported to be the leader of the street community. I doubt that they have a leader, but his ability to generate publicity has established George Kimball as their spokesman. He is running for sheriff of Douglas County. (The incumbent has a withered hand; Kimball promises to be a "two-fisted sheriff." Kimball also is pledged to "keep an eye on everyone"; he has one glass eye.)* "Kimball is crazy," someone said, "but he's not stupid."

It was after midnight and as we watched the milling crowd, the fire trucks, and the cops, word came that the east side was quiet. "Sure it's quiet," Kimball said. "They got a pig, didn't they? They got what they wanted. The law of Hammurabi—they got what they wanted. Now they're even. It will be quiet for a while."

SATURDAY MORNING

Officer Williams did not die. By morning he had been transferred out of the intensive care unit. The four men at the adjacent table in the Holiday Inn speculated whether this would be enough or whether they would "go after another one tonight."

I introduced myself and joined them for coffee. The four men had lived in Lawrence all of their lives. "I just don't understand," one of them said. "There's a black working now in every bank. Go into any big store downtown and you'll see a black working there. The school superintendent told me last week he is looking hard for black teachers. I really don't understand. These people were my friends. I went to school with them. Yesterday not one of them would talk to me. Not one." He shook his head and drank his coffee.

"I had a call last night from ——," a second man said. "He's on the Support Your Local Police Committee." The committee and the John Birch Society have been collaborating publicly. "They want me to join. I can't see it. It's not that they're mean. Most of them are just scared. Honest to God, I don't think anyone knows what to think."

I went to the library to read about Lawrence. Even there the talk

* In November George Kimball received 2,089 votes to his opponent's 18,000.

is the same. I heard one man in the stacks say: 'Preservation is the first law of life, and I aim to obey it.'"

The proslavery forces from Missouri were determined in 1855 that the first territorial legislature in Kansas would approve slavery. Every election district in Kansas was to be taken over by Missourians. "Kansas much be secured for slavery by fair means or foul," former U.S. Senator David Atchison had said. More than 1,000 of his henchmen came to Lawrence for the election armed with guns, rifles, pistols, bowie knives, and two pieces of artillery loaded with musket balls. There were 1,034 votes cast in Lawrence, although there were only 369 legal voters in the district. It was a clean sweep for slavery. The administration in Washington condoned what had happened by refusing to back up antislavery forces protesting the chicanery. The free staters decided to repudiate the fraudulent legislature by ignoring its laws, and in Lawrence, on the Fourth of July, Dr. Charles Robinson, who had led the first group of settlers, made a speech that was to resound across the state:

"I can say to Death, be thou my Master, and to the Grave, be thou my prison house; but acknowledge such creatures as my masters, never! Thank God, we are yet free, and hurl defiance at those who would make us slaves. . . . Let every man stand in his place. . . . Let us repudiate all laws enacted by foreign legislative bodies, or dictated by Judge Lynch over the way [in Missouri]. Tyrants are tyrants, and tyranny is tyranny, whether under the garb of law or in opposition to it. So thought and acted our ancestors, and so let us think and act."

Lawrence became an "abolition nest," whose people "were a law unto themselves." It became an armed camp under threat of attack from Missouri, and during one siege John Brown made his first appearance in Kansas, to help defend Lawrence. If he rode into town tonight, I thought, no one would be surprised.

In 1863 William C. Quantrill led his guerrillas into Lawrence, the sixteen-year-old Jesse James among them, to plunder and kill in one of the bloodiest episodes of the period. In four hours some 150 innocent people were murdered by raiders moving from house to house. One of the casualties would be a relative newcomer, Judge Louis Carpenter. The raiders first robbed him of his valuables, "but his coolness and self possession, his genial manner and tact every time diverted them, and they left him unharmed. Towards the last another gang came. He accosted them in his usual pleasant way, hoping to engage them in conversation. One of them asked where he was from. 'New York,' he replied. 'Oh, it's you New York fellows who are doing all the mischief,' the Quantrill man said. He pulled his gun and shot the judge to death."[*]

I left the library and walked one block to the police station for an appointment with Richard Stanwix, the chief. He had been called to city hall for an emergency meeting. As I left the station I met more than a hundred blacks marching down the sidewalk chanting: "I am SOMEONE. I am SOMEONE." They turned up the walk toward the police station and the chant became: "We want—ALL the pigs. We want—ALL the pigs." Four young men left the main body and entered the station. They were tall, silent, and tense. I followed them, although the crowd tentatively resisted my passing through it. The young men asked to see Stanwix. There was a long silence when they were told he was out. Finally one of the blacks said: "He'd better come back."

"He is," the officer behind the desk replied. "I told you he's in a meeting at city hall."

"I just said he better come back."

There was silence in the corridor. Outside the crowd began to chant: "We want Super Pig. We want Super Pig."

I went to a landing up the stairs and looked down at the crowd. They were young—university and high-school age. The chanting subsided and a youth near the door said something about a man calling who wanted "to put flowers on Tiger's grave." A girl replied: "Might as well donate a plate of peas. He can eat those peas as well as he can smell those flowers."

It was not a time to smile but some of them did. So did I. The girl looked up and saw me and began a chant which the crowd quickly picked up: "We want you. We want you." With each chant they pointed in my direction. When the chanting died I mumbled something about their not wanting me because I was only passing through.

"Honey," one young lady said, "you better keep on passing."

"Where you from, baby?" asked the girl who had suggested peas. And as I started to answer I remembered the story of Judge Louis Carpenter, which less than an hour ago I had read at the library— he was one of those "New York fellows . . . doing all the mischief." I know it sounds ridiculous; there I was safely although accidentally ensconced

[*] *History of Lawrence, Kansas,* by Richard Cordley, D.D. (eyewitness to the Quantrill Raid). Lawrence Journal Press, 1895.

in the police station and I could only think of what had happened to a New York carpetbagger more than a hundred years ago.

"I'm from Washington," I said, which was true in a way. "And Texas," I added, which was also true. And then it just came out—"And New York."

"Honey," she replied. "You've come to Little Harlem and the fire is burning." And they began again to chant: "We want you. We want you."

Downstairs Chief Stanwix had returned and the young men presented him with a petition demanding that Officer William Garrett be immediately suspended and that an investigation be made into the events leading to the shooting.

"I understand how you feel," Chief Stanwix said. He is a Lawrence man who is well regarded for his amiability. "I'm sorry it came to this. We've got to stop the violence." He was sympathetic but firm. "I don't want any more trouble," he said.

The four blacks left and the crowd marched away chanting: "I am SOMEone. I am SOMEone."

At lunch a young photographer said: "Things have changed. It used to be that when you walked down the street people would smile at you. They're nervous now. They glance but they don't smile. It's like everybody's got a hundred-pound monkey on his back. I don't think it's just the local thing. Hell, you look at the front page of the paper—two cops killed in Chicago, that black politician gunned down in Kansas City, the cost of living is up, and every Thursday they bring in another body count from Vietnam just like the man comes to read the meter in your house. Nobody is saying, 'We're better than this. We got to get together, all of us, and pull out of this rut.'" He finished a Coke and said: "I'm just as good as I am bad, I think. I think all of us are. Nobody's speakin' to the good in me. No wonder nobody is smilin'."

SATURDAY AFTERNOON

I met Keith Wood, twenty-three, who graduated last year from KU and is teaching in the Lawrence junior high. His father is a doctor in a small Kansas town. Young Wood is a Republican, moderately conservative, and having been elected a precinct committeeman when he was twenty-one, aspires to politics and government.

"We've always had a certain amount of tension here," he said. "Early

111

in this decade Gayle Sayres [the Chicago Bears' football great] led a sit-in in the chancellor's office at the university and the campus police had to carry them out. Some white agitator sent a paper-sack effigy that said, 'You will Die, Racist Pig' to a professor who led a fight to get an integrated swimming pool. I think there is more irritation now. That's the best word for it—irritation. Things were coming along pretty well—jobs were opening, the barbershop finally agreed to cut Wilt Chamberlain's hair, the restaurants began to open up. When the blacks at the university finally got a black cheerleader, the kids at the high school started wanting similar things. Then it was one thing after another.

"I don't think many people feel much remorse over that shooting. A man I work with right here in this building, a printer, said they should have got all the other Dowdells when they got Tiger. These people feel the law and the courts have broken down in this town. Several times in the last two years the guilty verdict has been returned, both by voluntary plea and by jury, and the defendant has been put on probation or given a suspended sentence. This has been the case with the Dowdells and the Mumfords [another black family]. Some of them have received two or three convictions and yet they get suspended sentences on top of each other. Call it what you may, this is what people mean when they talk about law and order. I confess that I feel a little upset when I see a news report of court action and a Mumford or a Dowdell has been put on probation for one charge in court when the day before he has been caught robbing a gas station and already has a suspended sentence for something else. Dowdell belonged to a troublesome family. It's no wonder to me that people feel very little remorse over the shooting.

"There are about eighteen black kids in the junior high where I teach. The thing I remember most of all is the time I assigned my class to read from a civics book. It began with the sentence, 'You are an American citizen.' This black kid—thirteen going on fourteen—opened his book and said aloud: 'No, I'm not.' I said, 'What did you say?' He said—his voice hadn't changed yet and it just blurted across the room—'I said, No, I'm not. I'm not an American citizen.' I asked him what he meant by that and he said: 'I'm supposed to be an American citizen but I'm not treated like one. I was even forced to come here through slavery.' I was aghast. This was my first year as a teacher. I had never run into anything like this. Some of the white kids were upset. I decided to do the best I could and I asked for a general discussion on what he had said. He was the only black student in the room. It was a vigorous discussion. He finally ran out of answers. He couldn't defend his position. He could go out and get a job at A & W Rootbeer like any other kid his age. He was on the basketball team. He just couldn't defend his position. I don't really think he believed what he has been fed. We weren't trying to break him down but he came as close that day as he's ever come to admitting he doesn't really believe this stuff about racism. I'm worried about him, however. He's a kid of average intelligence. But he's hotheaded and susceptible and he could wind up dead in some alley like Dowdell."

SATURDAY NIGHT

A black man in his mid-twenties came into Dick Raney's drugstore with a prescription for a drug. The prescription was written by a Kansas City doctor and the man gave his own address as the Holiday Inn in Lawrence. "Do you know what this can do to you, fellow?" Raney asked. 'It can send you right up the wall."

"Don't worry about that, man. I ain't gonna take no overdose tonight. Tonight I got to keep cool."

But East Lawrence was cool that night. There were some arrests for possession of firearms and narcotics and a shot here and there; but a kind of peace reigned.

On Mt. Oread people from the street community pulled a swing set into the intersection, piled trash around it, and lighted a fire. Then they opened up the fire hydrants in the area to decrease the water pressure. It was like a carnival, I thought, like something from the festivals of Rio. A frazzled young man with glazed eyes stumbled past me and said, "Come on, man, join the revolution." But there was no revolution here. Fire trucks and police came and someone tossed a string of firecrackers into the darkness and people dived for cover because for all their zeal they were not prepared to die.

★ ★ ★

At 3 A.M. there was a knock on the door of my room at the Holiday Inn. I opened it and squinted into the faces of three young black men.

"Are you the cat doing the thing for the magazine?" one of them said.

113

I hesitated. I tried to see if I recognized one of them from the scene at the police station. Then I nodded and said, "Yes."

"Well, put this in there so all those smart folks who read magazines will know what it's all about," he said as he tossed a piece of paper into my room. They turned and walked away.

It was addressed to "Apolitical Intellectuals" and it read:

> One day
> The apolitical
> Intellectuals
> Of my country
> Will be interrogated
> By the simplest of our people.
>
> They will be asked
> What they did
> When their nation died out
> Slowly,
> Like a sweet fire
> Small and alone.
>
> No one will ask them
> About their dress,
> Their long siestas
> After lunch.
> No one will want to know
> About their sterile combats
> With "the Idea
> Of the Nothing."
> No one will care about
> Their higher financial learning.
> They won't be questioned
> On Greek mythology
> Or regarding their self-disgust
> When someone within them
> Begins to die
> The coward's death.
>
> They'll be asked nothing
> About their absurd justifications
> Born in the shadow
> Of the total lie.

On that day
The simple men will come.
Those who had no place
In the books and poems
Of the apolitical intellectuals,
But daily delivered
Their bread and milk,
Their tortillas and eggs,
Those who mended their clothes,
Those who drove their cars,
Who cared for their dogs and gardens
And worked for them.

And they'll ask:
"What did you do when the poor
Suffered, when tenderness
And life
Burned out in them?"

It was signed: Otto Rene Castillo.

By this time I was fully awake and I walked hurriedly out of the room to the courtyard of the motel. The three young men were gone.

SUNDAY MORNING

"If it's not a revolution, what is it?" George Kimball asked. I had gone by the small frame house in West Lawrence, near the university, where he stays with his girl, the pretty daughter of a Kansas farmer.

"It's a frolic," I said. "It's a perpetual frolic. You were having a ball out there Friday and Saturday nights. You weren't expressing solidarity with the guys in East Lawrence. You're not radicals. You're bacchantes—you follow Bacchus, not Marx."

"Cut out the crap," he said. You can never be sure you know when George Kimball is taking himself seriously. You are not even sure he knows. But enough townspeople take him seriously to give him stature with the street community.

"That is really unfair," he said. "I spent most of my time last night in the black areas of town. It may not look like we've been together on this, but you see, what the white people up here were doing for the most part was drawing heat off East Lawrence. That's what we're into. During the curfew back in April that's what we were doing. We ended

115

up—when we tried to draw some of the heat off, we drew it all off. But the theory was the same. We're all the same people, the black people and our people, but at the same time I and we have no control over what they're going to do and they don't have any control over what we're going to do. We make our decisions separately and try to coordinate them when we can. But we're held together by something you middle-class mothers will never understand. We know what it is to be o-u-t. We know what it is to be hassled. We know what injustice is. That's what makes us one, our people and the black people in East Lawrence. We don't have to pick up the phone to be in touch. We're in touch just because of what we're all up against.

"Bacchus, crap." He was wounded. "The governing principle behind us is the only major policy statement I've made so far during my campaign for sheriff. I read the Declaration of Independence on the Fourth of July. Have you read that closely lately?"

No.

"Read it. You don't have to be stoned to understand it."

The aim of the people who wrote that document was pretty specific, I said. What's your goal?

"The whole thing has to come down," he said. "And it's going to. The whole power structure. The whole country is steeped in racism. It's so firmly ingrained in the minds of the people. That's what racism is. It is innate prejudice towards a certain race of people. I keep thinking about my mother. She considers herself liberal. This is a woman who is teaching a black-studies course at a university. Two years ago she would point to her maid as an example of a fine colored person. Now that's racism. I called her up on the phone the other night and I asked her why the hell they were letting a racist teach a black-studies course."

What did she say?

"She sputtered a little and denied it. I told her not to worry—I would always love her even if she is a racist. My mother and I make some sort of vague attempt at communication, which doesn't get to very much. We have certain common interests and we tend to exclude everything else. My father gave his heart, body, soul, and organs to the military a long time ago and would rather believe that I never existed. I thought he'd like it when the White Panther party made me minister of defense. But I don't guess he sees me in anybody's Pentagon."

I suggested that he might make a better minister of agriculture. He has organized a collective that buys foodstuffs in large quantities from farmers and sells it to the street people for half the price they pay in grocery stores. He also has a conventional approach to the nation's farm problems: "I'm going to encourage subsidies to people not to grow marijuana," he said. "Marijuana is potentially the biggest crop in Douglas County. I think if someone doesn't want to grow marijuana, they should get paid for it."

SUNDAY AFTERNOON

I stopped by Dick Raney's drugstore. He was having coffee with the Harold Stagg. Stagg is forty-five, a graduate of Grambling College and a lab technician in the microbiology department at the university. He also manages a tavern and restaurant called The Gaslight on the edge of the campus. Mrs. Stagg, a Texan, works in a local department store. They have been moderate influences in the black community. They were talking about the events of recent days.

"The kid that got killed," Mrs. Stagg said, "was supposed to have been the best Dowdell of the bunch. Maybe he was doing something he didn't have no business. But the thing about it is this: he wasn't one of these poster men you see posted around in all the states, vicious and this kind of thing. As tall as these Dowdell boys are, there's no point in nobody saying that they couldn't have shot that boy in his leg trying to stop him. You could have shot him from here on down. I can't shoot, but I could have hit him in the leg. I mean killing somebody when it's not necessary."

How has it affected you, I asked.

"I don't feel like I felt three years ago," she said.

"A lot of things have happened," her husband said.

Mrs. Stagg interrupted. "I don't believe in black supremacy, I don't believe in white supremacy. I feel like every man should share the power. But in the event that I see that there isn't going to be equality, like a lot of people are saying this weekend there won't ever be, you know where I'm going. I'm going over on the black side 'cause I am black. You're going to the white side 'cause you are white."

"And if you don't go voluntarily," Harold Stagg said, "you'd be forced to anyway."

Mrs. Stagg reached into her purse and produced a note which she said her daughter received during the trouble in the high school this spring. It read:

117

Edith Stagg: You and those other black bitches in your English class better get weapons. You leave that class every morning; one day I'll get your black asses. Try and guess who I am, you lanky bitch.

She said: "I carry that around with me since April just to read sometimes when I'm not feeling very mad. My daughter likes that school. Ain't nobody going to force her to quit or to get scared off. She came home from junior high one day and said she wanted to try for cheerleader. I said, 'Is it important for you to be a cheerleader?' And she said, 'Mamma, if it isn't important, why do they have cheerleaders?' I had told her, Take it easy, don't volunteer for nothing, get your diploma and get out of that factory of the devil. And she said, 'Mamma, I am a part of this school, I am going to participate and I don't care what it costs.' I knew she meant it and I said, 'Okay, Edith, I'm with you.'

"The note hit her pretty hard. You know, why live? You don't really have that much to live for if this is the way you got to be treated the rest of your life. But she got over it. The thing that bothers her the most is that she would like to go to class and not discuss the racial thing. The first thing some teachers want to do is to start discussing race. You got maybe two or three Negro kids in a class of twenty or thirty whites. It's like you and ten friends sitting around and someone says, O.K., we will now discuss why Joe here is odd; tell us, Joe, what is it like to have big feet? Well, the black kids will enter in but as soon as they say something the class doesn't like—"

"The discussion's over," Harold Stagg said.

"And people are always asking, 'Are you a militant? Are you a militant black, Edith?' Because she's black everybody expects her to be militant. Look at Harold. He's growing a beard. And it's just like every white man that has long hair—people think he's a hippie. Everybody with long hair is not a hippie. Everybody that's growing a beard or an Afro hairdo is not militant. I wear a kinky hairdo when I get ready. I'm not a militant until somebody makes me a militant."

"It's like the scenes at high school last spring," Harold Stagg said. "I don't think you have a lot of militant kids in this town, white or black, but when they are pressured into being hostile, they'll fight back. I think you could say that Edith is a soul sister of those kids. I guess she proved that this spring."

How?

"The black kids went in to talk to the administrators and the officials would not listen. They just wouldn't listen. This got the black kids upset and things got pretty tense. I guess everybody was talking tough and some of the white kids promised the black kids that they were going to get them. The black kids weren't going to talk to their parents about it because they knew their parents would put dampers on them. They told us afterwards that they decided to fight back. The girls, I mean— the word was they were going to jump the girls. Edith and her friends very quietly put some things in their purses and when those white boys marched down to where the black girls were standing, they were surprised because those black girls fought like wild horses. One black girl had a spray can and a lug wrench. And she'd spray one in the eyes and clonk him on the head with that lug wrench, and when she got through the rest of them left, but they left about three of them boys there. The others just ran off and left. Edith was in this—we didn't know anything about it until after it was all over—but she was in it."

"And she's a skinny girl," Mrs. Stagg said.

"But she's got muscles in her arm and spunk in her heart," the father said. "But when she got home, I said, 'Edith, I wish there had been another way.' You don't want your daughter hurt, you know. I said, 'Don't start anything; if you see a crowd gathering, get out. If you have to run, run. Save yourself. But you got to defend yourself when you're attacked.'"

What happens now? I asked.

"Maybe it'll just go away," Harold Stagg said.

"That's what the average man thought when this school thing collided," his wife said. "It will not go away until some of these problems are solved. They'll wait for a certain length of time and then it's going to flare up again."

The lab technician in Harold Stagg spoke up: "Yes, you might say the fever will recede but the disease remains."

★ ★ ★

The young man who took me to the airport in Kansas City had been a colleague in Washington several years ago. I did not know until this last day of my visit that he is teaching at the university; we met unexpectedly as I was checking out of the motel. He is middle-of-the-road politically, a strong family man, and he speaks warmly of Kansas.

"The average Kansan is not a dumbbell," he said. "People in this town are not know-nothings and they're not vicious. Sure, there are some racists here—I don't know any white man who isn't a racist to one degree or another today—but most of the people here are just afraid and angry and ready to believe anything. My neighbor called last night and

119

said, 'Turn on your lights.' She said the police are expecting trouble and the lights will help. I live way over on the west side and white people were expecting black invaders to come pouring in. When people are afraid, they say the awfulest things in the quietest tones, without venom, like: 'If one of 'em comes up to my door I'll shoot him dead.' As matter-of-factly as if you asked someone to pass the butter. They don't commit evil; they condone it. They won't go out of their way to attack it. They believe the worst about people they fear—'Why was Dowdell running away if he wasn't guilty?'

"Lawrence to them is a little oasis and they can't understand why the blacks can't be happy with their lot. Their whole view of the world is being threatened. Their frustrations reach out at any conspicuous example of unconventionality. They don't like the university, but they know the town wouldn't exist if these kids didn't come in here and buy their goods.

"The town got terribly excited in the spring when Chalmers met a crisis by turning the other cheek. He was making deals to keep the university open and to stave off confrontations and he was successful. The university stayed open. The radicals were furious. They wanted Chalmers to deliver them an issue. Chalmers outsmarted them. But the conservatives in town and in the state had to have a clear-cut victory. They can't live with ambiguity. In their book, somebody always has to lose and somebody always has to win. There are some things I don't like about the chancellor—but I'll tell you this: he knows the whole purpose of a university is defeated when it is closed down. And I think he understands that you can't just put your foot on the neck of a radical and stomp him to death.

"So now everybody wants Chalmers' neck because nobody thinks he is altogether 100 percent for their view. If a shrewd conservative administrator like that, who is working to keep the university open and to prevent an all-out confrontation, is going to be harassed because he is soft on 'them,' what will happen?

"There are conservatives in this town who could become reactionary. People are angry—and not just the Wallaceites and the hardhats. There's something in the air that stings. You might call it mutual paranoia."

★ ★ ★

Two nights after my departure from Lawrence an eighteen-year-old white student from Kansas City was shot and killed in a confrontation between police and young people on Mt. Oread. Another student was wounded in the leg and a police officer was injured by a rock. It was the same story: fires, open hydrants, tear gas. This time the police opened fire for reasons that are still debated. One bullet pierced the back of the neck of Harry Nicholas Rice and came out through his teeth. He died a few minutes later on the floor of Harold Stagg's tavern. Young Rice had come to Lawrence to see his girl friend, who lives one block from the scene of the confrontation, and there is no evidence that he was taking part in the action. He was, as they used to say, an innocent bystander. As I write, the bullet that killed him has not been found and there has been no identification of his slayer.

The governor declared a state of emergency and ordered twenty-five Kansas highway patrolmen into Lawrence. The city manager blamed the street people "for taking advantage of last week's racial unrest." The street people and others said the police did not have to open fire. The city manager said: "Our policemen are mentally exhausted. They are fighting guerrilla warfare out there." More than a hundred private citizens volunteered to ride in patrol cars with police. "The law should start cracking down," one of the volunteers said. "The only thing that will cure this situation is to get tough."

Three members of the University of Kansas board of regents thought so, too. Encouraged by politicians in search of scapegoats they tried in a secret meeting to fire Laurence Chalmers. The effort was led by a Topeka regent who supported California's Ronald Reagan for the 1968 Presidential nomination and believes that Chalmers is unable "to control events in Lawrence." The move failed by one vote.

The President's Commission on Campus Unrest sent a five-man team to Lawrence. One member of the commission said there is "an incredible lack of communication" in the town. On the day after it arrived two Negro organizations denounced the commission for "grotesque racism" because its staff called first upon Chancellor Chalmers and then upon city officials. As a result many blacks refused to speak to the commission team during the two weeks it remained in Lawrence.

★ ★ ★

I once asked a reporter who had just returned from two years in Vietnam: "Who's telling the truth over there?" He replied: "Everyone's telling the truth. Everyone over there is witnessing to the truth as he sees it. But they all see it differently."

So it is with Lawrence. The town is large enough to harbor several communities with their own ways of life. It is small enough for every citizen to feel the impact of colliding values. The people I met lookéd at events through the lens of their own personal experience and defined truth by what they saw: the townspeople who feel threatened, the blacks who feel oppressed, the street people who feel harassed, the students who feel misunderstood, and the police who feel abused. So fiercely had each adherent sworn loyalty to his part of the whole that the idea of community—of a place where people exist competitively without malice— would be hard to repair. Some were determined to try. The death of two young men and the injury to others had brought home to Lawrence the words of William Allen White: "Reason has never failed men. Only force and repression have made the wrecks in the world."

☆

I headed west feeling relieved to be on the road again and guilty that a traveling man can so easily walk away from trouble. The trials of Lawrence were actually not that quickly forsaken. No sooner had I buckled the seat belt on the plane than the man beside me said: "Looks like you been traveling."

I have.

"Where you going?"

Denver. Cheyenne. Boise. Seattle.

"Where you been?"

Lawrence.

"Been hot there."

Yes, I said. It was 103 degrees yesterday.

"No, I mean with the colored folks."

Well, it's more complicated than that.

"My son went over and looked at KU last year but he decided on Kansas State at Manhattan instead."

Oh?

"Yeah, he liked the smaller classes at Kansas State. Then he said there was too large a foreign element at KU."

Foreign element?

"Yeah. Kids from the East and colored fellows brought in to play foot-ball and a bunch of hippies. We went over to Kansas State with him for parents orientation and I asked one of the deans if there were any people likely to make trouble there and he said, 'If you give me an hour or so I might be able to rustle up six or seven hippies.' I was mighty glad my boy had decided to go there."

125

*He was a friendly man with the worn and marked face of the rousta-
bouts among whom I spent two summers many years ago in southern
Oklahoma. He said his name was Bob and that he worked as a salesman
for National Cash Register out of Kansas City. He chainsmoked Kools
and constantly twisted the seat belt as if he were uncomfortable. I was
trying to complete my notes on Lawrence but he wanted to talk.*

"I think we ought to face the fact that the Communists are behind
this trouble in the country. They picked out the two groups that are the
most vulnerable, the preachers and the teachers. We had an army colonel
come and talk to us at Kiwanis the other day, a highly decorated fellow
who didn't have any more room for fruit salad on his chest. He's stationed
at Leavenworth. He said that in 1939 the Communists were set to take
over the country and the war delayed their strategy for five years. Now
they're back at work, he said. He said he thought the Communists had
stirred up the trouble at Kent State.

"My son came home after Kent State and I asked him what he
thought. He said they got exactly what they deserved. I agreed with him.
If I had been a member of the National Guard I would have shot to
defend myself."

I pointed out that the victims were all bystanders.

"Let me put it this way," he said. "If there's trouble on campus and
you stick your nose into it, you're likely to catch it. When trouble
comes the best thing to do is to run to the boiler room and stay there.

"I like Agnew because he stands up to the Communists. I disagree
with him about Vietnam because I think the best advice there came
from the Smothers Brothers. They said just announce we've won and
pull out. That's what I would do. But I still like Agnew. I like him
better than I do the President. Agnew speaks his mind and Nixon hides
his."

*He spent the remainder of the time talking about business machines.
I remember that he said:* "Machines will make it possible for you to get
a number when you're born and take it right with you to the end. Like
the fellow in Cincinnati who runs a funeral parlor and next door runs
a store that sells baby products. That fellow's with you from the cradle
to the grave."

Denver, Colorado

THERE IS EXULTATION IN SEEING AN OLD FRIEND AFTER MANY YEARS, especially if your relationship with him has survived Washington, D.C. Blair Butterworth and I became friends ten years ago when he graduated from Princeton and joined the Washington staff of the Peace Corps. Wanting more action, he soon resigned to go to Africa as a volunteer teacher in a secondary school. After two years he returned to become West Coast director of the Economic Development Administration. He left government in 1967 to join a private social-action and research organization in Washington. He is a large man whose fervent resolve to correct the wrongs of society is balanced by a jolly sense of humor. Periodically the restlessness in him stirs, that part of him that is the son of a peripatetic diplomat says, Move on, and now at thirty-one he has taken a leave of absence, bought a camper, and is working his way across America "just to see the country again."

We will travel together for the next thirty-two hundred miles. There is no better way to cross the spectacular plains and mountains of the West than by sitting with a friend in the open cab of a pickup truck high above the road, a stereo tape console between you, and the freedom to go where your curiosity leads.

Butterworth greeted me at the airport wearing a straw stetson, striped bell bottoms, white bucks, and curly locks. "Some fellows in Alabama wanted to cut them off," he said. "I walked in the bar and one of them hollered, 'My, my, we have got a live one here! Hey, *Sarah*, the barbershop is across the street.' 'As long as you're buying me a haircut,' I said, 'let me buy you a drink.' And I sat down and we talked five hours. If

I had closed my eyes I could have sworn that I was talking to a black on Fourteenth Street in Washington. The urban black and the white Southerner both talk about power over their own lives. The white talks of states' rights and the black of community control, and I admit the white includes keeping the black man in his place when he talks about states' rights; but both of them don't have any hope of any control over the important things in his life. They don't think their voices matter in the big context of the country. The Peace Corps gave you and me the belief that we mattered. Most people I've met think everything's being decided for them. When the black's talking about community control he's talking about being free of the white man's definition of what is right for him. The white Southerner wants to be free of the government's making his social arrangements for him. I'm putting it coarsely, but I've traveled over ten thousand miles so far this year and listened to a lot of people, and most of them have one thing in common. Black and white, North and South, they feel they're diluted. They feel like flotsam floating down some polluted river and disappearing in the ocean with nobody giving a damn."

We were driving north toward Wyoming. The Great Plains begin to merge and shape here for the long sweep eastward. To the west are the high ranges of the Rockies, outlined at this hour by the fading sun and the stark A-frame of a pizza hut. Since my last visit the open land around Denver has been giving way steadily to patches of suburbs with fancy names. The West has played a role in our history far out of proportion to its population. Now that the people are coming in an ever-increasing flow, I wonder how long it will be before a man ceases to experience a sudden sharp feeling of excitement as he breaks through the last ring of split levels and spies the sign pointing to Cheyenne. In some parts of this country it is still possible to imagine the shouts of the point man on a cattle drive. Or is that Chet Huntley barking instructions to a construction gang putting up a dude ranch?

A cream-colored Cadillac limousine passes us. On the rear bumper is the sticker LOVE IT OR LEAVE IT. "If he doesn't love it," Butterworth said, "at least he'll leave it in style."

Cheyenne, Wyoming

THE ANNUAL FRONTIER DAYS CELEBRATION BEGAN ON THE DAY WE ARRIVED IN
Cheyenne; five exuberant days of parades, horse shows, rodeos, and
fairs. Having already been to these festivities twice during a long love
affair with Wyoming, I stopped in Cheyenne this time only to have
lunch with an old friend, Bob McCraken, publisher of the Cheyenne newspapers. I remained long enough to learn that Miss Frontier, a student at
the University of Wyoming, is allergic to horses. With the help of
inoculations and pills she survived the week. "I love it," Miss Frontier
said, galloping off into the sunset. In the true spirit of the Old West, I
think she did.

During lunch I met a man from another state who in his pleasant way
embodies what young people talk about when they discuss the generation
gap. He is a very cordial and rich man, a member of the board of directors of two Western newspapers, a large university, and a major airline.
A native of Kansas, he was interested in my report of events in Lawrence.
He declared that he "cannot figure out what got in the coloreds; we always got along real well when I was growing up there. I guess the
chancellor just let them get out of hand." He said he could not understand
why black football players at the University of Wyoming refused to
play against Brigham Young University last year because of Mormon
attitudes toward Negroes. "Out there on the playing field if you're really
equal you prove it, and winner take all," he said. In one breath he condemned students and said—perhaps facetiously—that "if we would shoot
a few more of them, maybe the country would settle down"; but in the
next breath he put his hand on my arm and said imploringly: "Tell me,

what are they *really* like?" I asked him if as a trustee of an important university he had ever met with many of the students, and he said no. I felt for him. At one time he could have made a real difference. But, for all his wealth, contacts, and opportunities, this engaging, successful man is nearing seventy years of age as isolated from the forces changing his country as if he had never lived here at all.

"You know that song 'Walk a Mile in My Shoes'?" Butterworth asked as we returned to the camper.

Yes.

"I'll split the cost and let's send that fellow a copy."

We accidentally discovered upon our return that someone had removed two of the hooks that secure the camper to the pickup. The culprit must have known that his vandalism could result in serious damage on the road. It was an act of pure meanness, and for the next hour we drove in silence and considered it.

Pine Bluffs, Wyoming

THIS LITTLE TOWN OF A THOUSAND PEOPLE SITS RIGHT ON THE WYOMING-Nebraska border and at one time was the main Union Pacific loading station for cattle off the Texas trail. It has known some boisterous days. They were over long ago and Pine Bluffs now is a quiet service community for the wheat farmers and cattle ranchers who live in the surrounding countryside.

Just a few days ago Pine Bluffs received its first national publicity in years. An Ohioan named Russell Oliver brought his family through in a covered wagon on a trip to retrace the route of the pioneers to Oregon. After reaching Cheyenne he complained publicly that in Pine Bluffs his party was refused water for the horses and "in so many words was asked to leave town." A news service carried his complaint throughout the country without checking with officials in Pine Bluffs. The people in town tell a different version. They claim a welcome had been planned for the Olivers but the family decided to camp on down the road. Butterworth and I listened to the arguments at the local drugstore and voted 2-0 in favor of the Pine Bluffs version, without checking with the Olivers.

The Oliver episode has not been the only excitement in Pine Bluffs during the last decade, but it is the only one to receive national attention. There was a train wreck four years ago and after that a hailstorm. Miss Gretchen Soule upset everyone last Sunday when she fell off her horse during a cattle drive sponsored by the Pine Bluffs Roping Club. She was shaken up but not seriously injured. Fighting at the local dances is routine and creates nothing but a little gossip.

My purpose in coming to Pine Bluffs was modest. All over the country small towns like this are having trouble locating and keeping doctors. Bob McCraken's brother, Bill, who is a trustee of the Cheyenne hospital, reported that Pine Bluffs had attracted a successful physician. I wanted to meet him. I wanted to know what happens in the life of a modern country doctor.

"Nothing romantic," James Stoetzel said. "Absolutely nothing that would make a movie or even a television show." He was not putting me on. For Dr. Stoetzel leads a simple life: he belongs to the Lions Club, plays bridge and drinks beer with his friends, goes to bed before eleven every night, and only charges $4 for an office call. He is also the mayor, which office he obstinately sought because—"I don't know; it was just there, I guess." He lost the first two times he ran; "I figured they'd get tired of me running and finally give it to me out of sheer desire to have me shut up."

James Stoetzel is a nonhero. There is something of a reformer in him— as mayor of Pine Bluffs he has tried to introduce cost accounting into the town's bookkeeping system but the city clerk of fifteen years, who is the husband of his secretary at the medical clinic, has been resisting such innovations. But he is content to push matters rather gently. He delivers health care—and rather well, according to his reputation in Cheyenne— performs his civic duties, and goes home to his family. He is like the people I know who work for IBM. Huge corporations that succeed and small towns that survive apparently have in common a reliance on nonheroes.

We were up at six each morning of our stay in Pine Bluffs to drive in Dr. Stoetzel's Ford pickup to the hospital in Cheyenne forty miles away. He has been making this round trip at least once a day seven days a week since he arrived in Pine Bluffs ten years ago. With the help of the Sears Roebuck Foundation the townspeople were searching for a doctor to settle in the community. Stoetzel, then a physician for the Public Health Service among the Paiute Indians in Nevada, wanted to enter private practice. That people in Pine Bluffs were raising money to build a health clinic for a new doctor impressed him. He arrived with his family to be greeted by bands, banners, and the governor of Wyoming himself, so grateful were they all to see him. "In three months we were meeting expenses and a little more," he said. "I think I make slightly more now than the national average for doctors. I have to. I'm buying the clinic from the town and I'm mortgaged to Pine Bluffs for a long time. You can make a good living if you know how to organize your practice and if you can tolerate an isolated life."

He is a stubborn and ordered man with the habits of an efficiency expert. His schedule seldom varies: Cheyenne early in the morning, office hours from nine to five, as few house calls as possible (he discourages them by charging $6 plus $1 a mile over two miles). "People have come around," he said. "They had to get used to the idea that a small-town doctor can only make it if he's efficient, and you can be efficient only if you build your practice around a clinic with a laboratory. I handle thirty to forty patients a day now. I couldn't do that if I spent all day driving over country roads. It took some getting used to, but the people learned that if they don't use a doctor this way and he leaves, the next one will be ten times as hard to get."

We stopped at the Cheyenne hospital. He had five patients to see. One was the mother of six children whose seventh had just died in birth ("My obstetrics load has been cut exactly in half since I came here ten years ago," he said. "The Pill has done that."). Another patient was ninety and had been in a nursing home. "She's ready to die. I find that most of them who live that long and are in a nursing home are ready. Funny thing about Pine Bluffs. They're superstitious about threes. We'll go a long time without anyone dying, then we'll have three people go in a matter of a little time. Once the first one dies, everybody in town gets nervous until the third one has gone and then they all relax."

As we drove back to Pine Bluffs Dr. Stoetzel said that many of his patients ("maybe more than half") suffer from emotional problems. "Seems especially troublesome among adults from the mid-twenties to the early fifties. What doctors used to call 'an old-fashioned case of nerves.' Women particularly. Partly it's the isolation, although we've got good roads now. There is a high incidence of girls who get pregnant. I don't know exactly why that is, unless there's just too little to do and too many places in the hills to park. I've always urged them to have the baby and either keep it or adopt it out. Usually they get married and right there is the beginning of hell. They marry a boy they don't love, and they marry him before he's a man. They fight a lot, they're lonely, and they're scared—the years are slipping by and they are in a rut, bored to death, and getting older and uglier. I've always been against abortion. I wonder. I don't know that I could ever perform an abortion myself but I've been asking myself about referrals. Isn't that better if the girl is willing than a lifetime of misery in a marriage that is hell on both of them and winds up ruining the life of a kid they didn't intend to bring into the world anyway? I don't know. We've got other girls who marry young because they want to, and then when they're twenty-four or twenty-five with three kids hanging on their skirts, and living out there in the country, they're beginning to feel it, too. Loneliness. I think there's a plague of it."

I asked him about the several air force vehicles we had seen on the road. "There's a Minuteman missile site just west of here. We've got a lot around the area. They put the Atlas missiles in here first. When they deactivated one two miles outside of Pine Bluffs, we thought it would be a good fallout shelter for the entire eastern end of the county [about three thousand people]. None of the bids were accepted and now I think a construction firm uses it for storage. People sort of felt then that they would be the first to get it in a war, with all the missiles around. After the Cuba thing two families in Pine Bluffs built shelters. Most people don't even think about it any more. I never hear it discussed. With all the sites we got around here, what would you come out of a shelter to?"

We stopped at the post office for him to collect the mail. "Sometimes when I go in there I'll see a patient coming out of the chiropractor's office which is next door," he said, pointing to the post office. "I'll sort of look at them—you know, tch, tch, tch—and they'll look sheepish and smile a kind of faint smile and they can hardly get a 'good morning' out. I think they all wait now until they're sure I've picked up the mail."

When he returned from the post office a woman in hair curlers, who had been stabbing weeds with a hoe in her back yard, walked over to the pickup and said, "Mayor Doc, that golf course is a disgrace to the town. Weeds are taking over. It's a damn shame." He joked about a rough that is really a rough and promised to look into it.

While Dr. Stoetzel received patients Butterworth and I explored the main street of Pine Bluffs. A summer rain had delayed the wheat harvest and several of the ranch hands were shooting pool. The Pastime Theatre was dark but a sign promised that it would be open on Friday and Saturday with *The Horse in the Gray Flannel Suit.*

We stopped at the small white building on the corner that we knew was the office of the other doctor in town. We could see him reading inside and pushed open the door to introduce ourselves to Martin Luther Morris, M.D. "Sit down, sit down," he said. "All I've got is time."

He is eighty-seven and has been a doctor since he finished medical school at the University of Louisville in 1910, third in his class of 221.

"I'd like to practice three more years," he said. "I've already made arrangements for my retirement. Bought two lots at the cemetery and paid the funeral director in cash for two funerals. When he exercises those options, I'll be finished. Until he does, I'll be here six days a week, nine hours a day, just like I've been. Just because a man grows old don't keep him from gettin' hungry or havin' to wear clothes. I still bill about three, four hundred dollars a month. Don't collect all that, of course. Never have. You know how much I'm carryin' on my books?"

No, sir.

"A little over $125,000. Absolutely worthless. Never could collect. Had a woman out south of here that owed me $80. Wanted to pay me in eggs, two dozen a week. I agreed. She said she sold her eggs at 25 cents a dozen. I said I wasn't any good at accountin' and she'd have to keep the records. When the price of those eggs went up she stopped bringing them in. I never did collect that bill. 'Course if you never had it you don't really miss it.

"But we didn't think as much about money then as they do today. We cared about sick people. I think we think more about money today. I get a dollar now for consultation. Just don't feel right chargin' more than that. I charge 'em for the medicine. I still do my own dispensin'. Want to see my place?"

He led us down rickety narrow steps ("Careful. Don't fall down these stairs. I don't want 'em all messed up") into what looked like the ruins of a nineteenth-century apothecary. Large rolls of cotton lay open and exposed. Broken bottles littered the floor. Bottles of every description— black bottles, green bottles, brown bottles, bottles with no identification, bottles with no tops—thronged the shelves. Butterworth and I brushed cobwebs out of our eyes. "There's $15,000 worth of medicines down here. My nurse is on vacation and I'm too old to clean up," he said. "How's that for an excuse?"

We went back upstairs. Everything in the crowded three-room office was old. He bought the examining chair with the black metal stirrups sixty years ago. The slightly creased operating table has not been used in years. "I used to do surgery in here," he said. "I still make house calls, especially in the country." On an early-vintage radio that no longer works sat a pair of baby scales loaded with musty medical books. "I don't have any more babies to weigh," he said. "I delivered a baby north of here in January and I got one due out east on the second of August. I deliver 'em in the homes and then the baby doctors take over." He pointed to a framed photograph on the wall taken in 1953 on "Dock Morris Day." "All those people in there were some of the babies I delivered over the years," he said. There were more than a hundred.

There was a picture of a bedside scene with a doctor leaning over a patient. The caption read: KEEP POLITICS OUT OF THIS PICTURE. He pointed to a picture of Franklin D. Roosevelt and said: "He presented me that himself when he came to Wyoming. I always voted for the man, never voted a straight ticket. Cast my first vote for William Jennings Bryan. I think this President we've got now is handling this Vietnam thing right. Especially this Cambodia situation. If there was a bunch of hornets a-bothering you and they was a-buzzing just over the fence line in the other man's property, I think you're justified in goin' over there and swattin' it down."

He sat down in the ancient brown leather chair in the front office. Hair oil had turned the head rest black. He is a short man with a lock of gray hair that falls down his forehead. Although it was hot he wore a vest crisscrossed by a gold watch chain. He smoked his pipe with a little smacking sound. A film of ashes covered the floor, covered stacks of magazines and the drug promotions. "Medicine is big business," he said. "Quack medicine is bigger. I get a laugh out of these ads. I used to get a new ad toutin' some new drug and I'd try it just to see if it worked. More people take too much medicine than take too little. Lots of people, though, enjoy poor health. Makes 'em feel good to be sick."

He saw me light a cigar. "Let me have that band," he said. "I want it for a kid that is collectin' 'em." He dropped it in an old pipe jar almost overflowing with cigar bands.

The door opened and two middle-aged women entered.

"Hi, Doc," one of them said. "You got any rubber corks?"

He got up and disappeared into the rear of the building. When he returned he said: "Nope, not a one."

"Well, heck," she said. "Fellow at the store said you might have one in some old bottle."

"Sorry, I'm fresh out of bottle corks."

"Why do you need a rubber cork?" Butterworth asked.

"We're making some wine. Makes real fast this time of year. But I sure need a rubber cork. They're best," she said as they left.

Martin Luther Morris put a match to his pipe. "I sure don't like not havin' what people want when they come in," he said.

"I got people come over from Cheyenne just 'cause I've been treatin' 'em so long," he said. "There are doctors over there better than I am, or over in Kimball, and that young fella we got in town—my lord, how we needed him. But they come, some people do, because—well, medicine is more than pills, you know. There's an old man in town not more than a few months younger than I am. He don't miss a day comin' in here 'cept Sunday. I don't do anything for him 'cept listen. Some folks still think they need me even if they don't. So I'll stay here as long as I can."

I asked him what he thought about the young people. "I was young once and hotheaded," he said. "That was a long time ago. But we had juvenile delinquency then and we got it now. Only thing that cures it is growin' up. You know, the best thing about the stage of bein' a juvenile is that it's so short-lived. I've been older a lot longer than I was younger."

As we left he showed us a plaque commemorating his service in the Lions Club. He has an unbroken attendance record of forty-eight years. Once he drove six hundred miles to make up a meeting he had missed.

★ ★ ★

We stood in the back shop of the Pine Bluffs *Post* and talked with the owner, James H. Lee, who with his wife has been publishing the weekly since 1937. The sons who once helped are in college and do not plan to carry on the business. "We haven't made much money but with the boys we were our own overhead and what we had was in the family. With them gone I'm thinking of unloading and going back to just being a printer. There's not much to hold young people around here. One of my boys is studying to be an engineer but he already says there are no jobs around here so he'll go to St. Louis or New York. That happens to a lot of them.

"I guess you'd say Pine Bluffs is predominantly Republican. Except for some diehards people don't really get very mean about their politics. Most folks would tell you they believe Nixon is slipping us out of Vietnam about the best way he can. Johnson eased us in without talking much about it. I guess Nixon ought to be allowed to ease us out in the same way. No, there haven't been any boys from Pine Bluffs killed over there.

"The most important thing about Pine Bluffs is that it's independent. Most people here make a decent living. I guess the doc and the banker are the best-paid people and they probably don't make more than two, three times as much as most other people. We don't like government interfering with us here. Lots of us would rather the government not take a chunk out for social security. We think we can handle it better than they could. They've turned it into relief, not security."

At lunch with the Stoetzels, in their modern home on a bluff over-looking the town with a view far across the plains, he scolded his thir-teen-year-old daughter for riding in a car with four other kids. "She's not supposed to be in cars with someone else," he said. "She's going to be my problem child [he has five children]. I know that already." But he said it affectionately.

"The biggest problem with the kids in town," he said, "is beer. Right across the line in Colorado, twelve miles, they serve 3.2 beer to kids. You have to be twenty-one in Wyoming. We decided to crack down in Pine Bluffs and I asked our three policemen to get tough. They arrested two kids with beer in the car and fined them $50 for possession."

How can you be sure they aren't carrying it home for their parents?

"That's part of the problem. We'll catch them and we know they are breaking the law, and the parents will come down and say they put it there, so we have to let the kids go. I think that when kids are growing up they should learn to accept the consequences of their acts."

I asked him about the story in the paper announcing a curfew of 11 P.M. in the town ball park. Who's responsible for that?

"You're looking at him," he said. "The games were running too long, lasting until eleven-thirty or midnight. One night I was awakened at eleven-thirty to treat a fellow who'd been hit by a bat. That kind of thing makes me mad. At the next city council I proposed the curfew. We told them they could start their games earlier."

You just lost the athletic vote, Butterworth said.

"That's better than losing sleep," His Honor the doctor said.

We drove to Cheyenne for dinner. The Stoetzels do not often get away for an evening. If they leave for a weekend he places an ad in the news-paper announcing that he will not be available. They hope to go to the mountains at Christmas. "Any time we plan something like that someone decides to have a baby," Anne Stoetzel said. "I am tempted to run an ad nine months ahead of time which will say, 'Dr. Stoetzel will be gone Dec. 21–28. Please take notice and precautions now.'"

After the Stoetzels had retired Butterworth and I walked down the farm road almost a mile to a narrow gravel lane that led into a pasture 150 feet to the west. A chain-link fence surrounded what appeared to be a sewage-treatment plant protruding above the ground. The moon was now quite high and to the north we could see two farmhouses with barns and windmills. Beyond the simple concrete shelter were the wheatfields of Nebraska. The air force indeed had chosen a peaceful setting for the Minuteman missile nesting with its megaton of payload in the ground beneath our feet.

★ ★ ★

On the road north we soon encountered again what has become a familiar sight: a diesel cab pulling the frame of a trailer home to a "permanent" location. The load was too great for the highway. It extended from the shoulder of the road into the opposite lane just over the center stripe. There was no way for us to see oncoming traffic without encroaching dangerously into the other lane. All over the country people with influence have been obtaining such exceptions to the standard weights and sizes of commercial traffic moving on our highways. In Michigan I read of the senate majority leader who forced through the legislature a bill to permit truck trains up to eighty-five feet long to use the highways. The highway department, the state police, the state commerce department and the secretary of state had opposed the bill because the longer trailers will be a danger to motorists. They also will increase the need for repairs and the cost of maintenance. In Washington there is a movement to increase from 96 to 102 inches the width of buses that can travel within states on the interstate system. The assault on our highways continues.

The evening news reports that two hitchhikers are being held in Montana for the murder of a man who had given them a ride last week near Yellowstone Park. I have picked up several thumbers along the way, usually a boy and girl traveling together. In Ohio I gave a lift to two couples going from Maine to St. Louis. They delighted in discovering the size and eccentricities of the Middle West. Upon reading a warning that state police were monitoring speed violations from airplanes, one of the youthful riders said: "Man, when Mitchell told Nixon he'd keep an eye on us, he wasn't kidding." But after this radio broadcast it will be a long time before I stop for even the most innocent-looking hitchhiker. Not only does the newscaster say that the motorist was murdered. Part of him was eaten. "I have a problem," one of the accused said when police arrested him. "I am a cannibal."

★ ★ ★

Many people in Wyoming refuse to boast about the grandeur of the state. They do not want to encourage a migration of newcomers. Privately they express relief that the population in 1970 is smaller than it was ten years ago. They want to keep the mountains and prairies and rivers as free as possible of the excrescence of urban progress. Tourists are welcome because they come and go, gracing the state with their money and their departure. I hardly blame the natives. I even hope they succeed.

"They'd better hurry," Butterworth said. We were watching dirty white smoke signals rise against the silver-tinted sky of central Wyoming. This is the Little America Refining Company welcoming us to Casper.

Clear Creek Valley, Wyoming

TEN MILES WEST OF BUFFALO WE TURNED OFF THE MAIN HIGHWAY AND followed a dirt road through a meadow, over the crest of a hill, and across the swift waters of the narrow creek that gives this valley its name. There we turned sharply to the right and eased down a barely sufficient path which ran between the creek on one side and a perpendicular wall of rock on the other. In less than a mile the path suddenly became a trail. We stopped the pickup beside a small cabin marked "Hobohemia." Seven years ago I had called to tell the couple now standing on the porch that their son was dead. Today I was to meet them for the first time.

Phillip Maggard was twenty-two in March, 1963, when a DC-3 in which he was a passenger crashed into a remote ridge on the island of Mindanao. He had been serving with the Peace Corps in an elementary school in a small Philippine logging camp. "I have been raised in the most delightful environment to the extent that I have been unquestionably spoiled," he wrote before his death. "Nevertheless, I feel that I have begun to develop a sense of values on how I should live my life." Once he had determined to be a priest. After six months among the people of Lianga Bay he was talking more and more about medicine.

In the hours after his death I read everything I could find about him in the Peace Corps files in Washington while I waited for confirmation from Manila that he was indeed aboard the plane. In later years Phillip Maggard became a very distinct image in my mind of a generation moving in the early sixties from complacency to deep social engagement. Sometimes it would trip over its own simplicities but it was a generous and

141

feeling generation and like Phil Maggard it never had a chance to finish what it set out to do.

"Don't worry about us," his father had said that morning when I expressed by telephone the sympathy of the staff in Washington. "We've always known there would be risks. Phil did, too. He died doing what he wanted to do. I only hope this doesn't hurt the Peace Corps." I never forgot his response or the courage it revealed. For seven years I had been determined one day to meet Phillip Maggard's parents in person.

Merida Maggard has retired after forty years of schoolwork in Buffalo, the last twenty-one of them as superintendent. His round face is still tanned from the hunting trips he took with his sons before his heart attack two years ago.

Mrs. Maggard has also retired. She taught second graders in Buffalo for thirty-one years. A small puckish woman with silver hair, she spends much of her time watching over her husband. "The doctor said he could have bourbon at five o'clock every day. I let him have a little three times a day. I look at my watch at three different times and figure it's five o'clock somewhere in the world." They have been married forty years. "I can't remember him not being around," she said. "Why, he had a dream the other night that we were in a car wreck and were put in separate rooms in the hospital. He kicked and screamed so much in that dream that they had to put us in the same room."

We sat on the porch of the log cabin which was built in 1917 by her grandmother. In all their summers here they have continued to use the outdoor privy. "This place just wouldn't be the same without it," she said.

She, too, has been a hunter. "Phil thought we were barbaric because we would kill something like that," she said, pointing to an elk head on the wall. "He would say with a tease in his voice but he meant it, 'Mother, how can you aim a thirty-ought at eyes like that?' I tried to tell him what it is like to stalk an animal of that stature, but he never understood. He loved music and art. He spent three summers up here writing an Anglican mass for the organ. See that old Reed pump organ in there? My mother had given it to the church and when they bought a new electric model they gave us the old one. Once Jack [another son] and Phil were painting a new fence around the yard in Buffalo and they were painting it psychedelic colors. At that time I thought it was a little wild but it was very modest compared to what would happen to it now. Jack sent Phil downtown to get another quart of paint. Hurry, he said, because the sun is bright and we want to finish it today. Well, Phil didn't come back and didn't come back and Jack was getting madder and madder and after about two hours he showed up, and Jack said, 'Just where in the hell have you been? You said you were going to get the paint.' And do you know what he said? He said, 'I got it, Jack, but on the way back I passed the Catholic church and it has a new pipe organ and I just had to try it out. I had the best time,' he said. 'I didn't mean to keep you waiting.'

"He couldn't kill," she said quietly. "I don't think he would go as a soldier today. He wasn't a kid and he wasn't running from the draft and he wasn't a sissy. It really made me mad when people called the Peace Corps a 'kiddie korps.' Why do you have to pack a gun to be a hero?"

We walked up the trail toward the mountains. The valley teems with lilies, bluebells, mouse-ear chickweed, wild mustard, and Indian paintbrush. "You should see it in June when the side of that mountain over there is filled with forget-me-nots," she said. The north and middle forks of the creek come together here and we stopped to drink with cupped hands from the clear, cold water running under tall ponderosa pines and quaking aspen. "There are big corporations moving in and buying up the ranches around here," Mr. Maggard said. "I heard that one of your big companies from New York just bought seven or eight ranches over that way"—he pointed northeast. "Those places have supported families for generations. They won't be family places any longer, though. I sure hope those companies don't come in here and turn this country into a closed society."

At lunch, seated near the old pump organ, we talked again of their son and events since his death. Butterworth asked them how he might have looked upon the peace demonstrations today.

"I don't think he would approve of the way they've gone," she said. "I can't see him throwing rocks and shouting obscenities. The only four-letter word we know around here is w-o-r-k and we avoid it any time we can. I may be too narrow-minded. He loved peace. He was working for peace when he died. Senator [Milward] Simpson called the American Legion in Buffalo and said that Phil Maggard died for his country just like a soldier and they should fly a flag on his grave every Memorial Day. They do, too."

"The whole country is more militant," Merida Maggard said. "Young people used to have a sense of responsibility toward their government that they don't have today."

"The flag, the country, and the President," she said. "I don't think young people today have an affiliation for them."

"The biggest crisis I ever had at the high school happened along this line just before I retired," Mr. Maggard said. "We had a Veterans' Day program and when the flag was marched in everybody stood except for one young teacher in the school. He refused to salute the flag. Then the program was closed with prayer and he didn't stand. I investigated it for a week or two and studied it and I decided that I had to let him go because the people of the town and most of the kids felt I should. Some of the kids disagreed and were going to have a protest. I heard about it and the night before I called the ringleader and said, 'You have been here long enough to know what we stand for and that teachers take an oath to uphold the Constitution of the United States. My office is always open to your grievances but if you stage any kind of protest tomorrow you won't be in school the day after.'" His voice was low but firm. "That stopped it.

"Do you know that this kid's father called me from St. Louis—he was from there—and said he didn't blame me. He said he didn't know what had got into his son and he asked me to kind of keep an eye on him. I went to see him in his apartment. I've never seen such a disorganized place in my lifetime. You could hardly crawl over things. He apparently would just pull off his clothes and where he was standing let them drop. He had ski equipment. And dirty dishes. He was only about twenty-five."

"But wasn't he a pretty good teacher?" Mrs. Maggard asked her husband.

"I'll put it this way. He was a brainy individual. He was smart. That impressed me. But he was a little far out for a small community like this. He had troubles after he left, and his mother came to visit with me. She was a very nice person and wasn't bitter at all. I guess he was all mixed up about the war. The war's the thing that has brought so much of this on."

Mrs. Maggard said: "I think most people feel it really isn't a war, just a fight between the people of Vietnam. We just got in their mess."

"Yes," he said, "their war, not ours. I don't think Phil could ever understand killing other people. Don't you think we're all that way? I don't pretend to know about the war. We made the mistake of going in in the first place, but I guess we can't desert the boys after we send them there."

Butterworth recalled Mrs. Maggard's statement about the flag, the country, and the President. He asked: "Is it possible that those things don't command allegiance because they don't stand for the same things they used to? I mean, the kids think the war is wrong and the war goes on although as you have just said no one wants the war."

"Yes," she answered. "They certainly do seem to think the flag and the country and the President have let them down."

"This war is such an immoral war to them. So much devastation," Mr. Maggard said. "People getting killed, losing their limbs and their eyesight. I can understand why they feel that way."

"I've been so upset because the Peace Corps has lost its momentum," Mrs. Maggard said. "I just wonder if it has anything to do with people not feeling they could be proud to represent their country after all the things that have happened."

"We were in Tokyo when President Kennedy was killed," he said. "We had gone over to the Philippines to see the place where Phil had taught school and where he had died. We had been in the Philippines on the day before the election and we were advised not to travel that day because of all the turmoil involved in the elections. There was a lot of killing. I said to myself, What a great thing to live in a country where that sort of thing would never happen. When we heard in Tokyo about the assassination of the President I really felt bad after telling all those Philippine people that we didn't murder our leaders or politicians. I guess the young people are seeing us as we really are."

She: "I think maybe many Americans may have used our professed ideals as a way of hiding our failure to live up to them. Maybe we're finding it very hard to live with all the problems we thought didn't exist. Young people know about these problems. They are so much more knowledgeable today than they were when I was in high school and college. I don't think I could go through college now."

He: "Oh, yes, you could. The difference is that we grew up in a textbook world. The teaching was pretty well limited to those textbooks, to what some author said was true. We accepted what he said as fact even when it wasn't. Young people today get their ideas from so many other places than textbooks."

She: "Television, for one. The last two years I taught the second grade I could see that the children were so much sharper. I had to lift my teaching a little bit. It wasn't just 'The apple is red. See the big horse.' And all that rote stuff. Today they want to feel something before they believe it's true."

He: "I know there wouldn't have been a big stink about the killing and stuff in Vietnam if it hadn't been for the kids. Most of us were confused, or just said what the people in Washington were saying, and the kids were trying to hit against a washtub to wake us up. I just wish they hadn't started throwing things."

She: "That's where Phil would have stopped. He didn't want to hurt anything. He just wanted to do what he could to help people live. Soon after he got to the Philippines he was working in the little hospital there with people who had been injured—he'd help patch them up. That got to him. Then he gave artificial respiration to some kids who almost drowned. He got real interested in medicine and was going in that direction. We had always thought of Phil as a little bit squeamish but he wasn't squeamish when he got to the Philippines."

And Mr. Maggard said: "He enjoyed the peace of this valley. All three of our boys enjoyed it but Phil in a different way. He would take a back pack and go up alone and the others would go on horseback. I remember one pack trip that he and Chuck, our second son, made with me once. We had three saddle horses and a pack horse. The pack started to slip on it and I stopped and Chuck and I got off our horses and went back to take a look. I called to Phil to help us. No action. No action whatsoever. I called him again and nothing happened. I was pretty angry. I shouted the next time for him to get back and help. Afterwards Chuck said, 'I don't think you should have done that, Daddy; he's looking at those mountains and he never even heard you. When he gets up here he's seeing something that you and I don't see.'"

We were quiet. He got up from the table and said, "Excuse me for a minute. Some of that beer is getting to me." But I could see through the kitchen door out to the back yard. He did not go to the privy. He leaned his shoulder against the white bark of a quaking aspen and wept.

Bondurant, Wyoming

THE AMERICAN FLAG AND THE PENNANT OF THE COCA-COLA BOTTLING COM-
pany flapping from the same pole told us we had made the right turn back
at Del Creek. This was the Little Jennie Ranch. Waiting at the gate, with
the Gros Ventre Mountains and a sumptuous swimming pool behind
him, was Robert Wagstaff. He must have thought we were expecting to
find a sod house with an old black kettle simmering with varmint stew
because he apologized sincerely for "not having a place where you have
to rough it." I assured him that the Simonses in Lawrence, who had suggested that I drop by to see him, had not misled me about the Little
Jennie. I wanted a working ranch and not an impoverished one. "Sometimes they're the same," Bob Wagstaff said.

He lives successfully in several worlds. In Kansas City he is president
of the Coca-Cola Bottling Company, a director of the Federal Reserve
district, a lawyer, and the highest lay leader in the Episcopal diocese.
He owns a ranch of approximately five thousand acres in Kansas. Here
in the Del Creek Valley about forty miles south of Jackson he has turned
another five thousand acres of fenced land into a profitable mountain
ranch. By every material definition of American success, Bob Wagstaff, a
handsome man with a beautiful wife, has made it.

"The mistake most city fellows make when they buy a ranch is not to
stay on top of it," he said. "You've got to get on a horse and ride the land.
No one had better get into this business who doesn't want to work like
hell." His own hands are hard and brown from the sun, his boots worn to
a dull surface like an old chamois rag. He was dressed in Levi's with a

jacket that was ripped twice in the back at the level of the shoulder blades as if they had torn in the lifting of some heavy object.

We drove in his jeep toward the higher mountain pastures. "I just signed a contract yesterday for an October sale at thirty-nine cents a pound," he said. "There used to be a time when a handshake closed a deal. Now you have to have a contract. Ranching has changed in many ways, especially with the machines, but in its essence it hasn't changed at all. We're simply trying to convert hay and cheap feed into meat. Actually I'm getting the best prices I've had since '51. People want choice cuts today and the per capita consumption is higher. The feed-lot people are butchering the cows at a thousand pounds now when they used to wait until they got up to about fourteen hundred. The big cows had more fat, more waste. If we don't get hit real hard with the imports from Australia, this is going to be a good year. It's funny. With the economy the way it's been people seem to be drinking more Cokes and eating better beef. Damnedest thing, isn't it? I don't know how to explain it."

Although it is midsummer his mind is already on the winter. The snows come early and by the 15th of October his calves must be out of the valley. "I wish you could have been here early in April when we started calving. Snow all over the ground. Thirty to forty degrees below sometimes. That's why the cattle up here are a good breed. They've read Darwin. Only the best survive. We'll get fifty to sixty calves a night. You can't imagine how hard the men work. They're on duty twenty-four hours."

We were passing hay as high as our shoulders. "We'll be baling it next week," he said. "Those stacks will weigh sixty to seventy pounds each and picking them up is rough. Can't get college students to do it any more. There's a fellow brings over a team of high-school kids from Idaho Falls. One of these days they won't want to do it either. I'm already planning to get a self-propelled windrower—costs between $6,000 and $7,000—that will do the work of the four mowers and three rakes we use now and cut us down to six men instead of the twenty it now takes for baling. I figure in three or four years the windrower will pay for itself. Got to have it. It takes about two tons of hay to get one cow through the winter. I only lose about 5 percent of my eleven hundred cows during the winter. It used to be that we were almost immobilized during the winters here. We had to use horses and sleds and there were times when they couldn't get to the cattle. Now we've got snowmobiles—ski-doos—for the cowboys and there's no place they can't go."

We had reached the highest grazing land and were driving among lodgepole pines, Douglas firs, and spruce which line the meadows. "The thing about ranching," he said, "is that you get land crazy. You see your neighbor's land and you say, I've got to have it. This place up here was in other hands and because it was the last spread between my place and the crest of the mountains I really wanted it. I was finally able to get five or six parcels from the daughter of the elderly fellow who owned it. He died after being up here all his life. We closed the deal down there at the house and she came up here for one last look. She was looking out over the place—and you'll have to agree it is a spectacular view —and she just fell over dead. Less than ten minutes after signing the contract she died. The oldtimers around here said it was no wonder, selling her father's land like that.

"It won't be long before this land will be out of reach. Ten years ago my place would have brought $100 an acre. Now I could get more than $500. North of Jackson it's bringing $3,000 to $4,000 an acre. But I'm not here just because of the land. I wanted to do something with it. I always wanted to operate a ranch. I didn't know a thing about it. For four years I read every book and every pamphlet I could on the subject of raising cattle. Then I hired a county agent to teach me everything he knew. It's been the hardest work I've ever done but I love this country up here. It's pure and clean and you can see to Christmas. I know it's selfish but I want like hell to keep it this way. I love it."

"You and Lyndon Johnson are a lot alike," I said. He almost drove the car into a big lodgepole pine. Literally. He stopped the jeep, turned around and asked incredulously: "What in the hell did you say?" Bob Wagstaff has been a Republican all of his life. "I wasn't thinking politically," I replied. "I meant that he talks about the land the way you do and both of you look at a cow with the eye of a swooning lover. I'd even say you subscribe to his philosophy that the best fertilizer for a place like this is the footprint of its owner." But he continued to mumble skeptically about Democrats as if he might never recover from the injury.

We changed from the jeep to horses and rode through the mountain trails with Bill Allen, the foreman. We were about eight thousand feet above sea level. Allen is fifty-five and has been a cowboy all of his working life. His skin was long ago tanned into a vintage brown and his eyes look out through a permanent squint. He refuses to observe Daylight Saving Time at the Little Jennie because it "screws our work schedules all to hell. Hay and cows can't turn back their clocks." Not many of his kind remain: combination cowboy, veterinarian, mechanic, botanist, horseman, leader of hard-drinking men whose own breed is diminishing like the wild mustangs that still roam parts of the West.

"Our biggest problem is gettin' help," Allen said. We were riding single file through a nest of Indian paintbrush and he had shouted back to Wagstaff that "your lady might want to see these." "Fellas just don't want to be cowboys any more. Can't take the hard winters and the lonely life. Their wives don't like stayin' out here by themselves. We give 'em a place to live, a side of beef, their utilities and milk, and usually $350 or $375 a month, and they can save money 'cause there's no way to spend it. But it's hard to keep them. Those fellas we do get these days don't want to stay with it. I had to let one go yesterday that wasn't worth the powder to blow up. When he left he was pullin' all his possessions in his kid's little red wagon and his wife was carryin' the baby. I guess he'll keep on driftin' till he finds something. His kind won't last at any job."

He stopped and pointed Bob Wagstaff in the direction of some cattle. "See that one over there?" he said. "She had a momma who didn't want to nurse. The little thing just went over and laid in the snow. We got to her in time. She survived but she shrunk."

I asked him about the winters and he said: "Used to be meaner than now. Now we get 'round on the ski-doos just like we do on horses in the summer. You oughta see some of the fellas go down these hills. The most fun is chasin' coyotes. They're just critters, you know. A menace to the deer and cattle. One blow of a ski-doo will stun a coyote. You run him down and then you run over and over him until you've got him pressed down in the snow and the ski-doo can pass over him without even a bump. Now there's a sport for you."

★ ★ ★

"You were at Lawrence?" Bob Wagstaff asked at dinner. "I graduated from the University of Kansas. It's hard, it's really hard for someone like me to believe the kids there are doing any good. Or anywhere. They are challenging all the values I've built my life around. This country has been good to me. I've worked hard in Kansas City and here to get what I have. This ranch didn't spring full grown from the mountains. I worked *hard* and the rewards came. Isn't that what America offers? Next to my family, my country means more to me than anything else. I guess that is why I sometimes think I'm having a bad dream when I see what is happening."

"Do you think outside influences stirred up the situation at Lawrence?"

Mrs. Wagstaff asked. She is a lissomely handsome woman who does not look like a grandmother. She walks several miles every day for exercise. "I don't think what happened in Lawrence required any outside provocation," I said.

"No Communist influence?" she inquired.

"I am sure that if the Communists were there Mr. Hoover would know about it."

"Yes," she said, "I think that's right."

Robert Wagstaff quizzed Butterworth intensively about the students he had encountered on his trip. Then he said: "I never heard of the establishment until I was put in the position of having to defend it. And I guess I started defending it without really knowing why. When the kids started attacking, I started defending. Maybe they don't know any more why they were attacking than I did why I was defending. I'll say this—the young people have really claimed the attention of everyone else. All of my friends are shaken. Suddenly they have kids with problems. They just assumed their children would follow in their pattern. They're not. They're having confrontations right there in their living rooms in Kansas City. You can't go to a dinner or a party at home without this being the major topic of conversation."

He got up and walked around the big room with the picture window that looks out over the swimming pool and the mountains.

"My own children turned me around on civil rights," he said. "They convinced me that there was no room for equivocation. I had always heard it said when I was growing up and then in the fifties that we had swept something terrible under the rug and if we ever looked under there it would destroy us. Well, the kids lifted up the rugs—you know, with the civil-rights marches and the petitions and the sit-ins—and boom! I worried about it because I wasn't sure where we would wind up if people got the impression that they could disobey the law if the cause was right. But I've got no more hangups on civil rights. I owe that to my kids.

"Kansas City got all stirred up one year about Saul Alinsky's coming there. I was asked to head up a group to see why he should or shouldn't come, to look into him. My friends all sighed with relief when they heard of my appointment because they were sure they had a friend at court. But I found there simply wasn't any reason to keep Alinsky out. I don't like Alinsky or his views, but there was absolutely no reason to keep him out of the city. Some of my friends haven't gotten over it yet. And, furthermore, the threat of his coming did some good—it made the city fathers sit up and take notice of some problems.

"My kids' generation wasn't awed by the economic imperative like mine was. My generation kept asking, 'How are we going to make it? How are we going to succeed?' But the kids today aren't obsessed with career or status. I keep saying to myself, But everybody has to make a contribution! And then I'm told that that is what the argument is all about—who makes a greater contribution, the president of General Motors or the leaders of the peace movement? We used to know the answers to questions like that without any doubt.

"I'm worried about the country. There's so much discord. Everybody puts everybody else in a strait jacket. How do you break out of a stereotype once you're in it? No one seems inspired. My own party is organizing itself around its negatives. You know—we can't tell you what we're for but we damn sure can tell you who we're against. Unless you have a great national symbol like Eisenhower, you need someone who can say, 'This is what America is all about.' I guess I'm a Republican without a leader. We need some inspiration. We don't have it. I really think business will finally take care of pollution, waste and congestion—things like that. But you can't look to business for philosophical leadership. Business leaders are innately selfish. I'm innately selfish. You can't expect our kind to give you the design of the best possible world. Where can we look? I think this is what the young people wonder. I'm sometimes afraid of them but I think this is what they're talking about, deep down."

He realized what he had said. "That's some confession on my part. Believe me, I want to understand. I need to understand. I don't want us to lose our children. I don't want our children to leave home and never come back."

And he sat down. "Damn," he said. "I haven't talked that much since I was in college."

Idaho Falls, Idaho

THE MORNING PAPER CARRIED A GALLUP POLL REVEALING THAT GEORGE Wallace continues to have support in the nation although his victory in the Alabama primary was narrow. I asked the man seated next to me at the counter in the coffeeshop if Wallace enjoys any following in this area.

"Yes," he said, "I think a lot of people who agree with what he says wouldn't vote for him as President. But they think he is saying things they wish they could say and get as much attention as he does. It's not a race thing as much as it is what he says about all those people who are disrupting the country and tearing up the colleges."

I asked him if there had been much campus disruption in Idaho.

"No, hardly any. But people are concerned about it." I made a mental note of an observation that was to become a truism on this journey: the farther some people are from an issue, the more intensely they feel about it. Leaving New York I was skeptical of another poll reporting that people felt more strongly about campus disorders than they did about any other issue. Fewer than 7 percent of the nation's twenty-three hundred colleges and universities experienced incidents of violent protest in the troubled year of 1968–69, and after all, I reasoned, men were methodically dying in Vietnam for the most obscure reasons, inflation cheats a little more every month from a man's earnings, and pollution affects millions. "But those things are different," the stranger said when I raised them. "The kids will tear the country down if we don't stop them." By the time I got back to New York I was no longer skeptical about the accuracy of the survey.

"Most people up here agree with what Mayor [J. Bracken] Lee did down in Salt Lake City," he said. There was to be a pioneer day parade. Two leaflets had been distributed the day before, one proclaiming a "Yippie Nude-in" ("Five thousand stoned Salt Lake freaks will strip and strut their stuff") and another purportedly issued by the Weathermen.

What did Lee do?

"He said there will be no protest demonstrations—period. He's not going to have all those naked people running about Salt Lake City like they did on the Fourth of July in Washington."

The man wanted to talk. He was outgoing and friendly, a Mormon, conservative, with very short hair. He asked me about New York and I gave him the usual quick diagnosis: poor housing, power failures, smog, garbage, the middle class moving to the suburbs leaving the city with the very rich, who are few, and the very strapped—people on welfare and the workingman on a fixed income—who are many. "Yeah," he said, "after all the spending of the last thirty years that's where we are. I never could see all those programs the bureaucrats came up with to solve problems like that. I've always said, Show me an ultra-liberal and I'll show you a man who is tightfisted with his own money. The only good program the ultra-liberals have discovered is Head Start. If you can get the kids early enough, you can turn 'em around. But by the time they're fourteen or fifteen, it's too late. It's like Agnew said—once a slum addict, always a slum addict."

I paid for my coffee and his—"At least you're not tightfisted," Butterworth said. As we returned to the camper I thought of the man at the counter: "He has the potential to be an extremist if any of the issues ever really touch his home, but he tried earnestly to find something positive to say. He seemed a little weary of defining himself only by his animosities. In a way he's up for grabs. The country is so uncertain and precarious because there are a lot like him who can go either way.

★ ★ ★

Crossing the Snake River plains in southern Idaho we turned south at Burley to inspect damage inflicted upon the crops of Magic Valley by a hailstorm two days earlier. The potatoes, sweet corn, and barley looked as if Paul Bunyan had walked through the fields wearing saw-toothed spurs. Damage was close to $8 million. An old man with a colicky face who was filling out some forms in the local Farm Bureau office said it was "like puttin' your head through a hole at the county fair and lettin' people throw baseballs at you. I got in the potato warehouse and then told myself that I'd almost rather be stoned to death than get driven out of my mind by them things poundin' against the tin. When it was over and I came out it looked like they'd been shellin' my place with howitzers. My wife said it reminded her of the pictures them fellas sent back from the moon—with them craters and things."

From the radio came a song we were to hear often in this part of the country. It is called "The Minutemen Are Turnin' in Their Graves," or something like that, and the vocalist—whose name, so help me, is Stonewall Jackson—sang:

"I can't condemn the man who feels that taking life is wrong.
But I fail to understand the man that won't defend his home.
Dear Lord, I've got one little prayer I'll pray in years to come—
Don't ever let those kind of people serve in Washington."

Cascade, Idaho

PASSING THROUGH BOISE WE HAD STOPPED FOR BREAKFAST WITH DICK HRONEK, the managing editor of the *Idaho Statesman,* who honestly believes Idaho is the land of milk and honey described in the ancient scriptures, who gets mad when careless people abuse it. He told us that the South Fork of the Salmon River, north of Boise, is closed to fishing this year. Twenty years ago thousands of summer chinook and steelhead salmon stirred in their spawning beds in the waters flowing beneath larch pines and ponderosas. Most of them are gone. Tens of thousands of cubic yards of sediment carried down from the mountains every year have filled the spawning beds and choked the oxygen supply from the river. Nature contributed to the strangulation of the stream with cloudbursts that poured silt into it. But man did most of the damage. Half of the silt accumulated as he built logging roads into the forests and roads for his recreation. The soil loosened and was carried away. Too much grazing of cattle and almost a quarter of a million people using the land for a playground every year also disturbed the soil and made it more vulnerable. Dick Hronek shook his head sorrowfully as he said that the Forest Service has banned all fishing in the South Fork in order to protect the remaining salmon. He said the stream is one of the most "sylvan pictures of beauty" he has ever seen. Hronek is a man of understatement, and Butterworth and I determined we must see the river for ourselves.

We negotiated the twists and turns of Horseshoe Bend and arrived in Cascade less than two hours after leaving Dick Hronek still lamenting the lost salmon. At the district office of the Boise National Forest we talked to Val Simpson, the chief ranger, who said the South Fork of the Salmon is worth saving from silt even if the chinook does not survive; the Forest Service is asking Congress for $4 million for the project. Simpson is one of the people who work for all the rest of us. We pay him $16,000 a year to manage 250,000 acres of our land.

"We have learned from our mistakes," he said. "When we realized what was happening with all the silt coming down, we set out to find out why. We had to. The Boise National Forest yields almost four million acre feet of water annually. You can lose a lot of soil with that much water. So three years ago we began the first full inventory of the South Fork. It was like putting a piece of the moon under a microscope, only this was earth. And every expert we could get looked into the scope: foresters, hydrologists, landscape architects, geologists. What each of them saw was put together into one package and for the first time we could say, 'This is what we have in this piece of land. This is what we need to do with it.' We began to develop a management plan that makes sense."

An important participant in that study was John Arnold. Although it was his day off he volunteered to take us to the river, a fortunate gesture, as it turned out, because John Arnold is a remarkable man, part Jeremiah, part Machiavelli.

"I was born and raised in Bergen County, New Jersey," he said. "Once I got out this way during the war I knew I couldn't ever go back East. In the navy I had lots of time to think during those long midwatches. I read a lot on ship. Mostly about the universe. Watching the stars at night and just knowing anything about statistics will convince any rational man that there have to be many places just like the earth with similar conditions for life. That means we're not as important as we always thought ourselves to be. If man was really superior, he wouldn't be ruining the earth. Powerful people throw their weight around, take advantage of everybody else. Superior people don't. I think nature is the superior creation. After all, the cockroach was here before us and I figure he'll outlast us. As soon as man started modifying his environment too much, he sealed his fate. But he was too dumb to know it. Or too greedy to care. I said to myself, 'O.K., Arnold, if we're doing such a darn poor job, go do something about it yourself.' I did. I didn't have the brains to be a true scientist, a physicist or chemist, so I chose this work. The proper term is 'Batholith Liaison Officer' for the United States Forest Service; wouldn't you know some bureaucrat back in Washington would come up with a job description like that? Actually, I get paid for making trouble. I joined the service eighteen years ago and I've been fighting ever since."

We stopped at a Ranger check station and the guard waved us on. There were gray trees among the Douglas fir on the side of the hills; they were the tallest and they were dead. The bark beetles were at work with an uncanny ability to select the best of the firs.

"Write down this sentence," John Arnold instructed me. Speeding up the side of a mountain at fifty miles an hour is not the best condition for taking dictation, but I managed to be a faithful stenographer. The sentence read: "The main concern in managing the slopes is with their hydrologic function, stability of the soil mantle, and structural strength of the slope itself."

"It took me two years of work to write that sentence," he said. "And half the time I was up there in the mountains, alone, scratching the soil and following little crevices where the water ran. My whole life's work is bound up in that one sentence." He must have seen me holding the sentence upside down because he said: "My whole philosophy, which you've got right there in your hand, is this: Know where the sources of sediment are and you've got the whole problem licked."

It's not Rousseau, Butterworth said from the back seat; will it sell?

"It took me less time to figure it out than it did to sell it," Arnold answered. "I had to bootleg it. That's a sad commentary on bureaucracy. You think you have support. You have support, yeah, as long as the boss is smiling. As soon as he stops smiling, it's back to the mountains again.

"It was worth fighting for, though. I had an operation once for bleeding ulcers; it was close. I came out of it and I decided that being me was the important thing in the world and to hell with the rest of it, and if I didn't make a difference now I might not ever make a difference. That's when I settled down and got on this land-management thing. We've been managing timber in the Forest Service, not land. It was time to look at timber as only one part of the land. And the key to land, I knew, is our aquatic environment. The stream system is the answer. You can measure a nation by the condition of its streams. And the way we've been treating our streams, we should all be fried."

He was quiet for at least a mile. Then he said: "This gets down to the religious thing. I don't believe that man is the ultimate that God can do. I think man thought up the idea that he is in God's image. Who wrote Genesis?"

There is considerable argument about that.

"Well, I'll tell you this—it was written by a human being. He decided to make himself important, so he wrote that he was God's favorite creation. The hell with that. Nature existed before man. And nature existed for nature's sake, not for man's. Man came along, the arrogant boob, and invented the idea of his importance in God's eye so's he could justify what he was about to do to nature."

What about those lines in Psalms, I asked: "For thou hast made him a little lower than the angels, and hast crowned him with glory and honour. Thou madest him to have dominion over the works of thy hands"?

"I'm not familiar with the gentleman who wrote that," John Arnold said, "but I'll bet he was a two-legged, self-righteous, pompous little bastard who thought he was lord of the manor. That's what man wants—*dominion*. Does that mean man has the right to destroy, to rape, to insult nature? Dominion, friend, is not the privilege to trespass on the rights of others. Don't you think nature has rights, too?"

His voice was angry. We were speeding along the highway and Butterworth, nervously eying the steep cliff to our right, looked as if he would prefer to be back in the camper.

"You know that old saw that God invented man for fellowship, for communion?" Arnold asked. "That's our egotism, too. If you have ever communicated with nature, you know something about the kind of communion God must have enjoyed before man started running around like a maniac with a blowtorch."

Do you consider yourself a religious man?

"You're damn right I am," he said, "but I don't always come out that way. I've heard too many sermons justifying the arrogance of the saw-mill operator to believe a lot of the stuff I was told. But I've got something going with God, if that's what you mean.

"See those lodgepole pines?" he said, pointing to the side of a mountain across the valley. "Nature invented those. Man didn't. Man can cut them down faster than he can grow them. And he can get sanction for doing it. The politicians have just been saying to the special interests, 'Here it is, boys—come and get it.' Why, did you see that Thor Heyerdahl said the whole Atlantic is polluted? The politicians could stop that. They could make the penalties so high the shippers would find a way to stop it. When are the politicians going to say, 'It's not yours for the taking. It's not yours to destroy. Find another way. . . .'"

"Look at this road we're on. This road from the top of the pass to down here will have provided to the South Fork of the Salmon about 150,000 cubic yards of sediment. This one road." He repeated himself, with emphasis: "This ONE ROAD!"

And that didn't have to be?

"Hell, no!" The car swerved as if to make its own exclamation point. "If we had had the information then that we have now, this road could have been made one mile longer and prevented about 70 percent of the silt. We would have had the knowledge of the best place to put the road. The engineers, the lawyers, and the bookkeepers built this road. The engineering mind says this is what we can do, and never asks whether we should do it. The lawyer says this is how you can avoid the spirit of the law when you do it. And the bookkeeper says this is the cheapest way to do it. That may sound pretty stuffy, but I've known too many engineers who thought about a project without regard to its wisdom, and too many lawyers without regard to its morality, and too many bookkeepers without regard to the consequences. I'd be willing to make this road five miles longer to prevent what happened here."

What about the argument between those who want to protect the spawning beds and those who say the salmon can go elsewhere?

"Gee whiz, this is something you've just got to save. The salmon belong here just as much as we do. Maybe more. They were here first. But the white man is determined to apply to every inferior species—I mean inferior because they don't have the firepower we do—the same policy we applied to the Indian."

Without any explanation he had slowed down to twenty miles per hour. "Up in that high country is the most fragile soil you can imagine. There's a short growing season up on those slopes, which means you don't have much time to recover if you disturb the vegetation. When the vegetation is injured, the soil isn't going to hold the water. There's one year in a hundred when things are going to be just right and you can begin to recover the conditions that protect the soil and keep it from running off.

"I was up there on horseback once during this study and I heard people coming down the trail. I looked up and it was the worst thing I ever saw. There were about 150 people riding through the high country on horses. That's the most sensitive country we've got. I could feel the soil breaking up and shifting under those horses. I shouted at them: 'What in the hell do you think you're doing?' And they said they were members of the Sierra Club out for a ride. Can you imagine? Up there a group of 30 or 40 horses is okay, but 150! Now I work with the Sierra Club and we do a lot of things together, but you can kill something you love if you're not careful.

"You've heard of crop rotation? We're going to have to manage these lands like that. If we want timber for scenery, we've got to plan for it. It takes longer to grow trees for scenic purposes than for cutting. And we're going to have to tell the lumber industry that we cannot cut these lands over as rapidly as they would like because we have to build access roads at a proper rate and remove vegetation at a proper rate or we'll upset the hydrological function of the slopes. They'll also have to come up with other ways of getting the timber out, once it's cut, than by road. They use balloons up in Washington, I think, and they're going to have to do that here, too. Just lift the logs up and out. Fifty years ago it was the public against the interests. It still is. But we've got to protect these lands against abuse and overuse by the public, too. They're going to ruin it through ignorance. I mentioned crop rotation. There's going to have to be people rotation on our lakes and in these parks. People will scream, but every generation has to give up something for the sake of the next."

If you could get the people who want to do something about conservation and preservation into one big stadium to speak to them, what would you say?

"I'd like to get the whole damn country in there. I'd like to say to the whole damn pot of them: Put your money where your mouth is and get with it."

We pulled off the road just before it crossed the South Fork of the Salmon. We were alone. The only sound came from the cold mountain water washing the rocks and the roots of dark green pines and firs along the banks. When Butterworth spoke, he whispered; it was that kind of place. "It looks clear and beautiful," John Arnold said. "But it's full of sand. The soils that come down don't have much clay so you don't get color in the stream. Used to be holes in there so deep you had to swim across them. Now you can walk across. The sand has filled them up. It just sandblasts everything in there. A river can be dying while you look at it, and you can't even see death coming. The sand is choking it. There are still some salmon spawning in there. Not many, but some. We've got to hurry or there won't be any left. Then the river will look just like it does now, but it won't be the same."

161

We said goodbye to John Arnold, who was taking his family into the mountains for the weekend, and headed toward the panhandle of Idaho. The highway dropped suddenly out of the mountains and we were driving on an alfalfa pool table toward the town of Grangeville. This is the Camas Prairie, where the Nez Percé Indians assembled at harvest time for the men to hunt and the women to dig and prepare the starchy purple bulbs which were a staple of their diet. It is also a reminder that some things never change. For in June, 1877, according to the sign before us, "Indians under white pressure to move to the reservation camped for council at this familiar place. The council chose peace but on the 14th *angry young men* of Chief White Bird's band broke out *to avenge past wrongs*. Their raid sparked the Nez Percé war." The italics are added.

★ ★ ★

Our intention was to drive steadily through the night to reach Seattle by noon on Sunday. But at a café in Lewiston, on Saturday night, I noticed in the local newspaper the following announcement:

"Whitman County residents and university students are invited to the first meeting of concerned citizens about campus unrest," Delbert Logsdon of Cheney, temporary chairman of the new organization, said Friday. Logsdon is a Cheney motel owner.

The meeting will be at the Whitman County Fair Grounds Sunday at 5 P.M. and is open to the public.

Purpose of the meeting is to help Washington State University "Get back on the right track" regarding campus unrest, a spokesman said.

"It sounds like a New England town meeting out West," Butterworth said as I read the item aloud.

"Let's find out. Seattle will still be there Monday."

"If there's anything I can't tolerate with things the way they are today," Butterworth replied, "it's an optimist."

Colfax, Washington

BY 5:15 EVERY ONE OF THE 550 SEATS IS TAKEN AND PEOPLE ARE SITTING on the floor along the walls or standing shoulder to shoulder at the rear of the big room with the concrete floor. Outside another hundred persons have arrived too late to get in. Some of the older men are joking with the deputy sheriff of Whitman County, a stocky man who wears his gun on his left hip for a crossover right-handed draw. The wheat has been harvested and the fairgrounds are surrounded by stubbly hills. The stock barns and the rodeo grounds are as neat and modestly prosperous as the people whose cars and trucks now cover the grassy parking lots.

There is a hum inside the auditorium. Neighbors who have not seen each other for a spell are catching up on their gossip. Something is wrong in one of the local churches and two women seated behind me are certain the preacher made a mistake to take his vacation "right now in the middle of everything." Two women and a man, who I surmise is a school official, are discussing a statewide poetry contest for grownups. The participants are asked to submit poems that reflect "the goodness of America." One knot of men grumble about the latest census figures. Whitman County's population has dropped in ten of its incorporated towns but in Pullman, where Washington State University is located, the population has increased by 50 percent in ten years. "The damn university has grown too fast," one of the men said. "Yeah," another answered. "That's why we've had so much trouble. The more people you got, the harder it is to control them." Most of the women are dressed as they probably were at church this morning. The men are wearing short-sleeved shirts with open collars except for a few in suits and some who are wearing ties without coats. The rows are dotted with gray crew cuts. The men and women of the towns and farms of Whitman County, in the rich wheatfields of southeast Washington, are here in goodly numbers to put their university "back on the right track."

About a hundred of their adversaries have come: students and faculty members from Washington State University who have made the thirty-minute drive from Pullman to Colfax "to attend our own lynching," as one of them put it. The students are seated along the left wall of the auditorium facing the stage and in a group in the first few rows of seats. There are several mustaches but few students have really long hair. Most of them are neatly dressed. A beautiful girl with blond hair is walking to her seat in a polka-dotted miniskirt which brings a few stern looks from some women in the audience and more than one furtive glance from the corner of a husband's eye. One student with a rampant beard seats himself beside a middle-aged woman in a print dress who draws her lips tightly and stares ahead. I am not sure whether she is tickled by the adventure, or frightened.

Delbert Logsdon of Cheney, motel owner, has moved to the podium. He is a small, round man in his fifties, with blue eyes set in a full-moon face. He is very nervous. His hands clutch the microphone until they are white as he begins the first meeting of Concerned Citizens:

"I'm happy to see such a crowd today. It means one thing to me, that people are concerned. I've been asked, 'Who's sponsoring this?' There's no particular group. Just a bunch of citizens who are interested in our universities and colleges in this state. It's just what the name implies, Washington *State* University. The taxpayers of the state are the ones who are footing the bill. We're not as a group of citizens trying to raise hay over on the campus. We think there are things that should be done over there and can be, but there are enough rules and regulations over there on the books if they'd be enforced. This is one thing that our group is going to insist—that the rules be enforced. This group that is causing a lot of noise and seems to be heard the loudest is a very small minority. You the general public have not taken an active part. This is what has hexed the legislators as well as the board of regents and the college administration. It's happening all over the country. It's not the students, but it is the appeasement, appeasement and capitulation. I can remember when Chamberlain tried appeasing Hitler. We ended up in World War II. Appeasement didn't work there and I can see no evidence of appeasement working here. It's time to end it."

There is a burst of applause from the audience. None of the students I can see are clapping.

State Senator Elmer Huntley is the first speaker. He is a tall, broad-shouldered man wearing a dark green suit with a modest tie. His forehead runs all the way back to the crown of his head. He begins with a confession:

"Actually I've been in such a quandary for the last week. People have been asking me what the meeting was all about, what I was going to say. Frankly I was called and asked to be here, and that's all I know about it, period."

Delbert Logsdon looks like a man in need of a very strong drink.

"Since I am on the platform," the senator continues, "I'm going to take the prerogative of saying just a few words about what I'm sure you're all interested in today. Living right in the middle of this district, I've been called on many, many times by the citizens of the district to go over and straighten that school out over there. That isn't what I was elected for. I was elected to make laws, not to enforce them. I have spent many hours over on the campus giving them my ideas for whatever they were worth, meeting with students and with the staff. I tried to impress upon them that there are going to have to be some rules and regulations laid down, a code of ethics if you please, and it should come from the regents. We were afraid that if this didn't happen some legislator would take it in his own hands. I would hate like the dickens to see a code of ethics or rules and regulations written into law. You put these things into law and the college staff and the regents don't have any flexibility. I think that I've said about all I have to say."

Delbert Logsdon introduces the next speaker as Representative Robert Goldwater and the audience laughs. His name is Goldsworthy.

"I've been called lots of names [laughter] but this is the first time Goldwater [laughter]," he says. "That's all right; I voted for him [laughter and loud applause]. Not only that, I'd vote for him today [more laughter, more applause—enthusiastic applause]."

Representative Goldsworthy is also tall and he is also wearing green —a checked sport coat and dark slacks. He has a long, square face like a Prussian general. He stands very straight and does not touch the podium or the microphone as he speaks:

"This issue that you're all here for today is going to be one of the biggest issues we're going to face this fall. And I'm saying this knowing that on the ballot there'll be tax reform, the abortion bill, nineteen-year-old voting and all that. But I want to say this is not peculiar to Washington State University, the University of Washington, the state of Washington, or the United States. We're rather newcomers to this problem. For many, many years the students at the University of Mexico, the University of Tokyo, Seoul, in the Philippines—all have made their voices heard and have done it through violent methods. Now we're seeing it spread to this country. We're certainly not pioneering anything new in the United States. I hope this helps you to see that passing more punitive and restrictive legislation is not the answer. Firing the president of the college is not the answer, either. I get many calls and letters to cut the appropriations to the school, and this is not the answer, either. The answer is to keep open the lines of communication. Now this has got to go both ways, not just from me—the middle-class, balding, middle-aged establishment-type person—but from you young folks here who feel strongly on the other side. It's all right for some of you to tell us we've got to listen. But it's got to go both ways. You've got to listen to us, too. The answer to the thing is not a closed mind on either side."

As Robert Goldsworthy sits down he is vigorously applauded by the townspeople and some of the students as well. It is about the last time they will be together. For it is State Senator Sam Guess's turn at the microphone and he is not an equivocal man.

"This is the most serious problem that has faced America since I've been in public office, certainly since I can remember, even back in my high-school and college days," he begins. He has put his left hand on the podium and will leave it there throughout his speech. He is a big man with a crew cut and eyes that peer through black-rimmed glasses directly toward the students. He speaks quietly in a monotone that belies the force of his words:

"We passed a bill in the legislature exactly as the president of Washington University had suggested to give him the power to control uprisings and riots on the campus. Did it stop the situation on the University of Washington's campus? No. Did it stop the situation on Washington State's campus? No. Now if the administrators will not administer, what can you do? The legislature is going to have to do something. I am going to put in a bill that will establish rules and regulations to guide and regulate the conduct of students and faculty members on campus."

[I later obtained a copy of Senator Guess's bill. It provides for the immediate dismissal from the university of anyone "gathering on or adjacent to the campus in a manner which causes damage to public or private property, causes injuries to persons, or interferes with the orderly functioning of the college or university or the normal flow of traffic"; or, among other things, for "inciting students (or faculty) to violate written college or university policies and regulations."]

"I feel that it is my duty as a legislator to furnish the money and the guidelines to the board of regents. I think it is the duty of the board of regents and the administrative staff hired by the board of regents to create on campus a setting in which a student may learn and equip himself in order to be a good citizen of the United States. I do not believe that a university is created by the taxpayers of the state of Washington to be the hotbed of anarchy. I do not believe that we taxpayers pay our money for our children to be infected with bad ideologies and i-de-ologies that are foreign to what has made America great." With the last three words he abandons his monotone and raises his voice for emphasis.

A voice from the crowd: "RIGHT ON!"

There is loud and sustained applause.

"I do not believe that a faculty member violating a professional code has any right to remain on campus."

More applause. A man at the rear shouts: "Give it to 'em, Senator. Let 'em have it."

But Guess returns to his flat way of speaking. "Under this bill any administrator, faculty member, or elected official, including senators and representatives, may submit a written complaint to the board charging any faculty member with unprofessional conduct, specifying the grounds therefor. If the board determines that such complaint merits consideration, the board shall designate three members to sit as a committee to hear and report on such charges. *Upon filing of a complaint* the pay of an accused faculty member shall be suspended until a final determination is made by the board."

Someone behind me shouts: "Guilty until proven innocent, huh?"

Guess: "These are—"

Another voice: "That's a hell of an America."

Guess: "These are conditions that are merited by the situation. The board has the power of subpoena. There will be due process."

A chorus of protesting voices rings from the students.

"What happened to the courts?" a girl asks.

"Jee-sus," another girl says. "I must be having a bad dream."

Guess: "Due process is in here." He has not raised his voice.

Voice from the audience: "Read it to us."

Guess: "You know what it is. This is a time that calls for stern measures." And he sits down to long, hearty applause.

Chairman Logsdon is back at the microphone. "Is there a Thomas Young here?" he asks.

"Yes, right here." A young man stands up behind me.

"Thomas Young contacted me and asked for permission to speak at this meeting and he said that he was a participant in the strike at Washington State last May."

Groans rise from the right side of the auditorium.

The chairman continues: "And I don't know but I think it's right we listen to Tom—or Thomas—and I'd like to have him come up here and let us open-mindedly hear his side of the story."

Two or three people applaud lackadaisically, but Thomas Young does not move. He speaks across the room to the chair: "When I called you, I had a different impression of the meeting, and now that I'm here, I have changed my mind. I do thank you that you responded to my offer, however."

Delbert Logsdon is relieved and hurries to his next introduction: "The past editor of the *Washington State Evergreen*, the college newspaper, Gary Eliassen. Come on up, Gary, and give us a speech."

Angry voices and catcalls from the students are drowned out by applause. The muttering continues after Eliassen, wearing khaki pants and blue shirt, with a straight haircut, his voice cracking nervously while he shifts back and forth on the balls of his feet, says:

"As a student at WSU the past four years I have seen irrational student dissent grow until it reached a climax this spring with the sit-in at the university administration building and the student strike. For the most part, this behavior occurred despite students being allowed an increasing number of freedoms and responsibilities. The president of the university made many attempts to involve students in decisions. Some of the students answered his efforts with ultimatums, demands, and even threats of violence. They made the university a political arena rather than an educational institute. The student movement at WSU has become an absurdity of generalization, rumor, threats of violence, and oversimplification. Those who didn't participate in the recent student strike were quickly labeled racist by some of the demonstrators.

Those merchants who didn't put up WE OPPOSE RACISM signs were simplified as either supporting racism or being ignorant. Anyone who opposed the sit-in at the administration building was called an oppressor of the people's rights to assemble. What about the students who wanted the freedom to attend classes, who protested the president's decision to cancel classes, and whose pleas were ignored by the administration? What about the six hundred students who supported President Nixon's decision to go into Cambodia in a poll taken by my newspaper?"

"That's tellin' it like it is," comes a shout from the audience.

"By God, that boy is right."

Cheers and applause fall upon young Eliassen's ears. His hands are in his pockets and he is rocking back and forth. He still appears very nervous, but I am sure that the turbulent cries of approbation escaping the throats of the majority of his audience at that moment are a sound he will never forget. He is new to the experience. Should he smile? Pause? Raise his arms? He plays it like a professional: he lowers his head and waits for the applause to die away. I wonder if he will ever write another editorial. For in such moments are politicians born. Gary Eliassen has met the people and they are his. His peers only glower.

Now he continues: "If we are not going to allow our college campuses to become an arena simply for political action, irrational dissent, and violence, the taxpayers, students, and most importantly the university administration are going to have to take a long, hard look at the jobs they have been doing. The university must be firm in dealing with both college disrupters whose intent and purpose is not in education but merely to create confusion and bring about confrontation. Taxpayers will have to take even more interest in who they are electing to the legislature [applause]. Students too will have to become even more involved, for I am convinced that we have not seen the end of student unrest at WSU [a few claps from the left side of the room]. In essence, the so-called silent majority must begin speaking. If we stand by we will allow minority rule a free hand on the campuses. Thank you."

And they cheer mightily as Gary Eliassen leaves the stage.

Delbert Logsdon again: "I've been informed that since Mr. Thomas Young will not speak there's another member of the student strike steering committee here who would like to say a few words. Her name is Miss Nola Cross."

Actually it is Mrs. Nola Cross. At first glance I would have guessed her to be a high-school junior, but she is in her early twenties, tall, with hair flowing down to the small of her back. In her manners she is very austere, and I expect to hear a rather harsh voice when she speaks. But it is soft and not at all abrasive.

"I did not intend to give any speech, but due to the nature of this occasion I think it is important that I come and speak now. I was chairman of the strike at WSU and editor of the school paper there in the fall. We've heard a lot of talk about students who want to get a real education, who don't want to be disturbed, who want to go to classes and hear lectures and read their books, get their degrees, and go out and make money. But I think there's more to an education than simply going to classes. I know I have rarely missed a class. I know that I have a 3.5 average, but I also know that during the strike I skipped every class that week—"

The students are listening intently to her. There is something about her they respect. Her role last spring must have been commanding. If we ever have a revolution in this country, I conclude, it will be led by women like this wearing baggy old caps and thick cotton jackets storming barricades in the winter snow while their husbands tend the babies.

"—I skipped every class that week and I learned more than I had ever learned in any other week of school [applause]. I learned about political pressures and political ideas and this sort of thing, but I also learned about being an American and how to adjust to being a citizen, a concerned citizen—"

The plagiarism did not go unnoticed among the audience.

"—a concerned citizen, of the United States. I learned that I must speak out as a concerned citizen and do whatever is in my power to change the system, to make the lives and the system, be it in the university itself or in the nation as a whole, more suited to the quality of all those who live within the boundaries [applause]. A democracy means that all citizens should participate in the decisions of the government, and all students should participate in the decisions of the university.

"As far as the strike is concerned, it should be made clear that there were absolutely no threats of violence during the strike by the strike committee. All decisions were made by the strikers in large mass meetings, and there was no bar to attendance. The decisions were made and the actions taken by what one might call a true democracy.

"Please look at the goals of the strike. The people who were striking were striking in particular to support the Black Student Union and the

Mexican-American students who live on campus in their struggle to obtain equality with other white students on campus."

There are no blacks in the audience.

"By equality they meant securing classes which were suited to them and would help the rest of the students at the university understand their situation. There are only about sixty black students in a university of thirteen thousand, and that makes them very much of a minority. But that doesn't mean that the white students on campus shouldn't take classes, be allowed to take classes, in Afro-American history so they can learn about the background of black students. The Constitution was intended for a majority of the people in the United States to be able to make decisions but not at the expense of the minority. We were striking in support of the minority and there were no threats of violence by any members of the strike.

"I am troubled by the legislation being discussed here today. When you are talking about whether or not a student is suitable to remain at the university or whether an instructor's conduct is suitable for a professor at a state university, you have to watch the wording in the bill. How vague is it? How specific? What exactly does it mean for a professor to be unsuitable? Does it mean he's not allowed to take part in any kind of protest? Even a legal protest? I think that a number of professors at WSU are not going to try to stay here under those conditions. They are going elsewhere where—"

Loud applause erupts in the center of the room.

"—where they'll have the freedom of expression. You're going to see a decline in the quality of education—"

From the crowd: "That's what we want." More applause. Loud applause.

"—Well, if what you want is a decline in the quality of education this bill is one way to secure it. But the university is no longer going to be a place of freedom of expression. It's no longer going to be an academy. It's going to be a place where you can come to learn cold facts by memory so you can get a job and not to become a citizen of the United States."

"Go home, go home," someone shouts. There is a buzzing through the auditorium. They want her to quit. She does.

As she leaves the stage Delbert Logsdon says: "I think you've got plenty of courage to stand up for what you feel is right and I admire you for it."

171

There is another angry rumble from the audience and Logsdon, the motel man, does not like it. "It took a lot of nerve for that young girl to come up here and speak," he says angrily. "We don't all have to agree with her, but she still is courageous." His words sting and the audience responds meekly.

Other speakers follow. Mrs. Margaret Hurley, with her brown hair in bangs, wearing large white bracelets, her glasses far down on her nose, is also a state representative and the only Democrat present. She speaks sweetly:

"People in my district and all over the state are saying that the administrators should keep their place and act responsibly, and the students should keep their place and act responsibly. I think that word 'responsibility' is the key to the whole thing. Act according to your role. If you are acting according to your role, you are keeping your place."

There is a growing murmur from the students and someone asks: "What about the niggers?"

"When I'm not in the legislature, I'm a teacher, and I find that no teacher can teach unless the students are in order, and that order has to be maintained. And the responsibility of the teacher or the administrator is to maintain order. If you students actually really and truly want to learn, you will help to maintain that order."

A titter runs up and down the front row and Mrs. Hurley is nettled. She responds indignantly.

"You children can laugh because you haven't sent any children to college yet. I have sent four to college, and it costs a lot of money. And don't minimize this money thing. It costs a lot in sacrifice by your parents. People who are living out in the districts are darned well fed up with what's happening. . . . Just this last week when I heard over the radio that the University of Washington had named a certain young person as part of their recruitment committee, to go out into other states and into other areas of the nation and bring minority groups into the state to go to college, I thought how ridiculous this is. We have our minority groups. They are welcome at our colleges. I think they deserve an education just as well as any of you down here who are not part of a minority group, but to go out and recruit more minority groups seems to me a very senseless thing to do, and I think that we should demand that this halt immediately."

There is tremendous applause.

The young man sitting in front of me turns to an older woman—I

172

take her to be a member of the faculty—and says: "This is incredible."

"I want to close with this point," Mrs. Hurley says. "It has to do with limiting enrollment. Now I know a number of serious students who really and truly want to get an education and are being eliminated from this because enrollments are limited. Well, I would suggest that they start limiting those people who don't seem to be serious students [applause]. We would cut down the enrollment to where the university could cope with it and we would have students that are interested in getting an education and eliminate those who are not. Thank you very much [applause].

Representative Carlton Gladder, an older man who leans into the microphone, his right hand glued inside his pocket, his left hand moving up and down as he talks:

"I think I was as idealist as any of you when I was young. But about the time I got out of college—I worked two and a half years between high school and college—there were a bunch of idealistic youths who had been revved up by a bunch of articulate and persuasive politicians in Germany. And when these brown shirts committed their pogroms of the Jewish people of Berlin and all over Germany and Austria, they were motivated by nothing else than idealism. So what I'm saying to you is this, that idealism is a great and wonderful thing, but cherish it a little bit and don't put it clear up on a pedestal and say that this is all that is necessary. . . . The students of America were rightfully and righteously concerned by the Kent State deaths. Violence exploded all over the country. Emotions were wrought up and people were climbing the walls, but I don't downgrade this a bit. But one of the things that does disturb me is that I didn't hear any cries of outrage when Jerry Rubin appeared on campus after campus after campus in this country and said, 'You must be prepared to go home and kill your folks.' Why didn't you rise up? Why didn't you rise up? Why didn't you shout?"

He is shouting.

"When two policemen were killed in one day for doing nothing but performing their duty, where were you? I mean, are you rounded? Are you sincere all the way? I'll tell you this, we're going to try and correct the situation on our campuses. The taxpayers of the state of Washington want us to establish some reasonable ground rules and we're going to. And I'll tell you this, too. Their ideas of what education consists of is going to be adhered to, to quite a degree, rather than what you, in your infinite knowledge, would set up."

"RIGHT ON. RIGHT ON," a student shouts, facetiously.

Representative James Keenly, a handsome man with graying hair and a ruddy face, dressed in a brown sports jacket and a gold shirt, from Spokane:

"I didn't come down here to put the vigilantes into shape. I didn't come down here to seek any scalp. I'm here as a father . . . and as a taxpayer. . . . I think the key issue of what we're talking about is this business of taxpayers and who is paying the bill. In the last few years we've seen a number of attempts on the part of some minority groups to rule, to try to gain their goals through anarchism. This scares me half to death. . . . These are rather well-trained, rather well-financed, and rather well-organized young people who aren't on the campus for the purpose of securing an education. They're there for the purpose of stirring up trouble in political ideology, and in the process they are enlisting and rallying up the support of a whole lot of other impressionable young men and women who are there and who do not have the proper background with which they can make intelligent decisions. I don't really think at this point the issues are really important—"

A girl down the row put her head in her hands and said with disgust: "Oh, my God. Oh, my God."

"—and I certainly am not going to talk about them. The issues are being used as subterfuge in many instances. Whether we're talking about Vietnam or Cambodia or final examinations or grades, it makes very little difference; they're subterfuges. If students want to worry about Cambodia, Vietnam, or grades, they can do it on extracurricular time like they do in football. Unfortunately some of our administrators really do feel that some of the theatrical radicals are the architects of a brave and compassionate new world. Some of these theatrical radicals that I refer to are able to spice things up with a little rock music, or a little pot, or a little acid, or the old Marxist idea of dictated equality, and it becomes appealing to some impressionable young people on campus. Some of our administrators and academicians had better learn fast how to contend with this kind of thing because the survival of our colleges and our institutions, the survival of our free-enterprise system, is most certainly at stake. . . .

"I have two fine young daughters. They've told me often what is on their minds and what's going on with their friends and I learned things I did not know. In many instances I changed my manner, I changed my method of doing things. But some place along the line somebody has to

174

call the shots. I'm the guy who pays the bills, and I'm the guy who's going to call the shots in my family. The same thing is going to happen in Washington. The taxpayers of this state, who are putting up the money, are ultimately going to call the shots, whether you people like it or not."

The young man in front of me says to his companion: "In the beginning was lucre, and lucre was God."

"And so," James Keenly is concluding, "if the regents and administrators do not do their duty, we in the legislature will take away the powers of the regents and administrators and place them in the legislature. We may even go further—maybe create a disciplinary board on campus with powers delegated directly from the legislature, to keep discipline. We will also have to let the police go directly onto the campus to deal with these problems. We are not going to hope our way through this or wish our way through. We need action. We want the regents and the administrators to make backbones out of their wishbones—and now."

And the longest applause of the day carries Representative James Keenly back to his seat. Not once did he raise his voice.

As the next speaker—a woman who teaches in the political-science department of Washington State—begins to lecture the students that the goals (of the strike) did not justify the means (of the strikers) someone in the audience shouts: "Then how do you justify Vietnam?"

"I did not come here to discuss the war," she replies, "and I remind you that I have the floor." The audience is on her side, but it is late. Delbert Logsdon moves back to the podium and she concludes hastily. Several students raise their hands to seek recognition. He looks past them and says: "This has drug on long enough. If you want to meet with individual legislators afterwards, you can get to them when we've adjourned. This debate could go on for hours and hours. We all know what we came for today and I hope you all realize something from it."

The students shout: "Let us speak. Let us speak. Don't stop now."

Delbert Logsdon of Cheney ignores them. He leans into the microphone as if he is applying mouth-to-mouth resuscitation and asks: "Is the silent majority ready to be heard?"

The roar that reverberates in the hall momentarily stuns even Delbert Logsdon: what has he loosed? He stands there, three-fourths of his short, round frame hidden by the podium, sweat running from his face, and suddenly he is no longer nervous. For the first time during the afternoon he is not gripping the microphone. His hands are on his hips.

175

"What about the minority?" a young voice cries from the floor. A professional-looking man turns to a student with long hair and says: "Now you see what we're up against."

Delbert Logsdon leans into the microphone and says: "I said you can come up here and speak to any one of the legislators you want to, but we're not going to stay here all night and listen to you. Goodbye." And he walks triumphantly away from the microphone.

They did stay. Small groups of students cornered the representatives and some engaged the townspeople. One young man in the midst of about twelve adults was asked if things were going to get worse. "Yes," he said, "I think they will." Another man, about thirty, with very short hair, said to the student: "You better watch out then, because if it does get worse, it's gonna get worse for YOU." A much older man with a slight European accent said he had heard that there were twenty outsiders now using official university rooms to plan next fall's riots. The student replied: "Look, man, we've come here. You've got to come to the university to see that that just isn't true." The man's wife said: "I'd be afraid to go and I'd be afraid to let my husband go."

On stage a young woman in a tight white blouse and a red miniskirt talked to the representative from Spokane. "Why did you bring up the war without saying that it should stop?" she asked. "It's immoral for anyone to mention the war without saying in the next breath that we must stop it. Don't you realize that for everyone who dies over there, Vietnam or American, this whole country dies? Some of my friends have died over there but I don't mean just them. The whole country is dying." She began to cry. The legislator answered: "I mentioned the war because it was one of the reasons for the protest. That's why I brought it up. But the real reason for the meeting here was what the taxpayers think about the university and not about the war." And she replied: "I am goddamn sick and tired of hearing about the taxpayers this and the taxpayers that. I am a taxpayer and I am an orphan and I own my parents' property and I bet I pay more taxes than anyone else in this room tonight. And I am goddamn sick and tired of paying taxes for these goddamn farmers not to grow wheat. Why didn't you mention that tonight? Why? I'll tell you why. The reason you didn't mention that was because the room was full of wheat farmers and you're a politician and you haven't got the goddamn guts." And the man from Spokane who had said issues were not really important managed to get out of there.

I located Mr. Logsdon. His eyes were bluer than they had seemed from the audience. He was quite happy. "I never said more than five words in public in all my life," he confessed. "Until today. And they said, 'Del, we got no chairman; you'll have to moderate it.' "

How did this meeting come about?

"Some of us was just having coffee one morning and lamenting what was happening to Washington State. The kids were destroying it. There had been this strike and the administration just threw up their hands and ran. When they got through running, they capitulated. I didn't go to Washington State but I have a niece over there and my father did and I belong to the Cougar Club. I've always boosted 'em in sports. And I just don't want to sit over at Cheney and watch the university get torn apart the way Harvard and those other places back east have been.

"I went over to the campus after the coffee session and asked a lot of questions, but I got no answers. We began to hear there's gonna be trouble in the fall and we decided to let the regents and the legislature know that it isn't just a small group of businessmen who are upset—lots of other people are, too. So we decided to have this meeting. I just didn't believe we'd have this many people, but I'll tell you—this is all the proof I need. Folks are fed up to their teeth." And he turned to receive the congratulations of his neighbors, who were coming forward with outstretched hands.

Seattle, Washington

CROSSING THE CASCADE MOUNTAINS TOWARD SEATTLE I READ CLARE WOFFORD'S note again and realized that I have not been doing so well. The more diligently I search for the humor, ironies, and humanness, the more I keep bumping into the problems.

No sooner had we checked into a motel than the desk clerk handed me a piece of pink paper with a mimeographed message from the Seattle Police Department. I read it aloud to Butterworth: "'Welcome to Seattle, and may your stay be a pleasant one.'"

"That's very nice of them," Butterworth said. "I really appreciate that. How did they know we were coming?"

But there was more: "Like other cities we have a problem of thefts from vehicles—particularly during the summer season. Criminals are well aware that travelers carry numerous personal items in their vehicles. They are also aware that many of these items are left overnight in vehicles. Please cooperate in preventing this type of crime by removing clothing, luggage, cameras, etc., from your vehicle. If it is not possible to remove all valuables, please place them in the trunk and lock it."

Butterworth sighed as he said, "I guess I'll sleep in the camper."

I do not intend to sully the good name of Seattle. It is one of the most beautiful cities in America. With the light falling across the buildings at certain times of the day Seattle is as pretty as San Francisco except that it does not have an old prison sitting in the bay. But already I was threatened with sleepless nights worrying about my friend out there in the camper. Truthfully, I was less concerned about Butterworth, since he weighs over 215 pounds and once held the entire Princeton security force

181

at bay while his girl friend scrambled out of his dormitory window, than I was about the general idea. There is no escaping our trials.

An hour later I hailed a cab and the driver turned the wrong way into a one-way street. He apologized very profusely and said: "I'm new to this. Two weeks ago I was working at Boeing, but I got laid off. I took this job because it's all there was and I just don't know the streets yet."

Suddenly I was upon a problem greater than those thieves against whom Butterworth is guarding in the camper. The problem is unemployment. Two years ago the Boeing Company employed 101,400 people in the Seattle area. Today there are 56,000 and by the end of 1971 there likely will be no more than 30,000. In three years two-thirds of the workers at Boeing will have been laid off. Already the annual loss to the Seattle payroll is about $475 million.

During the years I was in Washington we dealt with unemployment figures. They were always percentages—5 percent, 4 percent, 3 percent. Sometimes a government will actually cause people to lose their jobs and then conscript them as shock troops in the War Against Inflation. Only last week I had read an editorial declaring that "Administration officials can be forgiven if they take a little comfort from the latest employment figures. The jobless rate dropped in June—to 4.7% from May's 5%." Now I was in the midst of a vast number of people who are represented by those percentages, people who generally take less comfort from such situations. I decided to meet some of them.

I called first upon W. G. Cogdill, the manager of the Seattle Unemployment Insurance Office, which is located in the shadow of the Space Needle, that elegant heirloom of the Seattle World's Fair. Mr. Cogdill was once a Marine. He retains the crisp manner and the straight-as-an-arrow bearing of his former profession, but his silver hair frames a wide, kindly brow and friendly eyes and he acts very much like a civilian.

"Things were real good here the past few years," he said. "People weren't prepared for what happened. It came so suddenly and with such a shock. Right now they're running scared. You hear them talking to each other in the lines and they say, 'I've never seen it so bad.' Our problem right now in this business is space. We handle about twenty-one thousand people in a forty-hour week. We get about a thousand or more new claims every week. We keep telling ourselves that things are going to change, get better—hold on till next week, we say—but they don't.

"A person who's been laid off comes in here to apply, he fills out a form, and he's given a little booklet which he brings every week. We give him a certain hour to report according to his social security number. He's eligible to start receiving benefits after the second week and he comes in every week at the appointed hour and a clerk at the window certifies his claim. The clerk asks him the same questions every week: Did you look for a job last week? Were you able to work every day last week? Did you accept all offers of work during the week? Were you unemployed every day of the week? What were your earnings before payroll deductions? Then the person signs the card swearing that he is familiar with the contents of his identification booklet. We send this card to the state capital in Olympia and usually the check is sent within the next two days. His benefits can run from eight to thirty weeks, as little as $17 and as much as $72.

"People are pretty nice. Just today a fellow came in and said, 'I'm selling out and moving to California. I just want to thank you for your help. It's been a tough time.' Real nice fellow. People try to act cordially while they're in line. Some are in a hurry—they may have a job appointment and they'll try to sneak in line. We've had an altercation or two but nothing serious. See those young people at the door? Seattle Liberation Front is passing out pamphlets. Occasionally an old shipbuilder or a plumber or a lumberjack—you'd call them a hardhat back in New York—will want to give one of those kids a swat on the chops. They get uneasy with the bare feet and stuff like that. Some people will ask me to throw them off the streets but I can't do that. The streets are public. We get hippies who don't wear shirts or shoes or socks. But they're eligible as long as they're laid off from work. People come over to me and say, 'Why are you giving *them* benefits?' I say it's the state law.

"We get some strange ones. Northwest Airlines is on strike and a pilot came in last week. He had been making about $25,000 a year and all we could allow him was $72 a week, and that only after the two weeks. He said, 'If I have to wait, I wait—where can I get food stamps?' I couldn't understand why he hadn't saved anything. I guess he had a big house and a big car—lots of credit and no savings.

"I don't know what we're going to do for space this fall when the carpenters, fishermen, and construction workers start their seasonal layoffs. Our lines are too long already. Maybe some of these people"—he gestured to the large outer room filled with people—"will run out of benefits." He winced. "I didn't mean it to sound that way. I really didn't."

I believed him; but I have heard people in Washington say casually that a little unemployment will help the economy.

I walked among the long lines of people. The windows are identified by social security numbers (2000–2099, 2100–2199, etc.). Some people laughed as they recognized each other from the previous week. A few would not look you in the eyes—"they feel conspicuous the first time," Mr. Cogdill had said—but others were very relaxed. I counted 127 people in three lines, including three blacks, one Chinese, and two Mexican-Americans. A deeply tanned man of about fifty-five wore a red jacket with the emblem of the National Rifle Association. Behind him stood a youth of about twenty-four with a Mephistophelian beard, blue jeans, and white sneakers, talking to a very tall middle-aged man wearing a handsome charcoal-tweed jacket and gray slacks with expensive two-tone shoes. The young man said he had been on the security force at Boeing. The other man had been an engineer; it was his first visit and his height (six feet four) made him all the more self-conscious.

A clerk said: "All the eight-o'clock people to the front, all the nine-o'clock people to the rear, please." The newcomers looked at their little orange books to assure themselves they were at the right place at the right time. A matronly woman of sixty, dressed in a neat gray suit with a string of pearls, got to the counter too soon. "I'm sorry," the clerk said, "you're in the 8:45 group. This is the 8:30 group." With the bearing of a matriarch she walked to the rear of the line.

Fresh waves arrived every few minutes. As the nine-o'clock people came in they often smiled or waved or stopped to talk to friends and acquaintances. Conversations would end in the middle of a sentence if people realized their time had come and their group was leaving them behind. A blithe young man dressed like Zorro but with billowing yellow sleeves and sandals ogled a blond male in 2000–2099. An elderly man said to me: "I hit the bus service good this morning. The bus driver had a green light and I was stuck across the corner on the red, but he recognized me because I take the same bus down here every Tuesday, and he leaned out of the window and said, 'Come on, come on.' I wouldn't have made it today if he hadn't waited."

I stood in another line beside a Swedish woman with a heavy accent. She had lost her job as a motel maid in April. "I've been to every motel on highway 99 and no luck," she said. "Last year there were 'no vacancy' signs everywhere. Now they stand on the street begging people to come in." Her husband is retired with a small pension. "I've got to find something soon," she said, "because my benefits will expire and I don't want to go into that welfare office." She was getting $42 a week.

A grizzled man at least sixty said: "I've come full circle. I came here in 1931 off the ranch in eastern Washington. There was no money there but at least we ate and I should have stayed. But I came on to Seattle and there was a place grown up over by the tracks which everyone called Hooverville, where all the people like me stayed. We ate beans and we would stand in line two hours for them. Now I'm standin' in line for $42 a week. I pay $13 a week for an apartment—that leave me $29 to eat on and pay my other bills. If my wife was still livin' we'd be in a bad way." He worked in an anodizing plant until "people stopped buyin' appliances because of this economy thing. I told my friends two years ago they were votin' for a depression when they voted for Hoover's party but they were more scared of the niggers than they were of not workin.' Now they come and stand in line right beside a nigger. That'll teach 'em." He laughed so hard that people stared at us.

I talked to a man in his early twenties who had worked at Boeing almost five years as a machine tooler. "I'll never go back," he said. "Life is too uncertain, too many ups and downs there. When you see people with eighteen or twenty-five years being laid off, you know you can't build your life on that. I was luckier than most people because I had something to fall back on. I felt this was coming, and I saved a little money. I can go to September on my savings. My father owns a little machine shop and he offered me a job, but it would have meant his letting someone else go. I've written around the country but nothing's shown up. I'm in the reserves and someone said volunteer to go back in full time—there are some jobs in Cambodia. I told him to go to hell; at least I'm not getting shot at."

Through a friend who still had his job at Boeing I met three other men who had lost their jobs.

Robert Street is a small man who once had very large ambitions. "I set out to make a million," he said. "I ran a bridge club and taught bridge. I started playing bridge because I couldn't afford to go to the movies during the depression. I'd play bridge all afternoon and maybe win a dollar or two. Figures just sort of jump through hoops for me and I got pretty good at it. Just seven years ago, in June of '63, I played my millionth hand of bridge. I would have had to go East to make it big as a professional bridge expert, but I was born in these parts and I just couldn't make myself leave. So I took a temporary job at Boeing and wound up staying nineteen years until they declared me surplused in February. I could have made that million if I had gone East. I know it."

How much were you making when you lost your job?

"I'd struggled up to $10,300. I believed in the company and I still do. I even took a cut just to stay there last year and they dropped me down to $9,100, but then they let me work overtime, Saturday, two nights a week, to make enough money to get back up to where I was. It's kind of a funny system; they're firing people all over the place and I'm working overtime, along with a bunch of other people. I had difficulty getting raises before that. Obviously they finally didn't approve of me because they fired me. I just wish they had fired me many years before that, if they were going to. When I was first told that I was going to be laid off—these two fellows came in to see me on a Monday morning and as they were getting around to tell me, one of them said, 'Let's see, Street, you're the oldest fellow in the tax group, aren't you?' And I was. I was fifty-five then. I'd been paying Boeing's taxes a long time—I'm an accountant—and do you know, that was the first time in my whole life that I felt the least bit old? I hadn't had any time to get old, not with a boy to take care of, and golfing and fishing and wrestling with him. I just never thought of going into that rocking chair. When they told me I felt like I was a hundred years old."

He had to stop for a minute and I was glad that we were alone. I am sure that he would not have wanted anyone to see that he was upset. He is a shy man with salt-and-pepper hair that is thinning considerably and eyebrows that flare out like the wings of a butterfly.

"I took pride in my work," he continued. "I thought I did a good job for the company. A lot of other people did, too. If I wasn't doing a very good job in the tax group, it shouldn't take them all that many years to find out. Several times I had a chance to get out, but they didn't want me to go. Then when the chances were gone, I was unloaded. Just declared surplus. I said to the fellow who had put me in the job, 'How come you didn't talk to me about it, at least let me know a little bit ahead of time?' And he said, 'Well, I was afraid if I talked to you I might change my mind.'

"There was nothing to do but go out and look for a job. I filed applications everywhere I could think of, even went down to Portland, where I was born and raised, but things were tough in this area. Finally in June I found an accounting job with a firm that processes fish. Less money, but I'll prove myself and they'll give me a raise, I'm sure. It's like starting all over again, only I'm fifty-six and there's a difference. I went through the depression. I got out of school and I couldn't find a job. I feel badly right now about all the kids in this area, coming out of school, or on summer vacation, who can't find jobs. I met a lot of them in the unemployment lines. They're good kids but they need something to do. It's not good they are unable to get a job."

I asked Robert Street if he feels challenged in his new job with the fish company. He answered: "Oh, yes. There's an awful lot to learn about the fish. I'm learning something every day. Of course, a fish is not the same as a 747."

Neither is a used car, but I met a man who is selling them now. While he was being axed by Boeing he was in New York trying to sell Alexander's Department Store a used jet for $1,800,000. Now he is pleased if he sells a car for $1,800. While he is a handsome man—tall, tanned, with a silver-gray crew cut—he has the tired look of someone who has been swimming upstream for several months. He spoke in a voice so low that I could hardly hear him and he chain-smoked cigarettes. His name is Tom Carroll; he is forty-eight, possesses two degrees, once taught in college, and worked for a while as a budget analyst for the University of California. He had been at Boeing for four years.

"I came back from New York and there was a new organization chart without my name on it," he said. "My boss had just died and I felt unprotected. I went to see the vice president for sales and he was away on a trip. I asked everybody who was in general management but nobody knew. They sort of looked away. I kept getting madder and madder, and I finally found a guy who said he would find out, and he went down the hall and a few minutes later he came back and he said, 'Well, Tom, you've been laid off.' That's the problem with a huge company, you never know exactly where you stand. The human value can be pretty low. Like my terminal interviews were with a little twenty-two-year-old girl, you know, filling out the forms. You hand your identification badge to her and what does she say? She doesn't have anything to say. Just, 'Will you sign this, please.'"

Carroll laughed. "During all this I finally got to see a fellow high up on the chart—he might get to be president of Boeing. He's a wonderful guy. I went in and told him about my predicament and he said, 'God, Carroll, I'm sorry to hear that. I wish I could help you but my son was just laid off, too.' We laughed about that and he said, 'Have you had breakfast?' I said no and he had breakfast sent in. That helped.

"I filed for unemployment. Standing in that line I felt like a loser. I didn't really believe I was there. The first week was embarrassing, but the second week it didn't bother me. Hell, I had earned it. The thing that bothered me is the U.S. Employment Service doesn't do anything to help you find a job. They just process a bunch of papers. But there's no organized way to match up job requirements and skills. They'll send you to a room and say, 'Here's a bunch of newspapers from across the country' and you can look at want ads from Atlanta or Dallas or Miami. Very ineffective.

"It's funny, you know. My eighteen-year-old son was more upset about what happened than anyone. He was enthusiastic about my work because I love airplanes—I was a pilot in the air force—and I love aviation. I made a decision to stay there at the plant. I knew a lot about business and a lot about economics and a lot about the Department of Defense and how all these things tie together. My kid thought I got a really bad kick in the stomach and he said, 'See, Dad? In the end the system doesn't really give a damn about people.'"

I asked him if his style of living changed drastically.

He confessed that because of "my air force pension I wasn't hit as hard as the fellow with nothing to fall back on, but sure, you change your life style when you lose a big income like that. I'm working fourteen hours a day selling cars, and that's a change. When I lost my job I tried to go into business for myself as a management consultant. But every business has been hit in Seattle because of Boeing's situation and after three weeks I had made $180, which just repaid my original investment and my gasoline expenses. I couldn't pull it so I got this job selling cars. Two things I always hated: car salesmen and insurance salesmen. I can't stand them. Now I'm one myself.

"You should see the people who come in to buy cars. They're usually in their middle twenties and they have one or two kids with them. They're paying on a car that's a few years old and it's almost paid off and they've come to get another one. They don't have any money for a down payment and we send them down to the mouse [loan company] and they'll have to pay 20 to 30 percent interest overall to get what they need. They live paycheck to paycheck and when something like this recession we're in hits, they're in trouble. Much more trouble than I was because I have never lived beyond my means. I feel sorry for those people. You can see the mouse going back and forth collecting their assets—repossessing, you know. Every mouse in Seattle is working overtime this year. Did you know there's a shortage of one-way trailers for rent in Seattle right now? People renting them to move.

"What happened to Boeing? That's easy. When the economy was gorging itself a few years back everybody went wild. The airline companies started ordering planes like crazy and Boeing had to expand like crazy. They promised to deliver all those planes in a certain time, so they put on thousands and thousands of people. They were flying laborers in from as far away as Florida just to get that big building finished north of here where they build the 747s. This is another thing. When you build cars you can run maybe fifty million through one plant. There are only two hundred 747s on order and at the most optimistic prediction maybe a thousand will be built in all. Nobody knows how to build a building that you only need for ten years. There was a lot of waste. Everybody was grabbing for that big pie. Then the bottom fell out and a lot of people went right down with it. Including yours truly."

George Metcalf was also among them. He is a taciturn man. I could hardly picture him defusing mines and bombs in the Pacific, but he did during and after the Second World War. He went to Japan in 1945 to dispose of our old bombs and there met his wife, the daughter of a missionary. He is a graduate of MIT and had worked for Boeing since 1955. He got The Word early in February.

"I wasn't expecting it at that time," he said. "I had left the weapons division [where he helped to develop a photoscreen to detect the passage of high-velocity bullets] and had gone to the acoustics program. I understood that acoustics was going to be sound for the next couple of years. That wasn't meant to be a pun. I was really quite surprised to learn I no longer had a job. But I wasn't angry. If some of us have to pay to keep the economy going, I am willing to make my contribution. But I've been extremely discouraged the past few months. I make a weekly trip every Thursday to the unemployment office. I don't think I was made to stand in line. I haven't had to go to the welfare office yet. I hope I never have to."

Mrs. Metcalf spoke. With her husband out of work she has been selling home cleaning products—bleaches, water softeners, liquid concentrates, waxes—house to house. "The whole experience has had a big effect on the kids," she said. "They see a person like George who's had very fine training, who's been with a company for fifteen years and given them his best . . . it makes them wonder. They start thinking about whether they really want to do the same thing. We thought our son was going to be a scientist. He's a national merit scholar. On his science test he scored 800 out of a possible 800. But he's going to study Japanese and German philosophy and literature now."

To teach?

She smiled. "No, just to understand. That's where they're different from our generation. They're not as concerned with function, and what's happened to George makes them skeptical about just being a cog for some big machine."

George Metcalf said his situation "has brought our family even closer. One of our daughters has taken a job in a restaurant. Ellen, the other girl, was supposed to go back to college this fall—she'll have to borrow to do it, and the poor man that marries her will have a big bill on his hands. She was working in women's apparel this summer but lost her job last week because business is so bad. Our son Roger has been studying in Germany and we didn't have the money for his ticket. Do you know that Ellen sent him the money to get back? And her needing to go back to college."

He laughed. "You should have seen Roger at the airport. His hair was so long I didn't know whether to claim him or just drive on."

"Now, George," his wife said, "you knew the hair wasn't important. That was your son under there."

"Yes," he replied, "way under."

I asked George Metcalf what he had been doing since February.

"I applied to a lot of labs and places like that but things are slow everywhere. I'm running some experiments on a patent I have filed relating to the simulation of sonic booms and maybe something will come of that. I have lots of other ideas I'm exploring. Just takes money to get started. I've got this safety decal for cars—just a simple little reminder of safety habits that attaches to the driver's window, to establish good driving habits—little checks to make before you get in and before you get out. I spent three weeks trying to sell it—insurance companies, driver training schools, the Teamsters, Sears Roebuck. I've even tried to sell it through the newspapers, but I didn't get one response to an ad that reached 200,000 people on the comic page. It'll go one day, you'll see, but it's slow right now. I'd rather be doing this than what some of the fellows are having to do. I've got one friend who was twenty years at Boeing. He's on a fishing boat now. I couldn't do anything like that. The problem is that there doesn't seem a market right now for anything I am good at."

He looked at his wife and said: "I think we'll get through. Sometimes I wonder . . ."

"We'll get through," she said. "We're not going on welfare." As I left she handed me a brochure touting the products for which she is now the local representative. The brochure began: "Brighten your Life with . . ."

I went to lunch with four Boeing executives who were quite explicit about the causes of their discontent. One man said: "We foresaw the decline in government contracts in military and space hardware but we did not foresee the drop in the commercial market. The repeal of the tax investment credit came just before the economy started to cool and airlines began to lose customers while labor costs were skyrocketing. We had promised almost instant delivery of airplanes and to do that we had to build rapidly; we were hiring any warm and breathing body we could find. Then the orders were cut back and there we were: all dressed up and nowhere to go."

"It's a good lesson," another said, "on what can happen from over-centralization of economic means. Hundreds of thousands of people were tied to one company. I have a friend in the sign business who was expanding when we began to lay off. 'Your layoffs won't affect me,' he said. But now he has let half his work force go and he may have to close. There was a feeling in this town that the government would just not let Boeing go down the drain. It was a delusion. When times were good, some of us tried to get the city fathers to broaden the industrial base, to bring in more and varied industry, but they didn't see the need and they sat on their fannies."

"We've got to diversify," another man said. "We just got a $2 million grant from the Department of Housing and Urban Development to explore the development of 'new towns' using modular and prefabricated housing. Things like that have to be looked at."

"There's something deeper here," one said. "The national psychology that prevailed midway through the sixties was like the stock market: it was bullish. Everyone thought it would go on forever. The economists said we were in the millennium. People were buying and buying and buying. So was the government: guns and butter, butter and guns. We became a nation of gluttons, each man driving toward his individual ends without any concern for the whole. Now we know we weren't in the millennium at all. We weren't infallible. Now people are disillusioned. What made Boeing unique over the years was the feeling of loyalty and kinship that people here felt toward the company. Now they see the guy next door who has been laid off after twenty years and they worry when their time is coming. They feel the company has let them down. Don't you think that's happened to almost all of the institutions that held this country together: the schools, the churches, the hospitals, now the corporation? Nobody knows where to put his trust any more."

"Well," the fourth executive said, "I'm no socialist or even close to it and I don't believe in a dictated society, but we have got to have some national guidelines, some planning. Each President appoints a blue-ribbon commission to say this is where we ought to go, they come up with a five-hundred-page report that is published in the Sunday papers, and then everybody forgets. This country has got an enormous capacity to analyze problems and absolutely no apparatus to follow through. The fifty states go their own way, companies think all they need is the free market, everybody acts as if this is 1870 rather than 1970 and that a nation of two hundred million and more people can just go on developing as if everybody was making absolutely beautiful decisions and the system didn't need overhauling. An example? The federal government is spending billions on pollution but spreading it all over the lot with every agency in Washington competing for it. What we need is a NASA for pollution. We need a NASA for mass transit, and so on—agencies sufficiently endowed with money and authority to achieve a specific goal, like NASA got to the moon. Right now everybody in government and in industry is so busy doing something that no one is asking whether what they are doing is worth doing."

And then the conversation in that corporate dining room took a very surprising turn. One of these men, a very mild-mannered, undemonstrative person, began to speak: "Yes, what is the end of it all? Where is the country going? Where is each one of us going? I think this is what is bothering the young although I don't think they have the practical experience to know what to do about it. I feel that I have betrayed myself. What in the hell, I've asked myself, have I done with all those things you were thinking about in college? I know this sounds schmaltzy, but truthfully I haven't done very much. And I got to thinking about this after that first big layoff. I lost some friends in that, people who had put their hearts into this company. And one day they weren't here. I think rushing into that fantastic progress caused more heartache and suffering than it was worth. The people were saying, 'More, more, more,' so the airlines said, 'More, more, more,' and Boeing said, 'More, more, more.' We scrounged and grabbed and fought for dominance, and when we got it, we lost it. All this running and shoving to build a structure that suddenly we don't need. And look at all the people who got hurt. Business has got to change. I think it will because the children of so many businessmen are becoming hippies."

He was speaking very quietly but he was intense and nervous, and I am not sure that he was really talking to those of us who were at the table. Or maybe he was. It was with considerable difficulty that he announced: "A month ago my own daughter just disappeared. She left—no note, no word, nothing. Just disappeared. I've been lying awake at nights asking: Where did I go wrong? What happened? How come she didn't come in and say, 'I've got to go, Daddy. I'm going to pull out.' We've had a very beautiful relationship over the years. Oh, she got mad last spring because I wouldn't buy her a car—her friends all own one. But was that a reason to—to leave? She called last Friday night. She wouldn't leave a phone number or an address. She just said she was in New York, working as a typist for $100 a week. When her mother came on the phone she said, 'It's okay, Mother, I'm being a good girl.' I guess she thinks we're more concerned about her chastity than we are about her as a person. Maybe that's the problem. She's a sensitive child. We thought she had a suitcase full of clothes but it turned out to be full of books—Tolstoi, Dostoevski, introspective writers. We thought maybe she was going into a convent. Maybe she has, in a way. I asked her if she needed any clothes or any of her jewelry. She said no, not at all. I wanted a phone number, an address, some way to get in touch with her if anything happened. But she said not to worry and wouldn't give them to me. I can't figure out what happened. Where did I betray her? Where did I betray myself?"

The room was silent. None of us knew what to say. He appeared to be apologetic at having talked so personally. Our meeting broke up and he walked quickly to his office.

I left Seattle with an answer for Clare Wofford. I have been looking for the humor, irony, and humanness of America as if they existed apart from the problems, as the ancient Gnostics looked for a soul outside the body. But only in the midst of adversity—in the good-natured optimism of the people waiting in line for their unemployment checks, in the pride and courage of the Streets, Carrolls, and Metcalfs, and in the honest self-questioning of the man who bared his soul at Boeing—did I find those qualities which are the bedrock strength of America. They make it possible to travel the country in troubled times without losing heart.

On the Road in Oregon

WE DECIDED TO RELAX IN OREGON: DINNER WITH FRIENDS AT AN ECCENTRIC and superb French restaurant in Portland; a bottle of rosé at noon on the beach at Coos Bay; a round of old Southern hymns (although Butterworth comes from good New Orleans stock he was born in London, the resulting hybrid dialect rendering unbelievable violence to "Sweet Bye and Bye" and "Zion Stands with Hills Surrounded"). A merchant's sign —"We buy junk but sell antiques"—provoked a frivolous competition to collect examples of Americanese ("garden apartments" that have no gardens, motels with "queen-size beds" and "baronial bathrooms," hamburgers disguised as "Whattaburgers" and politicians who accuse one another of "untruthful lies"). We spotted a sign which announced "There Are No Billboards in Russia" and thus understood why there are no Russian tourists in America.

San Francisco

A FRIEND IN WASHINGTON HAS A DAUGHTER WHO RAN AWAY TO SAN
Francisco. A friend in Texas has a daughter who ran away to Los
Angeles. They asked me to try to locate their children. I failed. But at a
precinct in Golden Gate Park I saw the scope of the problem. An officer
had put forty-two fresh notices of runaways on the bulletin board.
Almost all of the pictures had been furnished by parents. They were
school pictures of freshly scrubbed youngsters. "They probably won't
look like that now," the officer said. "That's why it's so hard to find them.
Also there's just too many of them." Some are printed circulars: "Valerie,
17, blonde, dark blue or black sweater with bell bottoms or dungarees.
Subject withdrew $200 from savings account and took flight to San Fran-
cisco. Subject has no friends or relations there." Thirty-seven were girls,
only five were boys. All of them were white. They came from places as
different as Willmar, Minnesota, and Arlington, Virginia. The father of one
girl offered $500 to the police benefit in Tucson if his daughter was
located. Two sisters, young teenagers, had run away from their home in
Reno. The officer said: "They always claim it's their parents. I don't think
you can believe them every time, but that's what they say. Every time
we find a girl, it's almost always the same problem—they just gave up,
they lost faith in the family."

I went with Officers Juan Morales and Pete DiBono to the juvenile
guidance center where they rap once every week with the kids in jail.
This is part of the juvenile bureau's "community relations" program. "After
a while on the street," Juan Morales said, "you've taken so much abuse
that you throw a shell around yourself. Working with these kids helps to
tear that shell down. Nowadays the only contact between kids and cops

195

is on the street, when you're arresting them or dispersing or fighting them. Used to be you walked a beat and you knew the kids in the neighborhood. Nowadays a kid only sees a cop when he's in trouble. Or he sees some policeman on television knocking somebody over the head with a night stick. This contact in the guidance center at least tries to get back some human contact between the cops and the kids." Morales, who came from Mexico fifteen years ago, wore a gold tie clasp with a tiny blue pig on it. "If you can't beat 'em," he said, "join 'em."

There were eleven boys between fourteen and seventeen in the room. One of them said to Morales as we walked in: "Hey, I recognize you. You're the guy who hassled me." Several of the boys tried to convince Morales and DiBono to try pot. Morales asked: "If a man came running out of a store on Mission Street with a gun, and a lady ran after him saying he had shot her husband, do you think I could shoot that man if I was high on pot?" One boy replied: "You're not supposed to fire into a crowd." During the discussion another boy said: "Ninety-nine percent of the people on heroin started with marijuana but 99 percent of the people who smoke pot don't use heroin." DiBono said: "Ninety-nine percent of the people who drink milk die before they're a hundred."

One boy said he had run away from home in Phoenix two years ago. He was then fifteen.

How did you get here?

"I drove a car."

Did your parents let you go?

"They don't care."

You just split and you don't think they care?

"They never cared that I was home. Why should they care if I'm not home?"

Another had fought with his parents. When his father told him to go to his room, he walked out and came to San Francisco. "They didn't even call the cops," he said. "They were glad to see me go."

"Isn't it possible that you share in the blame for the trouble at home?" Morales asked.

"Oh, sure, man. I popped it to my old man every time I could."

Why?

"I mean, isn't that what it's all about today?"

★ ★ ★

Pete DiBono was new to the San Francisco police force when he was dispatched to the campus of San Francisco State College during violence

196

three years ago. After that, he almost decided to become a fireman. He told me of his experience as we drove around San Francisco. "I spent a lot of time talking to those kids out there and trying to explain to them that I'm just a human being, that my job is to get in the middle of opposing elements. I saw a cop get his neck broken out there by a rock. I never did see who threw the rock, but Jesus it was a mean rock, must have weighed a good two pounds, maybe more. Television only told half the story. The cameras didn't get that rock; they didn't see it coming. But they got us cops getting mad and reacting. After the rock hit the cop another policeman grabbed this person, right beside me, and that's the picture that got in the paper. The cameraman can pretty well anticipate what the cop is going to do. But out in a crowd he doesn't know who is going to do what or when someone is going to do something, because it's always spur of the moment. I don't believe the public gets both sides of the story. I don't doubt there's been overreaction by the police. I mean, I'm standing out there and the boss says those people are not to get on the college grounds. They're marching, right? Thousands of them. So we form a line to keep them off the grounds. This is our job. You get a crowd with fifteen or twenty people around and they'll box you in and start talking to you, and another twenty will see this crowd and come over, and you'll be joined by another policeman, and pretty soon some kid comes over who's militant. I got cornered like that out there, and they kept wanting to demand why I was there, and I explained to them that it's my job, I'm detailed to it. And they said, 'Don't you see that's wrong?' Well, gee, before long I had about fifteen people screaming at me. I just excused myself and took a hike. How can you talk when people are screaming? I'll never forget, a little gal about sixteen years old, she comes running up in front of me and I just try to look straight ahead and not pay any attention to her, because that's how you get into trouble. She comes up and she gives me the finger and she says, 'Up you, you pig.' Just screams it out. The prettiest little girl you can imagine, except her face was all twisted up and there was spite in her eyes. She just kept screaming, 'Pig, pig, pig,' and giving me the finger. Oh, man, I'd love to take her over my knees and whale her good. I couldn't do it. But I sure as hell wish her old man would."

★ ★ ★

There is no immunity for the establishment. As the large organizations of politics, education, and business do battle with new ideas, forces, and doubts, less conspicuous institutions are trembling, too. Even in the arts, so long the domain of the noblesse patriarchs of philanthropy and finance, new constituencies are seeking power and recognition. Quite by accident I witnessed one round of the struggle in San Francisco.

I had been trying to reach Loni Ding Welch, a young woman who could tell me about the changing ways of the Chinese in San Francisco. She is into many things and hard to locate, but I finally talked to her on the telephone and she suggested that we meet after a session of the San Francisco Art Commission which she was to attend that afternoon. To assure that we did not miss each other I arrived early. The scene more closely resembled a campus confrontation than it did an art commission. On the sidewalks people carried signs declaring DOLLARS FOR WAR, DARTS FOR ART, $$ IS POWER and THIS COMMISSION MUST GO painted with a grotesque skull and crossbones. Something called the Gorilla Band played discordantly from the street, many in the crowd were chanting "Power to the people. Power to the people," and two young men were passing out rolls of toilet paper made by the Crown Zellerbach company.

I pushed my way through the crowd into a twenty-by-twenty-five-foot room packed with members of the Art Commission, who were seated around a long table, and approximately one hundred protesting citizens who were forced by the size of the room to stand. I was jostled into a vacant seat at the table, and this led some of the protesters to conclude that I was a member of the commission and an equally abominable estab-lishment fink. The man into whose lap I almost tumbled looked familiar. He turned out to be Eric Hoffer, the waterfront philosopher, who is a member of the commission. Just as I was about to introduce myself he began to gesture forcefully toward the crowd jammed around the table. "There are too many people here," he growled. He squinted at the lights of the two television cameras in the room and said: "Goddammit, there are too many people here to show off for the cameras. Get those cameras out of here." A tall woman to my left said: "The press is the servant of the people." He waved angrily at the cameras and shouted at the woman: "They want us to play their dummies. They want us to play their dummies." His eyes were almost closed by the lights. The woman's voice turned shrill and she asked why people shouldn't be allowed to see the commission's proceedings. He yelled back: "Shut up, goddamn you. Who th' hell you talkin' to?"

"You shut up yourself," she said. And she asked him for his name.

"My name? My name?" he roared. "I don't have to justify myself to a mob. You are not supposed to come in here with lights in our eyes and give grist to their mills"—he pointed to the lights. "There is a way of doin' this and this is not the way and I'm not going to be part of it."

The chairman was banging for order.

The woman said to Eric Hoffer in a soft but emphatic voice: "Well, you can leave."

Other voices joined in: "That's right. If you don't want to be here, you don't have to."

And Hoffer said, to no one in particular, "Come on, let's get th' hell out of here." He stood up, smashed his longshoreman's cap down on his head, and made his way around the table, muttering to himself something about "playing this game." There was scattered applause. A woman said: "He hates people who disagree with him. If everybody had just kept still, he wouldn't have left." But a more kindly observer said: "No, he really believes the cameras make a circus out of something like this. Don't judge him harshly."

The issue was the Neighborhood Arts Program, a four-year-old effort to promote music, theater, dance, poetry, and film events in the neighborhoods of San Francisco. Until 1966 San Francisco, like other American cities, had been subsidizing art as usual: the support of downtown theaters, opera companies, and museums, which essentially served a narrow middle and upper class of enthusiasts. The Neighborhood Arts Program, proposed by university and community people to quicken interest in the arts among lower-income groups, minorities, and the poor, has been promoting activities in and by the communities where those people lived. NAP secured funds from the Art Commission, the board of supervisors, and some private foundations. But conflicts developed. The supervisors dropped their support in 1969 when they feared NAP was becoming too political. Disputes broke out over salaries, budgets, and programming between the NAP staff, headed by an iron-willed organizer named June Dunn, and the Art Commission staff, directed by Martin Snipper, a shrewd bureaucrat. The chairman of the Art Commission is Harold Zellerbach, member of an old San Francisco family, one of the three or four most powerful men in the city, and a patron of the arts. To the NAP staff he has become the Enemy, although he has supported their program and even contributed substantially to it from his own funds when the supervisors abandoned it. Privately the NAP people will tell you he is a decent, pleasant man but publicly they accuse him of trying to use the program to build support for a bond issue to build a new symphony hall and culture complex downtown. They want art facilities throughout the neighborhoods instead. The issues have escalated into swollen and impassioned rhetoric so contagious in America today. "The real question," said NAP in an attack on Zellerbach, "is, can a program responsive to the people be dismantled at the will of one very rich and very old man?" "Nonsense," one member of the commission told me, "the issue is whether the present staff is competent to run the program. Mrs. Dunn is trying to make her personal fortunes tantamount to the survival of NAP." In June the Art Commission voted to fire Mrs. Dunn and her staff. The issue is far deeper. It is a messy and confusing affair with as many layers as an artichoke, but essentially it is the same issue being joined throughout the country: how far and how fast will the establishment go to share power with people who demand recognition regardless of wealth or status?

Which brings us back to the meeting from which Eric Hoffer has so abruptly departed. Mrs. Dunn has brought her supporters from the neighborhoods to protest the commission's decision of June.

Already the establishment has committed one serious mistake; it scheduled the public meeting in a room it must have known would be too small for the crowd that would come. This gives the protesters a ready issue. "You're just trying to keep as many of us out as you can," one angry woman said to a commission member as she put her finger right in his face. "We are a very poor commission," he said. "This is the biggest room available to us." But he knew he was on weak ground.

No one can hear the chairman because of the Gorilla Band and the overflow of people outside. They are not being disruptive, merely annoying, since they have no idea of what is going on inside, and the room is so crammed that absolute order is difficult. The chairman tries several times to say that the commission intends to hold a public hearing on the future of NAP, but a young man at the door keeps interrupting him with shouts of "WE CAN'T HEAR." When he has yelled it the fifth time, in his own mind repaying the commission for the crowded conditions in the room, the chairman shrugs his shoulder, looks helplessly at the crowd, and asks: "Can't we do this like America?" A young black man replies: "Who're you to say what America is like, man?"

"If you can't hear us," the chairman says to the people in the rear, "it's not our fault because this is the biggest room available to us." A woman says: "I'm sure if you will call the mayor he will let you borrow one of his rooms. You can use the board of supervisors' room."

The chairman (Mr. Zellerbach is ill) tries to read a resolution which

the commission will act upon, but the young man from the door continues to interrupt him: "WE CAN'T HEAR. WE CAN'T HEAR." This time
someone near the table shouts at him to cool down and the rest of the
crowd signals its support of the suggestion. "This is an important issue
and people are concerned," one man says to the chairman. "Can't we
move to another room where everyone can hear? Half the people who
have come are out there and can't understand what's going on. Can't we
be democratic?" Some of the people begin to chant, "Serve the people,
move the meeting." The chairman tries to explain that the commission
will call a public meeting in a few days in larger quarters. "What happens to NAP in the meantime?" he is asked. When he says that it will
continue under the direction of Martin Snipper, he is greeted with boos
and catcalls. "No establishment cat's gonna tell us what to do," a black
man says. And several people take up the cry: "Why wait? Why wait?"
And the chairman, growing more exasperated, answers: "Because all the
interested people are not here right now."

June Dunn speaks. She is tall with very black hair, and she is tough.
She reminds me of Anne Wexler in Hartford. I would not want her as
an adversary. "There *is* no staff," she insists. "The staff went out of business
on Friday because of your action. Why are you afraid of letting people
discuss this in a sane environment? They have come down here to listen
to you and to have you listen to them. They can't hear. They truly can't
hear." And the chairman says to her, "Well, if they can't hear, we can't
have that kind of meeting. How can we have that kind of meeting if
they can't hear." June Dunn, flabbergasted, says: "But they can't hear
because you have called this meeting in a room that is too small." It is
a self-defeating cycle. A young man shouts: "Let's move out to the
street and hold this meeting on the sidewalk. Let's have it outside in the
spirit of creation."

The chairman says, "This is just a regularly scheduled meeting. . . ."

"But it's a public meeting, and you knew there would be a lot of
interest." June Dunn is speaking. "And this room is too small. We're asking
you for a favor—move to . . ."

"No, no, no," someone in the audience shouts. "It's not a favor. It's a
right. It's a right."

"You should be willing to speak to them," June Dunn continues. "Why
aren't you willing to speak to people who are willing to come to talk
to you?" She has the advantage on this issue and she is pressing it.

"I'll tell you what it is"—her voice is not loud, but it is direct and pointed to the man who is not there, Harold Zellerbach—"you knew damn well that if we began to get other money in there, as we were going to do, whether from other foundations or the government, the Neighborhood Arts Program would go out of the control of Mr. Zellerbach. You knew that. [The audience has become quiet. The Gorilla Band is silent.] You are a cipher commission and you have always been. This commission is owned by Harold Zellerbach."

An older man on the commission rises to his feet. His hands are clenched and his knuckles pressed against the table. He is no more than three feet from Mrs. Dunn. "Wait," he cries, but something catches in his throat and his voice is muffled. "You're wrong . . ."

". . . and it shouldn't be," she continues. "No public agency should be owned by one man."

Now the elderly gentleman has recovered his voice and from across the table he says slowly, each consonant falling on the crowd like a gauntlet: "P-l-e-a-s-e s-h-u-t y-o-u-r g-o-d-d-a-m-n m-o-u-t-h." I doubt that he has ever said that to a woman before and June Dunn looks as if she has never had it said to her. Her head snaps as if she had been slapped. I think they are both surprised. Is this art or is this politics? Or have the two become inseparable?

There is a bellow of anger from the crowd. Now everyone is shouting. Finally a man's voice rises above the din: "I think you ought to apologize to the lady. You're a representative of the people. Apologize to that lady. Apologize. Right now." The commands are spat out. The old man is still standing but he is shaking. Something to which he has given years of his life has been assailed by the people whom he thought he had been serving, and he has struck back wildly, blindly, in fury. He seems shocked at what he has said and by the belligerence of the response. He is silent as he sits down. He is still shaking.

Someone says sarcastically: "Our city in action. This is our city in action." And the old man who is shaking looks up and replies: "Yes, this *is* our city in action. You're our city, too. You're part of it. Is this any way to conduct business?"

"Swearing the way you were is not a very pretty picture."

His voice is very soft. He drops his eyes to his fists, which are tightly clenched. "I know."

Almost two minutes pass without anyone saying anything to anyone else. It is uncanny. No one seems to approve of what has just occurred and no one seems able to take command of the situation. "It was almost like the country today," Butterworth said later. "Everybody spitting at each other and ashamed of it all the time and wishing they were talking instead of spitting and not knowing how to stop the one and how to start the other."

Finally a Mexican-American member of the commission, a woman, says: "I think we should allow them the courtesy to speak." Back from the audience comes the high-pitched voice of a man, also Mexican: "We do not need the courtesy to speak. We have the *right* to speak. It is not something you can give us."

The impasse is broken and a woman says: "Look, what's happened is that you have no confidence in the program and the people in the communities of this city have no confidence in the Art Commission. You can't evaluate the Neighborhood Arts Program without involving people from the neighborhoods or you won't have a constituency. You'll have plans and blueprints and you'll even have money but you won't have a constituency. People don't want you to do things to them any more or for them. They want to do these things for themselves. Don't you understand that's what we're trying to say to you today?"

The Mexican-American member of the commission asks: "Why don't you just send a field representative to meet with us?" and is greeted by a chorus of noes. "We've had enough of that kind of representation," a man says. "The people must represent themselves."

At this point the fire marshal comes in, a smiling red-faced man with white hair, and says that most of the people will have to leave. No one does. He turns in a half circle, his hands upraised, and says: "Please, please, will you move out?" No one moves. He looks at the chairman of the commission, both men shrug, the marshal says: "I'm not very persuasive," and leaves.

A black man: "There is one thing we can agree on, one positive thought we can come together on, that the neighborhood program has been exciting and wonderful. Everyone here believes in it. We know there is creativity in the neighborhoods of San Francisco. Can we build on that? Let's start out fresh, together, in a new meeting."

Across the room another black responds: "You do not speak for me, brother. You do not speak for me. In my community the Neighborhood Arts Program was not positive. The blacks don't even have anyone sitting at that table." He points to the commission. Now the people in the audience are arguing with themselves while the commission remains silent. Finally another black says: "Wait, wait, we are going to destroy ourselves. We are eating each other and the commission is happy that we are." Still another black asks, "Do you believe these honkies are going to give you any power? Do you think they're going to let black creation build an audience out there in the communities? Never!" And the first black answers: "We are bickering, we are bickering." "You are right, brother, we are, but we are bickering about important things. The money is going to the staff of the program and not to the people. That is worth bickering about." But someone says: "You guys go outside and fight if you want. Our argument is with the commissioners. Our fight is to keep this program alive. Other things later."

A young woman with long straight hair speaks. "Mr. Chairman, I came here today representing the Haight-Ashbury children's center. I don't feel I have a chance to say anything in this room. I think you should postpone this meeting and do nothing about the Neighborhood Arts Program until you can set a public meeting and have the whole thing discussed. In the meantime, continue the present staff. Keep it going until the public meetings."

"Right on. Right on," the crowd responds.

"Yes," someone said, "let's have a spirit of reconciliation."

The tide is turning. Several members of the commission look as if a temporary truce is exactly what they want, too. I am sure they also know it will take a long time to leave there if they vote against the crowd. There is some haggling over the wording of a resolution which calls for the staff that had been fired to continue another month until a public hearing is held. This is what June Dunn and her supporters have come for and they appear pleased.

The vote is four to four. If Eric Hoffer had stayed, he could have carried the day. Now the chairman must decide the issue. He fiddles with a piece of paper in his hand and says quickly: "The chair votes yes." The motion passes 5-4.

As I watched people leave, a gray-haired lady in her sixties walked out, one who had been shouting "Right on!" during the meeting. I heard her say to several young people: "I would love to stand up and act with some dignity at a meeting like this but I guess you have to be a bitch to get anything done these days."

★ ★ ★

Loni Ding Welch smiled as she left the hearing. "I should have warned you that we would be meeting at the barricades," she said.

"I expect anything in California."

She laughed and said: "Expect it. Just don't believe it."

She is a spirited woman of thirty-nine who gestures with both hands as she talks. I have sought her out because she is in close touch with the currents running among Chinese youth in San Francisco. These forces are violating centuries-old traditions in the Chinese community and assaulting those stereotypes into which white Americans long ago molded Chinatown.

In 1960 the California Department of Corrections ordered a study "to find out why young Chinese-Americans stay out of trouble with the law." In the next five years the number of juvenile arrests per thousand juveniles in Chinatown increased more than 300 percent. Between 1964 and 1969 arrests and citations of Chinese youth rose 600 percent. Last year a committee of concerned Chinese in San Francisco identified eleven youthful "gangs" operating in Chinatown. According to one Chinese leader, "Although the number is small one of the dangers to the community is the rise of conflicts of interest between the 'gangs.' This can lead to overt acts and open 'warfare.' Certain of the tongs (gangs) are known to be seeking recruits from these rivaling groups. Threats are being heard of 'reprisals' for such 'raiding' of members." Many of the gangs have been started among recently arrived refugees from Hong Kong who do not speak English. They exist in isolated and bitter hostility among the American-born Chinese. One report showed that arrests of immigrant Chinese outnumber arrests of natives by two to one.

But statistics of rising juvenile delinquency only hint at deeper issues. Conditions in Chinatown are awful. More than thirty thousand people crowd into a twenty-block area with a housing density five times greater than that of the rest of the city. Three out of four dwellings are substandard and six out of every ten do not have separate bathrooms. In many of them heating and lighting are worse than poor, and the tuberculosis rate in Chinatown is almost four times the city's. Few jobs in Chinatown pay minimum wages. Women work with their young children beside them in the shops. Land costs up to $150 a square foot. Recreation opportunities are almost nonexistent. Discrimination is rampant.*

* For many of these insights and facts I am indebted, among others, to Paul Jacobs, an informative dinner host, whose new book, *To Serve the Devil*, contains the best concise account I have read of the lot of the Chinese in America; to Judge Harry Low; to the San Francisco Delinquency Prevention Commission; the San Francisco Chinese Community Citizens' Survey and Fact-Finding Committee; to the officers and men of the juvenile bureau of the San Francisco Police; and to two nights spent in a Chinatown tourists never see.

In the face of these pressures Chinatown is changing. A deep chasm is growing between many children and their parents. The young Chinese born in America rebels against the deference his parents have accorded the white tourists who come through the streets gawking and pointing their Kodaks. "My parents took their money but they hated their guts," one young man told me. Newly arrived youths from Hong Kong, speaking little English, unable to find jobs, rejected by whites and native-born Chinese alike, turn to the streets to scrounge for a living. And in the back streets and basements of Chinatown can be found a new rancor, nourished by the resentments of a generation that determines it will not be "the white man's yellow man."

Loni Ding Welch knows all this. She and one brother were the only two of seven children to make it "beyond the narrowest Chinese culture," and she feels loyal to both her Chinese past and her American commitments. She is married to an author, has taught social science and history at the University of California, is the mother of an eleven-month-old baby, and moves in many causes, including the Neighborhood Arts Program.

"My parents came to this country with the conscious intention of making a chance for the children to grow up in a Western democracy. They thought China was corrupt and backward. My father didn't think of America as the promised land. It was just a place where his daughters would have a chance to become real persons. He gave the matchmaker in China very specific instructions for the wife he wanted to bring to this country: she had to be a liberated, Western-trained Chinese lady. She also had to be young and beautiful. That's how he found my mother.

"They moved out of Chinatown because they felt that it represented the backwardness of China itself. They wanted their children raised in a white society—well, not white, but a Western society. I was about three. At that time there were restrictive covenants and it was hard to move out of Chinatown. The only reason we found a place is because it was condemned and no white family would live there. We were the only Chinese family living there. My mother once lifted up the rug in the living room and showed me a patchwork of flattened metal she had used to cover holes in the floorboards. I always admired the woodwork and thought it was glamorous and glorious because it was a red rich mahogany, but it was in fact rotted wood which had been painted over with I don't know how many layers of red lacquer and she would lean on it and show me how it would crumble.

"It was very clear to me in all sorts of little ways that our life as Chinese in this society was very precarious. You watched your behavior because you didn't want people to think badly of Chinese. We lived in a house with a month-to-month lease and we tried hard not to do anything that would jeopardize it. We lived above the whites and I used to listen to this music coming up through the floorboards of my bedroom—loud, loud music, and drunks would end up in our doorway, vomiting on our steps. And yet my mother had me very carefully dressed at certain times of the year, like Christmas, Easter, Thanksgiving, and would have me deliver a cake to the people downstairs. We were that nice Chinese family that lived upstairs, so don't make any trouble for them, you know what I mean? I said to myself, Why are we doing these things? We were better than the whites. We were more refined, we were more self-restrained, we could take insults with dignity. I felt singled out for my Chineseness, and I would get that Ching-Chong-Chinese thing, you know, like burning with anger when white schoolgirls would catch me if I came home and form a little ring around me while they sang this insulting ditty to me and knowing that my parents had forbidden me to get mad at them, and forbidden me to say anything to them, and I was seething with anger, you know, and feeling that I had to endure it with grace.

"I think that is one reason I never thought of being an American. Right up until the time I went to college I kind of assumed that I would go back to China. I thought there was no place for me in this society. Then in 1958 when I was a graduate student I went to Hong Kong for the summer. I worked a lot with the Chinese refugees, talking to them, revising and improving my Chinese, and I began to see that they did not think of me as just a Chinese, they thought of me as an *American* Chinese. I realized that I am definitely Western. I belong in two cultures. And when I got back from Hong Kong I headed for Chinatown, and the smells of the food and the old men and the street life, the variety of people, they were all tremendously exciting. My mother had never permitted me to go down to Chinatown when I was growing up except for language school, and I was cut off from it for most of my life and I was never really received into white society. I was glad to find that finally I belonged in both worlds. Hong Kong showed me that. That's why in Chinatown you'll find so many college students coming back searching for their roots. I mean Chinese-Americans who have gone to San Jose, San Mateo, Berkeley. They make it back whenever they can. Even though they don't speak Chinese—their parents made them learn English as mine did

—they're looking for something they know is there. A part of them is there, a certain vital part of them. You come to terms with life there. Everything is magnified in crowded conditions like that, the good and the bad alike. On the other side of those thin walls are neighbors, and you learn to react with them. You learn what people expect of you, and how to make all those little accommodations that make life possible and very real, too. Like the common pot from which a family eats meals. My parents wouldn't eat from it; they thought it was unhygienic—and not Western; and I grew up feeling better than the kids in Chinatown because my parents understood about nutrition and hygiene and all that. I know now there's something important about that common pot. A kid knows when he's eaten more than his share. He knows who the pig in the family is, and it may be him. He learns to ask if he is leaving enough for other people. Other people become very very real to you in Chinatown.

"There are some powerful emotions working now on the young people down there. Each group of young people has its own perceptions. Their feelings really depend on what generation the parents are—first or second or whether they were born in China. I know one sixteen-year-old boy whose father and mother run a curio shop and speak only village Cantonese. The only English they speak is that pidgin stuff they have learned for the tourists. This boy is very Chinatown. But he's also very hip, and his talk is all full of the black-teenage-youth-type talk. He 'digs' this and he 'digs' that. He speaks in fragments, not sentences. He has immense hostilities toward his parents but he also has a filial piety toward them; he's got to look up to them and protect them because he knows they are very vulnerable in this society because they can't speak English. They're going to lose their curio shop because the rent's going up. He's already having to worry about supporting them, although he is just an artist. That's his only skill. He does great drawings. I asked him once to do a paper movie on any subject he wanted to. He drew about tourists in Chinatown. It's so bitter—a savage denunciation of tourism and whites and their attitudes toward his parents in that curio shop. The board of supervisors would call it political art. Everything this kid's ever done he signs with fake names. He said his parents would run him out of the house if he signed his name. They're afraid of antagonizing the big families that make up the establishment in Chinatown and keep it the way it is because it's profitable. You see, that boy's parents believe the establishment will send the goons out to take care of you; they still live in fear of their own Chinese authorities—maybe they'll come in the middle of the night and get their boy or them. He shares this fear. He's got to find a way to get out at just the right time.

"Kids with first-generation parents like that know how fragile the life of their parents is. But kids with second-generation parents who speak good English are not as obligated. The parents can make telephone calls, catch a streetcar, move around a bit. In these families you find the same kind of battle going on as happens between any kid and his parents, over dress, freedom, staying out late at night, how you're doing in school, where you're going in life—things like that. But, while they are not as obligated to take care of their parents, these are the kids that worry me. They've been casualties of the melting-pot myth, see? They were expected to be Americanized—isn't that the myth?—but they haven't been. They know there's a lot of misery in this community, physical misery. They know it's going to be hard to find a job. They long to get out, they long for freedom, they long for the feeling of physical liberation, of being able to live at arm's length from everybody else. They're dying to have the same things everybody else has got—hotrod cars, bikes, making it with the girls. But where do you maneuver in Chinatown? There's no room. There's no public place, practically, for kids to meet, no coffee-shops, no hangouts. And most hangouts are for boys, like pool halls. They have no place to meet the girls and I think they're underdeveloped in the whole area of girl-boy relations. And what are they going to do about work? They don't want to run a curio shop and they don't want to grow up to operate a laundromat. They want a more manly image, right? They look at the men in the community—none of them are racing-car drivers, professional football players. They're insurance men, making a profession out of being Chinese, hired by the insurance companies to sell insurance to other Chinese. The kids regard that as a kind of humilia-tion. It doesn't represent the degree of freedom they want. There's no model for them to follow in the wake.

"I think this is one reason why some of them are putting pictures of Mao and Ho Chi Minh on their walls. These two are manly to them. After all, they've transformed a whole society, they talk like the fathers of nations, they're full of wise things about how to conduct your life, and they know how to use guns. They're patriarchs, and these kids have fathers who sell insurance for the white man, run curio shops, do laundry, cook, and wash dishes; Mao looks good to them. They have in common with young blacks the need for a strong model. This is why they have strong feelings about their ancestors who came over here to build the railroads. Yes, they were just common laborers to the whites; yes, they were victimized. But they were men. They knew who they were. They crossed the deserts, climbed the mountains, and carried the dynamite. And by God they built the railroads. They were poor but they left something behind them. They were tough.

"There's a group of kids like this, a small bunch, that has managed to find a vacant basement and open a center. They're big on this 'Asian Unity' thing and have a lot of Chinese music and literature. It's the ethnic thing all over again, the fight to say, 'Hey, look at us.' It's pride. They've organized a food program to deliver food to three hundred families. It's very hard work. They pick up and load the food at the warehouses, they do the delivery, they keep the books. There's a big sign down there that says: TO SERVE THE PEOPLE. And there's a picture of Mao on the wall. They're trying to prove themselves and they're trying to work out their vengeance.

"Then there are the Hong Kong kids. They're new. They're pretty sanguine about themselves as a group, despite the miserable discrimination they suffer. They're very aggressive. They are also very lost. The first group—the kids born here—doesn't know where it came from. The second group—who were born in China—doesn't know where it's going. They have the standard American dreams but no way to realize them. I have been very lucky. I'm at home with people I love. Everything in my life is a gift: my husband, my baby, my friends. I have structured my life so that I can walk away from what offends me. Those kids in those twenty blocks down there can't do that. Few of them figure they will ever break out of Chinatown. So in their mind they've got nothing to lose. When you're young and poor and vengeful and a victim and you have nothing to lose, who knows what you'll do?"

★ ★ ★

Some young people who have fled to California are beginning to question the extremes to which their renunciation of traditional values and concepts has carried them. Some even reluctantly admit that not every father is a fool. I do not want to exaggerate the point or even to call it a trend, nor do I want to suggest that these young people doubt the doubts they have held of American society. They are not repentant prodigals returning home to resume life as if nothing had ever happened, but some are beginning to search for more effective means of reforming the country.

Among them is Chris Kennan, the son of one of the country's most distinguished ambassadors, George F. Kennan, who is now a professor at the Institute for Advanced Study in Princeton, N.J. In January, 1968, Ambassador Kennan wrote for the *New York Times Magazine* a brilliant challenge to the radical left. He disliked their militancy, their certitude, and their drugs.* Not long after it was published his son Christopher became a radical.

We met through Butterworth, whose own father, himself a distinguished retired diplomat, now lives near the Kennans in Princeton. Chris Kennan stands at least six feet one inch; a slender, graceful youth with fair features and soft blue eyes. This summer he is working on a construction gang in the Bay area.

"I got really involved," he said. "It was largely emotional. I could have said where I stood but I would have had a hard time talking about why I was there. It started with the draft. When I got to college Joan Baez and David Harris came down to talk about the Resistance and they really shook me up. I came very close to turning in my draft card. From then on it was a progression of things and events. Reagan [Governor Ronald] came to the campus, and Max Rafferty. I was shaken just by seeing them. Having come from a school [Groton] where nothing ever happens of any serious social import, I was swept up in the emotion of the scene out here.

"I think a lot of it had to do with drugs. As far as I am concerned, they allowed me to feel emotions more deeply and not to worry about my actions in rational terms. When you're using certain drugs you don't

* Some samples: "I have seen more harm done in this world by those who have tried to storm the bastions of society in the name of utopian beliefs . . . than by all the humble efforts of those who have tried to create a little order and civility and affection within their own intimate entourage, even at the cost of tolerating a great deal of evil in the public domain. . . . It lies within the power as well as the duty of all of us to recognize not only the possibility that we might be wrong but the virtual certainty that on some occasions we are bound to be. . . . There is no pose more fraudulent . . . than that of the individual who pretends to have been exalted, and rendered more impressive, by his communion with some sort of inner voice whose revelations he is unable to describe or to enact . . . and particularly when the means he has chosen to render himself susceptible to this alleged revelation is the deliberate disorientation of his own psychic system."

have to think about what you're doing, you just do it. I would feel that the draft was wrong and that I should go out and burn my draft card just because it was wrong . . . without even caring what the consequences were or knowing if that was the best way to express my rage. If you feel it, do it—and think about it later if you think about it at all."

I mentioned a recent speech by the former chancellor of the University of California at Los Angeles, Franklin Murphy, in which he said, in essence, that many young people embrace the idea "I feel, therefore I am," to the exclusion of man's need to *think* and to *work* if he is to be whole.

"That's really it," Chris Kennan said. "I think that is a beautiful way to describe my own problem when I was so deeply involved in protest and drugs."

Past tense?

"Yes, I have begun to have some real doubts about what I was doing. I reached the apex of my activism during the People's Park thing at Berkeley. I was on the picket lines and I felt at the time that what we were doing was good, but I didn't understand really what was happening. I just felt it was right. It was like a party. There were tumultuous campus-wide meetings. We'd sit and talk all night about what we were going to do. It was very exciting, real togetherness—the only time I know of when the Santa Cruz campus was really united. It was a marvelous feeling. I think about it still because it was such a good feeling. But it was a feeling operating independently of reason. Until then the university was something other people controlled, you didn't. Now you were piping and the university was dancing. But I became skeptical of it partly because it was such a good time. It was more a power trip than a clear political statement. The issues were really confused.

"I still believe in the university tradition, see? If the draft thing weren't present, then you could really tell: students would either be in college for keeps or they wouldn't. I happen to think that the universities need the kids more today than ever before. Up until recently it's been the kids who needed the university. The universities will have to increase their recruiting of students just to get the tuition revenues to pay the staggering costs. But I'm not prepared to believe we are ready to function as a society without strong universities. I began to realize this last year when we were marching on that picket line. The universities around here ceased to function as universities. They just ground to a halt.

"I don't want to say that feelings are unimportant. They're very real to me. I think the feelings of activist students need to be felt. On some issues I think if you don't react emotionally it's almost immoral. The Kent State thing, for one. It really shocked me. I was out of school last spring and working back in New York. For a week after that I could hardly work at all. I walked the streets watching and listening. I was dressed in relatively conservative clothes for work. A demonstration was going on and an old man came up to me and asked which side I was on. It was a tough question because I can't identify any more with the things that are being done by the radicals and at the same time I know that some of the things they are trying to do need to be done, and some of the things the government is doing ought not to be done."

Did your conversations with your father influence your outlook on the student movement?

"Yes, they always have. There was a period when I didn't listen. I couldn't even understand what he was saying. He finds it hard to believe he's living in the age he's living in. He doesn't like it. But that's not unique to George Kennan or even to people his age. I have a young friend who is afraid of the year 2000. He wishes he was living a hundred years ago. He's my age. He hates airports and banks, the most modern institutions you deal with, because they're impersonal, computerized.

"I think my father and I reacted to each other this last spring in a way we never have. This spring was the first time in a long time I was home. He saw me reacting to these things. We had to talk about them. He had to understand that the bitterest day of my life was the day after Kent State. I rode in on that train from Princeton to New York with all the commuters. I watched them read about the shootings. Half of them paid no attention to it and half of them were saying, 'Well, it's too bad but that's what happens when kids throw rocks.' I was almost in tears. I think I felt more revolutionary at that moment than I have at any other time in my life.

"I began to think a lot about politics then. I know I have to be doing something about what's happening in the country and to the country. I hate to see this country ripped up. When I was deep in the movement we looked on the territory between the two coasts as hostile land. We'd drive through it fearful of stopping. The South we avoided like the plague. I don't think many people have realized what that last scene in *Easy Rider* says to the kids about the South. But that's wrong to have the country roped off into one big square of hostile territory and two tiny corridors along the coasts. I'd like to help change things like that. Part

213

of my disillusionment with student activism came because I felt power-less about it. That's curious, because the whole thrust of the movement is to feel powerful. But I felt like a nobody. I knew I couldn't affect the student activism any more than I could affect the establishment."

What about drugs?

"I was convinced they had the answers. I realized all the little gods I used to follow didn't have the answer. Drugs promised an answer, or at least they enabled you to live without one. But I ran into the fellow at Santa Cruz who became my roommate, who had been on drugs and come through the scene, and he kept telling me that reality is where it's at, not drugs. He felt the world is a beautiful place and it takes more than drugs to be able to see its beauty. If you're going to stand up and make it, you really have to appreciate the beauty of things when you're not stoned. If you can't make sense of reality on your own, without drugs, I think you'll go out of your mind.

"So I'm not interested in going back to drugs now; I'm enjoying life the way I am. To go back into drugs would be . . . well, it would be going back into a totally permanent emotional state of mind. It would be a total rejection of America, which I don't want to make. A lot of kids have said to me that I'm really playing it straight and I guess I am."

He laughed. "There was a time when I played it every way but straight. Last year I was completely devoted to the counter culture. I abandoned everything conventional. I had only one pair of blue jeans and wore them around all the time. I ate only health foods, and I believed those of us who ate health foods were infinitely better than those who didn't. You couldn't eat meat. You couldn't even eat a cupcake without feeling guilty. If you ate a candy bar you were really a bad boy. I thought that I wanted to go and live in the woods. I was really with it. At least I thought I was.

"I'll say this about drugs. They really separate fathers from sons. This bothered me. Drugs are hard to understand if you haven't used them. My father has asked, 'What is it about drugs that you can't explain to me. How can you go on a trip and not be able to tell me what happened?' Well, it's hard to imagine something you have never experienced. You haven't necessarily done all the things you can relate to, like traveling to Tibet or riding a motorcycle—but you can kind of understand what those experiences are like. But with drugs . . . you can't send a picture postcard from a drug experience saying, 'Wish you were here.' "

I asked, What does America mean to you just now? He thought several minutes, then said: "The country was beginning to mean less and less. What mattered was culture. For a while I just didn't think I was a part of the country. I still don't know where I fit in. With drugs you can extend things in your mind further than they actually go, and I had picked up a lot of hostility toward the country for that reason, especially toward official violence—violence done in the name of authority. Then I realized that I ought to try to do something about it instead of escaping from it." He paused again and shook his head. "But I don't really know how to answer your question," he said.

That night he called me at the hotel and asked if we could talk the next morning. We met over coffee. He said: "I've been thinking about that question, the one about America. I still can't answer it but I know why I can't. America to me is all the things that have happened to me, good and bad, for better or for worse. I can never sum up what all those things are, and that's why I couldn't answer your question. If I could tell you who I am, maybe I could tell you what America is. I'll know someday. Then ask me."

★ ★ ★

A letter from Chris Kennan awaited my return to New York. It contained an article addressed to radicals in *Rolling Stone*, a rock 'n' roll biweekly, written by the former music critic of the San Francisco *Chronicle*, Ralph J. Gleason. It said, in part:

> The whole "Don't think, feel" ideology really equals "Don't look, shoot!" It is stupid. Read, study and above all think, and if to think is to be linear, then damn McLuhan, for thinking is the only reliable weapon we have. Power doesn't come out of the barrel of a gun, what comes out is the ability of any fool with a firearm to kill you. A building burned down is a building you can't live in, love in or learn in. Thought out right, it may be possible to take it over some day and use it, and buildings are part of the planet's resources we must not waste, either. There's a bad moon rising, true enough, and doesn't look like much but bad times ahead. But the slogans and the hate messages do not help. They hinder.

Chris Kennan wrote: "There appears to be a split developing between out-and-out Weathermen type radicals, and those who believe that nonviolence has got to remain a prime factor in 'the struggle.' I feel that it is important that I let the 'Establishment' know that I waste no affection on them, that I let them know exactly what I think of them. However, I

think it equally important that those in the 'Movement' don't feel intimidated from criticizing what their fellow radicals are doing. Nothing
will defeat the 'Movement' faster than its own stupid mistakes and its
unwillingness to admit them."

★ ★ ★

The man who drove me to the airport was black. Like many Californians
he came from somewhere else. Where he came from has never let go of
him.

I'm not certain how the conversation began. We were talking, I think,
about Hurricane Celia, which had struck Corpus Christi, Texas, and I
mentioned that I was heading in that direction in a few days. He had been
in Corpus for five years in the Coast Guard, he said, and he liked it. He
said Corpus was a good place to be if you had been black in Mobile, his
home town. "They don't think much about your blackness in Corpus
Christi," he said. "That's all they thought about in Mobile."

There was a long silence as I concentrated on how I might find my
friend's missing daughter in Los Angeles. The driver started talking
again:

"Sometimes I wake up at night, sweatin', my fist clenched, my head
hurtin', thinkin' I'm back on that boat in Gulfport." He had been transferred
from Corpus to Gulfport for duty aboard a Coast Guard cutter. "It was
'45 and I was a young steward and there was a warrant officer who would
come down every morning at five-thirty and wake me up and say, 'Boy,
get me a cup of coffee.' I'd get up and start to fix him a cup of coffee by
heatin' the water on a pan on the stove, and he'd say, 'Boy, you know I
like my coffee in an urn.' And I'd say, 'But, sir, you know I have to fix
five gallons if I do that and the captain has given me instructions not to
serve the crew coffee that's over two hours old and the cooks will have
to throw all that coffee out when they serve breakfast to the crew at eight.'
He said, 'Boy, that's your problem. I want my coffee and I want it out
of that urn.' I fixed it every morning that way and the cooks would
complain and give me hell about throwin' out all that coffee, so after a
few weeks I went to the captain and told him what was happenin' and
he said, 'Well, Forrest, if that's the way he wants his coffee, you'll just
have to serve him that way.' This warrant officer hated niggers and he
kept harassin' until I decided to get off that ship by hook or crook.

"Now I have a stomach condition that is agitated by milk—if I drink
a glass of milk I'll get real nauseated—so I started drinkin' milk, two

quarts a day, and I got sick as a dog. We got back to port and I got permission to get to the doctor in Gulfport and I put on my white uniform because everything else was dirty and I was walkin' and weavin' my way to the doctor and this policeman sees me and say, 'Hey, boy, we don't allow no niggers to wear white uniforms 'round here; get back on that ship.' I told him that I was sick and he said they have just the place for sick niggers and started to arrest me when I got real sick right there on the streets of Gulfport and he saw I better get to the doctor. The other patients were white and the doctor made me wait until he finished with them. He said, 'Boy, you've got to go to the hospital,' and he gave me a slip signed by the doctor and I went back to the ship and started packin' and this warrant officer came in and said, 'Where you goin', boy?' I handed him the slip and told him I was catchin' the five o'clock train and he said, 'The hell you are, boy. I got my family comin' 'board for supper and I want you to serve.' I told him that I would die before supper was over and he said, 'You're goddamn right you'll die because I'm goin' to kill you myself if you try to leave this ship.' I was so sick I didn't care which way I died, so I didn't say anything, I just closed my bag and walked past him and off that ship, expectin' him to put a bullet in the back of my head. All I heard was him cursin' 'bout bastard niggers. I made it to the station. That's all I remember. The next mornin' I woke up in the hospital. I was almost dead, they said, but I got off that ship and I'm not ever goin' back to Gulfport, Mississippi.

"Not very long ago I saw the captain of that ship. He's livin' out here, too. All these years. He said, 'Forrest, I'm sorry about all those things that happened then.' I said, 'It's too late for apologies, Captain. You had your chance then and you blew it. It's too late to apologize now.'"

He was a mild-mannered man, the father of three girls who he swears will not "be bitter" if he can help it. We were strangers—he never told me his first name—and I don't know why he opened up the way he did as we drove to the airport.

Los Angeles

RUNAWAYS ARE HARDEST TO FIND IN THE PEOPLE SUMPS OF SUBURBS LIKE LOS Angeles and Long Island, and my effort to locate the missing daughter of my Texas friend was unsuccessful. In Greenwich Village and Berkeley —even in Washington, D.C., with its Du Pont Circle—there are starting points, places to which a youth in flight usually gravitates when he first hits town. It is sometimes possible to pick up his trail from members of the small permanent colony that will give him advice about where to go when he moves on. A city has a beginning and an end; suburbs go on forever. There are a hundred centers in the suburbs and no core. If you are lost there, you are lost.

I had said goodbye to Butterworth—he was on his way to Africa to advise the government of Ghana on setting up a national service corps of volunteers. I have a friend in Los Angeles who knows Groucho Marx quite well, and she suggested that we drop by to see him. I think I have seen every movie the Marx brothers made and this would be my first opportunity to meet Groucho in person. We went to Beverly Hills.

The mustache and hair, what is left of it, are mostly white. The voice has not changed. If Gabriel's trumpet fails on Judgment Day, I told him, you can stand on the steps and call and half the world will know who it is and come. "Yes," he answered, "but I'll be calling from the other direction." He was peppery but frail. There was no cigar and he did not drink. "That's all behind me now. I don't even go to these new movies or plays. Why should I go see people do on stage what I can't do at home? Everybody tells me I should read this new book that tells you everything you want to know about sex. I can't do anything with what I know now. If I'd read that book thirty-five years ago I wouldn't have had three divorces."

He asked me why I had enjoyed his movies and I said I did not know, maybe it was because they were funny. He growled and said, "Don't be serious." I said I was trying to be funny. He said, "That's why you sound serious."

He had run into Rowan or Martin, he said. "It was one of them. I can never remember which one has diabetes and that's the only way I can distinguish between them. He bet me he knew more lines from Marx pictures than I did. I bet. He won. These new comedians have studied those pictures. They would be fools not to.

"I have been amazed," he continued, "at how many kids are watching our movies, not only here but all over the world. I don't really know why except that our movies are slightly anarchistic. I think all of us are slightly anarchistic. The Marx movies were more so. We were always fighting the system. We had the authorities up against the wall. People think cops are getting hard times these days; they should look at what we did to cops. There was violence in our movies. I'm sorry if we contributed in any way to the behavior of kids today. I suspect we did, but I didn't think about it at the time. We didn't know enough to think about it. We were having too good a time. But we were hellions in those days. I think we were ahead of our time because we saw people in authority for what they were: inept, fatuous, and vain. Don't get me wrong. I'm very much against the violence and the burning. What they did at Columbia University in breaking into the president's office and seizing the building is abhorrent to me. That's for the movies. That's something the Marx brothers would do and could do because no one really got hurt. The problem with movies today is that there is nothing you can make a movie about that hasn't already happened in life. In our day we laughed at what might happen. Today people laugh at what is happening. There's a difference. Maybe that is why the kids are watching our movies. We tried to be intellectually honest in those films but we weren't malicious. I remember in one movie we had a character named Mrs. Rittenhouse and a cannon ball came through the porthole of her stateroom and I went over and pulled the shade down as if that would stop another cannon ball. She said, 'What are you doing?' and I said, 'I am trying to protect your honor and that's more than you ever did.' The kids love that kind of thing and I think many of them believe that is what they're doing, too."

He had a dinner engagement and it was time to go. He left with his date, a beautiful blonde in her thirties wearing a long black evening dress. Groucho Marx wore a white shirt with peppermint stripes and a black beret and carried a cane.

Later I mentioned to a young writer in La Jolla what Groucho Marx said about the kids and the movies. The young man had a different viewpoint. He is under twenty-five and groovy, as they say. "I like the Marx Brothers," he said, "because they're so absurd. No heavier reason. They're absurd, fun, mindless, unsophisticated, irreverent, playful—all the things I believe in but find it hard to be. I suspect that goes for many. If you accept my thesis that people tend to be weakest at that which they push the hardest, then today's youth who favor Marx Brothers principles are in fact serious, heavy, self-absorbed, and grim. We go to Marx Brothers movies and say, 'Wow. Yeah. That's where it's at. That's how I'd like to be.' And we try. But we can't. So we go see another Marx Brothers movie and try again. But we forget that even Groucho is morose and snide off screen, no better than we are at really being a Marx Brother."

Is nothing sacred?

★ ★ ★

It was an ordinary day in Los Angeles. Smog passed the alert level both days I was there and we were all warned against driving and exercising too much. The superintendent of swimming pools threatened to close the city pools if teenage violence and vandalism did not end. Disneyland announced a new "grooming and attitude" policy to try to keep out the long-haired troublemakers who had seized Tom Sawyer's Island and caused the park to shut down. The newspaper reported that a college student accused of throwing a bottle during a demonstration had been ordered to write an essay, register to vote, work with a political-party program in a deprived area and spend four hours a week riding in a police car for the next ten weeks. The taxi driver who dropped me at the Beverly Hilton for a luncheon date said he had never been in the hotel although he had lived in Los Angeles for ten years; "I'm afraid I'd like it," he said. A former movie actor was running for governor again and supporting a former tap dancer who is defending his Senate seat against the son of an ex-heavyweight champion of the world. It was just an ordinary day in Los Angeles.

Mathis, Texas

BETWEEN SAN ANTONIO AND THE GULF OF MEXICO, IN THE BRUSH COUNTRY OF South Texas, the status quo is cracking. It is being assaulted by forces that will echo from television sets in the next decade as surely as the sounds of student conflict and cries of "Black Power" reverberated in the sixties. The time of the Chicano has come.

I had forgotten what summer is like in South Texas. It is so hot that the caliche streets turn into a fine white powder that swirls berserkly in the wake of the cars. The flat one-story buildings with their corrugated roofs collect dust and heat until they become chalky little ovens from which the Chicanos emerge in the evening to sit on the porch until dark.

This town of five thousand people straddles the intersection of Highway 9 between San Antonio and Corpus Christi and Highway 359, which leads to Laredo and Old Mexico. The cattle baron who founded it was a pioneer from Tennessee, as so many early Texans were, and fought with the Confederates during the Civil War, as some Texans still do. Once the thirty-two-mile lake down the road was a great ranch across which rolled freight wagons carrying ironbound chests loaded with silver and gold from Mexico. Men now fish and pull skiers behind high-powered boats where once they played poker and drank and frolicked with the barmaids after long hours on the mesquite trails from the border.

Forty years ago fewer than a thousand people lived here, descendants of those early ranchers and the first farmers. Then came the war, and the demand for vegetables turned Mathis into the vegetable center of Texas. Thousands of carloads of vegetables went out by rail and by road, and Mathis prospered. But with the vegetables came the Mexicans, cheap help to do the stoop labor, and after the vegetables, cotton. By 1960

223

there were six thousand people in Mathis, more than half of them with Spanish surnames. But cotton, a treacherous ally, betrayed the town to machines. One mechanical picker wiped out the jobs of a whole company of stoop laborers. Now the vegetables are gone, leaving only the cotton and the descendants of illiterate laborers. Two out of every three people in Mathis—or is it four out of five?—are Chicanos. "The problem in this town," one Anglo businessman said, "is there are more'n three thousand Mexican people with nothing to do."

It is a poor town in one of the poorest counties in the nation. I met one Chicano with twelve children who earned $1,800 last year. Some of the men went to Houston, but were lonely and returned to Mathis. "They bought a little plot of land when the farmers sold out, just a shack on a postage stamp, but it's theirs and they'd rather stay than move," an Anglo said. Mathis collects $74,000 in property taxes each year while towns of comparable size in the area receive over $200,000. Last year the town issued $74,000 worth of building permits but no single permit over $2,000. New permanent buildings are not being built.

Of course, there is *some* money in the area. In 1969 the farmers in San Patricio County received $4,580,319 in direct subsidies from the government in cotton and feed payments. Thirty farmers got over $20,000 each, including three whose payments were more than $55,000 each. The Vahlsing Christinia Corporation, a diversified producer of frozen products, with sales of $18,424,535 last year and net income over $1,000,000, received $142,088 in subsidies from the government for its farming operations in the county. One-third of Vahlsing's equity is owned by Occidental Petroleum Company. Yet there are farmers in the area who will tell you that "welfare is ruining the Mexican."

The Chicanos do not like that word. To them "Mexican" is derogatory and "Spanish" is condescending. They accept "Mexican-American" or "Latino" but prefer "Chicano." "I hate that word," said an Anglo woman. " 'Chicano' stands for the same thing as 'poor white trash.' I like the old term, 'Mexican.' "

Perhaps a lexicon is in order:

Chicano. Corresponding to current "Black," "Afro-American."
Latin or *Latino.* Corresponds to current usage of "Negro" or "Black Folks."
Mexican-American. Corresponds to current usage of "Colored."
Mexican (if used by whites). Corresponds to "Nigra" or "Nigger."

Mexican (if used by Chicanos). Someone actually from Mexico, or a Chicano Uncle Tom.

Anglo. Non-Chicano Caucasian.

White (if used by Anglos to describe Anglos). A dirty slur to Chicanos, as it insinuates that Chicanos are not white.

White (if used by Chicanos). Nonblacks.

Gringo (if used by Chicanos). Whitey or The Man.

Gringo (if used by Anglos). Conservative, hard-line racist Anglo.

Mathis had always been run by Anglos. The Chicanos were not a factor in government except to be appeased with an occasional office proffered always to a "safe one." Then Esmael Alfaro got mad. It was 1961 and he was thirty-four years old. He had been born in nearby Robstown but grew up in Mexico with his father and worked as a boy in the fields. Soon after he started a junk yard in Mathis in 1956 Alfaro began to chafe at the treatment of his people.

"It is not the Gringo but the System I hate," he said. "In San Patricio County the Gringo has no love for the Chicano, but love is not necessary for living as neighbors. Jobs and work are necessary. The System would not let us live as neighbors. The System did not speak our language. The System did not hire our people. The System did not teach our children. There were no Chicanos in the Post Office. There were no Chicanos in the bank. Where was the Chicano? Mopping the floors for forty cents an hour. And this only ten years ago.

"In 1961 we go to city hall and complain about high water bills. They explain in English—never in Spanish. And they said finally, if we don't like it, we can move from Mathis. The city officials said I must close my business—that it was in violation of zoning ordinances. I got a lawyer from another town and we finally won.

"I had friends in Mathis. I talk to them. We realize we must work together, get all our people to pay poll taxes. So we ran a candidate for justice of the peace. He lost but we knew we were only beginning. The Gringo grew angry. The police began to drive by my house, the border patrol. They check me carefully. One day they stop me and ask, 'Alfaro, where is your passport?' I said I do not have a passport—I am American citizen. They say they understand I am wetback but I said I am American citizen, born in Robstown. This went on long time. The local car dealer stopped sending me business. I said, 'Alfaro, stay with it.' We formed the Action Party in 1963 and ran three men for council. We lost by only eighty-one votes. I think they were stolen. But we got ready for 1965."

That year the Action Party elected three men to the city council, including the mayor, Winston Bott, an Anglo. "We were under the System so long we had no qualified people—not even a high-school graduate," Alfaro said. "We had to take a chance on some Anglo. Bott was new to Mathis. He feel for the Chicano. He said he would appoint a Chicano police chief and fight poverty, and we supported him." Mathis became the only city government in Texas to be dominated by Mexican-Americans.

Stormy years of charge and countercharge followed, but by 1969 an uneasy peace prevailed and some people on each side hoped the political transition had been completed. While racial tensions still existed, they felt Mathis was ready to move forward. It was for that reason I had decided in May to come to Mathis before the summer ended. In the period between my decision and my arrival the truce had collapsed.

All the old wounds were open.

A bond issue to pave the streets in the barrios had been defeated (one-third of the cost of paving is borne by the city and the rest by the property owners on each side of a street). Anglos live mostly on paved streets; Chicanos do not. One Chicano councilman told me that the bond issue was defeated "because the Anglos don't give a damn." Although one white woman said, "We pay taxes to send them to school and we pay their welfare and we aren't gonna pay to pave their Mexican streets," I believe the primary reason for the defeat of the bond issue can be traced to the powerful dislike among the Anglos of Mayor Winston Bott. "We voted it down because we aren't going to give Bott any more money to waste before his term is up next year"—this from a prominent woman in town. People were bitterly reminded of the precarious balance of power in Mathis.

Then the four Lerma boys and their mother whipped the Mathis police force.

Patrolman Maurelio Contreras and Officer Mutt Jackson had been called to San Patricio Avenue, the main street, to investigate a minor accident between two cars driven by Chicanos. According to Mutt Jackson he was inspecting the damage "when the Lerma family pinned me in and Mrs. Lerma started in on me about a sideswiping that was done on their car on May 9. She said I never tried to catch who hit her car, and a lot of things. I told her not to try to run police business. I started to walk away, when one of the Lerma boys pushed me back and said not to talk to his mother that way. I told him not to touch me again and he did. I told him that he was under arrest, to get into the car and I tried to put him into the car. That is when it all started." The people who poured out of the drugstore and the café to witness the fight saw one of the Lerma boys hit Mutt Jackson over the head with a crutch [the boy was recovering from an injury]. Another hit him on the ear, knocking his hearing aid off and breaking his glasses. One boy struck Patrolman Contreras on the left eye, scratched him with his fingers, and grabbed him by his sling (Contreras had injured his arm in a wreck). An emergency call brought the Texas highway patrol within five minutes. Patrolmen K. R. Stafford and J. W. Byrd finally subdued the Lermas after a brief but angry round of fisticuffs and wrestling.

The fight occurred in front of the office of the Mathis *News*. Mike Singleton, the editor, saw it. "It was one of those things that should never have happened," he said. "Mutt Jackson is an Anglo cop who is hard of hearing, he has something of an abrasive personality, he doesn't speak any Spanish, and he doesn't understand the Mexican-Americans. When Mrs. Lerma asked him about the investigation into the hit and run, he put her off—you know, 'Don't bother me about that now.' The son took offense at the tone rather than the words, and as they say, push comes to shove. The Lermas have never been in trouble before—two of the boys were to graduate from high school that night. But they shouldn't have jumped on the police and, frankly, they got what they deserved." Most eyewitnesses agreed with his appraisal.

It was what happened after the Lermas were in handcuffs that shook the town—

Witnesses said they saw one of the highway patrolmen slap one of the Lermas while the boy's hands were handcuffed behind him. The Chicanos on the sidewalks immediately forgot that the Lermas had started it all and "got what they deserved" in a street brawl. They saw the handcuffs, the swinging hand of the uniformed Gringo, and the flinching of Juan Lerma. It was an instant replay in their minds of generations of brutality at the hands of Gringo police.

The report filed by Patrolmen Stafford and Byrd said: "Patrolman Byrd had handcuffed Samuel Lerma and Samuel started using loud profanity. Byrd told Samuel to quit cursing and Samuel continued. Byrd slapped Samuel in the side of the head with his open hand one time. After this Samuel quieted down and was placed in the patrol car."

Witnesses, Chicano and Anglo, said they did not see this incident. They say that Stafford, not Byrd, slapped *Juan*, not Samuel, Lerma. "I know Stafford and Byrd well," Mike Singleton said. "I've ridden with them on patrol. There's no question that it was Ken who slapped the boy. I don't know why Jerry Byrd took responsibility for it." Another Anglo witness testified before the Department of Public Safety investigating officer that he saw "Stafford slap this youth with his open hand and the youth quieted down." Mike Singleton gave a statement to that effect to the DPS investigator, but it did not appear in the report.

A former mayor of Mathis, Manuel Chavez, who owns the drugstore across the street, said that Stafford, "with his right hand gripping the hand-cuffs, moved Juanito Lerma toward the patrol car by alternately shoving him, then jerking his arms back by the handcuffs. . . . The boy turned his head around part way and said something [Chavez could not hear the words] . . . whereupon Stafford smashed him in the side of the face with a solid left hook." According to Chavez, this part of his statement was left out of the subsequent DPS report.

"At the time I thought it was just a fight," Mike Singleton told me. "But when I sat at my desk after it was all over I realized that the Lerma boy was handcuffed when he was slapped. The more I thought about it, the more I realized how wrong it was."

Others felt the same way. At Chavez's drugstore Chicanos talked in angry tones. "It is not the job of the police to hand out punishment," Manuel Chavez said. "That is for the courts. When that boy in handcuffs was hit, he was being punished by the police, not by the courts."

That night the Chicano majority on the Mathis city council passed a resolution requesting Governor Preston Smith to remove Officers Byrd and Stafford "from this area immediately." It was a shrewd political move on Mayor Bott's part. He is a Republican, and in the eyes of the large Chicano population of Texas he managed to put the Democratic governor of the state on the spot; in one move he also recouped Chicano support, which had been slipping away from him in Mathis.

Governor Smith asked the Department of Public Safety to investigate. The two patrolmen who had been involved in the incident accompanied the investigating officer on some of his interviews. He concluded that the slapping of "Samuel Lerma" was unfortunate but added: "Most witnesses agreed Samuel Lerma kept struggling, cursing, and yelling after he was handcuffed. . . . Patrolman Byrd did slap him once on the head with an open hand to get him to stop creating a disturbance while hand-cuffed." He concluded that Byrd and Stafford "handled this incident in the best possible manner." He did not mention the alleged slapping of

Juan Lerma and he did not recommend a transfer. "I saw Stafford slap *Juanito* Lerma," Chavez repeated. "And how much disturbance can a handcuffed boy create?"

The regional commander of the highway patrol forwarded the report to the state director, recommending that Patrolmen Byrd and Stafford "be commended rather than condemned for the actions they took in restoring order in a situation that had gotten out of control of the local officers." There is no doubt that Byrd and Stafford had handled a potentially dangerous situation without resorting to their guns or tear gas, but the sentence completely exonerating the patrolmen from the slapping charges enraged the Chicanos in Mathis. Their wrath was to spread to Mexican-Americans elsewhere in South Texas.

They were further agitated by a report made to Governor Smith by his executive assistant: "I have checked into the Mathis situation personally, *by telephone and through correspondence* [italics mine], with numerous citizens of the Mathis area who were involved [he did not talk to Singleton, who was an Anglo eyewitness]. . . . The incident which triggered the council resolution was relatively small. If the City of Mathis police force had been at full strength, the larger incident would never have happened."

"But it *did* happen," one Chicano councilman said, shrugging his shoulders.

The grand jury of San Patricio County also "investigated" the incident and commended the two officers "for their devotion to duty."

"Not one iota of understanding for the Chicano feelings," Mike Singleton said. "Not one."

Three weeks after the incident Governor Smith issued a statement in which he declared he would not transfer the patrolmen. He said: "It is apparently true one of the patrolmen did slap one of the persons involved with an open hand after he was handcuffed, but the subject was continuing to struggle and was in the act of committing another offense— the offense of loudly cursing and otherwise using abusive and obscene language toward police officers in the presence of a large crowd which had gathered at the scene—including numerous small children. . . . It is not the policy of the DPS and its employees to discriminate against anyone. I feel this is substantiated by the fact that the Department continues to employ increasing numbers of minority groups when qualified personnel can be found. An 'outsider' with a publicly stated grudge against one of the patrolmen who had arrested him on numerous traffic violations appeared before the Mathis city council and urged it to adopt the resolution asking for the withdrawal of the patrolmen." The "outsider" was Hector Gonzalez, of Beeville, who has been active in discrimination suits in South Texas. The Anglos do not like him, I was told by an Anglo who is friendly with the Chicanos, "because he is for his people." They consider him an outsider because he lives in Sinton twenty-two miles away. But they circulated a letter in support of the patrolmen from the director of a bank in Sinton. The letter read: "This fellow admitted he doesn't live in Mathis, but he said he was familiar with the situation there and knows most of the businessmen and leading citizens. He said he concluded from the conversation of the people he knows that this was just another political hassle. He even had the gall to say the policemen were being used as a tool of a minority of radicals." How do you like that? He's not an outsider because he's white. Gonzalez is an outsider because he's a Chicano.

"The issue," Manuel Chavez said, "is that they do not know the soul of the people who have been living in their midst for a hundred years. We are still strangers to them. They do not know what is here." He put his hand over his heart.

"What do you call what is happening in this town?" Esmael Alfaro asked. He was sitting in his bedroom beside a table on which rested a large bottle of acid-indigestion pills. "What is the word—polarization?"

And Patrolman Maurelio Contreras asked in his report:

When someone is interfering with officers, while performing their duty, WHAT'S AN OFFICER TO DO? Now-a-days, the police officer has his hands all tied up— Let the hoodlums do what they please— Or what the people would like—OR MAYBE THE PEOPLE OF MATHIS WOULD PREFER TO SEE A POLICE OFFICER DEAD?

This was the atmosphere in Mathis on the night of July 11, 1970, when Deputy Sheriff Eric Bauch fired two .375-caliber bullets into the chest of Dr. Fred E. Logan, Jr.

★ ★ ★

"Freddy" Logan, osteopath, was one of the few Anglos in Mathis whom the Chicanos liked. Part of their affection for him arose because he started a clinic to treat the poor. ("It would have made *him* rich," a prominent Anglo said.) Part of it was because he financed political campaigns for Chicano candidates. But much of their feeling was admiration for the way he lived in open defiance of Anglo traditions. He was a thirty-one-year-old maverick who drank heavily and wore long hair and a flamboyant beard. As a teenager he had been arrested repeatedly for disturbing the peace, after he came to Mathis he roared down San Patricio Avenue on his motorcycle in bib overalls, no shirt, a straw hat, and boots. For all the reasons Chicanos cheered him Anglos looked upon him with contempt.

"He had the soul of a Chicano," David Trevino, a young activist, said.

"He was a drunken fool," an Anglo businessman said.

He was dead, the coroner said when they brought his body to the hospital.

According to witnesses Dr. Logan had been at the Red Barn, a tavern and restaurant near Mathis, and was preparing to leave on his motorcycle for Corpus Christi, some forty minutes away. His Mexican-American friends tried to stop him because he appeared to be drunk and in no condition to make the trip. When they persisted he drew a pistol and fired several shots in the air. San Patricio County Deputy Sheriff Eric Bauch later filed this report of what followed:

> I asked him if he had a pistol and he finally told me he did but didn't know where it was. Another man said it was under the seat. Logan took two shells out of the gun and then pulled the trigger twice. I took him by the hand and told him to come on as we were going to have to go to Sinton. . . .
>
> We started down the west side of the Interstate heading for Highway 881 overpass to go to Sinton. He informed me that I was on the wrong side of the highway and I heard him unlocking the door. I stopped him and he did it again and then he wanted to know why I didn't handcuff and whip him. I assured him I had no reason to do so.
>
> He pulled the door open the third time and I reached back and closed it again. He did it again and I stopped on the overpass in park position. He was out of the car. He didn't run. Both the front and rear doors were open on the driver's side when I started to get out. He had his hands on both doors and had me hemmed in. I asked him to get back in the car. He then hit me with his left hand on the right eye and then kicked me at my waistline. As I tried to straighten up he swung at me again. I fired what I intended to be a warning shot and put the gun back in my holster. He then kicked me in the groin. I pulled the gun and shot him pointblank. It spun him around clockwise and he fell backwards on the pavement.

At the hospital the body was tested for alcoholic content. In a test of sobriety the standard maximum of alcohol is .10 of 1 percent. Logan's blood is reported to have had .18 of 1 percent.

The Chicanos were enraged. Dr. Logan's father called the death "politically motivated" because his son had joined actively in the effort to get Patrolmen Stafford and Byrd transferred from Mathis and because he had accused county officials of trying to thwart his migrant health program. (County Judge William Schmidt had called Logan "a liar" in one heated exchange.) The Mathis city council passed emotion-laden resolutions hinting at "a political murder" and calling for the resignation of County Sheriff Wayne Hitt and Deputy Sheriff Bauch and condemning Governor Preston Smith for "tacitly approving brutal treatment of selected prisoners."

Several questions troubled the Chicanos:

1. Why had Bauch's warning shot struck Logan?

2. If Bauch had holstered his gun between shots, why had both bullets entered the body from the same downward angle, one on the right side of the chest and one on the left?

3. Was Logan sitting, kneeling, lying, or bending down when he was killed? The angle of the bullets indicated such a possibility.

4. Why did the car disappear for several days after the shooting? Chicanos said officials wanted to clean up the bloodstains that would have disproved Bauch's story. Sheriff Hitt said Bauch's life had been threatened and he had told him to leave town for several days in the patrol car because his wife was on a trip in the family car.

5. Why couldn't Bauch have subdued the smaller drunken man by mace, tear gas, or force other than gunfire? (Bauch is more than six feet tall; Logan was five feet two inches.)

More than a thousand people attended Fred Logan's funeral. As the local Catholic pastor gave the text of the service in English, members of the Mexican-American Youth Organization (MAYO) from Houston marched in front of the church carrying placards reading: MAYO UNITES IN SORROW, MEDICINE YES—MURDER NO! The mourners walked in a long procession to the cemetery where during the graveside services members of MAYO circulated among the young Chicanos and urged them to organize.

They did. At a rally a few days later in the Chicano dance hall brown-shirted MAYO organizers told more than three hundred Mexican-Americans that nothing would be done for them unless they did it themselves.

The crowd responded with clapping and cries of "Viva La Raza," "Viva MAYO," and "Viva La Causa."

Manuel Chavez, the druggist, was master of ceremonies. He began the meeting in English. The people demanded that he speak in Spanish.

★ ★ ★

"Are you interested in telling both sides of the story?" Mrs. Betty Sutherland asked on the telephone. "Then I'll talk to you."

Her husband, Tom, runs a general-merchandise store in Mathis. They have been here a long time. Mrs. Sutherland is a friendly forthright-speaking slender woman who works in the family store. For twenty-eight years she has been the Red Cross in Mathis and for many years also served as the local welfare representative; she prides herself upon her benevolence toward Chicanos in distress. She is also a leader in an Anglo-dominated nonpartisan political association. She and her husband live in a modest house on a corner of two streets which are not paved. ("We had children in college and we just couldn't afford the money to pave them," she told me.)

"To show you that you're entering an unbiased house," she said as she greeted me, "that table is set up over there for a shower some of us are giving for a deserving little nigra girl in town." She invited me to sit at a card table covered with the clippings she has been keeping for years on the problems of Mathis. "Nobody ever listens to *our* side of the story," she said. "This is a wonderful little town with lots of good people in it, Mexicans and Anglos. It was a wonderful town, that is, until that awful Winston Bott took over as mayor in 1965. I am sick about what he has done to Mathis. He is an outsider who came here from Ohio and doesn't understand our community or feel any loyalty to it. There have been mistakes on both sides but Bott took advantage of the poor Mexican and has divided this town. The Mexican was really making progress until Bott came along. I've seen them progress so far in their methods of eating, sleeping, drinking—those things. They have come a long way. I don't look down on them because some of my best friends are Mexicans. Now I'm against intermarriage, but I have Mexicans in my home all the time. At this party"—she pointed to the punch bowl and cups—"there will be Mexicans. They don't feel discriminated against. Bott makes them think they have been. I wish I could figure him out. I've heard he was a Mexican hater—if I knew some of the girls that worked in his home . . . to find out how he treated them . . . how he treated the Latins that worked with him . . . It seems he sort of wants to get revenge on the city of Mathis for something. Oh, the antagonism . . . the venom . . . the false promises he made to all the Mexicans . . . Oh, how he has led them down the primrose path.

"You take this MAYO thing. I understand there was a very small group in attendance at the meeting. It really has no purpose. The majority of Mexicans don't want it. Just some of the young. The problem isn't the older Mexican. It's the young ones. The young MAYO people have been called Communists, you know. We didn't have them until Dr. Logan's funeral. He was a fraud if there ever was one. He was going to make a lot of money out of that clinic which the poverty program was going to give him. No one could see the applications he had submitted but some of us managed through friends to get them from the regional office, and all the salaries they were paying, and the high costs—he was going to clean up. Because we got to snooping around he resubmitted his proposal but he was still going to make plenty. And they made *him* a hero."

The Chicanos?

"Are you saying 'Mexican'?"

I mean—

"I don't get all these words like Chicanos and Gringos."

Mexican-Americans?

"The Mexicans? Yes, they made him a hero. They didn't know how hard some of us was working for them where it really counted. Like we had room mothers in school and one year there was going to be a banquet, a party, and it was just going to be for the Anglos, and I said if it's for the Anglos and not for the Latins, I'm not helping. I have to admit there was—I couldn't see that everybody was mistreated—maybe just overlooked or neglected—I can't find a word for it—I don't think anyone meant to be mean, but they really were, in a way. I wouldn't hurt a child for anything on earth. They didn't want to have a reception after graduation because the Latin children couldn't have clothes, they said. I said the Latin children will be better dressed than our children will. We had the reception and the Latins all had on their suits and the girls had on their pretty dresses. See, they buy clothes for their children on important occasions like this. They've come a long way. Now I don't like a common, lowdown trashy white person either, and I think that Bott is one of the most common persons I have ever seen—he is! And what he's doing to people, the way he mistreats the Latins by fooling them."

I asked her if Mathis has changed significantly in the last ten years.

"It's the unrest that's come. We were at fault. We left our Anglo commissioners in office too long. We let it go too long. We should have had some Latins on the board, we really slipped up there. I guess we just didn't see it coming. Then the Action party organized and Bott was elected. I think that people have learned, have bent more. I think that people are being—I still can't find that word I want to use about the way I can see that they're treating them—that they're being more considerate of the Latins. Because the Latins are elevating themselves to a higher level, see?

"No one has gone to City Hall any more than I have to take care of the Latins. That's what I can't understand. I read the Communist code one time—they have ten or eleven steps. They go after the young. But a little boy worked for us in the store, and one of his friends was the little Rojas boy. Well, the first thing the Communists seem to want to do is to turn their children against their parents. One of the little Rojas boys had run away from home. His grandmother came to visit and the little Rojas boy went home and during a talk that night his father made him see the light. So he moved back home the next day. He'd been disrupted by outside influences. That's what's ruining Mathis. It's the outside influence that has disrupted us. Those northern people at the Ford Foundation have come to South Texas and they're backing lots of things in the valley and around here. Foreign influences. Leroy Wheatley told me about the marches in Austin at the university and the capitol grounds. He said there were 350 dirty, filthy, nasty, long-haired, you know, common old hippies lying on our capitol grounds. He said it made him sick.

"Our good Mexicans in Mathis aren't like that. I've always advocated having Latin councilmen as well as Latin school-board members. I feel they deserve representation. It makes no difference to me of their color. But we do need *qualified* people. People that can't even manage their own families don't have any business trying to run a city. I'm sure you know that Bott has sacrificed his wife and his children—they're divorced, she left him—and we just can't see what right he has to be giving us moral advice about Mexicans. I know more about the Mexicans than he will ever know. The greater majority of 'em turn out to have the same attitudes and be alike. Now I've had the same girl working for me about thirteen, fourteen years. I had another girl working for me eleven years until she left town. We had another boy that worked at the store for twenty-two years. You can be—you're good to them and they become like part of your family, but the first thing you know you learn—well,

235

I've been too good and they're taking advantage of me. It's just like at my house today, with the party coming up. My girl came last week and worked extra quick—and her daughter came and helped—to get ready. Well, yesterday she had company so she called and asked me whether it was all right if she stayed home. I said yes. Well, this morning her brother's father-in-law died; she wanted to go to the funeral, so she called and said I'll be there as soon as I can. I've never docked her a day's pay in my life.

"There are a few good faithful ones that'll stand by you, but in the end —this is the strange thing—in the end the Latins we were trying to help and to get to work with us . . . when Dr. Logan was shot they got all stirred up, and it got the venom to running in them, and instead of turning against just the deputy that shot him, they turned against the race. That's the really strange thing. I can't understand that."

★ ★ ★

"I was one of the first Chicanos to run for office," Manuel Chavez said. We were drinking coffee in the rear of his drugstore. He is a native of Mexico and a graduate of the University of Texas. When he bought the drugstore from two Anglo women in 1962 he was welcomed by the Anglo community as a local entrepreneur—he even was asked to join the Rotary Club—but in 1963 his sympathies were openly for the Chicanos and he ran unsuccessfully as their candidate for councilman. He ran again in 1965 and won. "I lost 80 percent of my business in two months," he said. "They just pulled that red carpet right out from under me. I went broke. Only to this day I don't think they realize I went broke. I pulled in my hiring. I cut my expenses to the bone, I weathered it, and then little by little the Chicanos started trading with me. This had been an Anglo store. They didn't all beat a path to my door, but they gradually trickled in and before you know it I've got enough to make expenses, and last year was the first year that I made as much money as I could have made working for somebody else. It was a four-year fight.

"Bitter? Not by a long shot. A little cynical, perhaps, but not bitter. The people here are the ones who have suffered for a long, long time. They don't have too much to show for it even now. But the big gain is intangible. A frame of mind. The Chicano's approach to things is different from what it used to be. His behavior at work, what he expects from his boss and his job, is very much different. At school he is expecting and demanding a lot of things that were his rights to begin with and he never had. It is one thing to lose rights; then you know what you lost and you fight. But when you never knew you had rights, like the Chicano that come here long time ago to work in the fields, it take a long time to know you must fight. Look at the graduating-class pictures five years ago and this year. The dropout rate of Chicano children is reversed. More are staying in school. That is our big victory. It is pride, man, pride.

"I was lucky. My mother gave me a shove a long time ago. She wanted me to get into the mainstream. Get in the Boy Scouts, she said. Go to school. You are poor but you be something one day. But when you are stooping out in that sun half the year, how you going to know such things? That is why these people have had such a hard time.

"It is hard on Anglo, too. His own history made him what he is. He's caught in a web of tradition, prejudice, and misinformation. He must get out of that web. So must we. When I grew up I was the kind of guy who was ashamed to take tortillas and frijoles for lunch. I was ashamed because the Anglo kids looked down on anybody who ate tortillas and frijoles. They made it something nasty. Well, it wasn't, and we didn't have enough sense to convince them that it was even superior to what they were eating, dry bread. We didn't have sense to push our own cause, where we had damned good reasons to. Now the young Chicano is trying awfully hard to do what we never had the sense to do. He knows his lot is to be more than a dirty poor field hand."

He laughed and ordered more coffee. "It is funny that the Chicanos and the Negroes should be banging on the front door of the Anglo society trying to get in when the hippies are going out the back door because they have had a bellyful of it. I keep saying to myself, Suppose we do get in that door someday. I'm willing to wager that we're not going to like a hell of a lot of what's in there."

He laughed again, became suddenly very serious, and said, looking over my shoulder into the blank wall, "But we will get in. It is the only way to make the years of the past worth it. I remember to this day my wife going to the big bank in Corpus to ask for a job. I can see them laughing at her now. They didn't even go through the motions of giving her an application. This was way back. I was naïve. I thought maybe they did not need anyone. I was a fool. I started so late."

I asked him if anything in particular had changed him.

"One big thing. Soon after I come here the Mexican consulate came over, wanted to bring a big troupe from Mexico that was coming to Corpus on up here for the same program. We got a committee together and somehow I wound up as chairman. Everybody put in a tremendous amount of work because we don't have the facilities or capabilities for taking sixty people and giving them one meal. Forget about the school, they wouldn't lend us the facility. But the state park is near here and we could use that. On the morning of the fiesta the mayor came to me and says, 'Manuel, I want to ask you a big favor and I will make it up to you. Do me this one favor, don't raise the Mexican flag today.' I said, 'Why not?—the American flag goes up first on the right, the Mexican flag goes up second on the left. It seems like such a little thing,' I said. He said, 'Well, I have had calls all morning saying that if that Mexican flag goes up it is going to be shot down.' I said, 'I don't believe that, I don't believe things are like that in this town.' (Remember, I am new here.) He says, 'Manuel, friends of mine of forty years have threatened to run me out of town on a rail if that Mexican flag goes up.' And it wasn't even in town. It was in the state park.

"Well, it just so happens that on the superstructure down there at the park where this troupe was performing, I had already put an American flag. It was sticking way up in the wind, real high, so we didn't raise any flags at all. And I'll tell you what, man. I've done a hell of a lot of things in my life and I don't think I regret any one of them except that one. I've been kicking myself in the you-know-what ever since. That flag should have went up.

"It is a very subtle thing, prejudice in a town like this. The mechanics of it are second nature to people after so long. There are very few men of malice in this town. I think they think of themselves as good Christians, and I think that they have a certain responsibility to the social system, and they think they're being good citizens when they behave in such a manner as to sustain the system. I believe that if any one of them were to break down and admit, 'Damn, the way we've treated these people— maybe I should try to make amends one way or another'—I think he'll feel himself a traitor. This is why you don't get to first base by appealing to their compassion, reminding them about the brotherhood of man. I don't think they understand that language at all."

Then what gets you to first base?

"Power. You have to bargain with them from a position of power. It's the quickest return for our money. The people had to have a taste of victory or they wouldn't go on. That's why winning the city council was so important. We haven't touched the schools yet. The school district is an independent district—it includes much more territory than just

Mathis. The farmers in the county have more to say about the schools than we do. They've got the power. We have to go to them."

Manuel Chavez swallowed the last of his fourth cup of coffee.

"That will change," he said.

★ ★ ★

—— runs a small business in Mathis and would not talk for attribution. The Chicanos call him an Uncle Tomás and the Anglos call him "a good Mexican." He feels very uncomfortable these days. "My people have suffered, yes," he said. "But I do not think we can correct things by fighting with the Anglos. We have been running the city council off and on for four years, right? We have been no more efficient than the Anglos, right? My people say the issue is not efficiency but power and patronage. They did not have those things for a long time and I understand. But I am more interested in good streets and being sure the children of the migrant goes to school. We are not making progress in Mathis now because everyone is afraid someone else will get the credit. Something must give. We must not become two cities in one like we were for so long. We must become one city, working together. No more Gringo, no more Chicano—all one."

★ ★ ★

Adolph Bomer and I sat long past midnight talking about many things. One Chicano leader had described him as "the System Incarnate," but this night he was gracious and hospitable and reminded me in manner of my father, who had also gone as a very young man to California to seek his fortune, wound up "flat busted," and returned to Texas to work hard for the rest of his life. For men like this life has been one long struggle to recover from the thirties. It has also been a constant grappling with attitudes of race deeply rooted in the way of life to which they were born. They are men caught in what Manuel Chavez had described as "a web of tradition, prejudice, and misinformation."

At sixty-three Adolph Bomer runs the Mathis Feed and Seed Company. His heavy black eyebrows contrast with his crew-cut gray hair. He is a slender man whose hands are worn and hard, like an old pair of leather gloves. Mrs. Bomer worked a crossword puzzle as we talked.

"The agitation started early in the sixties," Adolph Bomer said. "The biggest part of the agitation has come from Anglos from out of the North [he specifically meant Winston Bott of Ohio], who have been coming into this area. We've had some trouble from some of the Latins, including some who are our people, and I still can't figure 'em. If one gets a little smart, I guess, he'll use the ones that are not so smart to his advantage and he don't care very much how he would hurt 'em. The good Mexicans who have been here for many years are upright; they don't believe in crime or this pot smoking or gettin' drunk and carousin' around. They're for law and order, all of those people are, and that's the way I am, I guess.

"I was president of the school board when we completely integrated the Mathis school system and I was instrumental in getting the first Latin that was ever on the school board. Lots of Anglos came to me and said, 'Adolph, you're crazy.' But I felt that it doesn't make any difference if a man's Negro, Latin, Jap, or Chinaman—as long as he's honest and upright I'm for him. I went to school with 'em from the very beginning—in a little one-room schoolhouse out here in the country. We lived on a farm and my playmates were Latin. There was one old colored man who lived there who ate on a separate table on the back porch. I used to go back there and eat with him. I was just a kid and he knew lots of stories. Neither one of us ever thought anything about it. Right now I have two colored men and two Latins and two Anglos working at the store. Before I have always had three colored, three Latins, and one Anglo. And then they say I'm prejudiced in favor of Anglos? It just wouldn't make sense. You can hardly ask a Latin in Mathis that don't know me and you can just go ask any of 'em if I haven't always treated 'em just like I would treat anybody else, customer-wise or else. We've got some screwball Anglos just like screwball Latins. There's Gringo haters in the Latin race and there are Anglos who deserve the word Gringo—they hate Latins. Both races got 'em.

"You can't force people together, of course. It's just like birds—when they go to roost, they like to roost together. The sparrows go to roost together, the doves roost together. That's more or less in my thinkin' a natural thing.

"But a lot of the Latins in Mathis are my friends (I think it's an insult to the average Latin to call him a Chicano). I didn't even intend to run for a second term on the council if it hadn't been for Latin people encouraging me. They're gettin' fed up with Bott, too. He's promised them so much, deceived them so much. The Latins got disgusted with him. I polled more votes than anybody last April and I couldn't have done that if a lot of Latins hadn't voted for me. They told me they'd been taken for a ride. By Bott. They have woke up. They know things have changed. After the hurricane had hit here [Hurricane Celia, which had leveled Corpus Christi the week before, damaged Mathis heavily, too, and ironically may have staved off the ultimate confrontation after Logan's death] a big milk truck pulled into town with free milk. I said to the Latins there isn't another country in the world where people come to the aid of people in distress like they do here. Don't make any difference whether you're brown or white, when you need help you get it. Even those who don't work can get it. I remember years ago, the average Mexican man probably married at twenty years old, eighteen or twenty, and by the time he was thirty he has probably ten kids and they're getting old enough that he can make 'em go work in the field and he lay under the tree. And that was their thinkin': 'Get a family just as fast as you can and I won't have to work.' But you got real industrious Mexicans coming along now. They know things have changed. Why, years ago that Lerma boy wouldn't have been slapped with an open hand—he'd been hit with the butt of a gun.

"We were gettin' along just fine until Bott came in here and started tellin' the Latins they had been mistreated and they believed him. They know better now. That's why I'm not necessarily worried about the town. We've got to get a coalition of good Mexicans and upright Anglos and straighten this thing out. We got lots of both here. Golly, I worked all my life right along beside 'em. I picked cotton. I chopped cotton, I picked corn, I baled and stacked hay. I done the same work they do. Family grew up that way. I never did ask any of my help to do something that I didn't feel like I could do myself. I don't think I'm too good to clean the restroom. If it needed cleanin,' I cleaned it, part of the time. I'm not any better than they are. Lots of people feel the way I do who are Anglos. And lots of Latins, too. So that by next election we might have a coalition that'll settle down and we can work together—without Bott."

★ ★ ★

Bott, Winston F. "That awful Winston Bott." To the Anglos he is a nemesis, to the Chicanos an ally or at least a useful instrument, to the traveler an enigma. One of his friends said: "He is either a hero or a nut, and there are times I think he is both." For certain the mayor of Mathis has divided his town at a price to him of position, family, and friendships. In the long run the cost will be worth it, he believes, "because the Chicano will have power and the one-party system of South Texas will be crushed." When he said it the gleam from the pupil of his right eye shone as from a laser.

From notes scribbled as we talked the paradox of Winston Bott emerges: "Everyman's Sunday-school teacher . . . small frame . . . right eyelid droops slightly . . . thinning brown hair . . . fiftyish . . . unlikely figure for controversy or martyrdom but has acquired both . . . frustrated Lutheran minister . . . depression shook him . . . idealistic or naïve? . . . modest, spare demeanor hides enormous ego . . . wise or just wily? . . . stoical? masochistic? Garibaldi or St. Francis of Assisi? No, Quixote . . . inscrutable, stubborn, singleminded Quixote, with Esmael Alfaro instead of Sancho Panza for counsel . . . analogy still doesn't fit . . . maybe none does . . . seems to share the Chicanos' pain but fiercely ambitious . . . whatever he has has helped to awaken one corner of one county of one state to the potential of power. . . ."

Winston Bott was born on a poor farm in southern Ohio. In 1948 he chose Texas as a place where any man might become another Horatio Alger. He first saw Mathis while working as an engineer on a nearby dam and decided to settle here because it was "the poorest town with the most potential." He did engineering and surveying, picked up a real-estate license, made connections with development money in Houston and was off and running. In two years he was president of the Chamber of Commerce and of Rotary and his wife was head of the PTA. Although it was a small town he was realizing his American birthright, he was an entrepreneur and a capitalist, and he was happy. Mathis, in turn, liked him, liked his hustle and dreams and connections to the outside world, and even forgave him the sin of being the only Republican in town.

Then came the collision. In his real-estate and development activities he found himself competing with several members of the local establishment over his proposed construction of a shipping center and other building projects. There were scrapes over zoning and permits, and the town officials, Bott says, sabotaged his plans. In one dispute, according to his version, he was told by a member of the zoning commission: "I'd advise you to save your money and don't bother to hire a lawyer. You can't win a case in this county." He fought back. He called news conferences, accused his tormentors, wrote letters. In return, he says, he was ostracized. The social invitations stopped coming. His business suffered. His wife and children were cut off along with him.

"I began to realize what it meant to be a Chicano," he said. "I became an outsider, like I had leprosy."

"That wasn't it at all," one Anglo businessman said. "Bott was a grabber, a wheeler and dealer, and when things wouldn't go his way, he was little and mean. Why, the things he accused us of doing he was doing himself. It was the old smokescreen—cover up your own faults by laying 'em on someone else."

Bott had not supported the Chicanos in 1963. But two years later they found him a qualified Anglo who had a score to settle with the establishment and he found in them the votes with which to settle it. It was a convenient mating. "Most of our people had no high school and could speak but little English," Alfaro said. "Winston Bott had been hurt by the system as we had. He knew what it was like. It was gamble on both side and it paid off."

"It was very fragile," Bott said. "They didn't really know me enough to know that I wouldn't sell them out real quick. I didn't have communication with more than just a few leaders. In fact, two years later Chavez wanted to run for mayor. I couldn't possibly be in a position of splitting up the Chicano power, so I ate a little crow and ran for a council seat instead. We won. Then we lost control in '68 when the Chicanos split over the police chief (there have been seven chiefs of police in five years). But we healed that one and I was elected again last year [1969]."

"The day after I was first elected in '65 the wife of one of the councilmen who was defeated came to our front door and my wife answered it. The woman was shouting and spewing profanity and waving her arms, and she said to my wife, 'Mathis is not going to wait two years to get rid of Winston Bott; we're going to have them Mexicans out of here in six months.' A couple of farmers started going around and telling taxpayers that the way to get rid of these Mexicans is just don't pay your taxes, then the city won't have any money. The outgoing council did some nasty things. They had just bought a new street sweeper to be paid out over three years. They took all the money that was available and paid that sweeper out right after the election so we wouldn't have any money in the treasury when we came in." (According to one report, the former mayor said the outstanding debts were paid off by his administration for fear that "the new council would repudiate the debts.")

"My own life got pretty miserable," he said. "We got dirty and vicious phone calls. They ridiculed my wife right on the streets. The Anglos wouldn't even speak to me. They called my children names." In 1966 his wife filed for divorce.

("If you believe that stuff you're crazy," one Anglo said. "He and his first wife broke up, too, before he moved here. That man just can't get along with anyone.")

"People like that just don't understand," Winston Bott said. "I don't pay them any mind. They're the minority anyway. Actually, we were beginning to make some headway until the Lerma incident and Logan's death. That got to the raw nerve—to the raw nerve of the whole of South Texas. It's been a totalitarian system down here based on police power. The evil was bred into it by generations of one-party, one-establishment control. Over the years politicians down here have condoned the kind of thing that men do to helpless people when they've got a uniform on. The only way to really change things down here, to get justice, is to bring about a two-party system. We've got one Republican Senator in Washington now from Texas, but even if we elect another this year we're a long way from agreeing that the two-party change which is needed is about to begin. I'm afraid the Republican party is making the same mistakes the Democratic party made a hundred years ago in the South, aligning itself with racist forces. The mainstream of the Republican and Democratic parties down here is white, conservative, and basically indifferent to minority groups. If the Republicans want to make a difference, if they just don't want to be carbon copies of the old reactionary Democrats who've been running this state from Austin for twenty-five years, they've got to understand that the Chicanos want power. They don't want to dominate the state, they just want their share of power.

"What the Anglo people of Texas don't understand is the way the Chicano feels after all his humiliation. Six years ago the Chicanos in this county had to beg for commodities because the Anglo power structure cut them off in the winter, trying to drive the migrant laborer out of town, back to be somebody else's problem. And the Anglos at the courthouse in Sinton fought Fred Logan getting his clinic to help migrant laborers. And there's always things like the Chicano who got whipped by the police recently because they thought he was resisting arrest when he was really having an epileptic seizure. There's always been three kinds of justice down here. One for the Anglo, whether it's the district judge's son or the prominent farmer's son who got drunk out at the Red Barn and the police took him home to his family instead of to jail. Then there's justice for the Chicano, two kinds. One for the kind of guy like [and he called a name] who gets into trouble but nothing happens, then they own him, the kind of people who won't vote in elections because they're paid. Then there's the third kind of justice. The kind Freddie Logan got, and the Lerma boy, and the epileptic. The only way to get better justice is to get political power. The Anglo has used power to keep the Chicano down, now the Chicano's got to use power to get up."

He laughed. "In 1965 I remember the Anglos saying, 'Why, we've never had politics in Mathis before!'

" 'Never had politics.' Why, politics is the name of the game down here. Who would think that a mild-mannered, self-effacing civil engineer would make waves in Texas politics just by writing a resolution to the governor! The one-party system has produced its own rules in this state and if you do anything that's a little bit not according to the system they say, 'Oh, you're playing politics.'

"You're damn right I'm playing politics. They've been in power so long that they don't know anything but power. But they're also in so long they're lethargic. That's why my cardinal principle is that whenever the system makes an obvious, provable error, challenge it. Chances are it hasn't been challenged in such a long time that it's going to be upset and rattled and they're going to make some more mistakes, and that's when you go for the throat. You understand?"

There was a long silence before he spoke again. "These people have suffered. My God, have they suffered. And if the Republicans don't recognize that, if one of the parties don't start dealing with these people with understanding, there is going to be one hell of a revolution in South Texas."

We left the city hall and stood outside. It was a quiet, hot, brush country night. We talked of minor things but he was thinking of something that had been said earlier by one of his adversaries, the one who had mentioned his divorce.

"What's wrong with me," Winston Bott said, "is that I set out to broaden myself as I went up. I guess I've broadened myself as I went down. People can't understand that. Sometimes even family can't. Man who sets out the way I have is going to find himself a scourge someday. I've gone broke fighting battles for Chicanos when they couldn't fight them alone. The Anglos hate me for it. And the day will come when the Chicanos will be ready to do it by themselves. There won't be room for me on this side and I got no home on the other side."* He fiddled with a rubber band in his hand until it snapped. Then he got into his

* In October, Mayor Winston Bott was stripped of his authority to hire and fire city employees. The 4–1 vote by the city council came after a dispute between Bott and some Mexican-American residents.

car and left. He was deep in thought and I'm not even sure we said goodbye.

* * *

Two days before my arrival in Mathis Carlos Guerra, national chairman of the Mexican-American Youth Organization (MAYO), had returned to visit the fledgling local chapter. After leaving Mathis he was arrested in Beeville by a highway patrolman who charged him with driving a car with only one rear reflector. The Associated Press reported that Justice of the Peace C. L. Cox had said that Guerra was "very arrogant and very haughty" when he appeared in his court. Guerra, who is twenty-three, said the officers asked him "a lot of what I thought were questions not essential to them, like where I was coming from, where I was going, and just exactly what I was doing, including my MAYO activities."

According to State Patrolman Leo Franco, Guerra "was kind of smart alecky and taking notes." Justice Cox said: "He acted like he was going to do anything he pleased. That don't go with me. And he came in with a pad and started taking notes." He could have given him a $10 fine if he had pleaded guilty, Cox said. Guerra was jailed for six hours before bond of $250 was posted.

* * *

When Hurricane Celia ripped through the barrios of Mathis people were left homeless and hungry. Members of MAYO, whose purposes were vague before the storm, have been working almost around the clock ever since. With food and supplies from the Red Cross, they have been preparing meals each day for 250 people and distributing supplies by truck through the barrios. The center of their operations was Cielito Lindo, a cinder-block dance hall. About thirty Chicano teenagers were working when I arrived.

"Relief was going too damn slow," Simon Guiterrez said. He is a huge young man who is the president of MAYO in Mathis. "The Gringo from the Red Cross had to have an interpreter and that slowed everything down. Now we bring a Chicano down and let him fill out the applications for the people and it goes like that." He snapped his fingers.

I asked several young Chicanos what had brought them together in MAYO. "Dr. Logan's death," one of them answered. "The Gringos did not like him but he was our friend, our compadre. He knew Chicano customs. He spoke Spanish without English accent. He even knew slang Chicano. He did not charge poor people for health. He fought for us. That is why the Gringos did not like him. He was not afraid of them."

"Now that he is gone," Simon Guiterrez said, "MAYO must work for our people. We're gonna prove to 'em that MAYOs are not just a bunch of hoodlums, long-haired hippies; we're gonna prove to 'em that we can work and do things honestly. Our parents were afraid to speak out. But we ain't got a damn thing to lose. Now we're gonna do something for our parents. My parents had to go through hardships, year after year, day after day, they had to work like dogs. They all worked so my generation could go to school. Any person over thirty-five in Mathis who is Chicano is less educated than a kid down here seventeen, eighteen years old. Our parents hardly know English. One old woman in here yesterday to eat said she could vote but she can't speak English. We find young people now who's not gonna be saying yessir-nosir to no Gringo, and we support them for office."

You're going to work in the political system?

"Oh, yes, no violence, none of that. In all of South Texas the Chicano has 15 percent of the vote. With that we got bargaining power. If we organize third party we go to the Republicans and ask them, 'What do you have to offer?' Or we can just as well go down to the Democratic party and see what they have to offer. We can be deciding point. That 15 percent gives great power. The swing, you call it."

Another MAYO, Lupe Garcia, spoke. "We're gonna concentrate on the schools, too. Long time ago cheerleaders and class favorites were chosen by popular vote. Then Gringos were majority. When Chicanos became majority they did away with popular vote and cheerleaders were chosen by Gringo judges who preferred Gringo children. Last spring we had elections first time in years. Students chose two Negroes, two Gringo girls, and one Chicano girl. It was democracy [the schools are 79 percent Chicano, 20 percent Anglo, 1 percent black]. We want to work for other things like that. We want to help make Chicano kids proud of their customs."

Guiterrez mentioned his parents again. "It is the old people we must help first. They have been sat on too long now. Just the other day a guy in town, a Gringo, would not hire young Chicanos at $2 hour. He said he could get older Chicanos for less. If everything goes well, we tell him, soon you not find any guys gonna work for peasant wages. We gotta have results like that. Some Chicanos say Gringo has screwed us so long we must screw him back—at least for little while. Rest of us say no, our purpose is not to hurt no one. It is to get for ourselves where we are not hurt."

★ ★ ★

I stopped at Adolph Bomer's grain and feed store. Milton Boatwright was there. He had lived in Mathis all of his life, much of which has been spent as a rural mail carrier. He was mayor until deposed by the Action party and Winston Bott in 1965. He teaches Sunday school at the Baptist church and is proud of the mission which was started for the Mexican-Americans on the other side of town. "It is booming," he said.

He was buying an axe handle from Adolph Bomer; was he trying to tell me something? "Oh, no," he said, "we don't have any Lester Maddoxes in Mathis. But the people who are causing our trouble are doing it for selfish gain. Bott wants to be appointed to something if a Republican governor wins, that's his interest. He says there has been discrimination against the Mexican-Americans. He's not telling us anything new. My ancestors were discriminated against, too. They were Irish.

"What happened in the slapping incident was unfortunate and Logan's death was a tragedy. But it wasn't a political murder. It's just been used by people with political purposes in mind. Sure, Bott. Let me put it this way—Bott didn't tell them how bad they had been treated as much as he told them how good things were going to be under him. But Mathis is just as poor as it ever was.

"We need a coalition government. We can get it. The Action party never could have got going without them abolishing the poll tax. When the poll tax was abolished, they didn't have to let go of any money to vote. But the Action party seldom wins by more than 100 votes and sometimes by as little as 50. There are about 1,600 registered voters and only about 350 Anglos on the list. So a lot of Mexicans are voting with us or against the Action party. We can get the coalition next year because the Mexicans will want it, too. They're getting sick of Bott. No one will work with him. He has to go."

★ ★ ★

David Trevino, twenty-eight, a veteran, with a neat, short beard and an ardent manner of speaking, and Simon Guiterrez drove me through the barrios in a Red Cross van. Several homes had been totally demolished. Roofs simply disappeared. We stopped at one three-room house which had lost both roof and toilet. Alfaro had come by earlier to hire the man for a job collecting debris. The mother and six children were home. The youngest child, one year old, lay on the bed sucking milk from a bottle. There were three large open sores on her legs. The woman said she feeds her family rice, potatoes, and beans every day. Occasionally she mixes meal with the rice. Her husband makes $30 a week when work is available. "It is a vicious circle," Trevino said. "The kids lead monotonous lives. When they get to school they are way behind. What happens? They come back to lives like this."

He pointed to a large picture of Jesus and Mary on the wall. "That is all they think they have that's worth looking forward to. It's been the excuse for doing nothing for a long time. They've been taught that they will be rewarded in heaven for being poor on earth. It's a Gringo lie—like that." And he pointed to the little three-year-old girl standing barefooted beside her mother. In her right hand she gripped a plastic Santa Claus doll.

Houston, Texas

FOR THE PRIVILEGE OF LANDING AT WHAT MUST BE THE WORLD'S MOST immaculately manicured airport the traveler must now ride twenty-five miles instead of twelve to get to downtown Houston. The time passes quickly if your driver happens to be a stocky woman in her early forties wearing a blue-green sports shirt and a blue-and-white net of artificial flowers around her red hair. ("I got 'em every color. Some people call 'em hats but I call 'em scarves. I wear 'em to keep my hair from blowin'.")

I gave her the address of my destination and she said: "That part of town—there's lots of colored people live there now. It used to be an exclusive area but it ain't no more. You sure this is where you want to go?"

When I confirmed the address she said: "You don't sound like no Yankee. You sure you got that address right?"

It's right, I said, and asked her how the races get along in Houston.

"Pretty good. Lots better than they do in the North. We had some trouble in Galena Park here a few weeks ago. The cops kicked a colored boy to death. [Two officers were subsequently indicted for murder.] Them's the exception to the rules. For the coloreds to have risen like they have here, I'd say relations are pretty good."

I started to ask her about a new building off to the west but she interrupted:

"I know some of them cops over in that Galena Park area. They wear them pointed cowboy boots with them sharp toes. They's enough to kick your ass to hell and back—pardon my French. And they's young boys and mean. Here about a year ago I was taking one of the boys home, one of the colored boys who drives for me. He was sittin' over

250

there well on his side of the seat and we was in Galena Park where he lives and the cops stopped me. We was goin' through the business district and he saw that colored boy in the car and he flat stopped me. He said, 'Let's go to the station.' I said, 'Why?' and he said he would tell me when we got there. I followed him and when we got there he threw this colored boy into a cell and I said, 'Hey, wait a minute, what are you doin'?' He said, 'We're gonna charge you.' I said, 'With what?' He said, 'We'll think of that in a minute.' And I said, 'Listen, you snotty bastard, I got the right to know what the charges are against me and I got the right to call my lawyer.' They think I'm some poor dumb cabbie that don't know the law and well, sir, he begins to get nervous and he and this other cop go off in the corner and begin to talk and they come over and say they have decided to drop the charges against me. I said, 'How you gonna drop charges you ain't even pressed?' I said to get that colored boy out of the cell and they did. This cop apologized to me and I said, 'Don't apologize to me, apologize to the colored boy.' And you know something, they did. Holy-cow-in-the-manger, you'da thought Earl Warren himself had thrown the book at 'em. But I won't go out there any more. No, sir, I ain't gonna get my ass between them pointed toes and the streets o' that town if I can help it."

How long have you been driving?

"Two years. I'm buyin' my own three cabs now. I got two boys drivin' for me. I had to work. Wasn't gettin' no child support from my husband and me with five children to feed. My oldest is out at the University of Houston studyin' to be a schoolteacher. I told her of all the damn things she could be, she had to go and study to be a schoolteacher. But I guess it's better 'n drivin' a cab. You ever drive a cab?"

No.

"You meet all kinds of interestin' people. The best drivers are people who are married and don't drink. Don't make any difference what color they are. Important thing is can they keep the cap on that bottle. I had to fire a boy last week. He was a hard worker, but he kept taking passengers the long way. The second time I caught him at it I had to let him go."

A white Ford raced into the intersection and my lady friend slammed on the brakes. "Damn the world to hell," she said. "That guy almost gave us a shave and a haircut. I'd like to give *him* a weekend in the Galena Park jailhouse. Man drive like that oughta get a pointed toe right up the ——." And I did not quite get the word she used.

We were passing the business district of what to me is one of the most exciting cities in the country. It is not as beautiful as San Francisco; it does not carry itself with the stately being of Chicago; New Orleans is more picturesque; and New York is more visceral—but Houston is astir with the future. Off in the distance I could see new buildings glinting in the sun and the steel shells of others under construction. Some predictions say it will one day be our largest city. The absence of fixed boundaries in the charter has allowed wild annexation of peripheral townships and acreage, and already 1.3 million people live in a metropolis of some 450 square miles lying a flat 41 feet above sea level. Still the city continues to spread. Its people earn $6 billion a year. And, although it is fifty miles from the Gulf of Mexico, a canal fifty miles long has been dredged deep and wide enough to admit ocean vessels into the city; Houston is now third among the nation's seaports.

"Here you are, Mister. This is jig town. You sure you got the right address?"

I did, and we pulled slowly up to the house. "I believe this is a colored house, Mister. By damn it is. Looka those two children." She pulled into the driveway, turned in the seat, and said: "Listen, mister, I'll wait here until you are finished with your business. I wouldn't want you to get stranded here. Been lots of crime in this part of town and you might not get a cab back late tonight."

"If you're not afraid to take one home to Galena Park," I said, "I'm not afraid to stay here. But I appreciate your interest."

One of the children walked over, smiled, picked up my bag without a word and started into the house. My lady friend wrote me a receipt for the fare and mumbled something about people not listening. But she winked at me and said to call her on the number of the receipt if I decided in the middle of the night that I had to catch a plane. I gave her a large tip, and as she backed out of the driveway I noticed on the dashboard a magazine opened to an article entitled "Rape Slayer and the Desert Nude."

★ ★ ★

Bill Lawson shook his head and smiled when I recounted the concern of my guardian in the taxi. "She was right about the crime. This is a transitional neighborhood. That means city services are being withdrawn. When street repairs are irregular, the streets get bad. When police protection is slowly cut back, crime goes up. This used to be the Riverdale of Houston—very swank and very Jewish. Then it cracked. No one remembers who went first, but houses that had been selling for $50,000 to $60,000 plummeted in value. You will see homes with tall trees and large lots, but you will also notice that the whole area has the indefinable mark of transition."

Roughly one-third of the population of Houston is black. They dominate 40 of the city's 125 census tracts. The largest number—75,000—live in the south-central ghetto which runs from the Gulf Freeway to the South Loop, from Main Street to Cullen Boulevard. It is to this area, to the home of the Reverend William A. Lawson, that the cab driver has just fearfully delivered me. The tour Bill Lawson would later give me would show it to be a diverse economic area with poverty and affluence living next door to each other. There are no large concentrated slum areas, however, and the poor maintain a low visibility. If the people were not all black this ghetto would resemble any city of comparable size with proportionate shares of young homeowners and elderly renters, rooted professionals and transient laborers, domestics and unemployed. But as the city services have receded crime, prostitution, and cheap night life have risen. "It is a vacuum," Bill Lawson said, "too new to be serviced, too laden with problems to ignore."

The real heroes I know are anonymous. They have therefore remained human and humble. They are also effective. Once a leader has become a media star he has been reduced to a stereotype easily communicated by a brief lead in a newspaper report or by a ninety-second television clip. He must forever thereafter conform to that image or lose the quicksilver base of his notoriety and power.

Bill Lawson, forty-one, of the Southern Christian Leadership Conference, avoids acclaim and seeks results. He has turned down offers from government, civil-rights programs, and larger churches to remain as the pastor of the four hundred black families who constitute the congregation of the Wheeler Avenue Baptist Church in the south-central ghetto. Many Negro churches remain the furnace rooms of the Black Pride movement, and Lawson is no pulpit-pounding, Bible-waving holy-roller Tomming Billy Sunday. In his speeches he is in the prophetic tradition of Martin Luther King, in his political awareness he is a cousin to Julian Bond, and in his understanding of the economic order of the black man he is a protégé of Jesse Jackson. But he is shy and given to contemplation, and television cameras, he says, are "sirens of destruction for all but a very few."

Some friends might call him slender or trim. The word for it is "skinny"—just as he was when I last saw him about ten years ago—and tall. He gets up every morning at 4:30 because, he said, "the facts require it."

The facts?

"Sixty percent of us earn less than $4,000 [he is speaking of blacks in Houston]. Forty-six percent of us are common laborers. On the average we have almost nine years of education each but 90 percent of our high-school graduates are unqualified for standard college freshman English or mathematics. Our per capita effective buying income is $954 against a median of $2,346.

"To be black in Houston," he continued, "means being consciously aware that you are excluded from most of the major decision-making processes that govern your life. It means probably being poor. It means almost certainly no access or relatively little access to many of the community services normally provided—from garbage pickups at your house to getting free samples that are sent out by companies in the mail. It means generally being sometimes gawked at, written about too much, talked about too much, having your own consciousness bombarded with a great deal of rhetoric about you and quote the problem unquote that you painfully recognize that you constitute or at least are a part of. It probably means that your children will give you some difficulty because if they are in the present generation they likely will be militant or at least angry in ways that you have not seen if you are part of the older generation. The generation gap which is normal between somebody whose philosophies were set in the forties or fifties and somebody whose philosophy is being set right now is exacerbated and made worse by the fact that there is also the gap between racial points of view of the old Negro and of the young black."

But Bill Lawson does not like "to whine." There is too much to do, he said, "to sit and bay at a moon you think you can never reach. You must keep trying to get there."

And the ways to get there?

"One response is the negative hostility of the revolutionary. Protests, boycotts, eruptions, undercover guerrilla attacks—to some blacks they are the normal steam valves of outrage. These people are grossly oversimplified by the media. It's been hard for journalism to find out what blacks think about the Panthers or what the militants themselves do when they're not on camera. Muhammad Ali was a newsman's dream, for example. When a reporter wanted to find something really rousing, all he needed was thirty minutes of Cassius Clay and he had it made. But if you ever saw him when he's in the neighborhood—he lived just down the street here—you saw him as a quiet, loving guy that all the kids just simply idolize, until suddenly a television stationwagon shows up and the guys jump out with their cameras. Then his shoulders rear back and his lip curls up and he puts on a sneer and he's ready to give a show to the newsmen. Once again he's the cocky, arrogant Muhammad Ali. As soon as they're gone, he goes back to petting kids and playing with dogs.

"What they see on the screen scares whites. I think that's why blacks do it. They know what shock value is. If nobody wrote about them, the average black youth couldn't care less about such things. 'Militant,' after all, is a term given to us by the white man, especially by the press. It implies a military alternative, the use of direct action to make a point. Sometimes the only language which the powerful understand is the language of anger, of contest. And sometimes you have to cuss not because you feel like cussing but because that's the only way to gain respect. I felt like it the day my little girl, who's now fifteen, first realized that she could not sit in the anteroom of the doctor's office and play with the toys like the white kids were, that she had to be in a separate room, a waiting room which had been reserved for black people. You can take hurt when you're the only one hurting. When your children are hurting, you want to cuss—and more.

"But, while the negative hostility of the revolutionary may have some therapeutic release, it's sterile and produces very little.

"Positively, there is the response of remedial programs, sponsored by government—the war on poverty—and by the private eleemosynary agencies' sometimes jerky reactions to riots, marches, or court decrees, and the idealistic or ulterior emergence of church or civic programs. These last briefly until the crisis which prompted them has passed. Then they gradually recede. They've done little but get wide publicity and produce new heroes. Minorities now distrust even genuine attempts to help, because we have seen this drama so frequently played out in our neighborhoods.

"There has to be another kind of response, a local and on-site response, and that's why I have stayed at Wheeler Avenue. If all black males leave the ghetto, especially those with college degrees, the ghetto will once again be a kind of never-never land to the child who needs to hope. I believe in building institutions in the ghetto. Eight years ago we started

with just thirteen families in a ghetto neighborhood with two universities on each side of us. We started out in the traditional way to provide
a traditional ministry to our people, but since the Black Pride movement
of 1966 we have broadened our commitment, we coach people instead
of pampering them.

"The heart of the black community is still its churches. Most of our people no longer attend or support the churches, but as yet they have no alternative institution of basic philosophy to determine human values and
courses. Most blacks still believe in a Transcendent Entity, recognize the
rightness of the principles articulated in the Commandments, and our
need for a Suffering Servant to redeem us. The raw material for commitment to Somebody Like Jesus is still strong with us—King as martyr
is loved, though King as civil-rights leader had begun to wear dingy on
our sleeves. Malcolm is read today because 'he died for our cause.'
So the ideals of the black church are still the center of the ghetto. Our
own church recognizes that we're going to have to create a whole
black theology. The church among slaves reflected the black community.
But for a century now it has been trying to imitate the north European
pattern of white churches. It became pietistic, individualistic, generally
divorced from 'secular problems.' It became Western, like the white
churches, because it was trying to forget slavery. But now has come the
consciousness that we are not simply former slaves whose background
has been the plantation. We are former Africans whose background
has been a whole complex of cultures on a different continent. Former
slaves imitate their masters. Former Africans will try to find their real roots.

"That is what the black church must do—spread again through the
veins of the ghetto like salt through flesh or leaven through dough.
These ideas are neither novel nor foreign to Christ—this was the core
of his own teaching. He spoke the language of the Eastern, not the
Western, world. The black church must be Easternized. That's the only
way we can escape wanting to be European. Generally the European
came from a place with few natural resources. Hard living and a kind
of acquisitiveness became a part of his life. An African came from a
place where there has been natural plenty, speaking generally, and he
didn't build up that kind of avarice. There's not been any special need
for him to conquer other countries for their tin or their iron or their
coffee, and he came to accept a kind of balance with nature. It seems
to me that the building of massive technology, which has enriched us
but at the same time is wrecking our nature, is a kind of European

hangup. I'm not claiming special virtues for the African, I'm only trying to say what I think are the values we have to try to rediscover in the black church.

"Look at the verbal tradition of the black church. The belief in spirit which gives rise to a kind of charismatic tradition is a part of it. The communal nature, which says that the entire tribe has to go into a kind of frenzy before it rains and the women are fertile, helps to explain why some black churches work themselves into a frenzy before the spirit can move upon them. As soon as you notate the blues and give them a Gershwinesque kind of score, you lose something; they have to be part of a dynamic living relationship between the guy who blows his guts out with the horn and the people who are sitting there listening to him. Tradition like that ties together individuals in a kind of charismatic commune of the spirit; it explains something about black people.

"We have to locate this in history and make it part of the present. Because one of the best things you can say to kids is that if you are black, you're black. Black pride is infinitely more viable than white pity or wrath on either side. And you don't need to hate your country or be ashamed of it once you are proud of your blackness. You can help to contribute to it as well as draw the best from it. These kids are proud to be Americans. They know the country has hangups, but they also know that they possess the strength to help solve some of these hangups. It wouldn't be enough for them to live a lifetime and leave the world no different from what they found it. But to love your country and to help it you've got to know where you came from. You've got to know who you are. You've got to know why you are you.

"This is why our church here even looks the way it does. That building over there is a little glass-and-frame perimeter of cubicles built around an open courtyard, the way a compound of African huts looks, with thatched houses encircling an open clearing where the cooking is done or the dancing or the village council meets. Our architect was trying to reflect a black reality. Which is what the church must do. It has to recognize where we've come from, and it must itself come closer to the Middle Eastern zeitgeist which produced Jesus Christ. Christ was not an institutionalist in the European Western sense. He founded a church that didn't leave very many structural guidelines for it. He was one who spoke to the personal experience. The hippie who tries to heighten sensitivity with his drugs, or the black who goes into a virtual frenzy over his blues are speaking the language of experience far more than they are speaking the language of structure. I think this is what's happening to blacks right now, and I think this speaks to the relationship between that early zeitgeist and the transcendentalism of the youth movement. Perhaps it helps to explain why it's possible for Black Panthers and SDS types to understand each other more clearly than Young Republicans and members of the NAACP can."

You're in a structure, I said, but the militants don't call you a Tom. Why?

"Some do call me a Tom and I'm not sure that I have any influence with them, but two or three things need to be said about militants. I don't think they really enjoy the fight as much as folks think they do They're fighting because this is the last resort. They've no place else to go and in their mind it would not be manly not to fight. In a real showdown they know I'll fight with them. I just hope that's not the only alternative.

"Then, a militant's a person who is basically a typical black: he's been reared in a home where hymns have been sung and gentleness has been taught, and the same mammy who cradled a white baby has cradled him. And he's not really as violent as his public rhetoric makes him sound, and when he gets in trouble, he still cries, and he still needs somebody to help him. He knows that he can fairly well depend on me to come and help him.

"Finally, I think the activist blacks know we are trying to achieve something here. With a tiny budget of $45,000 we run an infant school teaching self-esteem to thirty-six infants—integrated, by the way; our Boy Scout program has grown in five years to become the largest and most active in the Harris County area; we sponsor a college coffeeshop once a week and a high-school teen club every Friday; we offer tutorials for about two hundred secondary students having difficulties in basic skills; we show the classic children's films on Saturdays to interest youngsters from twelve down in literature. We conduct extrachurch and interchurch activities, including the renting and staffing of a neighborhood center called SHAPE, which involves young activists in free breakfasts, African and Afro-American history, recreation, and other activities which white Americans do not identify with these youths who are sometimes hostile. We have other activities on the drawing board: buying clubs or 'co-ops' to magnify the small buying power of food-stamp and welfare recipients, a rolling day-care center in a large van or truck or bus, a housing project that would be more than a colony of the poor, programs for exceptional children—do you believe there are no opportunities for the above-average black child within reach of Houston's poor, no way to sharpen genius as soon as it appears within our community? These are dreams at the moment. Our budget and supply of volunteers keep us from doing something about them now.

"Then there's Operation Breadbasket. Our church holds the Houston charter for SCLC and Breadbasket is headquartered here. We looked at the economic picture and saw that the black community loses its earnings to the white people and there's none of it coming back. So what we did was to begin to pressure white businesses, one after another, in a systematic way, to bring them to crisis about their hiring practices or banking practices or advertising practices. They have to give in to these demands or they stand a chance of losing their black market.

"We just went through with a confrontation with a soft-drink-bottling company. We had asked them to upgrade their black, brown, and poor white employees. We wanted them to establish a career ladder so that every employee at the company can know exactly what are the opportunities for advancement and how they can qualify for them. Those who can't qualify, of course, never will. Those who are eager to qualify won't be held back because their skin's the wrong color or they speak the wrong language.

"Second, we were expecting that company to invest in the banks in the black, brown, and poor white communities. The capital base of any community is its banks. We thought some of the working capital in banks throughout Houston should be transferred into these banks dealing extensively with these minority groups. The reason for this, obviously, is that when the Mexican-American furniture maker needs to borrow some money to buy wood or upholstery materials, he has to go to certain banks in town. The big banks won't lend to him because he doesn't have the credit rating or enough collateral. We want to see banks nearby with a base that can help him.

"Third, we asked the company to use some of its advertising capital in media that is owned and controlled by blacks and browns—radio stations, weekly newspapers, the giveaways they drop in grocery stores, barber shops, beauty shops. By putting ads in these smaller papers they become stronger papers. That builds up communication in the ghetto neighborhoods.

"Well, we were turned out cold when we first went to that bottler. They wouldn't even listen to us. They slammed the door in our face.

So we simply refused to buy his product. Our people drink a lot of soft drinks and we stopped. We said, 'All right, if you have the power to slam the door on us, then we have the power to change appetites on you.' That's exactly what we did. We took sixty thousand circulars and stood on the corners where the bus transfer points are all over Houston and passed them out to the maids and the porters and other people going to work. In all twelve ghettoes in Houston the word can be passed rather quickly. We have a lot of contacts. A soft-drink bottler operates a high-volume low-profit business and his profit margin is not more than 7 or 8 percent. In one week—one week—we cost him about 47 percent of his business. We virtually paralyzed him. So he called us back in. Only this time we wouldn't go to his office. We asked him to bring his people out here. He did. And he met our demands.

"Breadbasket is one way of making our anger work for us. Given some opportunity at least to face a man with your own strength, you feel good because at long last you don't have to say 'sir'—you have purchasing power on your side. And you feel even better when you can see your little bank getting bigger and bigger . . . your newspaper getting stronger and stronger . . . more and more concessions being made to other consumers like you. That's what Breadbasket does.

"But I wish it weren't necessary. I wish negotiations did not break down. Quite frankly, any time we have to utilize a selective buying campaign we haven't won, we've lost. It is not our interest to kill companies in Houston. Our interest is to get purchasing power for the black man. And if that can be done by rational men talking as gentlemen about a problem which is common to all of us, then we win. If the only thing we have left to do is to harm each other, then we've lost.

"Is integration dead? Integration as it was defined by the Supreme Court opinion in 1954 was dead to start with. Part of the wording of that decision said 'that which is separate is inherently unequal.' What it didn't say is what sixteen years of experience hence has shown, that white power is 'superior' and black power is 'inferior'; that when schools are consolidated usually it is the black principal who lost his job, or if there were children transferred from one place to another, they were black children transferred to a predominantly white school, almost never the whites to a black school. Integration meant 'We whites have set the standards and you blacks can therefore adjust to it, and you're welcome to the adjustment.' That kind of integration needs to die. But I don't believe in separation, and I recognize that the easiest reaction to phony integration is black racism or white racism. That's the kind of thing some fancy people are saying today—'It hasn't worked, so let's all go back home.' And that oversimplification plays right into the hands of the racists, the segregationists, the people who truly hate.

"Justice versus order? I don't think you can draw a line of demarcation there. The term 'order' usually means a kind of status quo in which people from a certain section of Europe have settled a nation, have taken it over, and have made its values and standards their own and have demanded that anyone who came in with them accept as given those values and standards. That's not my kind of order. Justice, on the other hand, is often used to mean that there should be privileges accorded to the underprivileged, and that's not what the underprivileged need. Man is made human not by privileges but by power. If he doesn't feel he can help to make decisions it doesn't matter how many benefits he's given. So that when people ask, 'What do *they* want?' or 'How much more do *they* want?' they're asking questions that sound very much as if they think they're Santa Claus, that they've got something to dole out and they're afraid their own bag will be left empty. When true justice and order exist there'll be checks and balances. There won't be anybody who will go all the way and there won't be anybody holding down somebody else.

"Until that day comes I guess we'll keep on having one crisis after another. But I can drive to Jackson, Mississippi, and stay at every Holiday Inn along the way—because of a crisis a few years ago. And I can get on a bus today anywhere in this country and I don't have to take the back seat—because of a crisis induced when thousands of people walked the streets in Montgomery. I guess that's the way it is. People don't change until they're forced to change."

We did not get to bed until almost 2 A.M. I heard Bill Lawson leave the house and drive away shortly before 5.

(From the Houston *Post,* Saturday, October 24, 1970)

ARSON SUSPECTED AS HOME BURNS

Arson is suspected in a fire Friday which heavily damaged the home of the Rev. William A. Lawson, pastor of the Wheeler Avenue Baptist Church and a leader in the black community.

Rev. Lawson, who was not at home when the fire was discovered at 12:30 PM, estimated the damage at more than $10,000.

District Fire Chief N. Blockmon said the blaze apparently started in a pile of papers in the garage of the two-story brick home at 3418 South MacGregor.

Chief Arson Investigator Alcus Greer said the fire is "highly suspicious" and is probably the work of arsonists.

United States District Judge John V. Singleton, whose court is in Houston, was a troubled man when he sentenced Dick Andrew Gee to prison for failing to report for induction into the armed services.

Gee had pleaded guilty.

> I cannot condone the killing of human beings [he wrote to Judge Singleton]. This is the logic of my position in its simplest form. . . . Our armed forces are engaged in an undeclared war in Vietnam in which part of the objective is to kill the enemy. . . . Our armed forces are killing women and children, too. I am not willing to judge whether I have more of a right to live than they do. Consequently, I will not participate in any division of the armed forces, because I will not assist in the killing in any way. . . . I applied for a conscientious-objector classification with my draft board, but they denied my request because my objection is based on a personal moral conviction rather than on religious grounds. Consequently, when I was called to be inducted into the armed forces on January 23, 1970, I refused.

When Richard Gee appeared for sentencing on May 7, Judge Singleton addressed him from the bench:

"I do not know what is going on in the world today. I do not know what is going on in the minds of young people. I cannot understand how an intelligent young man could, in his mind, living in this country, accepting the benefits of this free society, have the idea that he can substitute his opinion and his judgment for that made by the leadership of this country, and thereby act according to his own judgment and opinions in matters regarding national policy. I do not guess there is a single living soul in this courtroom—except maybe some of those charged with crimes of violence—that can stand killing human beings. That is your whole defense: that you cannot stand killing human beings. I cannot either. But a part of my obligation and a part of your obligation to society, to this country, for the benefits that you get from living here, is to respond when the leadership of the country says respond. . . . For every benefit there is a corresponding obligation. For the benefit of being able to go to school; for the benefit of being able to express your ideas freely; for the benefit that you have to go to religious institutions or not go to a religious institution; for the benefit that you have to be able to cast a vote; for the benefit you have of being able to take a grievance you have against your neighbor or government to a court of law and present it to that court or to a jury of twelve independent men and women—for all of those benefits there are corresponding obligations. These benefits do not come free. . . .

"I abhor killing just as you do. In fact, I guess one of the most chilling things that has happened to me in a great long time was the picture in the Houston *Post* the day before yesterday of National Guardsmen kneeling, firing live shots into a crowd of young people. But, at the same time, just because those people do not know how to handle their obligations does not mean that you should not know how to handle yours. . . . I have given every young man appearing before me and charged as you are the opportunity to change his mind. . . . I am offering it to you. I do not want to put anybody in jail. I do not know that jails, as such, cure any ills of society. I know that people who violate their neighbors' rights and violate society's rights have to be punished, but I am not at all certain that jails do it. I do not know. That is all we have open to us in the way of punishment. . . . I wish you would change your mind. I wish you would be inducted. This country is in terrible shape. I do not know why. . . . Maybe people have too much money. Maybe they do not know what to do with their leisure time. Maybe the government ought to spend more money teaching mankind what to do with his leisure time. Unfortunately, young man, mankind fights with each other. . . . Man just has to fight, and in any society the determination is made by the leadership as to where and when—and that determination has been made, and it is not for you or me to second-guess that. So you give me no alternative."

Judge Singleton sentenced Dick Gee to four years in prison. The probate officer had recommended two.

I went to see "Dub" Singleton in his chambers in the Federal Building in Houston. We had known each other from earlier days in Texas politics. Although we had not met since his appointment to the bench in 1966, I remembered him as a neighborly person, courteous and open. We differed on various points of political philosophy but he always seemed an amicable man whose principles were honestly held.

Some of his decisions on the bench have surprised liberal Houston lawyers.

When San Jacinto State College banned student beards to keep potential long-haired protesters off the campus, Judge Singleton declared the action unconstitutional and asked: "Aren't we dealing here with a form of McCarthyism—guilt by association or dress? Students are persons under the Constitution."

He riled the conservative establishment when he ordered the city to grant a parade permit it had denied to the Houston Peace Coalition for a demonstration against the draft and the war. City officials, he said, "may not deny such permits merely because of the controversial nature of the political thoughts they propose to express."

He refused the Internal Revenue Service access to all bank drafts and cashier checks at a Houston bank in an investigation of a suspected tax dodger. He wrote: "Government, businesses, labor unions and charities have gotten so big, somewhere somebody has got to protect the individual. Somebody's thumb has got to be in the dike, and that thumb is the federal judiciary."

"Some of us cried when Dub went on the bench," a prominent liberal lawyer said. "We feared he just had too many conservative friends. But in my opinion he's turned out to be just fine on the First Amendment." Judge Singleton told me his mail has been running six-to-four against his position in the Gee case. I told him that I had read his remarks to Dick Gee and that he had seemed rather mournful while also meting out a rather stiff penalty.

"Of course it bothered me," he said. "I don't like sending young people to prison. That's a very distasteful thing. But it was necessary in this case."

Why?

"Because I don't think young people today have a sense of responsibility. For reasons I do not know, they have lost respect for the institutions of government."

I told him about conversations with students on this trip. Those young people ask how they can be expected to respect a government that carries on a seemingly interminable war on the most tenuous legal grounds, with widespread killing not only of combatants but of civilians, and then sentences to prison for four years a young man who says that he cannot kill in such a war.

"I don't like the war either," he said. "But I know that my service in World War II in the navy helped me. It gave me a sense of direction. And I know that in Vietnam the President of the United States decided that it was in the interest of this country to take a stand. That's his responsibility. He has the information, the advice, the expertise available to him that we don't have. When the President asks us to serve, it is the same thing as the government asking us to serve, and I think it is our obligation, our responsibility, to do so. When the President makes such a determination and says that we must serve, I believe we have to follow blindly"—he paused and reflected on what he had just said—"yes, the word is blindly. We have to follow blindly along. He knows. We don't."

What is the individual's responsibility when a moral issue arises?

"Well, some people point to Nuremberg when that kind of question is raised. I don't think Nuremberg is analogous. I got letters saying it is. But it was a different matter. They had military orders to carry out an immoral act. Vietnam is not that. Vietnam is the government—your country—asking you to serve."

Some people do not see that.

"Yes, I know. But there has to be respect for the government and people have to fulfill their obligation when the government says it needs you. In great matters of foreign policy I think only the President can determine what is best for our country. When he makes a determination like that, we simply have to respond. It's like I told young Gee—that is what life is all about. You can't have one man interpreting his obligations this way and another that way and expect the country to survive. This is a dangerous world. The President's word on these things is final."

He changed the subject. "I am more concerned about the drift toward racism and fascism in this country than I am about the war. I'm afraid the average person in this country—the great Middle American—will take to racism and fascism if given a chance. I was at a party at the country club when the President said on television that the government will investigate the facts of Kent State. Hell, you don't have to investigate. All you have to do is look on television and see the National Guardsmen kneeling and pointing those goddamn rifles at those kids and squeezing those triggers.

"Listen, the most powerful man in the world is the man with a gun on his hip—that sonuvabitch is the most powerful man in the world. Most cops and state judges do not believe in the concept of innocent-until-proven-guilty and the administration is capitalizing on this. Just the other day the Deputy Attorney General of the United States of America made a speech to the judiciary conference talking about 'or-

265

dered freedom.' Now what in hell is 'ordered freedom'? That literally scares me to death. If you believe that mankind throughout history has measured progress in the creature comforts, those things which make life comfortable and bearable, this country has made more progress faster than any other country. Why? Because our government permits a man to move about with liberty and freedom. When you start talking about 'ordered freedom' the way the Deputy Attorney General means it, you're talking about something else. What they're doing is playing on the fear the plumber and the other working folks have of the Negro as a competitor. And of the students, too. That's what scares me. They're working on folks' fears. I think that is causing all the unrest and not so much the war."

Is the war contributing?

"Sure, it's a big part of the unrest. But that gets you back to the question of respect for institutions. It's not the beards and the long hair or even the pot that bothers me about the kids today. My brother made home brew in Waxahachie while Mother and Dad were away and I'd drink it. Marijuana is like that to these kids today, and I think it should be a misdemeanor, not a felony. The selling of it should be a felony, but that's the only way; the other way is too hard on the kids. As for the beards, look at those pictures on my wall. Do you see those six great jurists? There's Moses and Justice Holmes, Marshall, Coke, Solon, Justinian. Some have mustaches, some have long hair, some have mustaches and beards. Long sideburns, too. Hell, you can't hold those things against kids today. But those fellows in the pictures respected the institutions of society. They believed in law. And that's what's wrong with the kids today. If every man decided for himself which laws he was going to follow and which laws he was going to break, we'd have anarchy and society as we know it would completely collapse."

And that explains the four years for Dick Gee?

"There's got to be respect for our institutions," he repeated. "The young have no respect for Congress, for the Presidency, for the judiciary."

But you said in sentencing him that you didn't think jails cure the ills of society.

"I don't think they do. But there's got to be respect for government."

★ ★ ★

I decided to call on young Gee's parents in Beaumont, some ninety minutes east of Houston. This is historic country for Texans: down the

San Jacinto River in coastal lowlands the decisive battle of Texas' war against Mexico was fought and won. From Highway 59 at one point the slender white spindle of the San Jacinto Monument is framed by two towering oval signs advertising service stations. In this and other ways the billboard lobby has circumvented the modest success made five years ago to preserve scenic highway views for motorists. All over the country these signs have been lifted on stilts ranging from forty feet to over one hundred feet. From far down the road you can see them clawing the landscape and the sky.

It had been a tough fight, the billboard industry swarming all over Capitol Hill. Most people do not realize that a lobby can often summon more troops on a particular bill than the White House. I remember, on the night before the vote in 1965, seeing billboard lobbyists come out of a fashionable Washington restaurant with the chairman and two other powerful members of the House committee responsible for the highway legislation. There had been plenty of wining and dining, and the next day all three legislators capitulated to the lobby.

I also remember Phillip Tocker of Waco, Texas, president of the Outdoor Advertising Association of America. He would always defend the billboards in those days by pleading earnestly: "But we are a legitimate *business.*" Which we conceded. But he would only scowl when asked about the legitimate right of a family driving down the highway to enjoy the scenery. The difference is that the family doesn't have a Phillip Tocker taking Congressmen to dinner just before important votes.

Most of the more than one million billboards were to have been removed by July 1, 1970. Mr. Tocker and his friends so diluted the legislation and have so effectively opposed its implementation that by the deadline not one sign had come down. Not one. As I traveled I saw in those uplifted oval frames not "Gulf" or "Enco" or "Texaco" but the jubilant face of Phillip Tocker.

Beaumont, Texas

BOTH SONS?

"Yes, both our boys have gone to prison rather than go into the service," Mrs. John Gee said. She set a dish of hot blueberry pie on the table.

"George did sixteen months of a two-year sentence in '64 and '65, just as the war was starting. And Dickie just went in for four. Both of them have been reared in a church influence but they took the attitude that they didn't need a church affiliation to have a moral and conscientious conviction against killing."

"We lived in Texas City when George went in," her husband said. "He had gone to Austin to the University of Texas and he wasn't one to communicate with us at all. His last year in high school we were havin' to stay night and day with our daughter, who had a critical case of encephalitis and we thought would die, and George got a new freedom he hadn't known at all. Now he did his share of sittin' with Molly, but the rest of the time he was pretty much on his own. Then he went to Austin and sort of divorced himself from us altogether. We didn't even know his address. But something finally got to him, and in January of '64 he called us and asked if he could come home, that he was goin' to be drafted and was goin' to refuse to go, so he'd like to come home and wait until they picked him up."

Mrs. Gee chuckled. "We told him we'd come and get him."

"That's right," John Gee said. "I said, 'This is your home, George. It's the only place to go, you know that.' He sort of expected us to resent the fact that he would be arrested in our house, but we didn't.

268

We had prayed about this and already made up our minds that it didn't make any difference what he chose to do; we'd brought him up to make up his own mind, to do his own thinking."

What reason did he give you for refusing induction?

"That he was just morally against killin' and he thought that the war was illegal anyway."

Did you agree with him?

"No. I think he would have had less respect for me if I had agreed with him, because he knew I didn't feel that way. I had come out of World War II as a lieutenant commander and was proud of my service. We had three children when I went in, but I wouldn't have stayed out at all, because I felt it was my duty to go in."

Mrs. Gee interrupted. "George was thirteen months old when his daddy left, and he was more 'n three when he came back. And it didn't seem to affect him in any way. We never really had any trouble with any of our children as they grew up. That's why it's been such a surprise." She chuckled again and filled my plate with blueberry pie.

"Mr. Kirby, the FBI man in Texas City, was a good friend of mine because when I was assistant postmaster down there I associated with the U.S. marshal and different law-enforcement people. He came over one day and said, 'John, I'm looking for a George Gee—do you know anybody by chance related to him?' I said, 'Yes, that's my son.' He looked kinda strange and embarrassed and said, 'I've got . . . I've got to talk to him about the draft.' I said, 'That's him.' He asked, 'Where can I locate him?' I said, 'Just tell me where you are and he'll come over to talk to you. That's what he's here for,' I said. 'He's come home from Austin waiting to hear from you.' And the FBI fella said, 'I don't want to disrupt things around your house. Would you call and tell him when I drive up there to come and talk to me in the car?' I said, 'Sure,' and that's what he did. George told Mr. Kirby that he wasn't going to be inducted, and Mr. Kirby said, 'Well, you know what that means,' and he said, 'Yes, sir.' The night they came to pick him up before the trial it was just around seven o'clock. Mrs. Gee and I were gettin' ready to go to the church for our Bible study and George and Dickie were out playin' croquet in the front yard. And one of his classmates was a policeman and he came with a U.S. marshal to pick him up. George had on some old pants, so he changed his clothes and went with them. And they put him in jail."

"They sent him to Springfield after he was convicted," Mrs. Gee said.

"The judge [it was not John Singleton] said he wanted George to have a psychiatric examination. He asked George if he believed laws should be obeyed and George said yes. He asked George if he was going to obey this law and George said no. He thought there was something wrong with George and he sent him to Springfield for a presentencing investigation. They got the records fouled and kept him too long. Then they brought him back and kept him in Houston close to a month. In jail, in a tank up there in the Harris County jail. You know what those tanks are? Have you ever—"

No.

"Well, they're pretty awful. They have these little thin mats, one is right up against the other one, all around the wall, that the prisoners sleep on. There must have been about sixteen or twenty in this one tank. He got sores on him in there. And when you go to visit you see him through a glass about this wide and you have to talk to him through this grill down here"—she leaned her chin almost to the top of the table—"and you could only visit him just a very short time, about twenty minutes. He'd spilled some coffee up in Springfield and the side of his face got burned, and he tried his best to hide it but he didn't succeed."

How old was Dickie when George went to prison?

"Sixteen. He never did talk too much about George's being in prison. I used to tell him that George was wrong, that there were ways to change the law, that nothing justified breaking the law. But Dickie—I think he knew from that day on what he would do. He looked up to George."

Did either of them consider leaving the country?

Mr. Gee answered: "Oh, they wouldn't have done that. George had a friend who deliberately failed to pass the IQ test for the army. He wouldn't even consider doing that."

"The funny thing is that George just weighs about 120 pounds and he couldn't have passed the physical anyway," Mrs. Gee said. "He was just skin and bones."

"I was proud they didn't try to leave the country or pull some prank to fail. Both insisted that they were consciously disobeyin' a law that they didn't agree with and they were willin' to take their punishment."

What did your neighbors think?

"The ones in Texas City were a little bit surprised," she said. "The majority of them we heard from said they didn't altogether agree with

270

what George did but they said they were proud of him for standing up for his principles."

John Gee continued: "We moved from Texas City to Beaumont before George got out of prison and Dickie went. I made a firm commitment while George was contemplatin' gettin' out of prison that when I retired from the post office I wanted to go to college. We visited him at each place he was incarcerated, like we're doing with Dickie, and we called on him in Tucson. We went out there and I was talking with George and I said, 'You know, my time is comin' up for retirement and I'm thinkin' about retirin' and goin' back to school.' He said, 'Well' I just may go with you.' That tickled me to death. We felt real good about his wantin' to stay home and go to school. And Dickie at the time was in college here at Lamar Tech and I figured he could help me learn math."

Mrs. Gee laughed. "Last year we had all three of 'em in the same college. George was back from prison and finishing his work on a bachelor's degree in economics. Dickie hadn't gone to prison yet and was in school studying math. And John was struggling right along with 'em. All three of 'em made the honor roll."

John Gee blushed.

Why did you decide to go back to college?

"Go back? I'd never started in the first place. I finished high school in '27 up in Call—that's near Kirbyville—and when I got out I went to work for seventeen and a half cents an hour. That was a man's wages. Then you'd work awhile and you'd get twenty-two and a half cents and first thing you know you might get up to two bits. I couldn't afford to go to college but I always wanted to. I always kind of felt like I was shortchangin' the folks in Texas City because I was on the board of education for fifteen years and didn't even have a college education. They even dedicated the school annual to me down there because I'd been on the board so long and I said, 'By golly, I really ought to go get me a degree and teach school while there's still a little time.' My first year here was really tough. My old mind wouldn't click at all and I was a lot older than any of the teachers. But I'll be out in the summer of '71."

It was hot in the little frame house and we moved to the front porch.

"Before Dickie went to prison we used to sit right here and play forty-two up a storm [forty-two is a dominio game]. Dickie and me must

271

have been behind George and his mother for two, three years, and we're three games ahead now."

"Just wait'll he gets out," Mrs. Gee said. And they both laughed. She continued: "Just got a letter from him today. He said he sure does miss the front-porch talks. In those last days we'd sit out here many a night and just talk about everything.

"From the time George came back," she said, "our relationship was really something. He was so kind and thoughtful. I told him, 'George, I'm not ever going to be ashamed of what you did, you hear?' I told all our neighbors about it when we moved here and they know and they don't care. You feel like home here, 'cause that's exactly what it is."

"The only incident we had," John Gee said, "was when George had to go to the draft board and register after we got back. This old secretary there, who'd been there forty years, I guess, read him off. 'Are you the guy who burned up your draft card?' she asked him. And he said, 'I haven't burned up my draft card—I've still got the one that I had to carry—I carried it all through prison with me.' But she spent twenty minutes just reading him off. She said he was lowdown and would have to face this thing everywhere he goes—that people would know him for what he is. He didn't say a thing—he was on probation and he didn't want any trouble. But when I got back I could see the hurt on his face and I wanted to go back there and tell that gal off. But he wouldn't let me."

"He's not a criminal, no matter what she said," Mrs. Gee interrupted.

Her husband looked at her and said: "Well, he's a criminal in that he broke the law. All my life I've supported the law. I worked for the post office for forty years, and my father before me. And we've been spelling out the law to people all the time—'This can't be over seventy pounds,' and 'This needs more stamps because the law says it does.' No, he broke the law, there's no question about it."

"Yes," his wife said, "I know he broke the law. I just don't consider it criminal in the sense of a murderer or something like that. I still think it's wrong but I don't consider it the same. I don't know how you would differentiate."

"I'll say this," Mr. Gee replied, looking at his wife, "I wish the world had more criminals like our sons."

The frown had passed from her face and she said: "Well, after all, the judge didn't seem to like sending Dickie to jail. I think he knew he wasn't some kind of ordinary criminal."

"I told her," Mr. Gee said, "that I'm sure the reason the judge did it is because he feels there's more and more young people rebellin', and he's tryin' to set examples to sort of dissuade them from this rebellious attitude. I told her he was doin' it strictly as an example."

Mrs. Gee said: "I wish you knew these two boys. They think they are agnostics, but I have faith that God's gonna bring them back from that. Their sister's a missionary—the one that had encephalitis—in the Far East. Both of the boys have such good feelings for people. Year before last George was in charge of recruiting college students to tutor black children that couldn't make their grades over here at one of the schools—they were trying to get these children ready to come to integrated schools, and they needed some extra help. George enlisted students from the college to teach three days a week on their own time, without any pay. And he asked Dickie if he would like to, and Dickie said yes. George said, 'Well, let me impress upon you now that this means you'll have to do it three times a week and no excuses.' Dickie was working at the dock in his spare time—he became a longshoreman to help pay his way through college—and George asked him what he would do if some dock work came up. And Dickie said he'd put the teaching first. I had to be real proud of him because many times he got a call for dock work. During the whole semester, if it was his time at the school he went with George and they tutored these black children. He could've gotten $7 an hour at the dock. They had a good feeling about people, you understand? You can't have been raised in a Christian home and not be appreciative about killing. I once told my father when I was about fifteen years old that the Commandment says not to kill. He said 'Well, if a man comes in here and bothers you, I'd certainly kill him.' And I said, 'No, you're not supposed to kill him even under those circumstances, because the Bible says, "Thou shalt not kill." ' That's the way I felt when I was fifteen. How can I say George and Dickie shouldn't feel it now? I've never been—you know, a mother can't be very fair about her children. You can't really depend on what a mother says about her boys. I hope you understand."

I asked John Gee about President Nixon's handling of the war.

"Don't you believe he's tryin' to end it? I just never figured anybody really likes that war. That's the trouble with war, I guess. They're always easier to start than they are to stop."

Mrs. Gee said: "I think the President is doing the best he can do. The only thing that has really hurt me during this whole thing is we were at war with Japan and Germany, and we got in there and were through with it. Fought it and won it. But in this little bitty country we're not trying to fight and win and get it over. We're just keeping something going over there like we got all the boys in the world to spare. I don't understand it. Why we can't go over there and do something about it or get out."

Mrs. Gee walked to the car with me. "I get all mixed up thinking about it," she said as we paused under a pecan tree. "When I pray for Dickie I get to thinking how selfish that is. He's in prison because he didn't want to learn how to kill, and four years seems like a long time to give up just because you don't want to kill. But I think of all the other sons who need someone to pray for them, too. I prayed differently for Dick than for George. I prayed that George would be helped by it. I prayed that Dick would be spared from it. Two seemed too much. Maybe that's selfish, too. I just don't know."

She leaned into the window of the car and said: "You be careful and watch out on the roads."

The streets of the business district of Beaumont were decorated with hundreds of American flags. They were promoting something called the "New Orleans Sale." A few blocks from the Gees' I passed a large billboard with a flag and big letters that admonished: "Back It—Don't Buck It."

★ ★ ★

A few days later the Supreme Court ruled (in *Welsh vs. United States*) that men can be exempted from military service for personal and philosophical beliefs as well as religious beliefs. In San Antonio U.S. Federal Judge Adrian Spears ordered the army to release a soldier who had sought a discharge on conscientious-objector grounds; the request had been denied earlier because his beliefs were said to be insufficiently grounded in religious training. The Gees were financially unable to afford an appeal in behalf of their son. I mentioned this fact to W. V. Ballew, Jr., a friend and attorney in Houston, who in turn interested a twenty-eight-year-old lawyer, David Berg, in the Gee case. Berg then filed a plea with Judge Singleton asking him to set aside Dick Gee's sentence as a result of the High Court's ruling. Although I have yet to meet David Berg, I subsequently received a letter from him which read, in part:

The Gees, John and Gertrude, have written, called and come to my office on several occasions since I entered the picture. They do not fit well in all this: they should never have had to enter a court-

274

room at all, much less in a criminal matter. For my part, I find in the Gees something real and spontaneous which I have lost and regret losing, and although I cannot precisely say why, I feel protective toward them, and want very much for them, their son's freedom.

Judge Singleton announced from the bench during oral arguments that he will apply the *Welsh* decision retroactively, and decide if Dick qualifies as a conscientious objector under the new Supreme Court ruling. It is my opinion that he does qualify, and although he has not yet said so, I believe the Judge agrees. The Judge's conscience, he has said in open court, bothers him in Dick's case, especially since Gee would have been exonerated had the *Welsh* decision come down only one month sooner. I have brought and tried in Judge Singleton's court some of his most noted cases and I feel I know him well, though we have seldom spoken outside the courtroom. He is an enlightened man who does not seem to be influenced by fear of the community's reaction to his decisions. I disagree with his pre-sentence lecture to Dick, but I marvel at his self-doubts, the inner struggle that surfaces in his ambivalence toward sending this boy to jail.

Finally, there is Dick Andrew Gee, whom I do not know personally. His position is simple: based on his own personal moral code rather than on any particular religious belief, he has decided that he will not kill another human being. Because the basis of his decision was personal and moral rather than religious, he could not, at the time, qualify for conscientious objector status. And so, for his crime of conscience, he has been sentenced to serve a term in a federal prison. Perhaps I am exaggerating, but I feel the major issues of our time are inextricably bound up in a case such as this; I want very much for him to be freed, but if he loses then we have, each of us, lost, and the years we take from his life will surely diminish us all.

In mid-November, on the day this book went to the printer, Judge Singleton granted Dick Gee status as a conscientious objector, thus vacating his sentence and freeing him from prison on the condition that he accept employment in a nonprofit capacity.

The government planned to appeal the decision.

On the Road in East Texas

I TURNED NORTH UP THE TEXAS FOREST TRAIL AND HEADED FOR MARSHALL, my home town, in the northeast corner of the state. There were still two hours of daylight in the sky when my eye was drawn to a large crowd in the football stadium of the high school in Kirbyville, an inconspicuous but pleasant little town of about two thousand surrounded by piny woods. Deciding to investigate, I found a parking place among the pickup trucks and the yellow schoolbuses and joined the throng in the "Home of the Kirbyville Wildcats." The meeting turned out to be the annual gathering of the Jasper-Newton Rural Electric Cooperative. From all over the two counties families had come for an evening of food, entertainment, and progress reports. There were four generations in some families. Grandmothers with faces like hard pastry dipped snuff while their false teeth clicked, and tall pubescent boys in high-heeled boots sneaked away to the schoolbuses for a smoke. I observed that down here women over forty seem to have abandoned girdles as women under forty have abandoned bras in New York. The men pushed straw stetsons back on their heads and talked about the one subject that farmers always talk about: the weather.

And there was food—four long tables of barbecued chicken, beef, baked beans with thick juice like melted jelly, raw onions and pickles, home-made fried pies. I picked up an empty plate and someone slapped half a pound of sliced beef on it. Kids were throwing scraps under the stadium to the fattest, sleekest country red dog I have ever seen, the kind of dog that travels from one REA affair to another in the summer and sleeps it off all winter.

"Where you goin'?" a woman inquired of her husband.

"Git me 'nother one of them fried pies."

"Lord, Farrell, you done had three."

"Yeah, but I didn't eat but two helpin's' beef."

Ten years ago there would have been no Negroes here. They were abundantly present tonight. One white child and a middle-aged black woman reached at the same time for the spoon in the beans. The little girl looked up and her mother said: "Say you're sorry, honey." She did.

In the middle of the football field a flatbed trailer had been parked, decorated with green and gold crepe paper. The mayor of Kirbyville tapped on the microphone, looked around the field, and said: "Folks say things never happen around here but they sure can't say that tonight."

Another man introduced visitors and especially welcomed home "Mr. Willie Whitehead, who moved to Conroe and has come back to be with us tonight." Conroe is about a hundred miles to the west. Whistling and clapping, the crowd seemed happy to see Willie Whitehead again.

Mrs. Lilly Walker—I think that is what the mayor called her—had arranged the program for the evening, and the first performer was a preacher who sang "Galveston." The man sitting in front of me said: "Glen Campbell wrote that one." His wife replied: "I'd give two of my blackberry pies to see Glen Campbell in person."

Brother Jess Harper, Jackie Harper, and Betty Bass sang and played "Jesus Is Coming Soon" and "Jesus, I Believe What You Say" on the piano and the electric bass guitar. Brother Harper then told the audience: "It's not exactly Western and it's not exactly a hymn, so we're going to sing a country Western gospel song, Johnny Cash's 'Papa Sing Bass.'"

After their final number Brother Harper asked the people to stand and sing the national anthem. "Everybody now," he said. "I want to see everybody sing. I was in the position for about eleven months where it was forbidden to sing this song and I'd like to hear everybody sing it like you appreciate it." It has been a long time since I have heard an audience sing the national anthem with such enthusiasm.

While the co-op members went about their business I sought Brother Jess Harper behind the platform. A tall man with a distinguished mustache, he wore a dark blue shirt, a white tie, and a blue tie pin. I asked him where he had been during those eleven months when he could not sing "The Star-Spangled Banner."

"I was in a stalag in northern Poland. Got there by being marched for three months, three miserable months. Until recently I couldn't sing that song without choking up. Now, I'm not in accord with everything that's going on in this country but I still think we got to believe some of them folks in Washington know what they are doing. This isn't a perfect country and the government is made up of just folks, but I tell you—this is still a mighty good place to live."

What about the kids?

"They don't know, the ones who're spitting on the flag. They just don't know what price some folks have paid for it. They don't know what it stands for when you might have lost it. I don't hate 'em—they're our kids. But they're wrong when they spit at the flag and try to tear the country down instead of trying to change it 'n' make it better. Better to light a candle than to curse the darkness, I say. You spend eleven months in a stalag, Mister, and that song means something to you."

★ ★ ★

It was late and dark and I wanted one more cup of coffee for the last hour on the road. Somewhere past Center before you get to Carthage —I think it was around Teneha—I stopped at a roadside café. It was about eleven o'clock and the place was full of young couples having hamburgers and Cokes before they headed for the piny woods and the back seats. Several truckers were there. The waitress was harassed but friendly, and between orders she stood behind the counter and talked with me. I noticed through a square open window in the wall behind the counter at least four Negro men drinking coffee in a small back room that appeared to be part of the kitchen.

"They ever come up here?" I asked.

"Naw. That's their place back there."

I said, quite casually: "Did you know that's against the law?"

"Against the law?"

"Yep, the Public Accommodations Act of 1964 says you can't do that."

"You're pullin' my leg."

"No, no, I'm not. It's right there in the law. You have to open the same facilities to everyone if you run a business that caters to the public."

"That a state law?"

"Nope, federal law. Passed in 1964."

"I'll be damned."

" 'Course it's the owner that's liable. I don't think the fault would be on you."

She turned to her left and said in a very loud Shelby County voice: "Hey, Charlie, c'm here." And there arose from the table in the corner a vast square block of a man with his shirt collar open down to the hair on his chest and thick hard arms protruding out of the short sleeves of his sport shirt.

"Yeah?"

"This feller says it's against the law for us to serve them nigras back there."

Without changing his expression he said: "No shit."

"That's what he said. Said it was a fed'r'l law passed five years ago. Is that what you said? Five years ago?"

"Yes."

"Who says?"

"The government—the Congress—the Public Accommodations Act of 1964."

"Never heard of it."

"Well, it's there. It's there on the books."

He turned toward the square window in the wall, stabbed two fingers of his left hand into the corners of his mouth, and let out a loud throaty whistle like a hunter calling back his bird dogs.

The Negro men in the small back room looked up startled and glanced at each other apprehensively, and when Charlie motioned to them with a jerk of his head they got up and came through the door from the kitchen. They were nervous. Each appeared to be in his mid-forties, except for one, a much older man. I took them to be farm hands.

Charlie jerked his head toward me and said: "Feller here says it's against the law to serve you folks back there."

They were silent. I could not tell if they were more frightened than I was.

"Says it's something—what'd you say they call it, Mister?"

"The Public Accommodations Act of 1964."

"You ever hear of that?"

"Naw sir, never did." The older man was answering.

"You think it's against the law for you to have a nice place back there to eat so's you can talk among yourselves?"

"Naw sir, naw sir."

He turned to me and said: "They don't think it's against the law. And I don't think it's against the law. And nobody's told me it's against the law but you. Now what are you going to do?"

279

I said, "I'm going to hit the road." And I put down a quarter, which included a fifteen-cent tip for my recent friend, the waitress, walked out of the diner, got into my car, locked the doors, and sped away.

★ ★ ★

I was home for the first time in a year, and my parents and I spent a day driving through the back country along the Texas-Louisiana border, marveling at the recently black-topped farm-to-market roads. "They used to build those roads so we could go to town and come back," Dad said. "Now more people go to town on 'em than come back." We passed through Bethany, Four Forks, De Berry, Elysian Fields, and Deadwood, and I knew what he meant. "It's funny," he said, "but the more people we get, the more vacant land we've got. They just can't live on it any more." And he said it rather wistfully.

There was a small advertisement in the Shreveport paper placed there by Mrs. Cammie Sue Garrett of Heard's Café in Logansport: "Due to my health, labor shortage, employee vacation, food prices, and overhead expenses, I will not accept any outside trade beyond my usual regular customers. I cannot stock food and labor enough beyond my usual anticipation without 30-day notice. Please cooperate with me." I asked for Mrs. Garrett at the restaurant but she was not there; she was out for lunch.

Not far from the Sabine River, in a triangle formed by Keatchie, Carthage, and Gill, we came upon the final resting place of Gentleman Jim Reeves. He is buried in a park on more than an acre of land, and although it is in the "middle of nowhere," thousands of country-music fans come here to honor his memory. He brought class to the country movement, they say, and he might have gone as far as Johnny Cash has, but an untimely death cut him down in 1964 at the age of forty-one. Country-music fans never forget, and I don't know of another singer whose grave is marked by a lifelike statue standing at the end of a long walk shaped like a guitar, with robins and mockingbirds and crows fluttering in the hickory trees and liveoaks. It is here that the power and popularity of country music can be understood. There are over 650 full-time country-music stations in America and over 2,000 other stations that offer country music from two to sixteen hours every day; half of them seem to be right here in the pine belt of Texas—what a station down in Beaumont proudly talks of as "countrypolitan." But country music is no longer just a Southern rural phenomenon. There are two full-time country-music stations in Chicago, for example. And I know sophisticated successful businessmen in New York City whose car radios are permanently tuned to a country-music station in New Jersey.

Why? Because we are a nostalgic people. Next to loneliness the national disease is homesickness. Just about everyone in America is from somewhere else, and many are from the farms and small towns which run through country-music themes like aces in the hand of a Red River card shark. Charley Pride sings of a world "full of country boys out on the street" who have come from "the sticks of the country to the jungle of the city." When he wonders "could I live there any more," he is speaking for half of the nation who left it and to the other half who would like to discover it. Country music has become the poetry of the search for an irrecoverable homeland.

In the little park a man and woman in their fifties placed a bouquet of plastic flowers among a dozen other faded artificial arrangements at the base of the memorial to Gentleman Jim Reeves. They left after silently studying the inscription on the giant concrete guitar: "If I, a lowly singer, dry one tear or soothe one humble human heart in pain, then my homely verse to God is dear and not one stanza has been sung in vain."

My dad wondered if they would ever do that for Frank Sinatra. Mother said she did not know, but she thought they would for Lawrence Welk.

The road back to Marshall carried us past one small country church after another, most of them Baptist, most of them now abandoned. "There used to be more Baptists around here than people," Dad said. We fell to reminiscing about the little church in which I grew up. Today it is one of the largest in town, but twenty-five years ago it consisted of only a small group of people who had broken away from another congregation. "Where two or three are gathered together," Dad would say of Baptists, "they fight and split."

Once in that church we had an encounter group. This was before anyone had refined group sensitivity training, before Carl Rogers, before Esalen and Big Sur. At the time I was only thirteen years old, but I know it was an encounter group because even a boy that young knows when people discover who they are.

It happened during the annual spring revival. The church was filled and the kids, as usual, were sitting on the back rows. I was reading a copy of *The Reader's Digest* which I had smuggled inside the hymn book. The preacher was from a big church in Waco, I think, and while the grownups considered him very good even though he did not shout and thump the pulpit as much as the preacher who had conducted the annual winter revival when twenty souls were saved, we kids did not approve of him: his jokes were corny and he hated movies on Sunday. I cannot imagine *The Reader's Digest* condoning Sunday pictures in those days, but at least the jokes were good enough to make the long sermons tolerable.

Toward the end of this final evening service I spotted Brother Lamar Smith glowering at me from across the aisle, where the deacons took turns visually patrolling the back rows—they considered it hardship duty—and I closed the hymn book and tried to concentrate on the sermon. The preacher was lamenting the sordid spiritual condition of a church in which only four people, two of them eight-year-olds, had confessed their sins after thirteen sermons and prayer meetings in the homes twice every day. He would not take into account the fine harvest we had back in the winter revival because, he said, there was enough sin in our town to keep a stadium of preachers busy twenty-four hours a day until the Lord comes again. He felt something in that church right then, he warned, that was keeping the Spirit back, something deep down inside the hearts of the people that was working against a true revival. There were "back-biting" and "enmities" and "gossiping" in the church, he said—and no prophet ever spoke truer words, because half of the members had been trying to chase the pastor off and half of them had been fighting to keep him. Yes, the preacher continued, "the hearts of the people have ossified." What it meant to "ossified" I did not then know, but the idea of it happening to me was terrifying, and I remember the hymnal with *The Reader's Digest* beginning to get warm in my hand, like a quarter stolen from your mother's purse, and I leaned over and dropped it under the seat in front of me. It was too late, of course, because Brother Lamar Smith, the quisling, had already seen me; but I was no longer a stumbling block, and a revival followed. Within half an hour there was flooding through the crowded auditorium the most profuse torrent of confessions I ever heard. I do not mean the maudlin, cheap, superficial "I-Was-Down-in-the-Gutter-and-Jesus-Took-My-Hand-and-I-Will-Do-Better" spectacles practiced by the football players in the citywide revival services all the Baptist churches sponsored just before school (and the football season) opened every summer. Something very genuine happened in that service that night, something rare, basic, and, for the moment, healing. The masks people wore came off. People got up from their seats and started apologizing to their neighbors.

"I want to say that I have been a stubborn fool," one man, a leading pillar, said before the whole congregation.

"No more a fool 'n I've been," his arch nemesis replied, as they met at the pulpit and embraced.

One by one the stalwarts of that church pulled the motes and beams out of their eyes. Almost everyone who stood to give a "personal testimony" confessed to some grudge he had been harboring against someone else. Mabel White* laughed as she cried and said she had thought the dresses Myra Mobberly* had been wearing in the choir were meant to distract from the service and she was sorry she had thought such things, and Miss Mobberly, sitting in the choir, started crying, too. People were walking all over the auditorium to seek out the victims of their backbiting, to confess and be forgiven. The most touching scene came when the leader of the putsch against the pastor walked to the rostrum and without a word offered his hand and they hugged each other. I even felt kindly toward Brother Lamar Smith, although I recovered when later he told my father about *The Reader's Digest* and I caught hell at home. I guess no human being can forever escape his hypocrisies, because later they fired the pastor anyway and several people left the church. But that night a very honest thing did happen and all these years later I am still grateful for the memory of it.

* The names are changed to protect the guilty.

Little Rock, Arkansas

THE PICTURE IS ALMOST AS CLEAR IN MY MIND TODAY AS IT WAS IN THE newspapers on that Tuesday morning thirteen years ago. Two National Guardsmen, rifles slung to their shoulders and their wrists looped by leather thongs to billy clubs, framed the tall archways of Central High School. For the first time a Southern governor had called out the National Guard to interpose his state office against the authority of the United States Government. The Battle of Little Rock had begun.

Governor Orval Faubus announced late Monday night before the schools were to open the next morning: "Units of the National Guard have been, or are now, being mobilized with the mission to maintain or restore the peace of this community."

But the "peace of this community" had been violated only by the rhetoric of a minority of rednecks and by the rumors Orval Faubus himself stirred. At a public hearing a few days earlier he had hinted darkly at the violence, riots, and bloodshed that would come if the schools of Little Rock were integrated. When he called up the National Guard he acted, he said, because of telephone calls that had come to him expressing "fear of disorder and violence." Police, he said, had reported the sale of unusually large numbers of weapons in the Little Rock area and had taken pistols away from white and black students, and caravans were coming from all over the state to assemble at Central High School the next morning. Warning that forcible integration could not be carried out, he called up the National Guard to maintain forcible segregation.

Yet nobody had seen the caravans he reported to be on the way. A check of twenty-one gun dealers failed to find a single instance where the sale of firearms or knives had increased. The Little Rock chief of police said his men had taken no pistols from any students. The governor had promised to document his charges; he never did. There was ample evidence, in fact, to suggest there would be no trouble. Only five months before, voters had defeated two candidates for the school board who had openly pledged to fight integration.

But Orval Faubus wanted to neutralize the segregationist who was opposing him for reelection and who kept reminding him that in Texas Governor Allan Shivers had sent two Texas Rangers to prevent Negroes from enrolling in the schools of the little town of Mansfield. Needing an emergency, Orval Faubus simply declared that one existed. From then on it did.

The next morning 1,878 white students walked past the troops into Central High School. Fifteen-year-old Elizabeth Echford, who was black, was blocked by the soldiers. As she was turned away from the line of troops a crowd of two hundred people rushed to jeer and curse her. "Go back where you came from," a woman shouted. Another screamed: "Don't let her in our school—that nigger."

Three weeks later, after a mob of one thousand white persons forced police to remove nine Negro students who had slipped in a side door of Central High to attend classes under court order, President Eisenhower decided to enforce the law and to squelch sedition and rebellion in Arkansas. He put the National Guard under federal control and sent twelve hundred battle-equipped paratroopers into the city.

By this time Orval Faubus, whose favorite character in American history is Abraham Lincoln, had become a hero to the segregationists. The law had been undercut and moderates in Little Rock, who might have prevailed with Faubus' tacit help or even with his silence, were in disarray. The impulse to oppose integration, to obstruct the courts, had been encouraged from the highest office in the state. The high schools in Little Rock eventually would be closed for an entire year. A modest effort to begin the long road to equality had failed because political leadership failed.

★ ★ ★

"Is the situation any better than ten years ago? I think it's worse," John Walker said. "They stopped fighting us in the streets and started fighting us with the suburbs." Walker is the black attorney who has been arguing in court for faster and more widespread desegregation than the school board has proposed.

He is thirty-three, and was born in Hope, Arkansas, the watermelon capital of the world. He graduated from the all-black Arkansas A & M, earned a master's degree from New York University, received his law degree from Yale, and came back to Arkansas "to bust 'em up," in the words of another lawyer; "he was the first black man to shake 'em up since L. C. Bates in the fifties. But John had class, and pretty soon they were respectin' him. They hate him, but they respect him."

Since he returned to Arkansas, Walker has been pressing controversial civil-rights litigation and the school suits. He is a fashionable dresser; today he wore a green shirt with broad rose and gray stripes, a red tie, and a vest. He has a slim mustache and short hair, which he is constantly rubbing with his hand as he examines witnesses. In court he is the epitome of protocol, repeatedly addressing the bench with "Your Honor." Partly it is his color, partly his self-confident style that increases the edginess in the witnesses for the defense. "John Walker has beat 'em at their own game," the lawyer said. "It's the game of bein' a tough sonuvabitch but bein' a good Southern gentleman at the same time.

"When the whites saw that integration was inevitable," Walker continued, "they started moving west, building new suburbs out on the edge of town. They built a new high school out there just to encourage whites who could afford it to come in that direction. They built another new high school over where the blacks are concentrated just to keep them in that area. Out of thirteen new schools built in Little Rock since this whole thing started, only three have been put in the area where most of the blacks live. It was subtle and it was quietly vicious, but it was successful. Now we have integration accepted by law but segregation sustained by residence. The whites over here, because they can afford it, and the blacks over there, because they can't. We got almost nine thousand black students in Little Rock but most of them have to go to schools that are all or mostly black.

"The only way we are really going to get schools that cannot be identified by color is to transport black kids out of their neighborhoods to schools that are mostly white and to transport white kids out of their neighborhoods to schools that are mostly black. But that's what people call 'busing' and the white folks say we can bus all the black kids anywhere we want but no white kids are going to be bused anywhere. Well, that's unfair. We're tired of black families having to bear all the burden of integration. We think white kids and white parents ought to bear some of it."

John Walker and his associates, including the NAACP Legal Defense

Fund, have brought the Little Rock school board back into court to try to accomplish that goal. Their current suit is a continuation of the litigation that began when the Supreme Court handed down its 1954 decision and Governor Faubus thwarted a court-approved plan that would have totally desegregated Little Rock's schools by 1963. Negro plaintiffs and the school board have been in and out of court almost constantly. In 1966 a more or less liberal school board hired a team from the University of Oregon to prepare another long-range plan of desegregation for the district. The report recommended that the neighborhood-school concept be abandoned and the schools be integrated through a capital building program. Two incumbent members of the board who supported the Oregon Plan were defeated by two candidates who campaigned against it. In 1968 and 1969 other liberal incumbents were defeated and the school board is controlled now by people who the blacks charge are wedded to the status quo.

The blacks say they want only what the Constitution requires—"a school system not based on color distinction." "That is not the kind of system we have in Little Rock," John Walker said. "Every school in this district is clearly identifiable by race. We have high schools like Horace Mann with only two whites out of almost eight hundred students and another with only forty blacks out of almost fourteen hundred students. There are two whites in the Granite Mountain elementary school with eight hundred children and no blacks at all in the Fair Park elementary school with over two hundred students. Every time the school district has been told by the court to do something, it did as little as possible to inconvenience the whites. The pattern of separate enrollments is almost as strong today as it was ten years ago. When black children were moved they were moved principally into schools that were all black to begin with. White children were moved to schools that serve white neighborhoods. We still have, after all these years, what is in effect a dual school system. The board is an obstructionist group committed to segregationist policies."

"That's not so," the president of the school board, Daniel H. Woods, told me. "The people of Little Rock and the board itself are not in any way resisting integration or desegregation. We're resisting what we would consider to be far-out methods not in the best interest of education itself. The issue is neighborhood schools versus busing your children across town to school. People say that changing residential patterns have created a new form of segregation, but this has always been the pattern in most cities. It's not new that residential patterns tend to reflect people within their own kind. Little Rock is no different in that respect from New York and Chicago. People go with their own.

"I don't know why Mr. Walker always criticizes me in personal terms. He's on the defensive about me, I think, because the company I'm with [he is industrial-relations director for Timex in Little Rock] under my leadership and direction won the first equal opportunity award ever presented in this state and has received citations for our work in this area every year. We started our program long before any civil-rights pressure to do it just because we wanted to, felt it was right. We're one of the few companies in this state that has Negro men and women in just about every category of employment. Twenty-seven percent of our thirty-five hundred employees are black and less than a hundred of these are in service jobs. As a matter of fact, in my own personal office, where I have four girls working directly for me, one of them is black and she happens to be my lead clerk. The only category in which we do not have employees is professional. There are just no black engineers available, accountants, those categories.

"I have said as long as ten years ago that the answers to the problems relate themselves to employment opportunities more than anything else. Education is important, but I feel that where we educate them or who they happen to go to school with is not as important as the quality of education we give them."

Do you think that, say, a school 90 percent black can offer the same quality of education as a school more thoroughly integrated?

"My answer would have to be that today, if you evaluated it on the academic achievement of the students and nothing else, no. If you evaluate it on the basis of the type of instruction they get and the amount of improvement the students are able to achieve, I would say yes. Possibly there would be social advantages in putting certain black students from low-income areas into white schools, but I doubt that this would raise their education level. We have a school over in the east end—the Pfeiffer school [141 blacks, 1 white last year]—where we have been able to lower the pupil-teacher ratio to about 18-1. If we sent these black students to Forest Park [336 whites, 7 blacks] like Mr. Walker wants us to, one of two things would happen. Either the children in Forest Park would have to slow down to a pace the teacher is able to maintain with disadvantaged children or else the disadvantaged children would lose out. The problem is not that these children are born with less intelligence. The problem is the background in which they have been raised until they become school age. I've had white and black first-grade teachers tell me, 'Mr. Woods, our problem is that when we get these children we have to spend the first several months just teaching them how to go to school and how to be a member of a class, how to hold a pencil, how to sit in a chair, how to eat their lunch, how to go to the men's room —things they haven't learned at home.' This is the reason this school board in the last several years has opened all these kindergartens with federal funds. This won't break up the problem of their backgrounds but it will help. What's going to break up the problem is the economic status of their parents. That's why I said jobs is the answer. The Negroes will have to have the opportunity to get jobs and then they'll have to have the responsibility to accept the jobs that are offered them."

I asked him why the opposition to busing is so strong in a school district no larger in area than Little Rock.

"Two reasons," he answered. "First is the reaction to busing itself. Why send your child away from home if there's a school near him? It's as simple as that. Second is the type of neighborhood into which you're sending him. Meadowcliff [596 white students, 2 blacks] is one of our suburban areas. I'd say it's a little on the liberal side. When they came face to face with sending their kids to Granite Mountain [2 whites, 802 blacks], as Mr. Walker proposes, you see what happened. There was a petition with 690 names on it and some of those signatures were astonishing, considering they were thought to be fairly liberal people. If it had been the Terry School [479 whites, no blacks] I don't think they would have felt so strongly, although both schools are about seven or eight miles from Meadowcliff. The difference is that Granite Mountain is on the fringe of an area that has a crime problem."

Do you as president of the school board see a relationship between the neighborhood school and the quality of education?

"Yes, I do. You get a greater participation of parents when you have a neighborhood school, and when you get parents taking an interest you get better teachers and better curriculum. You find that without neighborhood schools you have a low amount of parental participation. This is true in black communities and white. We have some very active black PTAs. People will get behind the schools in their own neighborhood. Because schools are so dependent on tax rates, it is doubly important you have community support, and that's what you get with neighborhood schools.

289

"I think the Negro people and the whites in Little Rock are pretty well agreed on that. I think they all want their neighborhood schools. This city's changed in the last ten years. I think most people in Little Rock accept the policy of integration. The issue is how to do it and what's fair. The greater problem is housing, yes, but it's an unjust burden to place on schools to solve the problems of housing. Mr. Walker is correct when he says that our plan for this coming year would put the burden of integration on black families, but the school board felt that the judge meant it last week when he said he wants results. He threw out our latest desegregation plan and said come back with another this week. We didn't like having to do that but we have, and it provides for a lot of busing for the black children. We're closing down Horace Mann School in the black community and taking those children to other schools. If he wants results, that's the only way to do it. If we tried to bus white children to Horace Mann, they wouldn't go. They just wouldn't go."

"That's exactly the issue," John Walker said later. "They expect us to do what they refuse to do."

And so they have come to court—again.

★ ★ ★

In a case like this, the making of history can be dull, and the crowd of more than two hundred at ten in the morning dwindles to around thirty by dinner. U.S. District Judge J. Smith Henley prods the lawyers; the fall term will open in three weeks and the district still does not have an approved plan of desegregation. The Eighth Circuit Court of Appeals rejected the plan under which the schools operated last school year, and the revised proposal which the board submitted last week was so inadequate that Judge Henley stopped the proceedings when they had scarcely begun and told the school officials to go back and try again. The latest revision of the revision does not satisfy John Walker. It does not get at the segregation of the elementary schools, and the burden of busing is still on the black students.

"You live in the Leawood area, Mr. Woods?" John Walker asked of the school-board president, who was giving his deposition.

"Yes, sir."

"Would you characterize that as upper-middle income or middle-middle income area?"

"I don't know how to base a characterization, but I suppose that your characterization would probably be all right. I'll accept it."

"Mr. Woods, would you not say that most of the people in the area right now that live more than ten or twelve blocks from the school either furnish transportation for their children to get to and from school or otherwise have it provided?"

"Or they walk like mine do."

"How far do you live from Brady [elementary school—617 white pupils, 1 black]?"

"Oh, boy. The way they walk, not very far. . . . I would say five blocks."

"And how far would you live from Henderson [953 whites, 16 blacks]?"

"I would guess at probably a mile."

"And your child walks to school?"

"They don't walk to Henderson. They are car pooled."

"And if he—"

"It's not a he, but she—"

"And if he or she attends Hall [1,384 whites, 40 blacks], how will he or she get to Hall?"

"Well, this would be our first year in Hall and I don't know. That's Mrs. Woods' responsibility, but I assume that they will car pool."

"Okay. Now if you were to pair Mann and Hall in such manner as to have the pupils dispersed between the two schools, and a selecting system for determining which pupils attended which building was adopted, and it fell that your child was in the Mann zone [now all black], would you have your child attend that school?"

"Would I have my child?"

"Yes."

Daniel Woods, forty-two, the father of three, with an earnest face, turned to his lawyer and asked: "Is this a legitimate question? I mean, I don't know that my child ought to be involved in this lawsuit."

"You're president of the board, Mr. Woods," John Walker said.

"You can do as you want to on your deposition," Herschel Friday answered. He is the school board's lawyer. "If you don't know, you might say you don't know. You haven't made that decision, or you haven't come about it, or you might state otherwise. I'm not sure it is a relevant question. John, what is the relevance?"

"Well, I think it's relevant," John Walker replied. "Would the board send their children to black schools? The school superintendent has indicated about what would happen [the superintendent had said he expected less difficulty in getting black students from Mann to enroll in the predominantly white high schools than in getting white students

291

transported to Mann] and I think we need to know what the board's attitude about this matter was: would the board send their children to black schools. Now, Mr. Woods, why would you object to answering a question of whether or not you would let your child attend a formerly black school?"

"Well, I don't think that my child is involved in this lawsuit. This is the school board and I"—he turned again to his lawyer and asked: "What did you recommend, that I answer or not answer? I'll follow your advice either way on this."

And Herschel Friday replied: "Well, I think it's a matter of principle, you know, one way or the other. I don't know, I don't really think it's relevant as to what any particular individual one way or the other would do or maybe ought to be called upon to get into that type of situation. Now, if you want to show that this would color his judgment [as a member of the school board]—

"That's all right. I think it would color his judgment. . . . Would you advise him to answer or not to answer if it's all right? If your child was assigned pursuant to an arrangement whereby Hall and Mann were paired and it fell to your child's lot to be assigned to Horace Mann School, would you send your child to Horace Mann High School?"

"Don't answer it and we'll take it up with the court," Mr. Friday advised his client.

John Walker came at it another way.

"Now, if the court ordered that plan into effect, would you send your child to Hall High School?"

"Well, that's the same question in a different manner. Can we just defer that question, too—"

Herschel Friday said, "No, the question is would you follow a court order. I think you ought to answer that."

"But there are other alternatives," the president of the school board replied.

"It depends on if there is a court order, would you take any particular action?"

"Oh."

"And I say that you ought to answer that."

"Okay, if there's—I'm not talking about—you're not talking about my child. You're talking about putting the zone in Horace Mann."

"Mr. Woods," John Walker said. He turned, walked two steps back, and turned again. "Mr. Woods, I want you to do one thing for me from this point on. If your lawyer doesn't object to a question, you answer it, instead of asking him to object. . . . The question is as board president and also as a patron of the school district who has children attending the public-school system, would-you-send-your-children-to-the-zone-which-the-court-has-ordered?"

"I don't care to answer the question, Mr. Walker, until I find out the answer to the first question. I haven't made that decision. It hasn't confronted me yet and I haven't made that decision."

"Would you share the school superintendent's view that white people will not go into the black areas—to get education?"

"Yes, sir, I certainly do."

"Will you send your children into the black areas to get education—"

"He said he hasn't made that decision yet," Herschel Friday said.

"I haven't made that decision yet," Daniel Woods echoed.

Others had. During one recess a woman of about forty, her hair swept high above her head, wearing a bright-colored dress, stood in the corridor and said: "This crap is going on forever and they aren't goin' to settle anything. My child can walk three blocks to school and I'll be damned if I'm going to let her ride ten miles every morning. She's seven and I don't object to her goin' to school with colored. We have two or three colored pupils now, but if they put this through she would be going to school over in a part of town where they don't even let policemen in. Before I do that, I'd get me two, three jobs and keep her at home with a private tutor."

Another woman, about sixty, who was sitting on a bench reading *Women's Day*, looked up and asked: "Aren't we Christians?"

"I used to be a helluva lot more of a Christian than I am now. My child is not going to school with the criminals they have over there. I'm telling you that now and forever. I don't mind eatin', sittin' around talkin' to them, but they aren't gettin' my kid. They want the good schools and they want to give us the bad schools. They want to destroy us. They want to destroy our whole damn world." She lit a Virginia Slim.

"I've known some pretty nice ones," the older woman said.

"I've known some lovely ones. I was raised by one. But I'm not sendin' my daughter over to that colored neighborhood."

"Are you afraid she'll get a little charity?"

"I'm afraid she'll get a little switchblade. That's what I'm afraid she'll get." She squashed her cigarette on the floor and went back into the court-room. But she had touched off a lively conversation in the corridor.

Another woman, with red hair, wearing a cream-colored pants suit, said: "My older daughter was in that mess thirteen years ago and we scrounged until we found another school. We'll do it again before we send our younger daughter all across town. I'll tell you the way it is. My husband came out of the army and we didn't have a thing. We borrowed money and both of us worked and we finally were able to move out of *that* part of town just about the time the coloreds came in. We've worked hard for what we got and we *ain't goin' back*."

A man spoke. "They want to send my kid to Granite Mountain. By God, they're gonna wake up and find it's just a pile of rocks if they do." The red-haired woman laughed.

"I can't understand why they don't go after 'em up north," the man continued. He was young and neatly dressed, and he smoked little filter-tip cigars. "I know Cleveland. Eight hundred thousand people, surrounded by all those little suburbs. You think they'd put 'em in one district for racial balance? Hell, no. Them northerners are immune."

"Old John McClellan [United States Senator from Arkansas] was givin' John Mitchell hell on television last night," the woman said. "He said the South is bein' persecuted. He said there was a Jewish district in Boston that had a handful of coloreds a few years ago and it's about 90 percent colored now, but he said there weren't any whites willing to send their kids over there and he wondered why Mitchell didn't go up and make 'em do what they're tryin' to make us do down in Arkansas."

"It's a double standard," the man said.

"Yeah, that's just what ole John said."

The woman who had gone back to reading *Women's Day* put the magazine down and shook her head. "What ever happened to charity?" she asked. "What ever happened to the Golden Rule?"

"The Supreme Court said it was unconstitutional," the red-haired woman said, and they all laughed, except for the older woman, who picked up her magazine again.

John Walker walked out of the courtroom. A woman who said she was from the Terry school district (479 whites, no blacks) asked him if he had any children.

"Three."

"How do they get to school?"

"My wife drives them."

"So do I," the woman said.

294

"Then what do you propose?" John Walker asked.

"I don't know. I have no suggestions."

★ ★ ★

"Moyers? Are you the fella who danced the swastika up there in Washington?"

"The right man," I said, "but the wrong dance. It was the watusi."

"Watusi—swastika, what's the difference? Come on over and I'll buy you lunch."

R. W. (Bob) Laster has been in and out of controversy in Little Rock for more than a decade. He had been elected to the school board in 1958 as a diehard segregationist and had proposed several times during the crisis that the schools be reopened without Negroes. He was one of three board members who were recalled in a special election in May, 1959, after they had attempted to purge forty-four "integrationist" employees of the city schools. He was once photographed wearing two .45-caliber pistols and told the reporter: "Anybody with no more friends than I have ought to wear two pistols."

He is forty-seven now, a little heavier, a little grayer, a little mellower, but he still carries a gun. "This is my Saturday-night job," he said as he unstrapped the brown leather shoulder holster and put the .38 in his desk drawer before we went to lunch. His wife accompanied us.

"I believe in facing the issues, facing the facts," he said of the old crisis. "By God, either integrate or segregate, do it all at once or don't do it at all. But they wouldn't go that fast either way, they did it like the Vietnam mess, and they got everything all screwed up as a result."

"This town is not segregated by God or by law or by design," he said when I asked him about the current situation. "It's segregated by choice. It's like Washington, D.C. They're all going to the suburbs. We have de facto segregation just like you do up north. There is no order this court can make that will integrate our schools. If I had to, I would send my kids to a damned private school, not to keep them from going to school with colored people but to keep from having to haul them a hundred miles and make them wait in rain and snow out there until I have time to come and get them. If a client walks into my office at four and he will sit there until seven, I have got to stay with him, and I am certainly not going to expect a seven-year-old child to get on a bus and have to transfer twice to get home. We're in an income bracket where they won't provide a school bus. We have to provide our own transportation."

"If people are willing to put their children on a bus and haul them across

295

town, this is their business," Mrs. Laster said. "But we aren't going to do it."

"I happen to get along well with colored people," he said. "When I was growing up I used to get an ice-cream cone with my colored friend— two dips for a nickel in the same cone—and he liked one flavor and I liked another, and we'd sit on the side of the street and I'd lick my flavor and he'd lick his."

What did you do when you came to the cone?

"Now you're splitting hairs."

His wife said: "It all has to do with attitudes. I don't want a colored coming up to this table and pulling up a chair and sitting down and saying, 'O.K., you and I are going to eat together.' [We were eating in a private club.] I don't want you to do that, either. I don't mind eating with a colored or with you but it has to be my choice. Give people a choice. Don't force them against their will. That's not democracy."

"Do you think a banker wants to have lunch with a mechanic?" Bob Laster asked. "They don't have anything in common. It's attitude, too. If you're nice to me, I'll be nice. I don't believe in forcing anybody to do something against his will."

Is the black man saying that he wants the right not to be told he can't do what you and I can do?

"If he wants to buy a house out where I live, let him come on. But if he can't, I don't want to be told my children have to be taken to where he is."

And she said: "They've got schools in their neighborhoods. I think each neighborhood should have a school and the kids should be told to go to their school."

"Here's an example," he interrupted. "This girl—now I've committed a faux pas—I should have said this black woman, if I'm going to be modern —this black woman that works for us, do you know that my kids call her Mrs. Whiteside? We teach them to say that. It's respect that counts. You can't force it and you can't legislate it."

"The thing that's really sad about the whole thing," Mrs. Laster said, "is that the majority of these colored people don't want to be associated with whites. They don't want to go to white restaurants, for example. They want to go where their group hangs out. It's by choice."

What is the responsibility of the majority to a minority in a city like Little Rock?

"It depends on how the minority behaves themselves," he said. "If they are radicals, if they wear white sheets, burn crosses, I don't think you have any responsibility to them. I don't believe in hanging people to trees, dragging them up Main Street behind a car. I don't believe in lynching. I believe in integration. . . . There's no such thing any more as integration or segregation. It's a matter of personal choice. I entertain my colored friends—the term is 'black' now—I entertain them in my home. I go in their home, sit at their table and eat. Why, hell, I can show you some white people you wouldn't want to get within twenty feet of. But you can't legislate morals. You can force five hundred blacks, five hundred whites to go to this school. Within six months' time all the white parents will move to another neighborhood. It's not prejudice. It's just fact. That's the way it is. Period."

How do you think the administration is handling the school situation?

"Nixon? If I had not been a Democrat born and raised all my life, I would vote for Richard Nixon. I can't vote for him because I took an oath to support the Democratic party, and that holds. I have never voted Republican because I am a Democrat. I wouldn't vote for Wallace because he is a little chihuahua running around nipping at the heels of a great Dane. I would not vote for a damned blueblood Democrat; I would refrain from voting. I stayed with the Democrats in '52 and '56. I voted for Adlai because he had a sense of humor."

I had read in the newspaper clippings that while he was a municipal judge Bob Laster had acquitted an eighteen-year-old white boy charged with spitting in a Negro girl's face at Central High School. He had said that such occurrences are common in all schools and that President Eisenhower, not the boy, was to blame, anyway.

I asked him if he would do anything differently if he could live those days over again.

"I'm a lot more mellow. I'm no longer as radical as I was. I used to be a crusader. I went out and picked a fight because I liked to fight. I still do, I'm just getting too old, but I'll fight anybody that wants to fight, doesn't make any difference to me who he is. I've had my ups and downs. I've gotten kicked around, I've won a few, I've lost a few, and I don't regret a minute of it. But in those days I was right and you were wrong and that was that. You're probably still wrong and I'm probably still right but today I'm willing to split the difference."

Is there any possibility that Little Rock would have another upheaval as it did in '57?

"Do you know that we have had more killings, shootings, and murders in the last year that are unpublicized, and it's among the blacks. When I was a kid, a girl could walk anywhere in this town at any time of night and be perfectly safe. There was a story in the paper the other day that crime has increased 224 percent in Little Rock in ten years."

But my question—

"Yeah, I know: could we have more trouble? I was trying to tell you we got trouble of another kind with that crime. But as for the school thing, naw. Everybody's learned how to delay nowadays. That court will find some reason to keep putting off the final solution. The damn courts are dilatory, you know that. Hell, they've been going at this for almost two decades. They'd go out of business if they settled it."

★ ★ ★

In one of those geographical paradoxes of the South, the office of L. C. Bates, field representative of the NAACP, is only a few blocks down the street and around the corner from the office of Robert Laster, his old nemesis. The floor is bare, and yellowing newspaper and mimeographed sheets are piled around the two-room office. There is a sign on the wall which warns: "Don't talk politics in here unless you're a registered voter."

L. C. Bates has won some and lost some, too. He moves deliberately now, like an aging veteran who does not want to stir an old injury. He is thin, with very short hair, and he wears the dark suit of a Southern preacher, with a white shirt, a narrow tie, and two-tone black-and-white shoes. It does not seem possible that he was a smokejumper in the fierce brush fires of the early civil-rights struggle in Arkansas. But at one time L. C. and Daisy Bates, his wife, "shook 'em up," as the saying goes down here.

They published a newspaper called the *State Press* which "raised hell by asking that the Constitution be made real." Bates pushed the circulation up with a column called "Mornin' Judge" which simply printed the overnight police blotter. "Unfortunately," he said, "it caused a lot of divorces because wives found out their husbands were in jail for disturbing the peace at some wild party when they were supposed to be in Fort Smith on business. The lawyers wanted to sue me but they couldn't 'cause the stuff was true. I hated that column but in eighteen months we went from two thousand circulation to fifteen thousand." He laughed.

In the 1950s the Bateses became targets for racial hoodlums. Bottles and rocks were thrown through the windows of their home and crosses were burned on their lawn. Circulation agents for the *State Press* were threatened and intimidated until they stopped delivering the paper. Only one company, Standard Oil, continued to advertise. "Lots of people wanted to keep on gettin' the paper but they wanted it wrapped in brown paper and we just didn't have the money to pay the more costly postage that way," he said. The *State Press* folded in 1959.

"There wouldn't have been trouble like that if Orval E. Faubus had been a bigger man," Bates said. "This town went to work on a desegregation plan right after the Supreme Court decision in '54. Folks here weren't happy about buryin' Jim Crow but the majority accepted it as necessary and wanted peace. I am convinced we could've opened those schools peacefully in '57 if Orval E. had kept his mouth shut. Folks knew federal law supersedes state law. And the kids were ready, 'cause they said, 'Let the Negroes come, we can have a winnin' football team if they do.' We were ahead of the other Southern states till Orval E. sold us down the river.

"Why'd Faubus do it? He's an opportunist. He's never been a racist, just an opportunist, with no backbone. Also he hates those 'ristocratic people in the upper classes who never accepted him, looked down on him, and he saw a chance then to put it to 'em, if you know what I mean. If he'd gone the other way in those days, shown a little courage, things'd be different today.

"Very few districts are adherin' to the law today. Every one of the districts has made a pledge for the unitary system this fall but few are followin' it, and the folks in Washington are makin' the same mistake they made in '57—they are not pressin' 'em. The Little Rock system is tryin' to get a racial balance without inconveniencin' the white folks. Hell, *we've* been inconvenienced for decades. Our kids were bused forty miles one way to perpetuate segregation. Now the shoe is on the other foot and pinches like hell. I have no sympathy for these school districts. Whatever problems they have they brought on themselves. They've been spendin' all kinds of money to avoid doin' what they know they oughta do. God knows how much money it's cost us in legal fees and all that. Makin' the Negro pay twice—payin' to offend themselves and then payin' to defend themselves.

"This is why I'm not too critical of the black kids today. I don't condone the militant actions but I sure can understand why they feel that way. They're frustrated. You take a youngster five or six years old in '54. His mama said to him, 'John, you won't have to go to that old raggedy school with the potbellied stove and rain comin' through the roof. You can go to that nice brick school where Mr. Charlie's boy goes 'cause the courts have said you can.' That kid's nineteen or twenty today, he's in college or he'd like to be, and he knows what his mama told him sixteen years ago just ain't so. What would you do? Huh? What would you do?"

He opened another package of cigarettes, leaned back in his chair, and said: "But for all that, I challenge you to find a better city to live in than Little Rock. We got some hellraisers and some rabblerousers, but we got some openness here. I'm optimistic enough to think that whatever progress we make now will depend on the Negro. If we keep pressin' and workin' and bein' fair I think we can set an example here for the whole Southland."

★ ★ ★

Floyd Parsons, the school superintendent, sat in the window outside the courtroom during the late afternoon recess and said yes, he believes that the neighborhood school is important to education because "we depend on parents for the special committees to assist the professional staff. Matters arise occasionally where parents need to be contacted, and this is not to say that they couldn't drive seven or eight miles to take care of these matters, but it is far more convenient for them to go to the neighborhood school and their children to be in the area."

Parsons was very much the man in the middle. He is bald except for a swath of hair that curves from one ear to the other. He wore a brown sport coat, a blue shirt, and a white tie, and he spoke in the accent of the west Texas from which he came nine years ago. He had the air of a man who knows his answers are not going to make anyone really happy.

"Yes, it's largely a matter of convenience, but for a school that serves a widely scattered community involving people from eight, nine, ten miles, you would have to add facilities and programs to get the communication and understanding about school problems that you get in a neighborhood school now. Mr. Walker argues that our country's public schools were started so all the kids could have a common experience—rich, poor, middle class, lower class—and nowadays they don't get it in a suburban middle-class school where everybody's alike. He's right. I have to admit that. He's right. I wish this weren't true, but it is, and now everyone is asking education to solve the problem that has arisen because of the residential pattern. I think we have some responsibility there, which is why we've tried to have some pupils of all levels of income involved in many of our schools. We're not a segregated school system by any means. We are a well-desegregated school system—not well enough, I'm sure.

"Sure, Little Rock has changed in the last nine years. Tremendously. Go in that courtroom over there and you find those people not shouting at each other. I think the vitriol is gone. There's an atmosphere of communication. I think the passions are spent and people can hear what the other man's saying. They aren't opposed to integration like they were in '60 and '61. They're opposed to the artificiality of creating situations that will result in integration, but they're not opposed to integration that comes naturally."

★ ★ ★

I sat that night at dinner with a young black man in his early twenties who will within one year receive his law degree from the University of Arkansas. He was smartly dressed, with Italian boots and fitted slacks. He intends to return to the small Arkansas town of his birth and practice law. He knows exactly what he wants to do:

"I'm going to get thrown in jail for contempt of court the first day, 'cause that judge is going to do what he normally does—call the black lawyer by his first name and the white lawyer by Mister—and I am going to say, 'Your Honor, I find it difficult to plead in a racist court.' I'm going to stop all that crap, and the reason I'm going to enjoy it is that I know all those guys—the judge and the bailiff and the sheriff—'cause when I was growing up I worked at the country club they belonged to, and I took it from them right up to here." He drew his hand across the point of his trim beard.

I asked him if he agreed with L. C. Bates that Little Rock can be an example for the South. He replied: "I think Mr. Bates is a great man. He put it on the line when it counted. But it don't matter what happened in 1957. Right now things are not worth a damn. We're going to make them better. That's all I been living for ever since I went to work at that country club. You aren't going to like this, being a white man, but I need a little vengeance. Way down in me something just begs for it. Whatever it is, those fellas at the country club put it there. When you've had it given to you as long as I have, you don't feel bad when you give it back."

★ ★ ★

The hearings continued until almost midnight and resumed the next morning. John Walker pressed the point that the district's plan would work a hardship on low-income Negro families who would have to travel across town to school. Floyd Parsons replied that pupils from families below the poverty level would be given bus tokens purchased with federal funds. Walker said some of the children in Horace Mann School came from families just above the poverty level and still had trouble buying lunch because of financial problems. He wanted to know if the board's plan meant that those children would have to place getting to school ahead of eating lunch. And the school superintendent answered: "That would be their decision to make as to which would receive priority."

Herschel Friday, a well-built, balding man who looks over his horn-rim glasses when he cross-examines, a polite interrogator with an accent that seemed more Deep South than others in the courtroom, urged Judge Henley not to order any plan into effect that requires busing to achieve racial balance until the Supreme Court rules on whether busing is required. Norman J. Chachkin, who oversees school-desegregation suits for the Legal Defense Fund and is an attorney for the Negro plaintiffs, said: "I think it's a false hope to think that the Supreme Court is going to clear up all these issues." He asked Judge Henley to order the school board to take immediate steps "to acquire transportation capacity" to carry out a comprehensive desegregation plan when school opens. The school board had estimated the cost at $726,120 annually and said it did not have the money. Walker and his associates claimed the amount would be between $200,000 and $300,000.

A witness for the Negroes, Dr. Ira Eyster, an education consultant from the University of Oklahoma, said desegregation of the elementary schools was "probably more essential" than of the secondary schools. Studies had shown, he said, that black pupils in a black school were not motivated as well as those in a predominantly white school. He told the court that the achievement gap between black and white pupils widens each year the black child remains in a segregated school, making the desegregation process more difficult if it is delayed until the secondary level.

Herschel Friday asked Dr. Eyster if the support of the community was not the essential factor in effective desegregation. Dr. Eyster said yes, but he added that the success of a plan "sometimes requires leadership which is daring and goes out in front of the community in the first stages."

★ ★ ★

"Vacillating leadership is the problem here and across the country, don't you think?" James Youngdahl was sitting in his law office beneath an imposing Indian headdress that hung on the wall behind him. It had been presented to him by the Tonka Indians in Oklahoma for whom he had once served as counsel. "Vacillating and often contradictory statements in Washington on integration, segregation, and civil rights have encouraged the reactionary cause. Given the fact that most people have substantial and important racial prejudice, and given the fact that the way society moves depends upon how the big middle is swayed by one side or another in whatever particular conflict, clear and uncompromising and stalwart leadership is essential to keep some kind of balance and stability and progress. As long as people think there is any hope of getting around being generous and responsive toward minority groups, they will evade and delay. When substantial authorities in Washington imply there are ways to get around it, they give the reactionary cause aid and comfort of a serious and substantial kind."

James Youngdahl came to Little Rock in 1959. He was born in Minnesota, grew up in Missouri, and received his law degree from the University of Arkansas. He was chairman of the Arkansas advisory committee to the U.S. Civil Rights Commission in the early sixties. But his views on race, his bold beard, and his offhand manner have not hindered him from becoming one of the most successful lawyers in Little Rock, especially representing the labor clients. He claims that he is so far from the Little Rock mainstream that he cannot be relied upon for a fair appraisal, but he doubts that any effective communication is going on between the races in the city.

"There are all the standard cliché situations—the power structure, financial and commercial, with a few house Negroes to whom they talk. They assume those Negroes talk to the rest of the Negro community, but I don't think they do. As far as any integrated communication pattern in the community, I'd tell you there's none.

"I live in Meadowcliff, a kind of middle-middle-class area where about once a month there's a rumor that a Negro family is going to move in, and it spreads like wildfire. I don't know whether it's just legitimate unhappiness over the prospect of their kids' being on a bus every day or whether it's just pure gut racial antagonism, of which there is a lot, but the people there are really uptight. And this is what I meant about leadership. Who's asking those people to be magnanimous? Who's saying we really have to do these things if we want to be a great country as opposed to just a rich country? It has to come from the top, from the national leaders. Once the leadership says okay to that guy in the poolroom, and he goes out and knocks somebody's block off, you lose a very important restraint on bad things happening. It seems to me all the guys in the poolroom are being tacitly encouraged to do just that. And people are letting their worst instincts control them. People have lost their sense of humor. The leadership is encouraging us to be narrow, suspicious, and mean. I guess you might think the national motto is 'Think Small.'"

* * *

Judge J. Smith Henley greeted me in his chambers although the hour was late and he had been in court for two very long days. From every side I have heard nothing but praise for his patience and good humor—the *Arkansas Gazette* described him as "an exemplar of politeness and charity." He had preached law in a small town in upstate Arkansas until he "did a little politicking for Ike," who then brought him to Washington for assignments at the Federal Communications Commission and the Department of Justice. His nomination to the bench was due to pass the Senate the very week Orval Faubus called out the National Guard, but he was roundly condemned as "that damn Yankee from Boone County," which has more Republicans and more Negroes than most parts of Arkansas, and was not confirmed until six months later. There was, he knew, "a good bit of irony" in his situation.

"The situation in Little Rock is so much better than when I came here," he said. "More and more I find that among the little housewives and even among the diehards there's a reconciliation to the idea of integration. It's the sending of their children into previously all-black schools that is hard for them to take. It is not just the schools but the neighborhoods, which unfortunately have high crime rates. They want to maintain white majorities in crime-free neighborhoods with a minimum inconvenience as far as transportation is concerned. You can understand that. You can also understand why the Negro parents feel the way they do. They want to break up the concentration of crime, too, and they don't like to send their children across town any more than the white parents do. All the forces of history collide out there in that courtroom and it comes down to one man trying to find some way to achieve equity. Wholesale opposition to desegregation has evaporated in Little Rock, but people can't all of a sudden step out of the boots they were born with, and the courts are left with doing what's right by the law and also what's possible given the way people are.

"What concerns me is that the higher courts have left us to deal with ambiguous guidelines. Does the circuit court require this court to achieve significant racial balance in *every* school? What is a unitary school system? How much busing is too little and how much is too much? If the higher courts could tell me, then I could tell the school board to go and do such and such. But nobody really knows. And the opposition depends on whose ox is being gored or whose baby has the measles."

So, J. Henley Smith said, "I'll just have to ask both sides to do a little more."

★ ★ ★

Hugh Patterson, the publisher of the *Arkansas Gazette,* one of the few crusading newspapers in the country, is an optimistic man. "We were hurt badly by the insidious leadership of Faubus, but we're coming back. He was in office so long, took control of so many commissions and agencies, that government became corrupt and indifferent to people. The economy slowed down and people with promise left for better opportunities out of the state. The old man stayed around and with age became irrelevant. We developed the original generation gap in Arkansas. Now, in the last two years, things are picking up. But for a long time after '57 and '58 we were like Europe after the First War—our young men were gone and only the weary and the collaborators were left in power. If Faubus wins again, Arkansas is finished."

★ ★ ★

Orval E. Faubus was speaking Saturday night at an old-fashioned political rally in North Little Rock. More than a thousand people came and they were his: open shirts, sun-red faces, eyes full of hope that he would indeed make a comeback and save their world. Since he was defeated four years ago Faubus has been head of Dogpatch, U.S.A., a kind of Ozark Disneyland, which has been a commercial success. These people love him for it; if he wins, they believe, one day the whole world will be Dogpatch and they will be free—free of the *Gazette,* free of the John Walkers, free of the damn bureaucrats in Washington who keep chiseling tablets of stone and hurling them upon the sweating, aching backs of the little white people of Arkansas.

"Shut up and sit down, you bastard," one of them screamed as a Faubus opponent, William Cheek, started to criticize Faubus. Cheek went off balance. A woman standing near the platform spat close to William Cheek's left shoe. "Go ahead," he retorted. "Go ahead. Vote for him. Vote for him. I knew this crowd was for Faubus before I came." And he departed with the dust rising from his heels.

Orval Faubus came to the rostrum, and suddenly, in that open-air gathering, everything the South has lost because men like Faubus betrayed it became sickeningly clear. For he talked of raising the salaries of teachers, of reforming the prisons, of building more highways so people could get in and out of the mountains, of things that common people understand, and they listened; his children listened. And you knew that at one time he might have led them out of the past, might have come down off the mountain like some ancient prophet and hushed their fears and pointed them across the desert to a promised land. Now, leaning against an old Pontiac at the edge of the crowd, you wanted to cry because Orval Faubus had gone the other way, and they had followed, and Arkansas had begun its backward journey.

When the speaking was done I waited until almost everyone had left, then I joined a small group of men and women talking to Faubus beside the vacant platform. Half an hour passed, but he seemed not at all anxious to leave until the very last voter had cleared the parking lot. He must have thought I was the last one because when he finished with the people around him he turned and grasped my hand and said: "I'm Orval Faubus and I'm glad to meet you." I asked him, "What's on the mind of people you meet around the state?" and he replied without hesitation: "Lawlessness and the schools." I asked him, "Do you mean blacks?" He studied me for a minute. Then he said: "That's what I tried to warn everybody about the first time around. If you start integration where's it going to end? Give 'em a little and they always want a lot. They're not going to stop. The ultra-liberals said, 'Let's give 'em a chance to go to school where they want to go,' and we did. Now they're asking we gather up all the white children and bring 'em all over to the colored schools. And after that they'll want something else."

I mentioned that only yesterday Judge Henley had said from the bench that the people accepted the idea of integration. He gave his head a big circling turn, threw his coat over his shoulder, and answered: "Henley doesn't know the people. Henley sits on the bench and talks to lawyers and the Supreme Court. I've been where the people are"—he gave a broad sweep of his hand toward the empty parking lot—"and if they're accepting it is's only because they think they have no legal choice. They aren't accepting it here"—and he placed his left hand over his heart.

I asked him to explain what he had meant in his speech when he promised to improve the National Guard and the state police because "they might be needed." He studied me again. I am sure he knew by now that

I was not at the rally because I intended to vote for Orval Faubus, and he replied: "I just meant what I said."

"Would you do again what you did in 1957?"

"Yes." He looked at me and repeated: "Yes. I would."

Then he turned and walked to the sidewalk, where his new wife and two children waited. They walked down the street like an ordinary family on an evening stroll. Faubus carried his coat back over his shoulder and held the hand of his wife, who is several years younger than he is. The children were scuffing at rocks on the sidewalk and I thought that it was quite late for them to be up.

Orval Faubus led the Democratic primary for governor with about 36 percent of the vote in an eight-man race. In the runoff he declared busing to be the major issue, but he lost decisively to a political unknown, Dale Bumpers, a lawyer from a town of 1,350 people. Bumpers refused to make an issue of race, busing, or the schools. In November Bumpers defeated the incumbent, Winthrop Rockefeller, to become the new governor of Arkansas.

★ ★ ★

On Monday Judge Henley handed down his decision. He permitted the school board to continue the neighborhood schools at the elementary level and said the Constitution, as he interprets it, does not require the massive transportation of elementary-school students for the sole purpose of establishing a unitary elementary-school system. He found the racial imbalances at the junior-high level to be "very pronounced" and ordered the board to eliminate them by the fall of 1971. He agreed to the closing-out of the all-black Horace Mann School and the busing of black students to other schools. The district, he said, "is going to have to have unitary junior high schools and high schools so that all children of both races will receive at least the second half of their public school education in integrated surroundings." He ordered a white ratio to be maintained in Central High School, where it had all started.

John Walker and his friends appealed for emergency sittings of the Circuit Court. They were disappointed, they said, by Judge Henley's decision. It left "the entire elementary complex totally segregated." It would merely turn Horace Mann from an all-black high school into an all-black junior high school, they said, and it delayed junior-high integration another full year.

The plan, the plaintiffs protested, "is insulting, demeaning, and degrading to black pupils and their parents." But the request for an appeal was denied by a three-to-three vote of the Circuit Court. One of the dissenting justices warned that further delay in hearing an appeal from the Negroes "will serve only to encourage the further movement of whites out of areas that now have integrated schools."

In September twice as many blacks would attend desegregated schools in Arkansas as last year. Some of the schools would have very few white children. No appreciable increase would occur in the number of whites attending desegregated schools.

★ ★ ★

"We have come a long way, nonetheless," L. C. Bates said after the decision. I had stopped for coffee at the Bates home. As president of the Arkansas NAACP Mrs. Bates had fought for years to integrate the schools. She had become, someone said, "as well cursed as any woman in the history of the South." She had been jailed, fined, ridiculed, and attacked, and their home still has metal-lace guards over the windows as a remnant of past battles. She is over fifty now and works with the poor in Arkansas. She still remembers the time when she was six and the butcher kept her waiting for almost half an hour while he served the white customers before turning to her to ask: "What do you want, nigger?"

"I was bitter then and I was bitter all through those years," she said. "I'm not bitter any more. I look back on the progress we have made and I know the bitterness was worth it. Not very long ago an old man came up to me at a luncheon and said: 'You've forgotten me, Mrs. Bates.' I looked at him and I recognized him immediately. He used to publish a racist magazine and called me a fieldhand nigger and every other name he could think of, and I said I could never forget him. 'Well,' he said, 'times has changed, Mrs. Bates, and people change, too.' He died shortly after that of cancer. They were bitter days, bitter, but I think they were worth it.

L. C. Bates drove me to the hotel. "When I lost my newspaper I thought I had lost everything. But I don't regret a thing now. I am not only an old man. I am an old *free* man. And you know, I think we owe more to Orval E. Faubus than I thought at one time. When he turned the National Guard loose on those nine little children, the press turned the spotlight of the world on Little Rock and everybody—I mean everybody —suddenly knew what was happening to the Negro in the South. I think that was the beginning. Nothing was ever the same after that. I guess maybe that's the final revenge on Orval E. Faubus."

Johnsonville, South Carolina

FROM LITTLE ROCK I FLEW TO CHARLESTON, S.C., AND DROVE NORTH ALMOST a hundred miles to Johnsonville, in the coastal plains of South Carolina. As I drove down the main street in Johnsonville I passed the small vacant brick building that once was the doctor's office. There were two entrances, one marked *White,* the other *Colored.* The building is in disrepair, but people pass it every day and are reminded of things they want to forget. The traditions of the past are deeply etched here.

School desegregation, for once, is not an issue. Over a three-year period Johnsonville has already integrated its schools, and without violence. One-third of the 1,297 pupils in the three schools are black. Fifteen of the 44 teachers are black. That part of the past has been wiped out.

I have come here because Johnsonville is a company town, and the company—Wellman Industries, a wool-combing and synthetic-fiber firm—is in trouble. Its sales have fallen sharply. They have fallen as textile imports have risen—125 percent since 1965, 33 percent in the first quarter of 1970 alone. Japan, the largest exporter of textiles to the United States, shipped more than $540 million worth of goods to this country in 1969. Those goods cost less than American products because wages in Japan are many times cheaper.

The consequences were beginning to affect Johnsonville as I arrived. I had come, in fact, to see what happens when a small single-industry town confronts such a problem. Until recently Wellman Industries employed about twelve hundred people, almost six hundred of them from the immediate Johnsonville area (there are about twelve hundred people in Johnsonville, of whom fewer than seventy are black; but there are some

twenty-five hundred people in what is known as the Johnsonville Planning Area, of whom six out of ten are black). For the last few weeks
Wellman's processing capacity has been down to less than 60 percent
capacity and the company has just laid off nine secretaries, fifteen salaried
managers and supervisors, and two hundred hourly employees. More
layoffs were expected soon. In a company town there are no other jobs
available, and next door is Williamsburg County, one of the poorest in the
country, with a high unemployment rate among a large black population.
Even in the middle of August in humid weather the thought of rising
unemployment at Wellman Industries is chilling. Throughout the South
other textile towns like Johnsonville were also beginning to shudder. And
in the empty mills of old river towns in New England many a ghostly
head might nod with sad understanding at the prospect of men out of
work at the textile plants.

"That's why we moved down here sixteen years ago," Bill Bullock said
after he surfaced from a neatly executed dive into the eighty-degree
water of his lighted swimming pool. Bill Bullock is in charge of buying
wool for Wellman Industries. He and his wife live splendidly in a large
house well off the road outside of town. There is a private lake in front
of the house, and the country club which Wellman Industries inspired
is just across the way.

"You have to have a good supply of relatively inexpensive labor to stay
in this business," Bill Bullock said. "We came down here looking for it.
Almost half of our people are black. If we weren't here they would still
be fieldhands or living in the ghettoes of Chicago or New York. That's why
I can't understand why they're trying to organize. Yes, two union guys
showed up across the highway one day, one black and one white, and are
trying to recruit our men. They did the same thing to the plants in New
England and there's virtually no textile industry there now. Wages are
low because profits are low. The Japanese work for forty-five cents an
hour or less, in Hong Kong they get less than twenty-five cents an hour,
and in Korea between ten and fifteen cents an hour. How are we going to
compete with these wages? And the problem is not just imports, it's
synthetics. Everybody's moving into synthetics and that hurts your natural
wool.

"This part of the country would be a lot worse off than it is if Wellman
wasn't here. But if imports keep driving the prices down and unions keep
driving the wages up, we'll be looking for new sites down in South Texas
or Mexico. Don't laugh. We came south once before. We have to keep
thinking that way: where can we get the labor? We have to go where we

can afford the people, and there is a lot of people down there." He nodded in the general direction of South America and dived again and Mrs. Bullock said it was almost midnight.

★ ★ ★

Billy Mace, a native South Carolinian, is personnel director for Wellman Industries. The next morning he told me that the average hourly wage in the textile business in South Carolina is about $2.40; he was not specific about the wages at Wellman but they "are in that general area." Certainly they are lower than in other industries with a higher profit margin, he said; a pulp operator in the paper industry earns about $5.03, a crane operator $4.38, and a shipping clerk—a job fairly comparable to a textile production worker—$4.30. "You can see how trying to meet foreign competition affects our people. But it's a vicious bind you're in. You raise the wages and you play right in the hands of the Japanese and pretty soon you drive the Americans out of the business altogether, and then where does the worker stand? He stands out of a job—on welfare."

Billy Mace said that out of approximately 930 workers the exact number of blacks was 44.6 percent. No, he did not know how many blacks were in the first group to get laid off, and no, they do not have very many black supervisors—he was not sure how many. "Most blacks are not willing to give up their security in production for the added responsibility of the supervisor's job, and for some reason blacks don't want to be supervised by other blacks—they seem to prefer whites. And another thing is that a lot of the blacks don't want to work more than forty hours because of the food-stamp plan—you know, if they earn over a certain amount they don't get the stamps."

Billy Mace reckoned that the union thing was a real threat. "The Textile Workers of America—it's almost all black—sent a smart organizer in here who had made his appeal on 'black power'—you know, join because you're black and we're black and we should be in this together. The history of the union movement has always been that the blacks are appealed to and will often bloc vote against you because these are the ones who have been led to believe they will get something for nothing. This doesn't exclude a lot of whites, too. This is what hurts the nigra—the blacks—all over the country. Companies are reluctant to hire them because they do this sort of thing. We try to give our employees benefits and wages that are as good as possible. We don't need a union to tell us that. We just don't believe in unions. But the sad thing is the nigras—the blacks —we have brought in here are trying to fight us now. They stand across from the gate and make the black-power sign—the clenched fist. One day last week one of the black employees went into the supply room and was talking to one of the supply-room clerks, who is white, and he said, 'All you white people who didn't sign cards to get the union are going to be sorry when this union gets here. You're going to lose your jobs,' he said. These are the tactics they use.

"We'd love to pay higher wages but we just can't afford it. We have expanded so rapidly in our synthetic-fiber division that the working capital of the company has just all gone into that. Then we got that real critical import situation and we really feel the pinch. The real question is: If you have a union, will you have an industry? The foreigners will drive us out of business, there won't be any jobs, and then they'll raise their prices.

"A company town? I guess you could call Johnsonville a company town because Wellman is the biggest employer here. But nobody, including Jack Wellman, throws their weight around. I'm on the planning commission, and one of our black hourly employees is too, and the mayor of the town works on our security force, and things like that, but we're not active in the town simply because we work for Wellman but because we live here and we want this to be a good town. When the Wellmans came here they brought sixteen people down from the North and they built sixteen houses and scattered them around because they wanted management to mix and mingle with the townspeople. Well, yes, a lot of those houses are over by the country club. There's always a problem getting professional people—chemists, people like that—to live in a small town like this. Almost a hundred miles from Charleston and Florence over half an hour away, you have to provide entertainment and recreation for high-level management looking for a certain standard of living or you won't get them to come down here. Some private citizens in town had taken over the responsibility for the club but they got into financial difficulties with it and the company bought it back. But it's run by a board of directors of local people. We prefer to keep the company in the background."

★ ★ ★

Mr. Turner at the grocery store was leaning up against the counter at the checkout stand when I asked him if business has yet been affected by the layoffs. "Started last week," he said. "Same people came in. Just spendin' less. You can tell people are nervous when they're workin' but not spendin'. Guy down the road got it last week, maybe you gonna get it

312

next week. Put a little aside while you can. Hold it. See if it's just a sprinkle or a gullywasher. If it's a gullywasher—" and he shook his head and turned to wait on a customer who asked if he had a large economy size of . . .

★ ★ ★

"Is theah feah heah? Is theah feah in this town? Oh, mah Laward, yes," Shay Hagan said. Because he is the most prominent realtor on Main Street —the only one, I think—and because he is a member of the town council, I had stopped by to ask him to assess the economic picture in Johnsonville. His one-story building is the newest on the street; this is one of the reasons Shay Hagan is deeply in debt. "Show me a man who owes a lot of money and I will show you a hustluh," he said. Every small Southern town has a Shay Hagan—and needs a Shay Hagan. He got the United States Government to finance low-income housing in Johnsonville not for ideological reasons but because, as he admits, he could "make a little" from it. No one else had even tried. Shay Hagan got two blacks rather than one on the town planning commission not because he is a liberal but because, "Hell, you got to give 'em someone to talk to." Shay Hagan is not a liberal; he is what my father calls a "vane specialist"—a student of the prevailing climates. But, sitting behind his handsome desk, dressed in a bright blue shirt with a dark blue tie and slacks the color of new rust, he talked in an open and disarming way and with a most serious expression. He is immensely likable, as most Southern hustluhs are.

"I'll show you what feah is. We got this city dump one block off of Main Street, you know? It has been theah for twenty-five years and we have been tryin' to eliminate it—to get the garbage out of town. We are goin' to start usin' proper land fill 'round the county like. But we have to buy the proper equipment, you know? And the total maximum cost is $17,000, which is a very big lot for this town because we have just been makin' our way. We had to figure some way to bring in additional revenue, to retire that obligation. So we figured how: in-town residents and businesses would increase theah garbage-collection rates $1 a month; those areas we are servicing outside the city limits we would increase theah garbage-collection revenues $2.50 a month."

Shay Hagan paused a minute, shook his head slowly, and then leaned across the desk and said: "I am tellin' you—I thought we were going to be tahred and feathered. Because everybody theah at the town meeting said they couldn't afford that dolluh now. A dolluh a month. They can't afford that dolluh-a-month increase because—look at how many of 'em are goin'

313

to be on unemployment income. That dolluh's gonna mean something. They begged us: 'Please don't do this—wait until this situation settles down heah at Wellman.'

"Well, I know how they feel. The average little fella workin' by the hour has obligated himself so fa' beyond his immediate ability to pay out—my Laward, theah is no tellin' what would happen to me if we went into bad times. I would have to find me a high-rise buildin' not for occupancy but to jump off. It has nothin' to do with the Wellman people personally, eithah. It is this heah overall situation. You cannot kick the hand that feeds you, and Mr. Wellman has brought this little community from zero practically to wheah it's gonna take off. It is hard to say anything 'bout an organization that has done that fo' you. What people are wonderin' is whether you can completely depend on that as a livelihood fo' so many people when you know it can fluctuate this way and that." He waved his coffee mug up and down.

"New industry? Only if the industry is first approved by Mr. Wellman and if it's a related industry, because a related industry is able to maintain the proper wage level. You take Union Carbide. Good Laward have mercy, if Union Carbide moved in heah it would practically send Wellman unduh. That is what they say and my inclination is to believe them. Nobody but them really knows what the profit margin is on textiles— family-owned business and all that—but they say it's very low. Since nineteen fifty-foah this area has grown so phenomenal that people have not got over appreciatin' what has come heah because of Mr. Wellman. And people'd rather have the low wages than not to have Mr. Wellman heah. I think we can anticipate this growth for twenty yeahs and then finally the unions will take over. The unions got to or go unduh. Industry's got to follow the labor, then the union's got to follow the industry. I know fo' a fact that theah was a fella sent down by Mr. Wellman to South America to look 'round. Whether it will materialize or not, I don't know. But I—I better stop right theah. Fella came in heah the other day and told me 'bout some rumor of somethin' goin' on in town and I said, 'Tell me more.' And he said, 'Hail, I've done told you more'n I've heard.'" Shay Hagan grinned and said: "And I've done told you more'n I've heard."

★ ★ ★

I went to lunch at the country club with Billy Mace and some of the Wellman executives, as congenial a group of men as I have met on the trip. It was a mixed gathering—Yankees and Southerners. The dining

314

room overlooking the golf course was almost deserted because most of the people were eating together in a separate wing. A luncheon was being held there of town and area businessmen to organize community support behind Wellman's fight to keep out the union. No blacks were present. The very tall and distinguished man whom I heard open the luncheon with prayer as I waited for Billy Mace and his friends said with bowed head: "And we pray, dear God, that everything we do in this meeting today will be to the best interest of our community."

★ ★ ★

The people in Johnsonville were apprehensive of talking with an outsider about Wellman Industries. They are aware of the contradictions of its presence, of the many jobs it provides and of the condition the town would be in if Wellman were not there. But they also know textile wages are low, which means the workingman is subsidizing the industry, and they fret about being so completely dependent upon one company. There are people who say that if Wellman "was on the inside instead of the outside of the city limits, and paid the taxes it should pay, this town could really do somethin'."

But the same man who said that also told me: "You won't hear a bad word in this town about Jack Wellman himself." To the contrary I heard him commended even by critics of the company. Realizing that blacks would be coming in from the tenant farms as the county changed from agriculture to industry, Jack Wellman knew they would need housing. He purchased a farm on the edge of town and turned it into an attractive residential area. Lots were made available to the blacks for $800 including landscaping, and more than twenty families have bought or built homes in the $12,500 to $15,000 price range. Wellman also threatened personally to withdraw his support from the Dixie Youth League (the local Little League) unless it was integrated; it was. And he has aggressively supported vocational training for blacks and whites in Florence County and throughout the state.

"But absolutely the best thing he did," one local businessman said, "was to bring in Fran Buhler. Fran Buhler is the greatest thing to happen to Johnsonville since the Swamp Fox."

Franchot Buhler is a national asset, I will agree to that. He does not seem to believe it himself; he is chary in conversation, shy, and answers questions laconically. He is director of the Johnsonville Community Planning Center, and he seems uneasy when he is asked why he is there.

315

"Well, I—there was a need for someone—they said Johnsonville is—people wanted to get together—a chance to—I—to do something worthwhile, I guess."

To make a difference?

"Maybe."

Have you?

"Maybe. A little. I don't know." And he shrugs.

It is hard to interview a man who will not talk, but Fran Buhler prefers to listen. He just listens. That is his strategy and talent: he listens to other people. He will sit and listen to anyone, regardless of race, creed, etc. Follow him on any given day around Johnsonville and he will be listening: in Delance Poston's office, in the rear of David Marsh's hardware store, in Reo Cooper's tobacco barn, on Billy King's front porch, under Mrs. Sophie's liveoak, in the school cafeteria, or on the corner there at the H & L Café. By the time he stops listening to whoever is talking, the man knows Fran Buhler is not going to solve his problems for him. Fran Buhler wants him to reach that conclusion and he leaves. It is a rare talent for a thirty-year-old radical.

Fran Buhler came to Johnsonville in roughly this way: Jack Wellman heard Blair Butterworth make a speech about the free-enterprise system's capacity to provoke community change if its leaders take the initiative. He brought Butterworth to Johnsonville to discuss his ideas with Wellman officials and town fathers, and Butterworth suggested that, since the town really seemed ready to get something done, they should bring in someone who could serve as a kind of city planner, a man to help them attack the problems of idle youth, economic growth, and other concerns, which in a large city, of course, would be promptly solved by highly paid experts. The town council said, 'Great, but we cannot afford even a modestly paid amateur.' Whereupon Jack Wellman agreed to finance the project if the town council would assume the leadership and he could fade out of the picture. And that is how Franchot Buhler of Tennessee, a graduate of Carson-Newman College and a former student at Union Theological Seminary, came in mid-1969 to occupy the shoebox office of the Community Planning Center on Main Street in Johnsonville.

His explanation of what happened after that is rather meager: "I just went around listening to people talk until they said something which we all realized made sense."

"He did not just come heah and sit on his fanny, if you know what I mean," Shay Hagan said. "Theah was mo' to it than that. In his own should I say rather quiet way he told it the way it does happen to be. Which is that if this heah town was goin' to be saved, it would have to save itself. He said it so softly we did almost not heah him, but we did."

The Johnsonville Planning Commission, with five whites and two blacks, which Buhler urged them to organize soon after he arrived, conducted a survey of the town's needs and problems in cooperation with state agencies. The result was a recommendation for a five-year program ranging from a $1 million public-works program (there is no adequate sewage system) to a Get-a-Dentist Committee. The town council approved the program and Johnsonville began the long lurch forward.

"The important thing is *they* decided," Fran Buhler said after he had stared into his Coke for five minutes. I wrote it down verbatim because at the moment I thought it might be the only sentence he would utter all day. (The report was so impressive, I learned from others in Johnsonville, that Buhler was invited to Washington to appear before a Congressional subcommittee on small towns; rumor is he arrived in the hearing room, sat down behind the witness table, and said: "Yes?" Congress was so astonished that someone was willing to listen that he was awarded a medal, which around Johnsonville is called the Order of the Big Ear.)

There have been reversals. The summer recreation program called for a youth choir to come over from Birmingham to live in the homes of Johnsonville people while conducting a music workshop for the young people of the town, but somehow the word got around among a few Christians in the community that its covert purpose was to bring about the integration of the churches, and the plan was abandoned.

"The real problem is for people to want to stay committed," Fran Buhler said in a remarkably loquacious moment. "Soon after all this started we had a town-hall meeting in the high-school gym and a lot of people came. It was the first time some people were ever in the same meeting. People got up and seemed excited about a chance to say what they thought the town needs. They talked about the bad drainage, the sewage, the lack of any adequate leisure program for the kids, the schools—you know, they were real proud of how Johnsonville went about integrating the schools. They even spoke up and said the town should look prettier than it does, that it should be cleaned up, all those

317

boarded-up buildings on Main Street torn down. People were talking with each other, not just listening to politicians. I myself felt as excited as I think I've ever been.

"A lot of those people haven't kept at it. Some of the leaders have, but like every other small town, people here can feel terribly satisfied —little hunt, little fish, groceries on the table—and what else do you need? What I've been trying to help them see is that, if we ever do get that sewer system, Johnsonville will have a sewer system and that's all, unless the people decide to keep hammering away at the job of self-determination."

And then he lapsed into that characteristic silence about himself. I plied him with more Cokes but nothing happened.

I did manage to purloin a letter he had once written to a friend. In it he said:

If the National Commission on Urban Problems and the President's Committee on Urban Housing can come up with 221 ways to save our cities, why can't we come through with one or two suggestions for the Johnsonvilles? On the way to becoming a livable community, Johnsonville has committed the unpardonable municipal sin: it won't fit into the neat categories of federal classification. With all due respect to the agencies, their programs, and the enabling legislation under which they operate, Johnsonville is not rural enough for Farmer's Home. It's not urban enough for HUD. It's not lagging enough its unemployment is not persistent or substantial enough, for EDA. It can't afford 8% interest and it doesn't want to go on welfare. . . . This is a town in transition. Tenant farmers have become foremen and the graveyard shift has replaced milking. . . . The profound thing about the transition is, and put this down in your ekistical notebook, it's rural-suburban. For those who are making it, the middle step in the traditional rural to urban to suburban pilgrimage is being omitted. This is the suburbs. These folks are here (I'm talking about those with a choice) for the same reasons social-worker types live in Maryland or New York copywriters in Connecticut. Attitudinally, they come out of the same place! Cities are crowded, dirty, evil, and no place to raise kids. . . . It's the damndest thing when you think about it. Johnsonville is more like suburbia than anywhere else, with the professionals in Country Club Estates, Wellman Heights, and Laurel Shores, blue collar in the trailer parks and a block off Main Street, and the agri-industrials—those who work straight 40 and farm on the side—in Vox and Possum Fork. . . . There are rural ghettoes here, too. Not like those you heard about in Soc. 101—they are more dispersed. Which means they aren't as obvious, don't stick out like Watts or Hough. They haven't exploded violently, so we conclude the frustration may not be as raw, nor the misery so acute. But I really don't know how bad it is in those shacks behind the cornfields and between the tobacco patches. When I visit one of these homes . . . I feel like I'm invading their privacy. The Man comes to hire you on or collect, not to talk about what you're up against. So they suspect me, tell me what they think I want to hear, and I'm glad they're so resourceful. Who knows what the next guy might be after?

[But] little things make a difference. My wife joined the women's club. While I was trying to come up with some profound way to create community support for the child development center we were starting, Nancy asked some of the women about helping with curtains for the center. Well, they couldn't make curtains without measuring the windows; they couldn't measure the windows without visiting the center; they couldn't visit the center without seeing the children; and they couldn't see the children without wanting to help. . . . I came here because I believe the problems of this country run too deeply to be solved by an afternoon march or a weekend demonstration. . . . Someone has to translate insights from the ivy-covered think tanks into the ethos and ethic of small-town America. When children have to play in back yards that border ditches where septic tanks drain and mosquitoes breed, sewerage becomes an ethical issue.

And the man who started this digression, who is not overly keen on social reform or the power of Wellman Industries, repeated his comment: "The best thing Jack Wellman did was to bring that boy in here." And Shay Hagan said: "Oh, mah La-ward, he is GREAT!"

I drove past the tobacco and the corn and a few miles outside of town I came upon Reo Cooper sitting in his dusty Ford Galaxie beneath a massive water oak. He stirred slowly from his midafternoon nap, shook my hand, and suggested that I sit on the fender of the car while he occupied the little stool leaning up against the trunk of the gargantuan tree.

He pointed above him and said he called it the Tree of Life " 'cause so many folks workin' in the fields or passin' down this ol' road stops and finds rest here in the shade. The highway department wanted to put a new road through heah and cut it down, and I said, 'Oh no, oh no, if

you hav't' cut down the Tree of Life, we can do without the road.'
An' the tree is still heah and folks are always welcome to stop."

Reo Cooper was born one mile down this road fifty-six years ago.
He worked for white farmers until he managed to buy the small farm
which is now his home. He also runs a grocery in an unpainted building
no larger than three Florence County privies nailed together between
the highway and the tobacco. He raised seven children here, six of
whom have gone north. Many years ago he helped to organize the
NAACP and then the Florence County Voters' League with the purpose
of registering black voters. He fought battles in this corner of the county
through long years when he felt "mighty alone," and he looks older than
his years. There is in his voice a deep richness, and in his manner a
dignity worn like a single medal on the tunic of an old veteran observ-
ing Armistice Day fifty years later.

But Reo Cooper has not retired. Although he is a private man who
shuns the stage, the legends of his influence abound. It is said, for
example, that after the schools were integrated several classrooms remained segregated. Reo Cooper was allegedly told by officials that
they could do nothing about it, to which he replied: "Then I will find
someone who can." HEW officials appeared shortly thereafter and the
last color bars fell. It is also said that when a restaurant over in the
next county refused to serve blacks even after the Public Accommodations
Act of 1964, Reo Cooper disappeared for several days, returned with
some kind of mysterious letter, which was then sent by messenger to
the proprietor, who, the story reports, sought a black who had been
refused service, took him by the arm, and led him into the restaurant.
I do not know if such stories are true. When Reo Cooper is queried
about them he merely smiles and wipes the August sweat from his brow.
A respected farmer and a member of the town planning commission, I
suppose, keeps such things to himself.

"Oh, theah was tough times," he said. "Sure, theah was. Plenty o' times
I left home I wasn't expectin' to get back. I am certain that I am heah
today because of the good white folks. One white man made the long
trip out heah once just to tell me about what some other folks was gonna
do to me one night. I nevah really paid no mind to it 'cause I figger a
man only got one life to live and one time to die and I wasn't supposed
t' die in nobody else's time." And he laughed and shook his handkerchief
at a fly.

"Things have changed. Things are pretty pleasant 'long that line. Our big problem is employment. Any decent job in these parts ain't goin' to a Negro if the white man can he'p it. Common labor, sure, but that's all. It's an ol' Southern tradition. Some of the young Southern whites got a different mind but we still got some old ones hangin' on the ropes. Get some of the dieharders out o' there and you can probably do pretty good. But I think a lot of things are workin' in our favor now. I don't reckon I ought t' say these things to somebody I don't know. You ain't one o' them Texas crackers, are you?" And he laughed and shooed another fly.

"Our problem [in his patois the *o* is long—"problem" is "probe-lim" and "Johnsonville" is "Jones-unville"] is that after all these yeahs the white man is still tryin' to say what the black man wants. You take that point you heard at Wellman's, that Negroes prefer whites to supervise 'em, or that Negroes will not work more'n forty hours, or that Negroes do not want to be supervisors. Lot of our problem would be solved if the white man would speak for himself and let the black man speak for himself. You will heah it said that the white man is lyin' when he says those things. They are only lyin' to themselves, because they are ignorant of the Negro, and most lies people tell themselves begin in ignorance.

"The problem at Wellman's is that certain jobs are relegated for blacks, certain jobs for whites. And the jobs for blacks are the lower-payin' jobs. Theah information on average wages is never broken down for the blacks by themselves. I talk to lots of Negroes who work theah. In the synthetic department Negro men are gettin' a low pay rate of $1.97 per hour and white women are gettin' a rate of $2.20 per hour doin' the same work. I know machine workers gettin' $1.87 an hour and wool workers gettin' $1.73, and the problem is they stay in those jobs yeah in and yeah out. They will tell you over theah that Negro turnover is high. It is high, yes, because Negroes get discouraged. If you believed you were doomed to be a hooker [a worker who moves bundles of wool in the processing plant] the rest of your life, you might quit, too. But the Negroes have not been shown at Wellman that they can move up. One o' my boys was workin' down theah when they was buildin' that plant. When they got started they gave the whites 'bout six weeks' schooling but not the Negroes. He left, my boy did.

"Of course they want a union. If you was black, you'd want a union, 'cause you goin' to want every dime you can get. You go down to Mr. Turner's store and you walk up alongside a white man from the plant who's makin' more 'n you, and you both want a pound of bacon that costs ninety-nine cents. That butcher ain't gonna sell it to the other fella for ninety-nine cents and then say he will sell it to you for eighty cents 'cause you make 20 percent less than the white man. No suh, the cost of livin' ain't no respecter of persons. And when you have been puttin' that hook into that wool fo' yeahs, and you ain't got more to show fo' it than a job you might lose any day to the Japanese, and you know the guy above you is goofin' off but is gettin' away with stayin' above you 'cause you is black, and the union come along and say, 'I'll get that job for you,' you are gonna vote for the union whether it delivers or not. You been fo'ced to vote fo' it.

"I don't think it is Mr. Wellman, no, I don't. I think it's people under him with that old Southern tradition. Mr. Wellman came down here and he has done good for everyone, he has, but he had to rely on local men, bo'n and bred in South Carolina, the ones who brag 'bout how many Negroes they got workin' for 'em although they all are common laborers. Common labor, go to it. Skilled labor, no suh, hands off, so-r-r-r-eee. When the whites start off so much ahead, theah is somethin' wrong, somethin' wrong. THERE IS SOMETHIN' WRONG!"

And it was the only time during the afternoon that he raised his voice.

"Thass why I can't much blame the young ones who get so mad. When a man make you feel that way, then you gotta feel that way. I'm really sorry, 'cause I don't feel that way at all. If I had wanted to do that I could've had gangs roamin' with me long time ago, but you can check my record and I don't believe you would ever find one man who said Reo Cooper believes in violence. They tried to get me in a little mob down in Hemingway. I said I had other things to do. I have always believed that votin' power is black power. A bomb can't think. A voter can. I'm fo' votin' power. They'll recognize you more for that than fo' anything else."

We moved from the Tree of Life to the porch of his house, sitting in the middle of the field. It had become hot again after a brief breeze had brought some relief from the humidity. Reo Cooper said something to his nine-year-old grandson, who is down from New Haven. Then I asked him if he is pessimistic or optimistic.

"You can't be satisfied 'cause theah are always problems. As the old fella say, you got to outthink The Man, always beat 'em thinkin'. Seem to me that every little thing the whites can throw in your path, they will do it. I'm not tryin' to put all the bad on the white, 'cause Negroes are bad, too. But it does seem that way—they's a-shovin' you back all along the way.

"But I'm hoped up. Yes, I'm hoped up. The young ones are a-comin'. And they will be different.

"You take when freedom of choice came along in the schools, me and my wife sat down and talked with my baby girl. I said, 'You can go to Johnsonville High School if you want to, but I don't want you goin' there for six months and then quittin' and goin' back to the colored schools.' She said, 'Well, Daddy, I'll go theah and stay.' And I know this, when she was goin' to the colored school she'd act as if she warn't goin' to school when she came home. Never studied. Never opened a book. Next morning she pick up her books and go back as if she had nothin' to do at all. She was gettin' good grades and passin', but still . . . When I put her in the white schools, brother! when she came back home she sat down on those books. She didn't even seem to get upset when some of the white kids said they was goin' to beat her up—she studied, she studied hard. It was a difference, see. It was a difference. I notice all the colored kids are studyin' more now than they ever did. They say they's gonna go in theah and not make bad grades in front of all them white kids—they say, 'I'm gonna show them I got some brains, too.' Makes all the difference in the world, yes. Makes all the difference.

"So I think when this gone on awhile, people will forget about this color thing and look at a person as a person. I think they stop sayin' Thurgood Marshall is a credit to his race and start sayin' he is a credit to mankind. When I was growin' up I was told the whites are this and the whites are that, and over theah in Texas I bet you was told the Negroes are this and the Negroes are that. Both of us didn't know any better. But I bet if we sat on this front porch and talked long enough, we'd be one people to another, and that is a difference.

"That's why I'm hoped up."

★ ★ ★

One reason Wellman's wool combing in Johnsonville amounts to 35 percent of the U.S. supply is because John G. Wellman, president and chief operating officer, arrives early and stays late. He had returned at midnight from a business trip to Boston and was in his office at eight when I met him the next morning. He is not a man for small talk or obtuse answers.

"Just because we're the biggest employer doesn't mean I want this town for myself," he said. "I believe that it ought to be a good town because I live here. If I lived in Boston, I would be taking as much an interest in it as I do in Johnsonville. I would like to see Johnsonville pick up and grow and do the things you want your home town to do. But if I started pushing people around, or the company started acting like the old coal czars did, nothing would happen but anger and resentment. Sure, we are the biggest employer in town and that's different from being the smallest, but that's a fact of life and not the result of dictation. I would like to see other industries in here. The town needs diversity."

Someone had given me a copy of the company house organ with a column in which Jack Wellman had written: "The greatest war on poverty is a successful corporation." In it he had also said that he was so impressed with the slogan "Fight Poverty—Go to Work" that he gave it to his wife to carry in her pocketbook. I asked him about it.

"It's true. If you've seen our ads urging public support for reducing imports, you've seen our point that 'America's payrolls have made her great.' I believe that. And when I consider what imports are doing to us, I realize that they are costing jobs. They are hurting towns like Johnsonville because they're putting people off payrolls and back on the welfare rolls, and I don't think that is good for the companies, the country, or the men and women who are involved. Look at what happened to the silk industry. It could happen to wool. There are people in Washington who say that if low wages are the only way to keep the textile industry in America, then let it go to Japan. I think that is very shortsighted. It is not a question of low wages. It is paying what the market will bear.

"Yes, I am aware of what some blacks say about some of our problems. But we're not paying low wages because there's a policy of paying low wages. In the face of our competition from abroad and our profit margin we would be out of business if we competed with other industries. Look at any textile operation and you will see that we're all in the same boat.

"We do have a high turnover of blacks—I'd say 80 percent on an annual basis. I don't think it is because they dislike the work here. Many of them just want to work long enough not to jeopardize welfare payments, which they can't get if they earn over a certain amount. When I check into the reason for our problem, it's welfare. I believe in some kinds of welfare but I especially believe in an efficient welfare system, not welfare that takes away the incentive to work. We have had training schools, night classes, and other programs, but we still have not been able to reduce that turnover. Many of them still want that welfare. Then, of course, there is migration. Some of the best, most talented Negroes have left this area. We've been left with many who are largely illiterate, poorly motivated, and difficult to train. We've tried to have black supervisors. My people tell me they have really tried, but the Negroes have been asked and they just don't seem to want the responsibility. There's always the problem of finding people with the mental competence to do these jobs. You just have to keep trying.

"The union? It's not really a complaint about wages, conditions, or benefits—it's this black-power thing; it's the mood with blacks all over the country. We're not immune from it down here.

"There are plenty of pressures. The union thing. The imports. Prices. I am going to have to lay off some more people soon, people who have been with me several years. You take the highly skilled wool buyers— it takes a man seven years to learn that business. They can't turn around and get another job in their field. I feel for them.

"Maybe I'm cocky or something but I think one way or the other we'll continue to handle wool in this town. That's why I guess I want to see it do things. That's why I was willing to help the planning project. The biggest problem in a town like this is apathy. You can shake it up with projects like the sewer thing, the housing we got over there for the Negroes—things that get people talking and pulling together. But this is a good place to live. I want to keep making it better for everybody, all races. As Johnsonville goes, so goes Wellman."

And vice versa.

★ ★ ★

I left Johnsonville reluctantly, for I was only beginning to know the town. There are stirrings here worth listening to. Problems hide within problems in a small town like this, and every time you strip one away another appears. But, however haltingly, an awareness has come to some people that it is no longer necessary or wise to keep things as they always were. And there are people here, black and white, who believe they can work themselves through the dilemmas of their culture, even if they have to do it by the seat of their pants. Some have fought hard battles and have been tempted to leave, but they remain. One day, I suspect, the abandoned clinic with the fading signs above the separate entrances will disappear altogether.

Washington, D. C.

ALTHOUGH I LIVED SEVEN OF THE LAST TEN YEARS IN WASHINGTON, THERE are parts of the city I never saw. On the last leg of a journey that had taken me in a wide circle around the nation, I decided to stop here before returning to New York.

At a kiosk on the Ellipse south of the White House I picked up a brochure which welcomed me to the capital.

It informed me: "In every age, there has been one city which has seemed to be the center of the world, which the Fates have chosen to be the guardian for the hopes of all men, to hold and control their aspirations, to determine the probability of their glory, or their happiness, or their misery, their bondage or their freedom.

"That world city in our time is Washington."

★ ★ ★

In the middle of the center of the world, in the Third Police District, ten blocks north of the White House and only a brisk walk from the fashionable parties being held at that hour in Georgetown and along Embassy Row, Officer Willie Lofton tested the siren on his patrol car. It worked. His companion, Robert Horan, said: "Willie, if they didn't furnish us with one of those things, you'd buy yourself one for Christmas."

Willie Lofton started to reply but the voice of the dispatcher interrupted: "Shooting reported in front of Republic Theatre on Thirteenth." Lofton turned sharply to the left and two blocks down the street we could see people running. "They're starting early tonight," Lofton said;

326

he and Horan had only begun the 8 P.M. shift thirteen minutes before.

A white Pontiac convertible sat in the street in front of the theater —the marquee proclaimed "A New World of Thrills Beneath the Planet of the Apes"—and Lofton and Horan ran toward it after we had pulled into an alley and stopped. From across the street someone had fired a shotgun at the driver. His woman companion had fled into a bar next to the theater. The driver, a large black man in his early thirties, was holding his left hand, which was bleeding slightly, and he did not want to answer any questions. Beneath the front seat of the car Lofton discovered a holster and a dozen .45 shells but no gun. The driver shook his head and said the ammunition and holster had not been in the car when he left home and, no, he did not know how they got here. Lofton did not believe him. The man replied: "That's your problem." Police searched the bar into which the man's girl friend had run but they did not find a weapon. While Horan and other officers escorted the man and his buckshot-riddled convertible to precinct headquarters, I walked with Lofton down the alley from which the assailant apparently had fired.

The alley was joined by a still smaller driveway running behind a long row of tenements. There are 448 miles of alleys in the world city. In this precinct—the worst crime area in Washington—most of them stink with garbage and are littered with broken gin and whiskey bottles. Lofton began to poke through the abandoned cars and cellar entrances, and among the garbage behind one stoop he picked up four empty shotgun shells. "The guy who did it would have been a fool to run from here with that gun still in his possession," Lofton said. "He's bound to have tried to throw it away. The idea is to get it, because if I can find that shotgun there's one more gun off the street that I don't have to worry about being used against me or some other officer." Shotguns were used to murder seven persons in the District of Columbia last year and were weapons in 79 aggravated assaults and 249 robberies.

Lofton unsnapped the flap of his holster and disappeared into an open basement. Three black teenagers came down the alley drinking strawberry sodas and one of them said to me: "Policemen have a ball? A ball? Who they tryin' to hassle now? Whose back they on this time?" And his companion said: "They can plow into any ol' body when they want to, right? They can just look at me—I don't look like no hero and they can just jump out on me and beat my round head flat." I asked if it had ever happened to him and he replied: "Naw, but it could." And they tossed the emptied cups into the alley and walked away.

"Why is this district so rough?" I asked Lofton as he continued his search.

" 'Cause we got everything. We got peddlers and pushers and junkies, and we got peddlers and pushers that want to muscle in on other peddlers and pushers, and then you got a pusher that fills someone with bad stuff and they come back to get him. It's a chain, a chain that's got no beginning, no end. But, in my opinion, it all adds up to one thing. It adds up to the dope traffic. And I just don't think there is anything much that a uniformed police officer can do about that."

He stopped at another abandoned car, tried unsuccessfully to open the rusty trunk, pulled some old bed springs away from a wall, and jumped back startled when three children about five years old came sliding down a mound of dirt and debris which they were using for a playground.

He knocked on the back door of a tenement and a woman appeared with a little girl who was holding a doll. "Yeah," she said, "I heard all that shootin' but I didn't see anything 'cause I picked up the girl here and ran for the house. I don't know who it was. It sounded like everybody out there had a gun."

"It's getting regular now," Lofton said to her.

"It sure is. It's gettin' regular and terrible."

"We need the help of people like you if we're going to get them off the streets. At least to get the guns off."

"It just seems like everybody has a gun," she said. "I don't know where they get them. It seems you can buy them just like candy in a store." According to official police reports, revolvers and pistols were used last year in 130 murders, 1,206 aggravated assaults, and 4,590 robberies—all in the world city.

"That gun has to be somewhere in this area," Lofton repeated as we walked along the alley. "He just couldn't be so stupid as to try to get out of here with it. Unless in the confusion he came back and got it." The largest rat I have ever seen jumped from the top of a garbage can and scurried in front of us.

Lofton leaned over and picked up a newspaper roughly shaped like a long-barreled gun. "This is what he brought it in here with," he said. "I sure would like to find that gun."

Horan returned from the station and said the driver of the car would not talk. "Apparently it was some kind of personal feud," he said. "Somebody tried to ambush him and he knows who it is. But he doesn't want our help. I think he thinks he'll take care of him himself."

We got back into the patrol car. "Did you notice something?" Willie Lofton asked of Horan.

"No, what?"

"I didn't use my siren."

★ ★ ★

We cruised between Q Street and Florida Avenue in a part of the city that I had only seen occasionally from a passing car during the seven years I lived in Washington.

Twenty minutes after we had returned to the car the dispatcher reported a robbery by two armed men one block from the Republic Theatre. Another car was sent to investigate. In less than an hour there were six robbery reports. There were 9,338 robberies and 898 attempted robberies reported last year. Only 1,799 of the robberies had been cleared. There were 18,256 burglaries. That is only the number reported.

One block from the police station a blue Chevrolet had pulled over to the side of the street and a man was rummaging through the trunk. "Did I see a gun on the side of his hip?" Bob Horan asked. We turned and went back and Lofton got out to check. He came back laughing. "It was a wrench; his motor's conked out."

Willie Lofton is twenty-four, a tall, slender black immigrant from North Carolina. The ease and coolness with which he carries himself led one of his fellow officers, also black, to say that Willie Lofton is conceited; I think he mistook aplomb for conceit. His companion, Robert Horan, is a native of Washington. He is twenty-two, a mild-mannered, introverted young man with thick neat hair, a mustache, and steel-rimmed glasses that give him the appearance of a graduate student in English literature. He is white. Both men live in the area they patrol. It is a black area; most of Washington is. When I came here as a summer student intern in 1954 just over 50 percent of the pupils in the public-school system were black. Their number had increased to 79.7 percent when I moved to Washington in 1960, and when I left, seven years later, they were 93 percent of the school enrollment. In many respects Washington is the largest plantation left in America, managed by an overseer named John McMillan, who as chairman of the House District of Columbia Committee exercises despotic power over legislation affecting the lives of his subjects. For twenty-two years he has considered the center of the world as his own private fiefdom, although his home is in Florence County, South Carolina. No man has fought harder to deny to District citizens the right of self-government. One of the Presidents who was thwarted in his effort to bring home rule

329

to the District said of McMillan: "He thinks he's Jefferson Davis, and he's spent his whole life using the Negroes in Washington as a scapegoat for losing the Civil War." Approximately 850,000 people live on his plantation, three times as many people as live in the State of Wyoming, which has two United States Senators and one Representative in the House. The world city has Chairman McMillan. Almost half of his subjects live in inadequate housing. One hundred twenty thousand of them earn less than $3,000 annually.

"You have to ask yourself," Willie Lofton said, "why is there such a high level of drugs. I think it's because there are just too many people and not enough opportunities for them to go about what you and I would call a normal existence. I don't mean that everybody who commits a crime is just a frustrated saint, but I do mean that conditions around him don't help things."

"I'd say our biggest problem as police is the courts," Bob Horan said. "There's a tremendous backlog. I understand that if we were to stop picking up juvenile offenders tomorrow and just allowed the juvenile court to handle what they have pending now, we could resume arresting kids in 1973." There were 3,511 juvenile arrests in Washington in fiscal year 1969.

We received a call to go to an apartment to deal with "an unwanted guest." The young white man who met us outside said that another man upstairs refused to leave the apartment. "Is he a friend?" Lofton asked. "Yes, but I don't want him there," he replied. When we reached the apartment the young man and his "friend," a black youth, broke into a heated argument and the black left. The young man who had complained began to weep.

"A lovers' quarrel," Horan said when we were back in the car. He and Lofton had not spoken more than a dozen words in the apartment. "In a situation like that the less you say the better," Lofton said.

"We get a lot like that," Horan said. "I'd say 80 percent of our time is taken up with noncriminal matters: family arguments, disorderlies, dog bites, taking drunks home, directing traffic at fires, and reports—sometimes I think the police department exists just to keep the paper companies in business." In 1969 the Washington police department spent 143,498 hours—an average of 393.1 hours per day, or 49 men "lost" per day—in what are called "Details Out of Unit." Every day police spent 264 "on duty" hours and 387 "off duty" hours in courts and hearings.

At the scene of a complaint of "two disorderly juveniles shooting fireworks" we were greeted by a hostile young man in his early twenties and three boys under ten. No, they had not seen anyone with firecrackers. No, they had no idea where you could get firecrackers around here. "There's where the corruption of the young begins," Bob Horan said as we left. "He'll teach those kids to say 'pigs' and to hate cops before they even know what he is talking about."

That provoked Willie Lofton to reminisce about the little town in North Carolina where he grew up. "I used to walk seven miles into town and the policeman downtown would always call me boy and I would always say, 'Ise sorry, suh,' or 'Scuse me' and bow and scrape out of his way. My great grandfather lived with us until I was nine and he would tell me just to stay out of their way, don't bother them now. But I could go all the way into town without anybody bothering me—sometimes I would do it on a mule—and I never worried about getting robbed or mugged or attacked. I only worried about staying out of that policeman's hair. You come in here to this city and the lights go out and you start walking some of these dark streets by yourself and you see what happens to you. On top of the ordinary crime you got the new situation with the radical blacks and the Panthers and the racist white and the racist black, and every once in a while there'll be a fight between them. You not only got the mugger and the rapist and the thief but you got to contend with the agitator now, on both sides. The town is uptight, I'd say that." And they mentioned the officer in plainclothes shot and killed by a fellow officer who believed he was an armed-robbery suspect.

I asked them about race relations among police and Horan replied: "There are lots of guys in this department with race hangups but the thing is, when you're in this uniform, everyone is the same color—not black or white but blue, and you become so much an object of dislike by everybody who isn't wearing the uniform, black or white, that you don't have time to get mad at your fellow cop. You sure don't get the same respect you got back home. This happens to a lot of white guys, especially, who come here from Pennsylvania and West Virginia and from the South. Police were looked up to there and a lot of them come to Washington with the idea that being a cop in a big town is romantic— like Jack Webb or *Adam 12* on television—and when they get on the line and people start hassling them—they start getting accused of beating up Black Panthers or something like that—and they can't take it. They quit. Like I said, we got some black cops that don't like the white cops, and we got some white cops that don't like black cops, there are cliques, but under the gun they all feel intimidated by the way the rest of the world looks at them. I'm a white man in a black majority, and sometimes I'd just like to be able to take the badge off and say, 'Hey! look, man—me is me.' But anyone who hates you racially isn't interested in what you say, and that's true of the black cop who gets it from the whites and the white cop who gets it from the blacks. And, in the end, the white cop and the black cop gets it from everybody."

We arrived at a duplex from whose occupant had come a call that "kids were fightin' in front of the house." The woman, who was elderly, said she had tried to stop them " 'cause I feared they might break someone's windshield or hurt each other."

Lofton said to her, "I want you to do a favor for me, ma'm."

"What's that?"

"From now on when there are kids fighting out there, don't go out and start bothering with them 'cause nobody cares about nobody these days and you could get hurt. I'd hate to see you get hurt out there trying to be a good citizen."

"That's the first time I done it," she said. "I was especially scared for the little one out there 'cause his mother is out of town and I was afraid he would get hurt."

"Next time you call us and wait, though," Willie Lofton said. "We don't want to get here and find you were the one to get hurt."

Three blocks down the street a boy of about ten raced his bicycle through a red light and almost collided with the patrol car.

"Hey," Lofton yelled, and the boy nervously came to the window on the far side from the driver. "Did you see that light?"

"Yessir."

"What color was it?"

"Red, sir. But I was tryin' to stop my tennis ball from goin' down the manhole over there."

"You ever been to a hospital?" Lofton asked.

"Nosir, nosir."

"Someone oughta take you over there and show you all those kids lying up there with broken legs and arms and all masked up because they were playing in the streets. I don't want that to happen to you, you hear?"

"Yessir. Thank you, thank you."

"Some of those kids won't ever walk again for the rest of their lives, and they're only nine, ten, eleven years old. They were just riding their

332

bike, rolled in front of a car like you almost did, and—bang! They won't ever walk again. You know what I mean?"

"Yessir, yessir, yessir."

"You watch it, hear?"

"Yessir, I sure will. Yessir."

We drove away and Horan said: "You take that kid. If we were in a smaller town we could take him down to the station, call his parents, and really try to get him out of the streets—here it is ten o'clock at night and he's still wandering 'round out here. But you don't have the time to stop. Usually you don't have time even to give him a warning, but Willie here is a nut about things like that. Usually you just holler at him to get out of the way and you move on. 'Course there's a fifty-fifty chance you wouldn't get any response from the parents if you called."

"Yeah," Willie Lofton interrupted. "My aunt raised me down South, and when I would get into a fight at school the teacher would call and my old aunt would say, 'Send him home, send him home.' Well, I would diddle and daddle and I would finally get home and she would whip me twice—once for getting in the fight and once for taking so long to get home." He laughed, threw his head back, and laughed again. "One time I waited until almost midnight and tried to sneak in but she was sitting up in the bedroom waiting for me, and she'd wait until I got off my clothes and was ready for bed and she would let me have it. But she cried 'bout as much as I did and I knew she loved me. I just wish we could get some of *that* kind of licking for kids today."

We were patrolling not far from Du Pont Circle, and stopped in a small park where a crowd had gathered around a woman who was sobbing. Lofton investigated and when he returned to the car he said: "The lady said her husband—or friend—was late meeting her. When he finally came and she protested, he just hauled off and slammed her in the face. She didn't want to press charges."

"He was probably drunk," Horan said.

"Or on drugs," his colleague added. "I really believe the stuff is killing us. What I'm going to say may incriminate me a little bit, but when you spend as much time as we do on the streets and you run into all manner of people who can't handle themselves because of the stuff, you get short-tempered with it. Like that report of the two eleven-year-old kids who died from shooting peanut butter and one who died from shooting mayonnaise. And in this narcotics seminar I attended the fellow said that 87 percent of all known heroin users first used marijuana."

"That's an interesting statistic," Bob Horan said, "but what does it prove?"

"Now wait a minute, you didn't get what I said. I said they first used marijuana. I didn't say they used heroin because they used marijuana."

"You're not giving me the line that marijuana is indeed the killer weed?"

"Let me put it this way, Bob, the guy at the seminar said marijuana is an hallucinogenic drug, and I know a lot of people who can't handle themselves out here when they're using it. So the scientists and the chemists say it don't do you harm. The scientists and the chemists don't know everything. If they did why did they make the atom bomb? I've been on the force long enough to believe the stuff is harmful. I believe if we could get these kids in just this one district to stop using the stuff, you would see a change around here. And that's enough evidence for me."

We stopped at a sandwich shop on the corner and Lofton went in for some food. "Dining in Washington," the brochure in my coat pocket advised, "is a delightful experience. Few other cities, anywhere, can match the cosmopolitan menus offered to suit the widest variety of taste and of budget. Among its noted restaurants are many that offer music, dancing, and topflight entertainment, featuring celebrated artists, to fit your every mood." Lofton came back with cheeseburgers, French fries and root beer. We ate in the patrol car and listened to the dispatcher.

At 10:46 there was a disorderly conduct in a restaurant on Connecticut Avenue seven blocks from the office of Spiro T. Agnew. Two young men had finished a meal and told the cashier they had no money to pay for it. Willie Lofton took them to the street, where he talked to them for thirty minutes. "They ordered the food knowing they couldn't pay for it," Horan said. "They've been here from New Orleans two weeks going from restaurant to restaurant like that. There's not much you can do with them. They're probably homosexuals and would prefer to go to jail. That's where they really get their kicks. Free food to boot. About the only thing you can do is give them a lecture like Willie is doing and let them go."

Lofton returned to the car and said: "I believe they really were hungry. They said they went to three restaurants and no one gave 'em

334

anything. I told 'em to get a job washing dishes or get out of town. Hey, my French fries are cold. . . ."

Lofton and Horan returned to the station to file reports. ("That's why I like *Adam 12*," Willie Lofton said. "You don't ever see them doing any paperwork, do you?") While they labored with the forms I eavesdropped on a conversation downstairs at the soft-drink machine. One black officer was telling a group of recent recruits:

"I was downtown typin' in Records all day. This cat says we've been lockin' up more people this month than ever before and the crime rate is still high. I said, 'Man, what you don't know is that every day there are three hundred guys comin' to town lookin' for jobs. They put their ten kids in a room with ten other folks 'cause that is the only place they can get, and then they walk the streets all day lookin' for work and on the way home they try to pick up a ham for the kids and that's where they get hit.' Other day a tall cat comes up to me on the street and says 'Lock me up,' and I said, 'Why?' and he said ' 'Cause I'm hungry.' I gave him seventy-five cents for coffee and a sandwich and told him to be on his way. The next night I got me a cat trying to walk out of a deli with a bottle of pickles, a can of meat, and a box of crackers and I said, 'Man, why did you come up here?' He said he needed a bed for his kids and I asked him if he'd ever seen the public housing in this town. He said, 'No, but you ain't ever seen what I left in Mississippi.' "

According to the tourist brochure, however, "Ample housing, no matter the season of your visit, is available in excellent air-conditioned hotels and motels affording accommodations suited to your means. Washington leaves nothing undone to make your visit most pleasant. Wherever you live, whatever your position in life, it is your privilege, your heritage, to make at least one pilgrimage to this Federal City . . . it's a visit you'll long remember and want to repeat—an event that will gladden your heart every time you recall its 'Welcome, neighbor.' "

★ ★ ★

Willie Lofton and Robert Horan were dispatched to deliver an alcoholic found in a hotel room to St. Elizabeth's Hospital for an m.o. (mental observation). They would be there the rest of the night. The midnight shift came on duty and I went off in a patrol car with Officer Sam Wofford. He was not inclined to talk, but I learned that he grew up in Chattanooga, went to New York to work, did not like it, came to Washington, is married, and has a two-year-old son. Officer Wofford is black. He travels alone in the patrol car because business is duller after midnight. Last year there were some 4,200 offenses between 10 P.M. and midnight, 3,700 between 8 P.M. and 10 P.M., and only 2,500 between midnight and 2 A.M.

We were cruising on Fourteenth Street when a woman hailed us to the corner. She pleaded with Sam Wofford to "go up there and scare my man. He's drinkin' and beatin' me—I can show you marks all over— and I need you just to come up and scare 'im, I don't want 'em arrested, just scared a little bit, please?" Officer Wofford said that he couldn't go around "scaring people."

"But just a little," she implored him. "Just walk in there and look mean, you hear? I know you can do that for me. I'm a lady just like your wife and I fix him real good food and he treats me bad."

"Why don't you leave him?"

" 'Cause I can't do no better, you understand? But that don't give him the right to beat on me. I go to use the laundrymat—do his washing, too—and when I come back he is drunk. You have to see the condition —you have to read between the lines, Officer. I'm a good woman. My daughter teaches Spanish and English . . . my son . . . I got something behind me, Officer. . . . I don't see no sense in my livin' with him, but" —and she looked at Sam Wofford with resignation—"I can't do no better. All I want the law to do is to tell him to keep from gettin' drunk and to keep his hands off me."

"I can't do anything, ma'm, unless you want to make a formal complaint. He's in your house. You're livin' with him and you don't have to."

"Pretty please?"

Sam Wofford shook his head and she turned and walked off.

"Woman attacked at —— " the dispatcher said, and when we arrived she was still screaming. She was in her mid-twenties, standing in the doorway of the second-floor apartment in a short pink nightgown, holding her left hand in a bloody sheet. "I woke up and heard someone in the room—came through the window over there, see how it's been cut?—and all of a sudden he leaped on me and I started fightin' with him and he cut me. I screamed and screamed and he ran out the door." Other policemen arrived and Sam Wofford and I drove through the area but there was no one who fit the woman's description. "Sometimes you think you're chasing ghosts," he said. "But ghosts don't carry knives."

Knives were used in 989 aggravated assaults in the world city in fiscal 1969 and in 560 robberies.

There was a report by the dispatcher of someone breaking the windows in the Black Panther headquarters on Eighteenth. "It could be a setup," Wofford said. In July two police had been injured, one seriously, and twenty persons had been arrested in a melee at a Panther information center. Police said they had gone to investigate "boisterous noises, chanting, and obscenities," the Panthers charged the police with brutality, and the situation has been uneasy ever since.

("I was in the second car that got there," Bob Horan had said earlier. "There was this policeman lying on the ground bleeding. He'd got a brick right in the face; three days later he still thought he was a fifteen-year-old kid and they don't know if he'll ever recover mentally. Then there were twenty human beings in blue uniforms and they waded in. Some officers got tough, I guess, but you could almost say it was righteous anger. The sad thing is it was interpreted as a race thing, but there were more black police swinging clubs on the Panthers than there were white. It was a white officer who had been hit and the black fellows who came up and saw him, the policemen, didn't stop because he was white. To them he was a brother policeman, and that's when they stormed in the building and hauled those Panthers out.")

Two blocks from the scene another patrol car rolled up beside us and a lieutenant said to Sam Wofford: "Hold up. They're just trying to suck us in there. We're not going to take the bait." Wofford took a long puff on his cigarette and said softly: "That doesn't make me unhappy."

On the radio we could hear a squad car reporting a robbery by three armed suspects, one with a knife. The dispatcher queried: "Which suspect was armed with the knife?" And the patrolman answered: "The gentleman with the green shirt." Wofford smiled and started to say something but the dispatcher interrupted to send him to a robbery. We arrived to find a sixty-year-old black woman. She was hysterical.

"Oh, my God," she screamed. "They got my purse. They got my purse." She had parked her car at the curb and before she could get out a young man had run to the opposite window, reached into the car, snatched the purse from the seat, and disappeared around the corner.

"The check—the check—I had a check in there," she cried. "I just got a check today from my boy in Vietnam. A fifty-dollar check. Oh, my God, they got my purse. Somebody get 'im. Won't somebody get 'im?"

And then she became angry. "I would've got 'im, I would've caught 'im myself, but somebody held me back. Somebody held me back."

"Yeah, I did," a middle-aged man said. "She was goin' after whoever it was and I stopped her. First I knew she could never catch him—he was a fast little booger—and then I knew that if she did catch him, he might pull a knife on her."

"Did you think of chasing him?" Sam Wofford asked.

"Are you kiddin'?" the man replied. And he seemed genuinely shocked at the thought.

"O-h-h-h-h," the woman moaned. And she was weeping hysterically again. "They got my check. They got the only dolluh bill I had. And my medicine was in there, I got to have my medicine."

Her eyes widened and she clapped her right hand over her eyes. "O-h-h-h-h, the letter! The letter!" And she started to run toward the corner, but Sam Wofford restrained her. "What letter?" he asked.

"There was a letter in there from my boy, he sent with the check. It was the first letter since he got to Vietnam. Oh, my God, Officer, I want that letter. I got to have that letter. Please get my letter for me, please, Officer, get my letter."

Sam Wofford cruised a long time through the streets and in the alleys of the area, flashing his light into garages and parked automobiles and back porches of darkened houses. He did not find the purse and it bothered him.

"Those are the folks who get hurt a lot," he finally said. "Poor folks. An old woman with a son in Vietnam who sends money home to her, and some damn thug steals it. And when you catch him, he's out on bail in hours. Hours. Hanging 'round looking for somebody else's purse. It just isn't right."

He put another cigarette in his mouth and did a U-turn on Thirteenth and from that particular vantage point at two in the morning we could see the Washington Monument and the Capitol. Both were lighted brilliantly and looked exactly like the picture on the brochure that welcomes the visitors to the center of the world.

★ ★ ★

Paul Fuqua put down his steak knife and shook his head. The very act made a marked impression on the people in the restaurant because Paul Fuqua's is not a head you can easily ignore. With his red walrus mustache and his balding crown he looks like a British Lancer at Omdurman.

At the moment, however, he is the public-affairs officer for the Metropolitan Police Department.

"I am not a hysterical man," he said, "and I think I know as much about the statistics of crime in this town as anyone, but yes, I have to say that I would not want my wife to shop downtown after dark. That is a helluva thing to say about the nation's capital, and I do not like saying it. But it is true.

"There are a lot of reasons for it. One is that we have a lot of criminals. Period. Human nature does have a dark side; some men will kill, steal, beat, and rape simply because that side of their nature runs them.

"But that isn't all. The man who says that crime is not aggravated in this town because of conditions social and political is a fool or a bigot. Jerry Wilson [chief of police in Washington] has an almost totally black constituency and a power structure that is dominated by Southern whites. The same congressmen who get up and say we have to send another $100 million to South Vietnam to help their fight for self-determination oppose every dime spent on self-determination right here in the nation's capital. Why, the General Hospital here ran out of penicillin, did you know that? Our court system is an abysmal failure, especially the juvenile courts. Our corrections program would do justice to the Stone Age. Schoolchildren are being taught in low-grade slums. Most of the best teachers have fled to the suburbs in Maryland and Virginia. Until three years ago we didn't even have a city college. But what do we do? We do things like tearing down the slums in the southwest part of town, which was a good thing, and turning that area into luxury living, which wasn't a good thing. We've got lots of households with two color television sets but Washington doesn't have a good rehabilitation center for kids in trouble. We've got lots of country clubs and Cadillacs but no narcotics-addiction program worth a damn in the capital. We've spent $356 billion in four years for national defense and more than $20 billion for highways and yet if you will look out there"— and he pointed across the dining room of the Hilton Hotel through large windows overlooking part of the city—"you will see the roofs of some of the worst slums in the country. When you and I shave in the morning, we're looking at the cause of crime, because we support a political system that keeps a city of close to a million living on scraps thrown it by people up there"—and he motioned toward Capitol Hill—"who deep in their heart hate the place. Right on over those roof tops you are in one of the worst crime districts anywhere. And although the crime rate is going down the last few months, it's still a bad, bad scene. I couldn't even tell you how bad it is because I am sure we don't get more than 25 percent of all crimes actually reported to us. And those statistics don't touch white-collar crime. One officer of a bank here told me that his bank's losses to robbery are only about 10 percent of what they lose through internal theft. But that doesn't make the papers."

He shook his head again. People at other tables were straining to hear him but unfortunately they were not close enough. Paul Fuqua said: "The District should be a model for the country. We're a model all right. We're a model of what has gone wrong in the country. With all the problems we have, everything's breaking down and we can't even govern ourselves right here in the capital."

I left to catch the plane to New York. The taxi driver turned down Fifteenth Street and drove around the White House. From here you can see tourists enjoying the sights of Washington and local residents playing softball on the Ellipse. You can see the gleaming monuments to Washington and Jefferson and the low wooded hills of Virginia.

You cannot see the Third Police District.

The driver said this was his favorite view; he came this way every time he could. He said he always enjoyed driving at night because when this place is lighted up it is the most beautiful view in the world. But he stopped driving at night two years ago; he said it got too dangerous. He would not go a mile north of here after dark if they made him President and gave him the White House. But he missed the view at night, he said.

It was time to go home.

One night in the midst of this journey I sat with a friend in Cincinnati *watching television, and heard a local announcer urge his listeners to* *"call with your comments about our programming. We want to hear from* *you. We want to know what you think.* Your message will be recorded and examined later." *My friend threw his shoe at the screen, and he had not* *been drinking.*

It is treacherous to tell people that you want to know what they think, *and then force them to speak to a machine. People want contact. They* *want to affirm themselves.*

I found that most people not only hunger to talk, but also have a story *to tell. They are not often heard, but they have something to say. They are* *desperate to escape the stereotypes into which the pollsters and the media* *and the politicians have packaged them for convenient manipulation. They* *feel helpless to make their government hear them. They were brought up* *to believe that each man can make a difference, but they have yet to see* *the idea proven.*

I discovered how unfair it is to call a man "bad" because part of his *culture still owns him. I found out how important it is to get that man* *to acknowledge that people different from him are also human.*

Most people want to be generous. They expect their nation to have *visions of justice even if they themselves act unjustly. They expect from* *their country an ethos, an honorable character and enduring beliefs,* *even if they resist a common set of scruples and a rigid monolithic ethic.* *There are people who can endure personal tragedies and private griefs* *exacted by the nation only if they feel the nation itself is worthy.*

People are more anxious and bewildered than alarmed. They don't know what to make of it all: of long hair and endless war, of their children deserting their country, of congestion on their highways and overflowing crowds in their national parks, of art that does not uplift and movies that do not reach conclusions; of intransigence in government and violence; of politicians who come and go while problems plague and persist; of being lonely surrounded by people and of being bored with so many possessions; of being poor; of the failure of organizations to keep the air breathable, the water drinkable, and man peaceable. I left Houston convinced that liberals and conservatives there shared three basic apprehensions: they want the war to stop, they do not want to lose their children, and they want to be proud of their country. But it was the same everywhere.

There is a myth that the decent thing has almost always prevailed in America when the issues were clearly put to the people. It may not always happen. I found among people an impatience, an intemperance, an isolation which invites opportunists who promise too much and castigate too many. And I came back with questions. Can the country be wise if it hears no wisdom? Can it be tolerant if it sees no tolerance? Can those people I met escape their isolation if no one listens?

71 72 73 10 9 8 7 6 5 4 3 2